Praise for *The Miracle*

"*The Miracle Detective* . . . is an adventure for any Catholic (new, life-long, lapsed, born-again) or skeptic alike. . . . Sullivan speaks to us in two voices: one fully immersed in mystical experiences as an ecstatic convert, the other as the skilled contemporary *Rolling Stone* journalist. He strikes the highest ground toward the end of the book, culling from the sage and scholarly."   —Meredith Rolley, *The Santa Fe New Mexican*

"Certainly the best [book about Medjugorje] I have read . . . Sullivan brilliantly situates the apparitions within the context of the Balkan war. . . . *The Miracle Detective* contains vivid passages, nicely rendered theological history, and suspenseful scenes."
                    —Tim Cavanaugh, *The Washington Post Book World*

"[*The Miracle Detective*] is a stunning mix of the personal and the historic, interviews and experiences, with Sullivan incredibly nimble at making the worlds overlap—in a way, just as visionaries do. . . . If what [he] writes about is astounding—sightings, healings, possession—the breadth and depth of his work is rather astonishing as well. . . . His writing draws readers into his search for answers, and soon we find ourselves sharing his excitement."   —Ilene Cooper, *Booklist* (starred review)

"Sullivan is there as both reporter and seeker. He brilliantly interweaves stories of his meetings with remarkable women and men, including the visionaries and the priest who serves as their 'spiritual director,' with incidents from his own spiritual turmoil."
                            —Vernon Peterson, *The Oregonian*

"An intrepid Portland journalist crafts a fascinating exploration of how the Catholic Church investigates purported sightings of the Virgin Mary; a globe-trotting, first-person spiritual odyssey that took him to northeastern Oregon, Arizona, Bosnia, the Vatican and beyond."
—*The Seattle Post-Intelligencer*

"[Sullivan's] tone here is droll, chatty and appealing, that of a curious skeptic who is willing, or perhaps waiting, to be convinced."
—*The Arizona Republic*

"Sullivan's journey is a religious one, a Christian one. But what happened on that journey and what it might mean to people of all—or no—faiths makes this book unique and valuable."
—Dan Hays, *Austin-American Statesman Journal*

"The reporter for *Rolling Stone* is a skillful writer on a subject that fascinates the faithful and skeptical. . . . Mr. Sullivan crafts a compelling narrative."   —Ira J. Hadnot, *The Dallas Morning News*

"[Offers] a fascinating glimpse at the paradoxes of religious faith. . . . [Sullivan is] a talented, intelligent writer. . . . Even before Sullivan gets to Medjugorje, a town transformed by the influx of tens of thousands of pilgrims, the project begins to affect him."   —Laura Miller, salon.com

"Sullivan's account of the six teenagers who witnessed the first of the apparitions in Medjugorje is fascinating, even to a non-believer."
—Lois Wadsworth, *Eugene Weekly*

"A remarkable book . . . A thin line—and a deep abyss—separates believers from the class of unbelievers such as Melville, who could "neither believe nor be comfortable in his disbelief, and who, as Hawthorne reported, had "pretty much made his mind up to be annihilated." Sullivan straddles this abyss and gazes both ways. This tension is the engine that drives *The Miracle Detective*."   —*The Oregonian*

"When it arrived, I flipped over *The Miracle Detective* to read the description of the author: 'Randall Sullivan is a contributing editor at both *Rolling Stone* and *Men's Journal*.' Oh, great, I thought: some hip, ignorant big city journalist, out to make fun of the Catholic Church. I opened the book to page one—and was still reading hours later . . . a laudable achievement by an unbeliever who started out investigating apparitions on a cynical whim, and ended up profoundly changed. . . . *The Miracle Detective* is exceedingly well-written, deeply involving and oddly inspiring."
—Kathy Shaidle, relapsedcatholic.com

"Plying his remarkable skills as a reporter and writer, [Sullivan] has written a book that operates and succeeds on a number of levels. It is an intriguing up-close look at the lives of mystics, an insightful study of the post–Vatican II Catholic Church and its institutional struggles with manifestations of the supernatural, a powerful documentation of the reality of miracles and demons, a detailed history of Marian apparitions and the context of the reported happenings in Medjugorje, and most of all a compelling story of personal conversion. . . . The result is a book of great scope and balance."   —Jay Dunlap, Catholic.net

THE MIRACLE DETECTIVE

Also by Randall Sullivan

The Price of Experience

LAbyrinth

THE
MIRACLE DETECTIVE

An Investigative Reporter Sets Out
to Examine How the Catholic Church
Investigates Holy Visions
and Discovers His Own Faith

RANDALL SULLIVAN

Grove Press
New York

Published simultaneously in Canada
Printed in the United States of America

FIRST GROVE PRESS EDITION

Library of Congress Cataloging-in-Publication Data
Sullivan, Randall.
    The miracle detective : an investigative reporter sets out to examine how
the Catholic church investigates holy visions and discovers his own faith /
Randall Sullivan.
        p. cm.
    ISBN 0-8021-4195-1 (pbk.)
    1. Mary, Blessed Virgin, Saint—Apparitions and miracles.   I. Title.
BT650.S85 2004
232.91'7—dc22   2003063631

Grove Press
An imprint of Grove/Atlantic, Inc.
841 Broadway
New York, NY 10003

05 06 07 08 09   10 9 8 7 6 5 4 3 2 1

For Steven Louis High, friend like a brother

CONTENTS

PART I

SIGNS AND WONDERS

Two ways of thinking, the way of time and the way of eternity and timelessness, are both part of man's effort to comprehend the world in which he lives. Neither is comprehended in the other, nor reducible to it, each supplementing the other, neither telling the whole story.

—Robert Oppenheimer

CHAPTER ONE

The first apparition had lasted twenty-four hours exactly and was witnessed by nearly one thousand people, most of them Mexican Americans, according to newspaper accounts of the event in northeastern Oregon. I read about it initially in the Portland *Oregonian* on Valentine's Day, 1994.

Shortly before sunrise on the morning of February 3, in the tiny, dilapidated trailer where she lived with her parents amid irrigated fields and arid rangelands in the high desert hamlet of Boardman, a young woman named Irma Munoz had been startled, then terrified, and finally enthralled by a glowing figure. The "stylized image," as the *Oregonian* article described it, had appeared in the upper right-hand corner of a landscape painting that hung in a master bedroom measuring five feet wide by six feet long.

Irma, then twenty-three and not at all religious, said she immediately recognized the glowing figure as the Virgin Mary. Irma's mother, whose name was Lourdes, saw the Madonna also, and fell at once to her knees. Irma's two sisters, summoned from their own trailers nearby, spread the word. Irma still stood behind her kneeling mother, staring at the radiant image, when first ten, then twenty, then thirty, then forty of her neighbors crowded into the trailer. They saw the Virgin also—or saw at least a woman wearing a veil—and most of them went to their knees with Mrs. Munoz.

There were, of course, skeptics. Two men raised the painting slightly to check its underside. Several people stood in front of the canvas, or ran their hands across it, to see if shadows would darken or disrupt the image. They even wiped the surface clean with a wet cloth. Finally, one of the men got up the nerve to lift the painting off the wall, to see if some strange play of reflected light was at work there. No matter where they moved the painting, though, or how they manipulated it, the glowing image remained. It would fluctuate in brightness, occasionally seeming to flare intensely, but this had nothing discernably to do with the painting's angle or position.

Someone called the Spanish-language radio station in Walla Walla, Washington, with the story, which was picked up that afternoon by a local TV station. By five P.M., several hundred people had seen the image, and outside the Munoz trailer was a line three hundred feet long; men, women, and children waiting in subfreezing temperatures for a look at the wonder. Inside, people sang, wept, fainted, and prayed.

Reports of the apparition in Boardman "have stirred many of the devoutly Catholic Mexicans in Oregon's Hispanic community," reported the *Oregonian* article. "More than 3,000 people have flocked to see it, some from as far away as Utah."

Later, when I met her, Irma Munoz said that what had hurt and angered her most was the way the media made the Madonna's appearance "a Mexican thing." Nearly half the people who came to her family's trailer in Boardman were Anglos, Irma said, but one never would have known that from the newspaper coverage. The *Oregonian* had consulted experts to interpret this "spiritual anachronism." Randall Balmer, the Columbia University professor who wrote a religion column for the *New York Times* syndicate, offered an opaque comment: "The power of faith is very real." The local authority who weighed in was the chairman of the religious studies department at a liberal arts college outside Portland, a man who had lived for eighteen years in Bolivia. Such sightings of the Virgin were examples of "syncretism," the professor explained: a marriage of Christian and pre-Christian beliefs in which the Madonna's apparitions either were linked to sacred sites of the Incas, Aztecs, or Maya, or in which the mother of Jesus had assumed the identity of some Native American fertility goddess. In other words, a Mexican thing.

The *Oregonian* article also managed to incorporate a brief history of Marian apparitions. Three such events during modern times had inspired worldwide interest among Roman Catholics. First among these, of course, were the visions reported during 1858 by the peasant girl Bernadette Soubirous in the grotto at Lourdes, France. The second had involved the alleged appearances and purported prophecies of the Virgin at Fátima, Portugal, in 1917. The third event still was in progress at a small village in Bosnia-Hercegovina called Medjugorje, where a group of children had been claiming daily discourses with the Madonna since the early 1980s.

It was the first time I remember seeing or hearing the word Medjugorje (Medge-you-gor-yi-a). My ignorance would amaze many of those I met in the months that followed, but none of the well-educated, well-read, well-informed people I knew back in 1994 had heard of the place either. This schism between the secular and the religious would become the consuming context of my life during the next several years, yet at the time I was far too temporal to see it as significant.

Any number of claims were made for the Boardman event. Most arresting was the claim that the apparition in eastern Oregon was the first appearance by the Madonna ever captured on videotape. I watched the video when it was broadcast by a television station in Portland. At first all I saw was a spectacularly ugly oil painting of a sunset in a Sonoran desert: segauro cactuses, crumbling rocks, and cirrus clouds, all rendered in shades of reddish orange and black. *Desert Aglow*, the artist had titled it. Then I noticed that there was, indeed, an oval of light in the upper right-hand section of the painting. Suddenly the light flared, and for a moment I could see . . . well, something. Maybe I saw a woman in a veil standing with her hands pressed together only because that's what I was looking for.

The television news reader reported that unnamed "experts" had speculated that the image might have been created by a holographic projector. Irma Munoz was still shaking her head over this one when I met her. "If we could afford a holographic projector," she asked, "do you think we would have been living in a place like that?"

The place Irma referred to was a trailer about two-thirds the size of my living room, which her parents had purchased for four hundred dollars five months earlier. Reporters who described the family's abode as "a small mobile home" were being polite to the point of misrepresentation. The trailer's painted aluminum skin was covered with scabs of rust and hung loose at the seams. It sat on bald tires among the broken branches of half-dead fruit trees upon which laundry was hung even during winter. Inside, the quarter-inch plywood that covered the walls didn't reach all the way to the ceiling, so that the wind (and in Boardman, less than a mile from the Columbia River, there is always wind) entered from both above and below. The roof leaked and the floorboards were so loose that one could see through to the ground in places. A propane heater was all that kept the temperature in the trailer above freezing during winter months. The bedroom where the apparitions had taken place was barely large enough to contain a double bed, meaning that those who inspected the landscape painting on that first morning had climbed across the mattress to get to it.

"My mom just let them," Irma recalled. "She didn't want to deny anyone the opportunity."

My meeting with Irma had come as a relief. To make contact with her, I went through an Anglo lady from nearby Hermiston who had assumed the role of mentor to the young visionary. This was Marge Rolen. Although Marge was entirely sincere, deeply reverent, and quite generous, she also was what most of the people I knew would have called a religious nut. Born and raised in rural Kansas, Marge had been homeschooling her children to keep them away from the sort of bad influences a town the size of Hermiston (population almost ten thousand) can breed. In her spare time, she had helped set up the community's pro-life Pregnancy Crisis Center, and for months had been engaged in "spiritual warfare" with her parish priest.

She was downriver in The Dalles with Dr. Rolen (an optometrist) when word of the apparition in Boardman reached her, Marge recalled: "My husband said, 'You may not go!' He knows I get carried away. I was thinking, 'I know I have to obey my husband, but how can I not see this?'" She consulted with a priest in Pendleton who suggested Marge offer the Munoz family some blessed salt and holy water to sprinkle at the apparition site, in order to expose any demonic presence that might be involved. Her husband, outranked, consented to a trip to Boardman.

Early the next morning, Marge was sitting with the Munoz family in their trailer, watching the video they had made on the afternoon of the first apparition. She saw not only the Blessed Mother, Marge reported, but also the face of Jesus, and the silhouette of St. Bernadette. Furthermore, her rosary had turned to gold. Marge showed me a string of beads that looked as if the tarnished silver finish had worn away to expose a metallic alloy containing, perhaps, a bit of brass.

Irma was an earthier sort, attractive despite being at least forty pounds overweight, with enormous eyes and a musical laugh—a young woman whose greatest difficulty was understanding why the Mother of God would choose a person such as herself. "I mean, I'm not exactly holy," she explained. Irma had been to church just once since her baptism, when her father was sick and her grandmother insisted the whole family must kneel at the altar and pray for him. "To me, religion was something old people talked about," Irma said. "It had nothing to do with me. Going through high school, I was taught about evolution, that we were monkeys, and there was really no God. That's what I believed."

Growing up in the Rio Grande Valley on the Texas side of the border, she refused to learn even the Our Father or the Hail Mary. Like her
parents, though, she would resort to prayer occasionally, when the family was strapped for cash. Irma prayed also after her tragedy, when she
went to the hospital in her ninth month of pregnancy and was told that
her baby had died in the womb. "My parents took me to this shrine of
Our Lady of Guadaloupe, down in the valley, and I had never seen anything like it," Irma recalled. "All these candles burning, all these people
praying. It scared me. I remember there was this couple kneeling next to
a little crib where their baby was hooked up to all these tubes and tanks."

She and her husband, an Anglo from Georgia, divorced soon after, and
in 1991 Irma came north for the summer with her parents. The family
went back and forth for three years, then bought the trailer in Boardman
to be close to Irma's older sister. The painting of the desert landscape they
had purchased for five dollars at a garage sale. "I hated the thing," Irma
said. "I was always telling my mom, 'It's so ugly and big. Get rid of it.'"

The morning the apparitions began, she woke up at four-thirty, which
was a miracle all by itself, Irma said. Her father, who worked for a local
rancher, left the trailer at five, and Irma was on the sofa watching TV
when her mother called from the bedroom to ask if she would fix a cup
of coffee. Irma said no at first, but then did as she was asked. "I was walking
into her room, toward her, where she was lying down, facing me, and I
was holding the cup of coffee, and then I looked up at the picture and
saw the light. I said, 'Mom! Mom! There's something behind you!' She
goes, 'What?' I said, 'The thing, the Lady, what you call—the Virgin.'
That's all I knew to call her. I didn't even know her name was Mary. But
I knew who it was the moment I saw her. My mom sort of shook her
head, but I kept insisting, 'Mom, turn around.' I was still holding the
coffee, and it was shaking in my hand; I think that got her attention. I
said, 'Mom, I swear to you on my son's grave. Please just turn around.' I
wondered if I was going nuts. So she turned around, and the next thing
I know she's jumping out of bed, and she's on her knees, doing the sign
of the cross, praying. And I said, 'You see it too?' And she said, 'I see it.'"

Everyone that day saw it: "The minute they walked in, they were on
their knees. I thought, 'Well, at least I know I'm not goin' nuts.'"

Irma worked as a nurse's aide, and hadn't missed a day on the job yet,
but called in sick that morning. "I didn't want to be away from Her. I
never did kneel and pray like the others, though. I was just standing there

watching, amazed by the love and devotion of these people, some of them getting on their knees way before they got to the door. Wow! And they just kept coming and coming.

"I was thinking, 'Why us?' People told me, 'Well, if She's here, so is the Devil.' That scared me really bad. I started crying, thinking, 'What did we do?'"

The image of the Madonna remained fixed for hours, changing only in brightness, fading and glowing. "Then She turned her head," Irma recalled. "It was almost evening, and She just sort of slowly turned Her head to the other side. Somebody said it was Her telling us to pray, to get closer to God. And that was when I realized how bad we were. We never went to church, never said a prayer."

By dusk, the line of people stretched from the front door of the trailer to the street nearly three hundred feet away. A team of sheriff's deputies arrived for crowd control; Irma's sister was furious when she heard one deputy say to another, "Hey, let's call Immigration—they could get 'em all in one swoop."

People kept coming all through the night, and Irma stayed up until the next morning, when the image disappeared at exactly the time she first had seen it the day before.

For the next forty-eight hours, the trailer remained full of those who wanted to see the painting or touch it. "They said they could still feel Her presence. It upset me. We couldn't take a bath or have any privacy. My mom, though, she left the front door open and let in anyone who wanted to see. People were jumping over my dad while he lay in bed to touch the spot where Our Lady had been, or to check if we had anything hidden behind the painting, or if anything was shining on it."

At least a half-dozen people who visited the trailer on the first day brought video cameras. Irma's parents decided they should rent a camcorder themselves, thinking of their relatives back in Texas. The Munoz video (the one that played on the local news in Portland) showed the illuminated figure in the corner of the desert landscape quite distinctly. All of the other people who aimed their cameras at the apparition, however, reported that the image of the Virgin they saw with their naked eyes had not been recorded. "Which was weird," Irma remembered. "Because it was very clear on our tape. We kept checking to see if it was still there, and it was."

The family made a second video when the image of the Virgin reappeared six days after the first sighting, at the same hour of day, and in the same place on the painting. Irma and her family kept quiet this time, wanting to have the Virgin to themselves. While they sat watching and waiting, someone knocked at the trailer's door. Irma told the man outside to come back another time, that her mother was ill and needed rest. When she returned to the bedroom, the image of the Madonna had disappeared. It was a lesson in unselfishness, Irma decided: The Blessed Mother's presence was to be shared with all who believed.

After this, the Munoz family accommodated visitors whatever time of day or night they arrived. The bed in the little room was removed, replaced by an altar loaded with candles and flowers. The video of the apparition played nonstop on the television in the living room.

For Irma, the overwhelming question had become "Why me? I knew there must be some reason She appeared to me, but I had no idea what it could be." Visitors to the trailer kept bringing her books and pamphlets, mostly about Lourdes, Fátima, and Medjugorje (she'd never heard of Medjugorje either). "People knew I was the first one who saw Her, and a lot of them, like, wanted to touch me." They asked if She told me anything. And I said, 'No, or if She did I didn't hear it.' I said I was sorry, but I didn't have any message. I kept apologizing."

By March 1994, Irma had partners in her search for meaning. Three women joined her to form a prayer group. The first of these was her coworker Kim Hickey. The daughter of a retired army officer well known in Hermiston, Kim was the first Anglo in whom Irma had confided, phoning her at home on February 2. "I wanted her to tell me if I was nuts." Kim had left the Catholic Church fourteen years earlier, but that afternoon found herself consumed by curiosity, and drove directly to the trailer court. There was a long line out the door, but she pushed her way to the front, telling those ahead of her, "I'm Irma's friend, let me in."

She squeezed into the bedroom, looked at the painting, and saw the Virgin immediately, Kim recalled. She stared at the "image of light" for a few moments, then approached the painting and touched its surface. "It was like my hand went through a cloud. You knew who it was because you could feel it. In fact, as soon as you saw, you knew, because there was this feeling that you had, not like any other feeling, a feeling of knowing, and of awe. And everybody who saw Her had it. "

Irma and Kim soon brought in another adult care worker, Irene Virgen. They tried not to make too much of Irene's last name, but still. . . . The three said the Rosary on their fingertips until Marge Rolen arrived with her strings of plastic beads and made them four. "We knew there was a purpose to what had happened," Marge recalled, "and so we prayed to discover what it was."

They weren't getting much help from their parish priest, Father Paco Vallejo. The Munoz family called him for counsel the morning of the first apparition, but the priest already had been notified by at least a dozen other parishioners. His office received more than 150 calls during the next twenty-four hours, Father Paco said; the telephone lines seemed to be ringing constantly. Yet the priest made no effort to visit the Munoz trailer, and from the start expressed not only skepticism but outright antipathy. "It happens all the time," he told the high desert's largest newspaper, the *East Oregonian*. "It's natural things that are thought to be supernatural. But God is always present—He's here right now." Father Paco was troubled by people more interested in a romantic relationship with God than in "the hard-core, day-to-day relationship" that a true believer maintained by regular attendance at Mass. His bishop had advised him to remind the people in his homily the following Sunday that even authentic apparitions were merely private revelations and amounted to little beside the revealed truth of Scripture.

Jesus Himself had said you could know a tree only by its fruit, Father Paco observed. "Call me Monday morning," he advised the newspaper of the Portland diocese, the *Sentinel*, "and see how many people come to church this weekend." Church attendance actually was higher than normal that Sunday, and Father Paco dutifully visited the Munoz trailer on Tuesday morning. "I went and saw nothing," the priest would tell me later, before adding archly, "but they said it wasn't happening that day." Patience and prudence were the best policies to follow in dealing with such matters, he reminded his congregation on the Sunday after that.

The priest had asked Mr. and Mrs. Munoz if he might take custody of the painting. "But all the people told my mom and dad, 'No, this is where She came,'" Irma recalled. "'This is where She wants to be. Keep it.' So we refused to give it to him. And after that, Father Paco didn't seem to want to have anything to do with us." Their parish priest was one of those people who believe such events should happen in church, and then only to someone very holy, Kim told Irma. "He thinks he knows the Blessed Mother," Irma's friend said. "But he doesn't understand Her at all."

While on the one hand she felt truly blessed, Irma said, the weeks that followed were among the most agonizing of her life. She was frightened by those who spoke of the Devil. Worst were the ones who said the apparition was itself the work of Satan, and that she was possessed. Her own brother, a Jehovah's Witness, told Irma she was a tool of evil. Strangers phoned in the middle of the night and threatened to burn the trailer with Irma inside. "Witch!" she heard shouted after her when she went into Hermiston. Even those who meant well upset her, warning that Satan hated above all others those who had seen the Virgin Mary, and that she and her family would be "under attack."

She started to think it might be true when a call came from Texas on February 11, informing them that Irma's grandmother had been found on the floor in her home, unconscious and bleeding from the head, apparently the victim of an assault. Mr. and Mrs. Munoz flew south the next morning, but by the time they arrived the old woman was in a coma. She died on Valentine's Day.

"People told me this was the Devil's work," Irma said, "and I was afraid it might be true. At the same time, though, I could feel that seeing the Blessed Mother had helped me, and my parents, too, deal with my grandmother's death better than we ever could have before. For the first time, I really believed there was a God and a Heaven. Her visit had changed me, changed us all."

Irma's parents stayed on in Texas through that winter. They called one evening to say they had visited a *guarandero* in Brownsville who said: "Your daughter, the one who saw the Blessed Mother; Our Lady wants her to prepare a shrine. When the shrine is standing, she will return." Irma and Kim made the best shrine they could in the bedroom where the picture still hung, assembling as many candles and flowers and holy pictures as they were able to find. "It seemed so pathetic," Kim remembered.

People from Oregon and Washington continued to make pilgrimages to the trailer in Boardman all through that spring and into the summer. Irma was sustained by the stories they told. One of her favorites came from a lady who had arrived at the trailer to kneel before the painting soon after the apparitions ended, to pray for her daughter, the one who had run away from home more than a year earlier. A missing person's report was on file, but there had been no word of the girl since the day she disappeared, said the woman, who did not know at this point if her daughter was dead or alive. In the Munoz trailer, the woman told Irma, she had begged the Blessed Mother to let her know that her daughter was well, and to hear the girl's voice at least one more time: That very night, her daughter phoned from California and said she was coming home.

The visitor who made the greatest impact was a young man who had been in a Portland hospital, dying of AIDS, when he saw the video of the apparition on the local news. He recognized the Virgin at once, the young man said, and in that moment knew She was blessing him. He had been told he never would leave the hospital, but the young man convinced his family to arrange for his transport in a medical van, where he lay on a stretcher, hooked to life-support systems, for the entire two-hundred-mile drive to Boardman. "They brought him in in a wheelchair, with all the wires and tubes and machines," Irma recalled, "and we let him sit alone with the painting. When we went to check on him, he was crying, telling us that She had come, that he could see Her clearly. I looked and didn't see anything, but that doesn't mean She wasn't there for him.

"My mom ended up getting very close to his family, and to him. He told us he had lived a very bad life, in crime, and had been on drugs, but that now he felt very happy and like his life had been worthwhile, because he got to experience this while he was still alive. And before he died, he asked if he could have the painting in his room with him. So we took it down, and he spent his last hours with it. I don't know what he saw, but he was smiling."

Apart from the man dying of AIDS, the only others who reported seeing the Virgin again were children. "They'd say, 'There She is. Don't you see Her?'" Irma recalled. "And I couldn't see anything." Kim said probably the pure of heart could see Her best.

The miracle of the peach tree astounded them also. Irma and her family thought the tree just outside their trailer's front door was dead, or at least dying. The year before, it had put out only a few leaves that turned yellow and shriveled. But that spring, the branches were covered with flowers, and in the summer, they were so heavy with fruit that Irma and her family gave away peaches by the bagful. "And the rosebushes that people had brought," Kim added, "every one of them bloomed huge blossoms that lasted even into the wintertime."

"Because of Her," Irma said. "We knew that."

The members of the prayer group still felt something more was going to happen. What that might be they had no clue, until April 1995, when a call came from a wealthy Portland land developer named Joe Locke. Back in May 1992, Locke had undergone a heart transplant, and for most of the next two years prayed every day that he might live long enough to care for his ailing mother until her death. One morning late in 1993, Locke awakened from a prophetic dream with the understanding that his prayers had been answered, and that in thanksgiving he was to do "something special."

His mother had been in a Portland hospital during February 1994, when she saw the TV news report of the apparition in Boardman. Knowing that her son owned property in Boardman, his mother called from the hospital, Locke said, and told him, "Joe, this may be the something special from your dream." She died two weeks later.

On the first anniversary of his mother's death, February 25, 1995, Locke felt compelled to retrieve the *Medjugorje Messenger* magazine he had received from a friend the previous September. He opened the magazine to a full-page photograph of the Shrine to Our Lady of Peace recently constructed in Santa Clara, California, and immediately felt a need to visit it. When he arrived in Santa Clara and knelt before the shrine, Locke knew what his "something special" would be: a shrine to the Blessed Mother in eastern Oregon.

By March, Locke had formed a nonprofit corporation to develop an Our Lady of Grace shrine in Boardman. Securing a site was a problem, however, and the project languished until a local Catholic family offered to donate ten acres outside Hermiston at the Umatilla Army Depot. At first, the idea that the Virgin's shrine would lay just feet from the entrance to the forbidding army base disturbed some supporters. Inside the depot's barbed-wire fences, behind its abandoned barracks, at the bottom of its deep concrete bunkers, was the second largest stockpile of chemical weapons in the United States: tanks of nerve gas and blister agents (most developed during World War II) attached to explosive devices that made them more deadly than any weapons on earth, after hydrogen bombs. The mustard gas in the canisters at the Umatilla base was alone sufficient to kill 90 percent of the U.S. population.

How, when, and where to dispose of the chemical weapons had been a source of contention in Washington, D.C., for more than two decades. And in the high desert of eastern Oregon, the dispute had produced some horrifying imagery. During my first visit to Boardman, I read a leaflet sent out that week by the federal government instructing locals to "shelter in place" should an accident occur that resulted in "leakage." Since it would be impossible to determine at once where a plume of the deadly vapors was headed, area residents were advised to do what they could to seal their homes (close air vents, stuff towels beneath doorways, turn off air conditioners, apply duct tape around windows, et cetera), then "await rescue." People shook their heads in outraged resignation when the *Oregonian* reported that their wait might be a long one, as local officials had no protective suits for rescuers, and that warning sirens installed around the depot were not at present functional. "They've admitted to us that anybody ten minutes downwind is dead," one local politician said.

After meditating upon the matter, most of those who had joined the Our Lady of Grace Shrine Corporation agreed that no more perfect spot could have been selected if they'd had the whole county to choose from. To see ground filled with poison transformed into a landscape of prayer and devotion would be a tremendous tribute to the Virgin, observed Marge Rolen. Like Marge, Irma saw much meaning in the fact that Kim's father had for years been commander of the Umatilla Army Depot, helping design the plan to incinerate the chemical weapons stored there. "I'm sure now that the shrine is the outcome, the reason for the vision," Irma said. Kim agreed: "This is about coming full circle, from war and division to unity and peace."

It still wasn't selling with the parish priest. The bishop had made it clear that the church would not support the shrine if it was directly linked to the supposed apparitions in the Munoz trailer, Father Paco said. The priest's position had softened, but he still was far from persuaded. He did not believe that Irma Munoz and her family were delusional or dishonest, Paco allowed, and even considered it possible that they had received some sort of private revelation. However, he saw no sign of anything more. The priest was particularly troubled that Irma Munoz and her family did not appear to have experienced a thoroughgoing conversion. "They seem to have become just slightly more religious," he noted. "One of the daughters asked to have her child baptized. The mother came to church a couple of times."

Irma became defensive when I repeated the priest's complaints. She went to church also, but in Pendleton rather than in Hermiston, Irma said, because she preferred the pastor there to Father Paco. "I can't say I'm a very devout Catholic," she admitted, "but I can say that what happened changed my life. I pray a lot more than I ever did before." Irma seemed to become suddenly very sad. "I don't know what everybody expects from me. Should I become a nun? All I can tell people is that I don't have any doubts that it was the Blessed Mother, and that there was a purpose."

Father Paco's personal stance remained "wait and see": "If I see fruits, I may change my mind," the priest explained, then added a remark that my friends would find far more amusing than I did: "Your interest is actually the most impressive thing I've seen so far." Only a few days earlier, the *Oregonian* had run a prominently displayed, enormously flattering review of my recently published book, and Father Paco regarded the fact that a noted author—one who wasn't even Catholic—might write something about the Boardman apparition as a significant development.

"You're fruit," he told me. "Real fruit."

CHAPTER TWO

One Tuesday afternoon not long after I'd read about the alleged apparitions in Boardman (but well before I'd spoken to Irma and the others), I was wandering through the stacks at the biggest bookstore on the West Coast, Powell's, in Portland. I'd come in looking for a travel guide to the South Pacific, but somehow strayed into a section never before entered by me, downstairs in the Purple Room below a sign that read "Religion and Metaphysics." The aisle with shelves marked Channeling, Astral Projection, Ghosts, UFOs, Tarot, and Witchcraft teemed with browsers, but there was not a soul in the aisle devoted to Christian Theology.

I found myself at a rack of shelves labeled Catholic Saints and walked past, brushing my fingertips along the spines of musty tomes that followed an alphabetical course from Aquinas and Augustine to Elizabeth Anne Seton and Teresa of Avila. The weight of all I didn't know seemed to pile up on me until my shoulders slumped with dejection. Near the end of the aisle was a shelf marked Virgin Mary. This was a subject in which I had shown not the slightest interest up to that point in my life, other than watching the first fifteen minutes of *Song of Bernadette*, a film I turned off because it was putting me to sleep. Without thinking why, I pulled down the heaviest and most authoritative-looking volume on the Virgin Mary shelf, a scholarly work published by the Princeton University Press. Opening the book to its middle, I began reading about a person named Mirjana Dragičević, one of the Medjugorje visionaries. Apparently, this young woman was playing a central role in the events over there, having been assigned both to keep, and eventually to reveal, what were described as the Secrets. These Secrets, which according to the book's author had been a feature of all major Marian apparitions during the twentieth century, were a list of ten events that would unfold in what sounded like an end-of-the-world scenario. They had been given to

Mirjana—by the Virgin, she said—during a series of private visitations at her parents' home in Sarajevo during 1981 and 1982.

The other seers, who had stayed behind in Medjugorje, also were to receive the Secrets, but at a slower rate, and when each of the six knew all ten Secrets, what had been foretold would begin to take place. Or so said this Mirjana, who had revealed that all would occur during her life-time. Through a priest of her choosing, Mirjana said, she would announce each event three days before its occurrence, as the Blessed Mother had instructed her to do.

I snapped the book shut without reading further and placed it back on the shelf. "Strange spooky shit," I muttered under my breath, and made straight for the door to the street. Even before I was outside, though, I had begun to shiver. A chill that started in the back of my neck ran up and down my spine like a current. I was shaking almost convulsively as I crossed Burnside Boulevard; my teeth actually began to chatter. I stopped in the first coffee shop I came to—there's one on almost every block in Portland—and dosed myself with a double latte until the trembling ceased.

It was as if I had experienced the physical sensation of premonition, but without any images or ideas to go with it. Religion was a subject best left to the religious, I reminded myself.

Yet there I was, back at Powell's one week later, in the same corner of the basement I had visited for the first time seven days earlier. I found a book about Medjugorje this time. It was your basic devotionalist drivel, written in breathless prose. The section to which I had opened the book, though, fascinated me, because it was about Mirjana's first visit to the United States, which had entailed just one stopover, in Portland, Oregon. While in Portland, according to the book's author, Mirjana had received a vision from which she emerged tearful and exhausted. It seemed that each of the Medjugorje visionaries had been given one group they were to pray for, and Mirjana was asked to carry the heaviest load, having been assigned to plead for the souls of "Unbelievers." In Portland, the Virgin had revealed to her some of what the Unbelievers faced if they failed to convert, Mirjana said, and the experience had devastated her.

This had taken place in 1990, right around the time I was moving back to Oregon from Los Angeles. Once again, I returned the book to the shelf and headed for the exit. I was shivering again, though not so violently as on the previous Tuesday. "What am I doing?" I wondered aloud. A young woman browsing the Witchcraft aisle heard me and flinched.

Later that month, my publisher flew in from New York to go over his suggested revisions to a manuscript that was to be typeset within ninety days. Over one of our early afternoon breakfasts, he asked if I'd been thinking about my next book. Without so much as a moment's hesitation, I began telling him about the reported apparitions in eastern Oregon. The Catholic diocese reportedly had placed the matter "under investigation," I explained, a phrase that started me thinking about how exactly one might conduct the official inquiry into such an incident. Drawing on what I had the audacity to describe as my "research" (ten minutes in the stacks at Powell's and what I could remember of a six-month-old article from the *Oregonian*), I began to outline an elaborate project.

I told my publisher what I knew about Medjugorje—he'd never heard of the village either—and suggested that the Church's investigation of events there might support the structure of a wide-ranging book. (I would discover eventually that the apparitions in Medjugorje had been subjected to perhaps more medical and scientific examination than any purported supernatural event in the history of the human race, but at the time had no idea this was the case.) At one point I described those who were assigned to investigate such phenomena as "miracle detectives," and by the flash in my publisher's eyes, I could see that the phrase had hooked him.

If I had understood what door I was opening, I would have slammed it shut immediately. But back then, I still imagined I might obtain what I needed by looking over someone's shoulder. Only when it was too late to turn back would I begin to understand that religion is one subject that can be engaged on only the most personal of levels.

By the late spring of 1995, it had been agreed that my publisher would finance an expedition to Europe, one that that would include a two-week stay in Rome and a month or so in Bosnia. If I could produce a proposal that worked for him, we'd proceed with a book. Over the next few weeks, though, the idea began to sound more and more far-fetched, actually laughable, when I tried explaining it to friends. "Bosnia" was all they could hear in most cases, and nearly everyone I spoke to seemed to have the impression that I was headed overseas to cover the siege of Sarajevo. To save face, I began playing along—even going so far as to obtain a war correspondent's credential through *Rolling Stone* magazine.

Then something unexpected occurred. The woman I was "scheduled to marry," as I found myself putting it, had paid a call on her old high school friend Janet Knez. During this visit, my fiancée, unhappy about my impending trip to Bosnia, bravely tried to explain to her friend why I was doing something so stupid and dangerous. I didn't know Janet well, but had attended her wedding out on the St. Helen's Highway in St. Birgitta's, an old Catholic church that was noted for its orthodox services and largely Croatian congregation. The priest who conducted the marriage ceremony, Father Milan Mikulich, was a character out of Tolkien, one of those spry little old men who has mastered the art of being ferocious and endearing in the same raspy breath, with his thatch of white hair, horn-rimmed glasses, and a set of bushy, bristling eyebrows that he employed to maximum effect. There was enormous charm and a vaguely chastening Old World integrity in the marriage-as-sacrament ceremony Father Milan conducted.

When she learned I was planning a trip to Medjugorje, Janet suggested that Father Milan probably could be of assistance: He had moved back to Croatia several years earlier, and lived in the town of Imotski, which was very near the Bosnian border. Furthermore, Father Milan had spent a good deal of time in Medjugorje and knew all the visionaries personally. He was especially close to the one named Mirjana; it was Father Milan who had arranged Mirjana's trip to the U.S. in 1990. Though she was no longer a practicing Catholic, Janet had made one of her infrequent trips to church to meet Mirjana while the visionary was in Portland. In fact, the two had been introduced in the little chapel next to St. Birgitta's only minutes after what had become known as Mirjana's "American Apparition."

Janet, who struck me as straightforward and steadfast, had been most affected by Mirjana's physical presence. The depth and luminosity of the seer's eyes, the chalky transparency of her skin, the serenity of her expression—they were like nothing she had ever experienced, said Janet, who sounded both moved and frightened by what she described. What really haunted her, though, was the overpowering scent of roses that had surrounded Mirjana; the aroma had been so intense, it made her feel almost drunk. She shook Mirjana's hand, and afterwards could smell roses on her own fingertips. The odor lingered for days.

I was relieved to learn that Janet's encounter with the visionary was not inspiring any pronounced renewal of religious practice. The experience had stayed with her, though; she found herself thinking about Mirjana still, and remembering that smell of roses. Janet then told me that I would have an opportunity to ask Father Milan for his help face-to-face, because even as we spoke, the priest was preparing for his first trip to the U.S. in three years, and would be in Portland two weeks hence. She would set up a meeting, Janet said.

Barely a week before I was scheduled to depart for Rome, Father Milan and I sat down in matching brocaded wing chairs at the plush suburban home where he was staying while in Oregon. The priest at once provided me with a bracing anecdotal insight into the history of the land I was preparing to enter. Mirjana's famous apparition in Portland had taken place at the Chapel of Our Lady of Sinj, which he himself had built, Father Milan said. Sinj was a city about thirty-five kilometers inland from the Dalmatian Coast, home to one of the most famous shrines in all of Croatia. This monument not only commemorated the heroic fourteenth-century defense of the city walls against Ottoman invaders, but was built on the very spot where, at the moment of attack, the glowing figure of a woman had appeared, hovering in the air, to scatter the Turkish horde in terror. Father Milan did not tell this story as if it were for him mythology.

The priest then not only pledged to arrange the introductions I had asked for, but gave me the number of a woman who would see that I had a room in Mirjana's own home during my stay in Medjugorje. I made a phone call the next morning, and a week later was on my way.

Another stroke of unlikely luck had given me somewhere to go after my arrival in Rome. This was the result of a call to an acquaintance I hadn't seen in some time, a language professor who for six years during his young adulthood had been a Jesuit priest.

Most of what I knew of the Catholic Church before I met David had been learned through my liaisons with women who were fallen from the faith, each of whom had demonstrated—and in remarkably similar ways—that it was a lot easier to stop attending church than it was to quit being a Catholic. Like them, David had left the Church disillusioned, but not disaffected. The Cabbage Monk, I nicknamed him, because shortly before joining the Jesuits, he had spent several months living meagerly on a small farm in Pennsylvania, reading Rilke in German and subsisting mostly on coleslaw as he harvested the crop laid in by a previous tenant, driving into Philadelphia every couple of weeks for assignations with the stripper who was his only companion during this period. He missed a lot of what the Jesuits had provided him, David said, especially the intellectual stimulation; the priests he lived among back then were far more serious thinkers and readers than the college professors who were his colleagues today. Also, most were homosexual, David said, a discovery that for him had been a shock, if not a scandal. Few of his fellow priests were sexually active, David told me, but the notion that for them celibacy was less a sacrifice to God than an escape from reality had disturbed him profoundly. Eventually David decided that he was ducking life also; he recanted his vows, married within a few months, and fathered his first child less than a year after that.

When I phoned David to ask if he knew anyone who could open doors for me at the Vatican, he suggested I try the head of the Oregon Curia, Father Steve Sunborg. Father Steve, it turned out, had returned recently from a sabbatical in Rome, and for me this contact was a gold mine: He provided numbers for people ranging from the Gregorian University professor who served as the main link between writers and the church, to the woman who headed the Jesuit Guest Agency. More to my purpose, Father Steve also gave me numbers for the two priests who were most involved in presenting proof of miracles before the College of Cardinals in the Vatican.

They were an Italian and a German, Fathers Paulo Molinari and Peter Gumpel, the chief "relators" for something called the Sacred Congregation of the Causes for Saints. Both, as it happened, were Jesuits, heirs to the legacy of the Bollandists, a society of Jesuits who more than three centuries earlier had undertaken to write the first biographies of the saints, drawn not from legend and literary embellishment, but based exclusively on historical records. The Bollandists intended to refute both the criticism born of the Protestant reform and the intellectual skeptics produced by the Age of Enlightenment. Their most formidable opposition, however, came from other Catholic clergy. Accused of heresy before the Spanish Inquistion, the Bollandists were placed under a censure that stamped them as schismatics for decades. They persisted, holding to their proud standards of scholarship, and produced a series of books on the saints (*Acta Sanctorum*) that today total more than sixty volumes. Perhaps the real achievement of the Bollandists, though, had been to convince the church, slowly but implacably, that historical documentation and critical investigation were no real threat to faith. By the time of John Paul II's election to pope in 1978, their methods had been formally adopted by all those at the Vatican charged with testing the miraculous and judging the holy.

* * *

It was a long walk in wet heat from my hotel on the Campo di Fiori to the Vatican. I made the trip even longer by taking the scenic route through the Piazza Navona, across the Ponte Umberto, and along the banks of the Tiber where it flowed foamy and murky green past the Castel San Angelo. As anyone who has spent even a night in Rome between early May and late June knows, during these weeks the eternal city seems gripped by a pandemic of sexual intoxication. Already preoccupied with apprehension of a wedding date that had begun to feel uncomfortably close, I felt more agitated and feral with each passing second. Even on the shady side of Bernini's stupendous Fountain of Four Rivers, my favorite Roman resting place, I found my gaze rising through the mist again and again to meet the large-eyed stares of lush signorinas who seemed to overflow both their summer dresses and their boyfriends' arms.

I started to sober up upon arriving at the Via della Conciliazione, the broad boulevard between raised walkways and sunken service roads that is the Vatican's main street, confronting each person who approaches with a point-blank view of St. Peter's. As instructed, I veered left at the edge of the cathedral square onto a narrow, shady street called Borgo Santo Spirito. Every trace of my voluptuary's reverie was dissipated by the time I stepped inside the coffin-sized, stainless-steel-lined, and torturously slow elevator that lifted me, literally inch by inch, to the floor where I would find the office of Father Peter Gumpel.

The antiseptic marble floors, the dim lighting, the heavy air of silence in which my footsteps echoed like whip cracks all lent the interior of the building an oppressively institutional air. One sensed that disturbing experiments of an arcane nature were being conducted behind the opaque glass of the doors that lined a broad but empty hallway. When I entered Father Gumpel's office, though, I found the priest seated at a magnificent hand-carved desk in front of a high window thrown open to reveal an exquisite garden that no one walking by on the street could possibly have imagined: The scene was a living homage to the possibility of perfection in which sculpted cypress trees stood embanked by flowering shrubs so perfectly groomed they looked as if they had been clipped not by garden shears, but with barber's scissors. It was an experience I would have again and again at the Vatican, this lonely walk down a forbidding corridor that led eventually to an open window filled with secret beauty.

Silver-haired and black-cassocked, Father Gumpel was a trim man with sharp features. He did not look seventy-one, an age that one year earlier had forced him to retire (by Italian law) after more than three decades as a professor of theology at Gregorian University. His collaborator, Father Molinari, was the enthusiast, I had been told, a suave and effusive man of great personal charm. Molinari was out of the country on sabbatical, however, and I had been lucky to get this allotment of time from Gumpel, a bookish man of precise speech who was regarded as one of the Vatican's leading intellectuals.

The old priest barely looked at me during a discourse that lasted more than two hours. Even when he turned toward the open window, Gumpel's gaze was abstracted, as if this task he had taken on—explaining to a non-Catholic author how the church attempted to establish divine intervention by scientific means—absorbed him utterly. That the processes of proving miracles and naming saints were inextricably tied at the Vatican, Father Gumpel assumed I knew. It was not, however, something I had even considered. He didn't appear to mind my ignorance; it seemed to please him, in fact, that he would be able to start at the beginning. Without dying a martyr's death, the priest explained, no person could be canonized unless at least two miracles attributable to the "candidate" had been demonstrated to the satisfaction of the Vatican's scientific consultants. What he and Paulo Molinari and each of the postulators assigned to a specific "cause" were required to show, as Father Gumpel initially explained it, sounded preposterous. In a nutshell, they needed to substantiate that prayers asking exclusively for the "intercession" of a dead person presumed to be in Heaven—but not yet canonized as a saint—had resulted in a blessing that could not be explained as anything other than "an extraordinary intervention of God."

As far-fetched as this sounded, I would discover that the Vatican's investigative process is quite rigorous. The interventions in question were almost always of a medical nature (there has been only one exception in this century), Gumpel said, which was why nearly every one of the Sacred Congregation's sixty-plus consultants was either a medical school professor or the director of a university clinic. Only organic diseases or physical injuries could be considered by the Congregation's medical board; anything arguably of a psychosomatic nature—shock and trauma, paralysis, or blindness—was excluded at once. Simply getting a case to Rome required the diocese where some supposedly miraculous healing had occurred to conduct its own investigation. This included securing testimony from not only the patient but every doctor, nurse, and technician connected to the case. Multiple witnesses were required, who could attest that neither the patient nor his loved ones had invoked during prayer anyone other than the candidate in question (which barred asking for the help of Jesus and Mary). If all this was accomplished, then at least two doctors had to examine the patient and submit sworn statements that all traces of the malady were gone and that no relapse was possible. Only at this point could the Vatican consider the case. Even then, 90 to 95 percent of the claimed miraculous cures that made it to Rome were disqualified during a preliminary investigation, "although many are quite extraordinary," the priest assured me. Of those few cases deemed worthy (by Gumpel or Molinari) to be considered by the Sacred Congregation, one third failed because of "insufficient documentation" or "unclear status." The cases that survived all this went to the medical board, which approved fewer than half. A board of nine theologians took over at that point to "ascertain the relationship between cause and effect," as Gumpel described it, and if two-thirds of them consented, the case went to a higher tribunal of bishops and cardinals, who also had to approve by a two-thirds majority. From there the matter passed on to the pope, who might, if he chose, decree that an intervention of God had occurred.

It was before the medical board, though, that miracles truly were tested. The members of the Consulta Medica include some of the most respected physicians in Europe. For a Roman Catholic doctor, an invitation to join the Consulta is the highest of honors. Yet very few of their professional colleagues ever learn of such an appointment. "They are concerned about being thought of as fanatics or bigots," noted Father Gumpel. The president of the *consulta*, Dr. Raffaello Cortesini, chief of surgery at the University of Rome Medical School, was among the select group of doctors on earth permitted to perform heart transplants and a man of near-legendary status in his field. Yet even he avoided publicizing his position at the Vatican. "There is skepticism about miracles," Dr. Cortesini had explained several years earlier to *Newsweek* religion editor, Kenneth Woodward (an interview I was told the doctor regretted). "I myself, if I did not do these consultations, would never believe what I read. You don't understand how fantastic, how incredible—and how well-documented—these cases are. They are more incredible than historical romances. Science fiction is nothing by comparison."

Among the central ironies of Peter Gumpel's work as a postulator was that the more fantastic a healing had been, the easier it became to prove as an instance of divine intervention. One of Father Gumpel's favorite cases—because absolutely nobody familiar with the facts would dispute that what occurred was beyond scientific explanation—involved a burn victim in Spain, a woman whose entire body had been covered by third-degree burns "of the worst possible nature," as Gumpel, who had seen photographs, put it. "The person was basically a lump of raw flesh," the priest said. At the hospital where she was taken to die, attending physicians told the burn victim's relatives that all they could do was relieve the woman's pain until her hopeless struggle to live had ended. However, one of these relatives placed a picture of a holy man, along with a relic, on the dying woman's bandages. "Overnight the burns were completely healed, without scars," Gumpel recalled. "Simply by what we know about the multiplication of cells we can say that this is beyond natural law. And in this case the skin was not only unscarred but like that of a newborn baby." It pleased the priest, I could see, to report that several doctors at the hospital had renewed their religious practice after witnessing these events.

Doctors of course never were asked to use the word "miraculous" to describe a healing, Gumpel noted; it was up to them to decide only if a cure had been "inexplicable." If the finest medical talents were unable to account for a cure, then by default a miracle was deemed to have occurred. This standard made some cases quite simple to resolve, as the senior American priest at the congregation, Monsignor Robert Sarno, would explain to me a few days later. Sarno, who often consulted with his brother, a New York physician, recently had handled the preliminary investigation of a case where a doctor died—"his heart was stopped for almost two and a half hours"—then came back to life after prayers for intercession, without any trace of brain damage or other residual effects. The attending physicians, some of whom were colleagues of this patient, agreed unanimously that what had happened could not be explained.

"Some complain that it's very difficult to prove that a cure that took place in a poor country is miraculous, because of the lack of medical records," Sarno would tell me. "But it can actually be much easier. Say you have a man with a bleeding ulcer out in the bush, where there's no hospital, no doctor, no equipment—yet he recovers completely. There's no other way to explain that but by divine intervention."

The cases that were really difficult—and really expensive—to follow to their conclusion, according to Peter Gumpel, involved cancer patients from wealthy Western countries. The most protracted case he knew of, Father Gumpel said, involved a young mother in Australia whose leukemia was so advanced she had been given no more than three weeks to live. After her entire family prayed for intercession, the woman recovered completely within a few days. The chief physician on her case refused to believe that the cancer was in full remission, and insisted she remain under observation. Fifteen years passed before doctors could agree that her healing had been both complete and beyond scientific explanation. "She was a grandmother by then," said the priest.

Because the intellectual climate of the twentieth century made it so difficult and expensive to prove divine intervention, church leaders had been persuaded to reduce the number of miracles required for beatification and canonization by half, from four to two. "There even is a push inside the congregation to cease requiring in all cases a fully approved miracle before proceeding to beatification," Gumpel noted (without telling me that he and Father Molinari were leading this "push").

Monsignor Sarno, though, insisted there was no chance that the Church would cease submitting miracles to scientific investigation. Born in Brooklyn and raised in the Bronx, clipped in speech and bustling in manner, Sarno did not conceal his disdain for "the soft-headed approach." Even those who knew his scorn recognized that the monsignor understood as well as anyone in the Vatican the process by which the church certified miracles and canonized saints; it had been both the subject of his doctoral dissertation and the main focus of his work as a priest.

Miracles, other than those wrought by Jesus himself, had meant little during the first three centuries of Christianity, Sarno explained. From the time that the "protomartyr" Stephen was stoned to death in A.D. 36 until the emperor Constantine's conversion to Christianity ended Roman persecution early in the fourth century, saints and martyrs were one and the same. Even Peter and Paul had been canonized neither for the wonders they worked nor for their leadership of the early Church, but because they died in physical torment as martyrs to the faith. These "red martyrs" still were ceded the central place of honor in the church. After Constantine signed the Edict of Milan in A.D. 313, the number of those crucified, stoned, torn asunder, or fed to wild beasts had dropped off considerably. Thus the concept of "white martyrdom" had arisen. The first white martyrs were the Anchorites, ascetic hermit monks who retreated into the wildest and most remote regions of Syria and Egypt, there renouncing food, shelter, clothing, and, of course, sex.

Eventually, certain fearless missionaries and zealous church leaders became saints, also, and during the Middle Ages, founders of religious orders began to be canonized as well. Since 1588, when the body now known as the Congregation for the Causes of Saints was created, the process had become codified down to the smallest detail. First, the promoters of a cause appointed a postulator, who in turn wrote a position paper, or *posito*. This went to historical consultants, who checked it for accuracy, then to theological consultants, who passed judgment on the candidate's "heroic virtue." If approved at these stages, the cause went to the cardinals, who then sent it—with their recommendation—to the pope. And if the pope decided that all had been done properly, he declared the person "venerable." All that remained then was to prove a miracle, and the venerable was beatified, thus becoming one of the "blessed." Beatification permitted devotion to an individual, but only canonization obligated the entire church to bestow "universal honor." And the entire difference between beatification and canonization was one more miracle.

Most Church leaders understood it would be an enormous mistake, Monsignor Sarno noted, in this age when educated people believed more in science than in religion, to suspend a process which again and again had demonstrated to the rational mind that even natural law was subordinate to faith. It was this obligation to appease skepticism and persuade impiety, apparently, that made so many in the modern church loath to address, let alone to validate, claims of miraculous intervention that did not lend themselves readily to scientific testing.

Even Peter Gumpel seemed uncomfortable discussing the one miracle of a nonmedical nature that the Church had recognized during the twentieth century, a "multiplication of food," as the priest put it, that had occurred on the evening of January 25, 1949, in a Spanish village called Ribera del Fresno. More than 350 years earlier, the town had been the birthplace of one John Macias, a Dominican venerated for his holiness, who died in Peru during the year 1645 and was beatified by church in 1837. The events ultimately accepted as an instance of divine intervention had taken place in the Ribera del Fresno parish hall, where each evening children from a nearby orphanage were served dinner, and where poor families from the village were invited to receive their meals at the door. On the evening in question, however, the cook at the parish hall had discovered there was barely enough rice and meat (slightly more than a pound and a half of each) to provide a meal for fifty-nine orphans, and nothing would be left for the poor. The cook knelt to pray for the help of "the blessed one"—John Macias—then proceeded to prepare the evening meal. Minutes later, she noticed that the boiling rice had begun to overflow the pot in which it was being cooked; she ladled some of the rice into a second pot, then a third. The woman stood by the stove for the next four hours, while the pot continued to overflow with rice. Both the pastor and his mother were summoned to witness what was happening. In all, twenty-two people swore they had seen this miracle; though it had cooked for hours, those who were present said, the last serving of rice was as fluffy and fresh as the first. Nearly two hundred people ate their fill. The cook and the pastor saved some of the rice; it was examined twenty-five years later by scientists working for the congregation, which in 1975 had approved the miracle that resulted in the canonization of John Macias as a saint.

Paulo Molinari, I had been told, was more disposed to accept nonmedical miracles than others at the congregation. A notable near-miss had come during the presentation before the congregation of a failed World War II raid by Allied bombers on a town called Kaufbeuren, in Germany. The intent had been to level several small cities just south of Augsburg, where military installations (including a dynamite factory) were located. There were no clouds in the sky that day; people on the ground could not only hear but also see the B-17s flying in formation overhead. A number of civilians knelt in prayer, invoking the Blessed Crescentia (Maria Crescentia Hoss), the former mother superior and reputed mystic whose body lay encased in glass under the altar in the convent church. They literally could see the bombs in the bellies of the B-17s, said those on the ground, but the bombs never fell—at least not on Kaufbeuren. The testimony of these citizens sat in file cabinets at the Vatican for almost forty years, until 1983, when the military archives of both the U.S. and West Germany were opened, making available the required documentation. The postulator assigned to the cause not only collected all available records, but interviewed every surviving American pilot, then turned his reports over to the German Defense Ministry, which, among other things, asked meteorologists if it was possible the pilots had been misled by a mirage, and checked with military engineers to see if the gyroscopes on the B-17s might have malfunctioned. In the end, the authorities in Rome decided that the failed bombing raid could conceivably have resulted from natural causes, and thus that no miracle had been proven.

A claimed miracle involving a mountain climber who had survived the fall that killed every one of his colleagues had been under consideration for more than a year, but few in Rome seemed to believe its chances were good. These same priests were even less sanguine about the efforts of certain postulators to pass what had become known as "moral miracles."

The test case was that of Matt Talbot (1856–1925), a Dublin dockworker who became an alcoholic in his teens but beat the bottle during his twenties, then went on to become a kind of working-class lay monk, one whose feats of prayer and fasting inspired and chastened a remarkable number of his fellow stevedores. Obscure during his lifetime, Talbot had inspired a cult of devotion after his death, first in Ireland, later in Poland, and eventually in the U.S., where several Matt Talbot clubs today provide support to recovering alcoholics.

Pope Paul VI had declared Talbot's "heroic virtue" in 1975, and Pope John Paul II made no secret of his desire to see the Irishman beatified as a blue-collar saint. More than a thousand testimonies from men who swore that Talbot's intercession had saved them from drunkenness had been collected and sent to Rome. The Congregation for the Causes of Saints, however, refused to accept alcoholism as a disease that could result in a miraculous cure. The Consulta Medica—and Dr. Cortesini in particular—were adamant on this point; only the healing of a "physical ailment" could be verified according to scientific principles.

Even claims of moral miracles, I would learn, did not disturb the slumberous peace that fills the Vatican's Palace of Congregations so much as the wonders worked by those individuals who for centuries have both nourished the faith of the humble and frustrated the rule of the exalted: the prophets of the Church, that is, and its mystics.

No Catholic who has lived in this century arouses such passion, such unease, such controversy as the man born Francesco Forgione, but better known as Padre Pio. During my first few interviews at the Vatican, I concealed out of shame my total ignorance of this man who, before his death in 1968, had been the most renowned "living saint" of the past several centuries. After a bit of reading, I began using his name as a provocation, marveling at the uniformly heavy sighs that any mention of this Capuchin friar from a small village in southern Italy would elicit out of those who considered it their task to distinguish the miraculous from the merely mystifying.

For the last fifty years of his life, Padre Pio was a stigmatic, bearing the wounds of the crucified Christ on his hands and feet. The bleeding, nearly continuous, was witnessed by thousands. From the time he was a teenager, the friar reported conversations with Jesus Christ, the Virgin Mary, and his own guardian angel. The holy man also spent many nights in what he described as violent battles with Satan, conflicts from which he regularly emerged bloody and bruised. After his death, the Capuchins claimed that Padre Pio had worked more than a thousand miraculous cures during his lifetime, the best known being the complete restoration of a laborer's shattered eyeball.

He was most beloved as a confessor. Padre Pio, those who sat with him said, read the heart and saw the soul; he knew one's sins simply by looking into a person's eyes. During the last years before his death, the lines outside his confessional were so long that the Capuchins issued tickets. When the sick or the penitent could not come to him, Padre Pio, it was said, went to them—without leaving his room. There is an astonishing body of evidence to support the Capuchins' claim that Padre Pio could "bilocate," that is, be in two places at once.

He was a prophet as well. Padre Pio's most famous prediction reportedly had been made in 1947, when he was visited by a young Polish priest named Karol Wojtyla. "Someday," he told Wojtyla, "you will be pope." It is a matter of record that in 1962, as the archbishop of Kraców, Karol Wojtyla wrote to Padre Pio asking that the friar pray for a woman who had survived a Nazi concentration camp, but who now was dying of cancer. Less than a week later, Archbishop Wojtyla sent a second letter to Padre Pio, reporting that the woman had been cured. In 1972, the archbishop lent his public support to those promoting Padre Pio's sainthood, and in 1987, forty years exactly after his first encounter with the Capuchin holy man, the Polish priest now known as Pope John Paul II celebrated Mass at the friar's tomb in San Giovanni Rotondo.

Most of those promoting his cause had assumed that Padre Pio would become a saint in short order. Yet more than twenty-five years after his death, the friar was nowhere near canonization. Despite the sworn statements of numerous doctors that the friar's wounds were not self-inflicted, "Padre Pio's stigmata [are] to us of no account," Peter Gumpel crisply informed me. The holy man's visions, prophecies, hands-on healings, and powers as a confessor also meant nothing, at least in terms of his sainthood: "All that interests us is if it is possible to demonstrate that after his death people have invoked his name and gotten a medical cure that is absolutely inexplicable."

This declaration of Father Gumpel's would ramify continuously during the next three years, reminding me again and again that what mattered to the heart (of the Church, in this case) might mean nothing to the head, and vice versa. Confronted by phenomena, such as those manifested by Padre Pio, intellectuals both inside the Church and out had inevitably resorted to parapsychology. Though they appeared reassuring at first glance, I was taken aback by how flimsy the experts' theories appeared upon closer inspection, utterly lacking in the empirical evidence that is the basis of good science. The prevailing attitude in the Vatican toward what are known as "mystical causes" seemed to be exactly opposite of the position taken on miraculous healings: What could not be explained, many of the priests seemed to be saying, must be ignored. Yet I sympathized, increasingly aware that nothing in this world has been better hidden from us than whatever separates holiness from hysteria.

About five days into my own version of Roman holiday, I spent an entire afternoon at Santa Maria in Cosmedin, where people still line up to thrust their right hands into the Bocca della Verita and be questioned by husbands, wives, and lovers, compelled by the legend that the Mouth of Truth will snap shut on one who answers falsely. Even at the end of the twentieth century, there are expressions of relief and smiles of satisfaction on the faces of those who walk away, permitting the next nervous, giggling couple to approach. On a bench nearby, I sat reading a compact biography titled *Short Story of a Victim*, which had been published in several languages by something called the Committee for Theresa Musco. Theresa, who had lived her whole life in a small town just north of Naples, began reporting visions of Jesus, Mary, and her guardian angel at age five. She became a stigmatic at nine, after a dream in which she saw herself nailed to a cross. Those who knew her best said Theresa could see the state of a human soul in a single glance, and she was given credit for the miraculous healing of a person dying from leukemia.

Theresa, however, spent her own short life in almost constant pain, enduring an astonishing assortment of ailments. According to her diary, Theresa at age six had tied a robe around her waist as a sign of penance and promised to give her life over to suffering in atonement for the sins of others. Eventually, she asked that she be permitted to feel the pain Christ had known on the cross. She also struggled against a brutal, bullying father, and a mother who eventually banished the girl from the family home. Short, plump, and unattractive, Theresa at thirteen reported a vision in which she had been instructed to consecrate her virginity. This she did during a ceremony in which she wore a white wedding dress.

Theresa did not begin to draw attention from outside her small town until 1969, when, at age twenty-six, she began to bleed regularly from her stigmatic wounds. She became a national figure in Italy during February 1975, the month when statues and holy pictures in her home began dripping blood whenever Theresa wept for the suffering of Jesus and the sorrow of Mary. Many witnesses, among them a number of priests, including the bishop of Caserta, testified to these phenomena. Theresa passed away in 1976 at the age of thirty-three, suffering from so many diseases and undiagnosed symptoms that no single cause of death could be determined. More than two thousand people attended her funeral.

The priests who head the committee promoting Theresa Musco's canonization assembled a huge file of evidence drawn on dozens of witnesses. Among those endorsing her cause was the immensely admired cardinal of Genoa, Joseph Siri, who described the Musco case as better documented than any other of like nature: "Facts are facts," Siri wrote, "and cannot be undone by mocking or ignoring them." Not undone, perhaps, but set aside, certainly. Although her cause had a postulator, Theresa Musco was regarded by Vatican officials more as a curiosity than as a serious candidate for sainthood. The evidence of a world beyond the visible that her life offers is either dismissed as unnecessary or shunned as morbid and "masochistic." Some, though, see even more ominous possibilities.

While the rational approach to purported supernatural phenomena is to assume that they are frauds or some form of not yet understood hysteria, the religious have a third option: demonic possession. Perhaps the most notorious instance of simulated sacred experience in the annals of Catholicism involved the sixteenth-century Franciscan nun Magdalena of the Cross. Magdalena lived in Spain during the same period as the most important female visionary in the history of the church, Teresa of Avila, and at the time not only was better known, but also more highly regarded. Magdalena's stigmata and her public levitations (numerous eyewitnesses reported seeing her float above the earth) produced an enormous sensation, as did her dramatic ecstasies and powers of prophecy. Bishops and great nobles of the era formed a virtual court around her at the monastery where she was named abbess. Every important Spanish theologian of that time came to investigate the purported visionary, and each one would conclude she was a genuine mystic of supreme significance. Even the nuns who lived under her charge believed the holy woman had existed for years without so much as a single bite of solid food.

Only in old age, near death, did the nun admit that it all had been a diabolical hoax. Her stigmata were self-inflicted, Magdalena said, and her decades-long fast an elaborate charade. Her levitations, like her ability to know the future, were real, the nun said, but far from divinely inspired; these powers, Magdelena said, had been granted her by Satan in exchange for her soul. On her deathbed, the nun received the rite of exorcism. For the next three hundred years, she would serve as a symbol of evil's power and a reproach to gullibility.

Nearly two centuries after Magdelena's death, the most exhaustive and enduring attempt to establish standards for judging mystics was written by Pope Benedict XIV. Visions, ecstasies, and especially manifestations of the supernatural, Benedict warned eighteenth-century Church leaders, could come not just from God but also from Satan. Benedict offered practical advice on distinguishing between divine revelation and the results of an unsound mind or a diabolical ruse. Mental illness might be supposed, Benedict wrote, if an ecstasy was followed "by weariness, by sluggishness of the limbs, a clouding of the mind and understanding, forgetfulness of past events, paleness of face and sadness of mind." The Devil's involvement was suggested when ecstasies resulted in "indecent" movements or "great contortions of the body," while "a divine ecstasy takes place with the greatest tranquility of the whole man, both outwardly and inwardly." And when the ecstatic "returns to himself," Benedict noted, he appears humble, cheerful, and secure, showing not the slightest pleasure in the attention of bystanders.

In outlining his recommendations for separating "human faith" from "supernatural faith," Benedict drew largely on his own work for what was then called the Congregation of Sacred Rites. His title with the congregation had been Promoter of the Faith—or "Devil's Advocate," as the position was more popularly known. In essence, it was the job of the Devil's Advocate (before the position was eliminated in 1983 by Pope John Paul II) to argue the case against a candidate for sainthood. For Benedict, the most memorable of the causes he opposed was that of "the flying friar," Joseph of Cupertino. It was claimed that Joseph had levitated on more than one hundred occasions. Obviously, only the testimony of "exceptional eyewitnesses," Benedict argued before the congregation, could validate such a claim. The claims of "frequent elevations" and "great flights" made on behalf of Joseph of Cupertino, were that rare instance, Benedict would concede, in which reports of miraculous feats were supported by the sworn statements of reliable persons.

Benedict had been most impressed by testimony from the Spanish ambassador to the Vatican court. The ambassador, his wife, and their entourage had asked to meet Joseph at the church near the friar's cell in Assisi. Refusing at first, Joseph relented only on orders from his superior. At the moment he entered the church, according to those present, the friar stared for a moment at the statue of Mary Immaculate near the altar, then flew a dozen paces above their heads and alit at the foot of the statue. After praying silently, Joseph let loose with his customary "shrill cry," according to the witnesses, again flew over their heads, then returned to his cell without speaking so much as one word.

"That ecstatic and rapt servant of God," Benedict called Joseph of Cupertino, when, as pope, he presided over the flying friar's canonization, an event that, even more than two hundred years ago, stood as a rare instance of the Church embracing one of its mystics without reservation.

Whether "it is better to believe than not to believe" in the revelations of mystics, as Pope Urban VII advised, has become a thornier issue in the Church with each passing decade, especially among theologians determined to accommodate the scientific revolution.

CHAPTER THREE

Before arriving in Rome, I had believed that there were three possible explanations for the raptures of religious visionaries: They were fakes, or they were hysterics, or they were telling the truth. A week at the Vatican had persuaded me that at least two more hypotheses must be considered. One, demonic possession, was something I found even more difficult to imagine than apparitions of the Virgin Mary. The other possibility was perhaps a corollary of telling the truth, an interpretation of these experiences involving some mysterious function of the unconscious that might be the means—at once symbolic and actual—by which a human being obtained direct experience of the divine. I knew Carl Jung had suggested something of this sort, and I was gleaning intimations of such a theory from several of the more cerebral priests at the Vatican. Every version of such an explanation that I heard or read, however, served better to trivialize than to illuminate.

One had only to consider the case of Alexandrina da Costa. No mystical cause before the Vatican was in its component parts more rife with fodder for psychological interpretation, or in its totality so far beyond mere analysis. Like Theresa Musco, Alexandrina had spent most of her life in bed. Born and raised in a village forty miles up the coast from Porto, Portugal, the young woman left school after less than two years in the classroom, to work on a neighbor's farm. As a teenager, she jumped from a second-story window to escape a sexual assault by her employer, and broke her back. Shortly before her twentieth birthday, total paralysis set in, and Alexandrina lay motionless for the next twenty-seven years—except during religious ecstasies.

Her first rapture, in 1931, was an appearance of Jesus, who instructed her, according to Alexandrina, that she must devote the remainder of her life to love, suffering, and "reparation" for the sins of the world, sins against sexual innocence in particular, especially those committed by priests. For the next ten years, she reported being tormented by Satan on an almost daily basis: The Devil appeared to her as a dog, as a snake, and as a monkey, Alexandrina said, tempted her to blasphemy, and proposed a variety of perverse sexual acts. Witnesses said that during these episodes the young woman seemed possessed, shrieking obscenities.

In 1934, at the age of thirty, Alexandrina reported a vision in which Jesus said He wanted her to assist Him in the redemption of mankind by sharing the suffering of His crucifixion. She did not become a stigmatic, but four years later began her "passion ecstasies." These commenced each Friday at noon and lasted three and a half hours. According to eyewitness accounts made mostly by physicians and priests, Alexandrina's body lifted—as if levitating—then fell to the floor. Once on the ground, she regained movement in her arms and legs (which lay inert the rest of the time), then began to heave and writhe. On her knees, Alexandrina would move through the stations of the cross, speaking the words Jesus had spoken in Gospel accounts of His torture and death. When it was over, Alexandrina collapsed into a semiconscious state, and once again became unable to move her limbs.

She did this nearly two hundred times, over a period of five years.

Stories of Alexandrina's passion ecstasies soon brought pilgrims from all over Portugal, then from Spain, and finally, from every part of Europe. Whatever else they believed, all those who knew her agreed that the young woman was not seeking attention. Alexandrina hated being put on display, but was anyway; Church officials selected those who would observe each Friday's ecstasy, and on one occasion permitted a camera crew to film her.

Alexandrina's last passion ecstasy occurred on Good Friday, 1942. She never left her bed again, and from that day forward refused food or drink, except the Eucharist. In June 1943, Alexandrina was transported to a hospital in Porto, where a team of doctors and nurses kept her under twenty-four-hour-a-day observation for six weeks. The medical team attempted to persuade the woman she should accept nourishment. Alexandrina, however, refused not only food but also medicine. The team leader, a specialist in nervous disorders and a member of the Royal Academy of Medicine in Madrid, testified that Alexandrina's ability to live without food or water for forty days was "scientifically inexplicable." Two other doctors testified that the woman's weight, temperature, breathing, blood pressure, and pulse had remained constant throughout this period, that she was perfectly lucid and showed an excellent disposition.

"The laws of physiology and biochemistry cannot account for the survival of this woman," wrote these two doctors, who then added their conclusion that Alexandrina's ecstasies "belong to the mystical order."

Alexandrina lived another twelve years without eating, the intensity of her visions increasing steadily. Eventually, she reported that she had been permitted to experience not just Christ's Passion but his Resurrection and Ascension as well. During the last few years of her life, as many as three thousand pilgrims would arrive at Alexandrina's home each day, pleading that she pray for them. "Consoler of the Afflicted," she was identified in the press after her death in 1951. According to witnesses, Alexandrina's body did not decay but turned to ashes, just as she had foretold, and these ashes, they said, filled the air with a perfumed aroma—the odor of sanctity.

The examination of Alexandrina's "heroic virtue" conducted to this point by the Vatican had been based less on the testimony of witnesses than on 3,650 pages of her own writings. Two consultants were employed to prepare the only *posito* that exists on Alexandrina da Costa. The first consultant's concerns were theological. He had been disturbed, this priest acknowledged, by Alexandrina's accounts of conversations with Jesus in which the nature of the "reparation" she was making (by her suffering) suggested something ominous, even punitive. Jesus had told her, "I must take revenge in you on those for whom you wish to atone," Alexandrina wrote during the early stages of her passion ecstasies: "Either you suffer, or I lose souls." The theological consultant was reassured by his discovery that these demands for "revenge" had disappeared from Alexandrina's writings after 1940. The first consultant was troubled as well by the descriptions Alexandrina gave of her battles with Satan, in particular her belief that the Devil had made her an object of his lust. While the lives of the saints were full of struggles for their chastity, this consultant noted, he knew of nothing of the like Alexandrina had reported. Nevertheless, the fact that Alexandrina had not willed these experiences, he wrote, was for him evidence that the visionary's struggle to remain pure had been "heroic."

The second consultant's perspective was principally psychological. Alexandrina's writings were insufficient to explain her passion ecstasies, this consultant observed. All he could say for certain was that Alexandrina had been "subjectively sincere" in believing her visions came from God. He found no indication of mental illness in Alexandrina's letters, which were full of wit, sound judgment in practical matters, and an impressive sense of irony. The second consultant admitted that he had struggled with certain "disconcerting details" in Alexandrina's diary. Her descriptions of receiving consolation through a golden "tube of love" that connected her to Jesus, and Alexandrina's account of Jesus using a pomade made from His heart to massage her own aching breast, both had "rather strange connotations," the psychological consultant noted. Despite these apprehensions, however, he agreed with his colleague that Alexandrina's writings "appear on the whole proof of uncommon virtue and of an often heroic commitment to fidelity and love of God."

The names of consultants employed by the Congregation for the Causes of Saints are not made public, but in 1988 *Newsweek*'s Kenneth Woodward had found the psychological consultant in Chicago. Father John Lozano was a Spanish priest with a doctorate in spiritual theology, but on his own initiative had taken advanced courses in psychology, and owned a familiarity with Freudian theories that was rare among Vatican consultants. Father Lozano did not dispute Woodward's observation that the "tube of love" Alexandrina described was a rather phallic image. "All the Freudian dogs were barking," the priest acknowledged. "It could very well be that her paralysis was a way of protecting herself from men. And look at her obsessions with the Devil. He appeared to her as a dog, a snake, a monkey—all of them Freudian symbols." He had not delved into this in his report, Lozano explained, because "in Rome they don't know what to do with Freudian psychology." He was stranded between psychiatrists who "attribute everything to sex," he said, and theologians who "attribute everything to God."

Father Lozano then made a statement to which I would return again and again during the months after I first read it: "The trouble is, we have very little dialogue between psychology and religion."

He was that rare priest who believed a visionary's experiences could be accounted for by psychological explanations, Lozano told Woodward. He did not believe, however, that Alexandrina da Costa's ecstasies were the result of psychosis or hysteria. Alexandrina had "healed" her obsession with the Devil, Father Lozano believed, through prayer: "Psychologically she was a sick person who was made whole again." The Church, Lozano reminded Woodward, "does not propose as saints perfect models of normality."

Among the things I learned at the Vatican was that while ignorance may be a crude facsimile of innocence, it enjoys many of the same advantages, the main one being that people want to educate you, and that in so doing, they inevitably disclose their deeper intentions. No less surprising, I found I was learning as much from those who shunned me as from those who drew me close. The doors shut in my face, the phone calls not returned, the claims that someone else was better qualified to answer such questions, and especially, the demands of confidentiality made by those willing to address even briefly certain "dangerous" topics eventually began to reveal a good deal about both the nature and the scale of conflict in the Holy See.

After ten days in Rome, what at first had seemed mere palace intrigue, the petty machinations of careerists in clerical collars, I gradually understood as something much more profound, a clash not only of ambitions but also of deeply held beliefs, one that many in the Vatican—particularly at the highest levels—regard as an apocalyptic struggle for the very soul of the Church. It heightened the drama that this struggle was coming to a climax in which the approach of the new millennium coincided with the failing health of a pope whom both sides saw as the central character.

Arriving in Rome as one for whom Pope John Paul II was less a figure than a figurehead, I was within a few days thoroughly fascinated by him. There was a personal regard—not respect, necessarily, but an unmistakable acknowledgment—this pope elicited from even his critics that made him, for me, an increasingly profound and mysterious presence. I encountered some who questioned his judgment, a good number who disputed his policies, even a few who seemed to resent his authority, but not one priest I met, pro or con, expressed even the slightest doubt about either the depth of his spiritual life or the strength of his moral conviction. Even those who all but wished out loud that he would die, and permit the election of someone more "modern," seemed wistful when they spoke of this pope, as if nostalgic for a world in which he would have been a better fit. Those known to oppose his leadership struggled, visibly and audibly, to comprehend how a man of such formidable intellect could live by a faith so simple, so humble, so "medieval."

I would learn months later that the Vatican expert Malachi Martin had designated the two main sides in the war being waged all around me as "traditionalists and conciliarists." The conciliarists, in Martin's view, no longer saw the Church as a sacred institution, but rather as a "stabilizing social force." They were globalists who wanted to relax Church doctrine in such sticky areas as divorce, contraception, abortion, homosexuality,

and vows of celibacy by priests—not out of moral conviction but because such policies would limit discord and controversy. Taking the
Vatican as a whole, conciliarists were about equal in number to traditionalists, but were better represented, Martin believed, in the College
of Cardinals, and were significantly more influential in the secular world
because of their alliances with academic, humanitarian, and governmental
institutions. They were certain they would win in the end, which would
come as soon as Pope John Paul II passed away.

Among the conciliarists, nothing about John Paul was so quaint as his
devotion to the Virgin Mary. The pope's relationship with the Virgin had
taken on the aspect of a mystical pageant ever since the attempt on his
life in St. Peter's Square during May 1981. The first shot fired by the
gunman, a fanatical communist with alleged ties to the Bulgarian secret
police, would have struck John Paul in the head, it was said (by him,
among others), had the pope not, at the very moment the trigger was
pulled, bent toward a young girl in the crowd because he saw that she
was wearing a picture of the Virgin of Fátima. The would-be assassin fired
twice more, and the bullets struck John Paul's torso, but he survived.

During his convalescence, the pope was reminded that the date of the
assassination attempt was the sixty-fourth anniversary of the first reported
apparition at Fátima. He meditated daily on the meaning of the Fátima
apparitions during these weeks, and even began corresponding with the
sole surviving visionary, Lucia dos Santos. It was reported that John Paul
might at last do what popes had been promising since 1960, reveal the
awesome third Secret of Fátima. Instead, like the three popes who preceded him, John Paul announced that he would keep the message sealed
in a wooden box in the papal residence.

What this pope did that none before him had was visit Fátima: He made
the trip on May 13, 1982, the first anniversary of the attempt on his life,
and the sixty-fifth anniversary of the apparitions in Portugal. He had come
to thank the Virgin for saving his life, John Paul explained.

For those who found this all a bit much, there was the consolation that
Fátima had, over time, taken on mythic rather than mystical significance.
It was in the past and posed no real threat to their plans for the future.
"You know what the third Secret of Fátima is, don't you?" one postmodern
priest asked me with a sly smile. "The bill for the Last Supper."

This priest, like others of his ilk, admitted being much more distressed
by the cult of devotion sustained in the present by those alleged appari-

tions that were taking place in Bosnia, and by the role John Paul seemed to be playing as "Protector of Medjugorje."

In its entire history, the Holy See has never recognized any apparition of the Virgin, not even at Lourdes or Fátima, Father Gumpel informed me during my first interview at the Vatican. This was something, the priest added, that even most Catholics did not know. Bernadette of Lourdes had been canonized, of course—fifty-four years after her death, and on the basis of four miraculous healings that were passed by the medical board. "This very fact gives more credibility to what she said," Father Gumpel allowed. "But the Church has absolutely refrained from making a public binding statement that miracles or apparitions or anything of this sort took place."

I recognized that Father Gumpel did not want to encourage my interest in Medjugorje; he seemed even a little disappointed in me because of it. It was not so much the controversy surrounding the apparition site in Bosnia, I sensed, as that the assorted conflicts might never be satisfactorily resolved. "There has been a massive investigation at Medjugorje that has resulted in a great divergence of opinion," he said. "Certain bishops are very much against it, and others very much in favor of it. It can be said, certainly, that Medjugorje elicits strong opinions and powerful experiences. There have been several commissions here in Rome to examine the evidence, but no final conclusion has been reached. It remains an open question." In a case like Medjugorje, science could be used to disprove fraud but not to prove authenticity, Father Gumpel observed. It was obvious that the inevitability of such "unclear status" troubled him. "You can get so many people who claim to have seen it, but we know there are cases where people see things which aren't there. We could collect one hundred statements, but is that of value?" Thankfully, the problem of Medjugorje and other apparitions of the Virgin belonged not to the Congregation for the Causes of the Saints, said the priest, but to the much more powerful and secretive Congregation for the Doctrine of the Faith.

The Catholic Church is far less inclined than its critics to see significance in the fact that this preeminent branch of the Roman curia was, at the time of its founding in 1542, called the Congregation for the Holy Inquisition of Heretical Error. The Inquisition by then had been operating for more than three hundred years, from the time of the *Excomunicamus* promulgated by Pope Gregory IX in 1231. The Inquisition is most notorious for how it functioned in fifteenth-century Spain, where the grand inquisitor Tomás de Torquemada supervised the arrest, torture, and execution (often by burning at the stake) of thousands of accused heretics. The operations of the Inquisition were more discreet in Rome, where the father of the scientific revolution, Galileo, was not executed for claiming that the earth moved, but merely given a life sentence and permitted to serve it under permanent house arrest. By the eighteenth century, less concerned with the suppression of heresy than with a scholarly vetting of theological doctrine, the Inquisition had become known in Rome as the Holy Office. Only since the Second Vatican Council, during the 1960s, has it been called the Sacred Congregation for the Doctrine of the Faith.

The current chief officer of the congregation, its prefect, was the German cardinal Joseph Ratzinger, a former professor of theology whom the American priests I met at the Vatican invariably referred to as "the pope's main man." Born in Bavaria to a policeman and a hotel cook, Ratzinger had been known at the time of Vatican II as a brilliant young progressive. In 1962, at age thirty-five, he was brought to Rome to aid the reform movement. Ratzinger was said to have changed a great deal since then, however, and now was considered a leader of the traditionalists.

It was Ratzinger's reputation as an important thinker that (even more than in the case of Pope John Paul II) made his fundamentalist faith so inexplicable to those within the magisterium determined to rid the modern Church of all they regarded as anachronistic. Among these priests, Ratzinger's reputation as a reactionary had been topped off by the publication in 1987 of a book called *The Ratzinger Report*. For those who opposed the cardinal's positions, *The Ratzinger Report* was an intellectual scandal that revealed the prefect as "a throwback to the Dark Ages." Describing the Church since Vatican II as prone to "dissension" and "decadence," Ratzinger laid most of the blame at the feet of theologians more concerned with accommodating the world than with defending their faith. The Church was too open to outside influences, Ratzinger complained, weakened by bishops who lacked the courage to accept criticism. He deplored the decline in moral values and especially the "conformism" that left many Catholics unwilling to oppose what the cultural elite presented as progressive, logical, and self-evident. The cardinal's description of the

Devil as an inscrutable but very real presence, possessed of superhuman powers and an unrelenting opposition to God, had been particularly embarrassing to many intellectuals. The horrors of the twentieth century were inexplicable without Satan, insisted Ratzinger, to whom it was obvious that the Evil One had gained more influence with each passing year.

The intellectuals were chagrined as well by Ratzinger's strong support for what was perhaps the main obstacle to reconciliation with Protestants, veneration of the Virgin Mary. The cardinal encouraged the praying of the Rosary and was lavish in his praise for the Lourdes and Fátima movements. Ratzinger did not mention Medjugorje, but it was common knowledge in the Vatican that the prefect—at the behest of John Paul, perhaps, and certainly with the pope's support—had blocked those most intent upon seeing that the devotions there were condemned.

In Rome, my own interest in that tiny Bosnian parish would increase each time I spoke its name aloud. There was no single word, I discovered, that so instantly could produce a rapturous smile, a derisive snort, or an uncomfortable silence in the Holy See as "Medjugorje." What fascinated me was that those who extolled Medjugorje as a sacred place of unparalleled power all had made pilgrimages across the Adriatic to experience the village firsthand, while those who scoffed knew only what they had read or heard. The priests inclined to dismiss reports of miracles in Medjugorje (first as an insult to their intelligence, and second as an embarrassment to the Church) all seemed curiously muted. I understood eventually that this was due to the pope's undisguised sympathy for the devotions in Bosnia. Though he had made no public statement on the matter, a number of bishops who spoke to John Paul privately reported the pope to be deeply moved by what was taking place in Medjugorje.

It happened that I was in Rome at a time when Medjugorje was appearing on the front pages of newspapers all across Italy, mainly because of its connection to the controversy that had arisen from the reported miracles in a small city called Civitavecchia. Just forty miles north of Rome and barely an hour by train from the Stazione Termini, Civitavecchia is a tough, grimy port city on the Tyrrhenian Sea with a population of sixty thousand and an unemployment rate of more than 20 percent. Before the previous February, when tears of blood first were found on the cheeks of La Madonnina's (The Little Madonna), Civitavecchia had been best known for the brutal gang rape of three young girls in 1993, in particular because the father of one victim became a hero to many Italians when he avenged his daughter by castrating one of her assailants.

La Madonnina was a sixteen-inch white plaster statue of the Virgin that had been purchased as a souvenir by Don Pablo Martin, the parish priest of St. Agostino's Church in the Pantano district of Civitavecchia, during a pilgrimage to Medjugorje in September 1994. He had been guided to select that particular statue, Don Pablo would say, by the spirit of Padre Pio, who assured him that "the most beautiful event of his life" would result. Shortly after his return home, the Pantano priest had presented the statue as a gift to a particularly devout parishioner, Fabio Gregori, to protect the man's family against evils. The statue had begun to weep tears of blood, it was said, on the evening of February 2, 1995, the Feast of the Purification of the Virgin. Fabio, an electrician by trade, was loading his two-year-old son into the car, headed for the evening Rosary at St. Agostino's, when his six-year-old daughter cried out that the Little Madonna was crying. Fabio went inside, saw wet streaks of bright red on La Madonnina's cheeks, and reached out to touch one with the tip of a finger. The moment he did, Fabio would say, "a great blast of fire" surged through him.

During the next six weeks, nearly sixty persons, among them Don Pablo Martin, two police officers, the commander of the local traffic police, and a newspaper photographer, claimed that they, too, had seen La Madonnina's cheeks bathed in red tears. By mid-March, all of Italy was caught up in the drama, which had been trumpeted in headlines from Milan to Naples. Pantano's parish priest declared that La Madonnina's tears of blood were prophetic, part of "a mysterious design" that would be realized during the new millennium. Don Pablo, however, had long been prone to "marvelism," according to certain newspaper accounts: The priest was a Spaniard who claimed that when he came to Italy in 1969, he had been answering a call sent from Heaven by the recently deceased Padre Pio.

The esteemed bishop of Civitavecchia, Gerolmo Grillo, publicly declared his skepticism. When Don Pablo refused to destroy the statue, as his bishop requested, Bishop Grillo phoned the police, demanding that they investigate the Gregori family, then dispatched his own family physician to take a sample of the alleged lacrimazioni. The tears were indeed blood, the doctor reported. Bishop Grillo promptly announced the formation of an investigative commission and took personal possession of La Madonnina. After performing an exorcism on the statue of the

Virgin, Grillo drove it to Rome to be tested by two separate teams of physicians, one headed by the leading forensic medical examiner in all of Italy. They, too, said the tears were blood, human blood.

By then the Bishops' Commission was only one of several groups investigating the Civitavecchia phenomenon, as well as more than a dozen other reports of bleeding statues that were surfacing from all over Italy. Skeptics were particularly incensed by the opportunism of Civitavecchia's mayor, a communist who hung a crucifix above his desk in city hall, claimed he was an agnostic, not an atheist, and scheduled a series of press conferences to proclaim his vision of a religious shrine in Civitavecchia that would create a commercial boom. After allocating more than ten million lire for improvements to St. Agostino's Church, the mayor revealed plans for a sanctuary in the shape of a lily that was open to the sky, with seating for a thousand and a parking garage next door. At one press conference, the mayor described how ferryboats might anchor offshore to accommodate pilgrims. The year 2000 would bring an unprecedented flood of pilgrims to Rome, the mayor observed more than once. Why shouldn't Civitavecchia siphon off some of that action?

By early March, the Church investigation of *La Madonnina* had been superseded by a criminal complaint filed on behalf of the Italian people by the country's largest consumer protection group, Codacons. The law invoked was one that had existed since the 1930s, outlawing "abuse of public credulity." At almost the same time, a group based in Sardinia that was better known for exposing religious frauds than any other in Italy (despite bearing a singularly cumbersome title: the Anti-Brainwashing Telephone Line, Against the Tricks of Wizards and Sects) forwarded to the Procura (public prosecutor's office) in Civitavecchia an anonymous fax it had received from a person who claimed, "I feel very deep repentance for Pantano. They told me it was a carnival prank, but instead I am the tool of fanatical colleagues."

Early on the morning of March 8, the Procura (with Bishop Grillo's assent) orchestrated simultaneous police raids on the homes of Fabio Gregori and five of his relatives, but found nothing incriminating. The head of the Anti-Brainwashing Telephone Line remained the main source of theories to account for the Little Madonna's bloody tears. A blood-filled syringe, encased in the plaster and attached to a small battery that could be activated by remote control, said Giovanni Panunzio, was the most likely explanation. Or perhaps the culprits had employed special contact lenses that would expand and release liquid when exposed to heat.

Separate CAT scans run on the statue of the Virgin at the behest of the Catholic Church, Codacons, and the Procura, however, showed that *La Madonnina* contained no hidden devices.

Every other report of a bleeding statue that had arisen during early 1995 by then had been debunked; in one case the blood had turned out to be olive oil; in another, red paint. Doctors who tested the red liquid lifted from the cheeks of *La Madonnina*, however, agreed that it was the blood of a human male in his mid-thirties. That was the age of Fabio Gregori, skeptics noted. It was also the age at which Jesus had died on the cross, answered the faithful.

Newspaper columnists spun increasingly outlandish theories. One suggested that someone had played a "macabre joke" on Don Pablo and the Gregoris that was spiraling out of control. Others blamed enemies of Catholicism (the Jehovah's Witnesses, for example) who might have staged such a "mock miracle" in order to embarrass the Church. There was even a claim—taken seriously by the Procura—that a secret organization of gangsters whose sole motive was financial gain lay behind the whole affair.

The *giallo* (thriller) took its most dramatic turn yet on April 5, when Bishop Grillo appeared on a national news broadcast in prime time to announce that three weeks earlier—March 15 was the exact date—he and his sister, her husband, and two nuns visiting from Romania all had seen *La Madonnina* weep a tear of blood. As he held the statue of the Virgin in his own hands, the bishop said, his sister had reached out to touch the tear with her fingertip, but as she did, the red droplet disappeared. Until that instant, Bishop Grillo told his television audience, he had hoped "the whole matter would just go away." For weeks he had been unable to sleep, and spent most of the night praying for direction. Now, though, the bishop said, he would be the star witness before his own commission.

La Madonnina was at that moment being prepared for a Good Friday procession to a specially constructed chapel inside St. Agostino's, equipped with halogen lights and bulletproof glass. The planned festivities were called off the next day, when the state attorney announced that he had quarantined the statue of the Virgin, sealing it in a cupboard at the bishop's residence. Also, he had asked the Criminalpol (the Italian FBI) to conduct new tests on the blood samples taken from the cheeks of *La Madonnina*, and to compare them to the blood of Fabio Gregori and the male members of his family.

Fabio, now officially charged with both abuse of public credulity and conspiracy to commit a crime, continued to display a calm that impressed even skeptics. He would provide blood, Fabio said, but only if ordered to do so by the Bishops' Commission. The other Gregori men said this would be their position as well. Bishop Grillo protested through the media that the state of Italy had violated its concordat with the Vatican by undue interference in a Church matter. Hundreds marched through the streets of Pantano to demand *La Madonnina*'s release in time for the Good Friday procession. The Procura refused to yield.

It was not until June 17, the day before my own arrival in Italy, that Bishop Grillo had been permitted to remove *La Madonnina* from the cupboard in his home and deliver it to St. Agostino's for enshrinement. During an emotional homily at the open-air Mass, Bishop Grillo seemed to express doubt about what he had claimed to witness three months earlier. He had suffered terribly since reporting that he saw *La Madonnina* weep, the bishop explained, and felt compelled to say that he could not be sure what had happened: "I never talked about a miracle," he insisted.

At the Vatican, the whole affair was causing no small consternation. Bishop Grillo, after all, was a churchman of considerable influence, one of the few priests below the rank of cardinal permitted to sit on the executive board of the Congregation for the Causes of Saints, and a man widely respected for his integrity. At the same time, the Italian press, both secular and religious, was making much of the fact that the bishop was also a noted *miracoloto* (recipient of a miracle). As a child of five, during rough play with friends in his native Calabria, he had been hit in the left eye by a stone. According to the family doctor, young Gerolmo had suffered a permanent loss of sight in that eye. His mother refused to accept this and knelt to pray outside the doctor's office, pleading that the Virgin ask God to permit a healing. When the boy's bandages were removed, the vision in his left eye had been restored.

Skeptics charged Bishop Grillo with a predisposition to credulity, while the faithful contended that his devotion to the Madonna was at the root of the miracles in Civitavecchia. By the time I reached Italy, pilgrims from all parts of the country were arriving by the busload at St. Agostino's, swooning and singing as they entered the church and approached *La Madonnina*. However, the Holy See and its official newspaper, *Osservatore Romano*, had declined to address the subject of Civitavecchia even once in public. "We are extremely cagey in such matters," Peter Gumpel said. ("Cagey" was the word Gumpel used again and again in describing the attitude of the Church toward miracles and mystics; whether he intended the meaning "wary" or that of "crafty" I never was entirely sure.) "We have not intervened in Civitavecchia, and we will not intervene. Our concern must be those hysterical, overimpressionable people who are prone to mistake a powerful emotion for a religious experience."

The day before I departed Rome, I learned that Bishop Grillo had been summoned to appear before the executive board of the Congregation for the Doctrine of the Faith, and that this meeting would be attended not only by Cardinal Ratzinger but by the pope himself. It distressed me to be leaving before I knew what had happened at this gathering. "Don't worry," a Scottish priest told me. "You'll be able to read about it over there; the Croatians consider Civitavecchia an important story. It's all about Medjugorje, you see, and nothing is bigger news than Medjugorje."

This dialectic in the Church that I believed I had discovered—the epic struggle between the liberals or conciliarists or secularists or sophisticates or whatever they were on one side, and those determined to preserve sacred traditions on the other, with the future of Catholicism hanging in the balance—was both an underlying reality and a broad generalization, one that created categories into which the majority of priests in Rome would not neatly fit. Monsignor Sarno, for instance, came across as entirely traditional in his faith and yet thoroughly rational in his approach to the world, persuaded by scientific investigation that miracles really happened, but skeptical to the point of intolerance about the claims of religious mystics.

One afternoon, Sarno drove me out to the beautifully landscaped compound in an upscale Roman suburb where he and many of the other American priests from the Vatican maintain their residences. We shared one of the best meals I've ever eaten at a restaurant just down the street; halfway through our second bottle of wine, I revealed my interest in Medjugorje. The monsignor shook his head. "You don't believe in apparitions of the Virgin?" I asked. "I wouldn't say that," Sarno answered. "I believe in Lourdes." Bernadette's canonization, which had required four miracles, was for him proof that her visions were real. On the other hand, only a few months earlier, the congregation had considered the causes of the Fátima visionaries, or at least of the two who were dead (the third and most important of the three Fátima visionaries, Pope John Paul II's correspondent Lucia dos Santos, was still alive), and had refused to approve them because the miracles attributed to them could not be certified. "And I tend to believe more in Fátima than in Medjugorje," Sarno noted, "because of the facility with which the Blessed Mother appears in Bosnia, and this whole idea of Secrets."

The monsignor still was talking about the Medjugorje visionaries an hour later, during our drive back to the Vatican: "My skepticism is not skepticism of their sincerity. But remember that they may be sincerely deluded." He was silent for a few seconds. "Of course, a crazy person can be right." Another moment passed before he added, "And God's grace can work through what in human terms is error.

"Is it objectively true? That is the question before us," the priest declared as we passed through an iron gate manned by armed guards. I nodded but said nothing as we followed a narrow road that wound through magnificent gardens to a parking lot enclosed by buildings on all sides. Slightly dazed by the majesty of my surroundings, I climbed out of the priest's little Fiat on shaky legs and found myself facing a massive stone structure. Overwhelmed, I stared up at it for a long while before realizing that I was standing, literally, at the back door to St. Peter's.

"When you get to Bosnia," Monsignor Sarno advised me, "bear in mind what the Lord said to His disciples about the hour of His return: 'No sign will be given, except for the sign of Jonah in the whale.'"

CHAPTER FOUR

The view from my window on the weekly Croatia Airlines flight from Rome to Split was of an engine on the wing that wobbled precariously—as if hung rather than attached—all the way across the Adriatic. I might have enjoyed the flight more had I known then how advanced a form the jury rig is in Eastern Europe, and that nowhere is it practiced with more dexterity than in Croatia. The pope himself had trusted Croatia Airlines to fly him from Zagreb to Rome aboard a jet just like this one only ten months earlier, according to the article entitled "An Event for Eternity," on page seven of my in-flight magazine. Which was a comfort.

Sipping my second Peroni, I decided that, instead of fretting about a plane crash, it would be more provident to worry about obtaining a visa at the border. The country I was about to enter, like its neighbors, remained under martial law. Some of the soldiers who served as customs agents took bribes, I had been told, but most didn't, and there were more than a few who would lock you up for insulting them with an offer of money. I had no idea what they were going to make of a solo traveler who did not speak the language and could show them only a U.S. passport, plus a credential from a magazine called *Rolling Stone.*

Fortune favored me again. My seatmate, an attractive, flirtatious woman named Carmen Sinatra, announced halfway through the flight that she and her pretty teenage daughter both thought I looked like a writer. The two were delighted when I said I was, though I clearly became less dashing after confessing that from Split I was headed to Medjugorje. The Sinatras glowed again, however, when I pointed out that the holy city had become the main staging area between the Dalmatian Coast and Sarajevo, not only for UN peacekeepers and European Union police, but also for humanitarian workers, mercenary soldiers, and black marketeers.

Carmen and her daughter clearly preferred me as an adventurer than as a pilgrim. Lucky they took a shine, because waiting at the airport in Split was husband and father Silvio, who was not only the offspring of an Italian father and a Croatian mother but also the Rome representative of Croatia Airlines, and thus a man of no little influence at the border. It was Silvio who introduced me to the commanding officer at the airport, secured my visa, arranged the exchange of dollars for kunas at a reasonable rate, and put me on the bus to the center of Split.

As our bus lugged along in low gear past stone houses and pigpens toward a vista of smokestacks, my fellow travelers glanced at me with confused expressions. Not one of them smiled. Disembarking from the bus at its last stop, on the harbor across from Diocletian's Palace, I hiked along the city's gorgeous seaport promenade, the Obala hrvatskog narodnog preporda, among magnificent palm trees planted by the Venetians during their occupation nearly three centuries earlier. It was dusk, and the sun seemed half-submerged in the silver-blue sea, a pulsing arc of orange haloed by rings of pink and gold. A Jadrolinija steamship, festive with running lights, was just at that moment nosing up to the dock. Above the grassy bank, gas lamps glowed among benches already taken by young lovers awaiting the cover of night.

I was in vagabond rapture for the first block or so, until I noticed that the people all around me, on the sidewalks and the benches, at the open-air cafés and the coffee bars, along the storefronts and in the doorways, were turning to stare, and that their expressions were far from welcoming. Animosity, suspicion, and undercurrents of violence were all I met for the next six blocks. I felt as if I wore the brand of abomination by the time I reached my destination, the Belvue Hotel, at the end of the street. The clerk at the desk greeted me with a cold glare and a long silence, then informed me in harshly accented English that the price of a room with a private bath was $120 a night. A Croat would have paid a quarter of that, and felt overcharged even then.

An hour later, I ventured out into the hot, heavy night air to get a beer and a plate of calamari, grateful to find soldiers on the street, although they, too, gave me looks of implacable hostility. I was shaken. It wasn't arriving at the point of entry to a war zone that rattled me so much as the abrupt realization of my vulnerability. I chose a café on the harbor and took a table with an unobstructed view. There was a group of six young adults seated nearby; as soon as I sat down, the young men all shifted the young women to chairs on the other side of the table, then faced me with forbidding frowns, as if daring me to sneak a look. So I did. One of the young women gave me a thin, taunting smile, while the other two wore blank, vaguely apprehensive expressions. The three young men seemed to become both angry and uncertain, as if my defiance had taken them by surprise. They glanced at one another, then brooded over their drinks, trying to decide, I imagined, whether beating me to death would be appropriate under the circumstances.

The waiter, despite my *molims* and *hvalas* (pleases and thank-yous), would give me no more than a curt nod. By the end of that evening I concluded it was lucky I had myself to talk to, since no one else would say a word to me.

At least not until the next day, when I met my travel agent, translator, and driver, Ratko Mikulić. "People think you're UN," Ratko explained to me over a beer at a café deep in the bowels of the palace. "Everybody hates UN. Now they see you with me, it will be better." Ratko was the nephew of Father Milan, who had brought him to Oregon as a teenager to attend Jesuit, the best Catholic high school in the state. He was the star of the soccer team at Jesuit, Ratko boasted, and had offers to play in college, but instead returned home to Split. Here, he was the married father of two children, and operated a business called Aquarelle Travel, which had been booming before the war. He still owned the bus he had used to haul tour groups to Medjugorje several times a week during the summers of 1988 and 1989. Now, he got at most one group a month, and even that was small. To keep afloat, he had been forced to take jobs like the one I offered him, 320 kunas—about sixty-five dollars—for a three-hour drive in his little white Opel across the border into Bosnia.

We agreed to meet the next morning at my hotel, where most of the other guests, Ratko told me, were either arms dealers or black marketeers. Over their breakfasts, these men spoke an assortment of Eastern European dialects that were indistinguishable to my ear, except for a pair of Arab businessmen who scowled at me over espressos, whispering speculations to each other about what I might be up to. "I would stay away from them," Ratko advised.

Bathed in sweat, suffering in the astounding heat and humidity, I asked Ratko where a good spot for a swim might be found. The best place was a cove about two miles away, Ratko said; he would drive me, but I'd have to hike back to the hotel. An hour later, I was perched on a huge, half-immersed rock at the edge of the Adriatic, reading intermittently from a three-day-old *International Herald Tribune* that would be the last English-language newspaper I was to see for the next six weeks. On the front page was an article about the big anniversary event during the previous week at Bijeljina, where Radovan Karadžić and Ratko Mladić and the rest of the Bosnian Serb leadership had gathered to celebrate St. Vitus's Day. The evening program of patriotic songs and chest-thumping orations had been a prelude to the parade of armed forces scheduled for the next morning. Daybreak had been announced not by military bands, however, but by air-raid sirens when the Muslims began lobbing mortar shells toward town, intent upon spoiling the Serbs' party. A week later, scenes of the Serbs scuttling for cover were still being shown on Croatian TV, and each replay brought down the house at the bars and cafés in Split. Bijeljina was, what, about a hundred miles from here? I thought, tossing the newspaper aside. Closer than Seattle is to Portland. That scarcely seemed possible.

I dove into the sea for another swim, then climbed back on the rock. Dangling my feet in the water and drying my body in the sun, using my eyelashes to diffuse the brilliant light reflected off the sea's surface, I wore the grin of a happy idiot as a huge army helicopter thundered into view, skimming the edge of the water along the shoreline as it flew toward me. A young soldier in the open doorway looked me over, then sportively aimed his AK-47 straight at my forehead; for an instant I could see his eye through the sight. He lowered the weapon as the chopper flew past, then smiled—not maliciously, exactly. It was more like, "Have a nice daydream, Americanski, but don't forget we can kill you if we feel like it."

It occurred to me a moment later that this was the Fourth of July, and that I was an American alone in a place where neither American nor alone was an advantageous thing to be.

I spent my second and last evening in Split wandering through the crumbling labyrinth of Diocletian's Palace. It is the most imposing Roman ruin in Eastern Europe, and among the most evocative monuments to Christianity's endurance that exists anywhere on earth. Emperor of Rome for more than twenty years (A.D. 284–305), Diocletian was a native of Dalmatia, an Illyrian. (Thirteen Dalmatians in all ascended to the empire's throne, including Constantine.) It was under his rule that power had been transferred from the aristocracy to the military and Rome replaced by Milan as the capital city of the empire. Diocletian is best remembered, however, as the emperor under whom persecution of the Christians was resumed.

Diocletian's own religion was Mithraism, a bloody and dramatic Persian cult that worshipped a warrior god, Mithra, said to have slain the divine bull whose decaying body produced all the plants and animals in the world that are useful to humanity. The religion was enormously popular among Roman legionaries; by the time Diocletian was enrolled, Mithra had become a god of the sun—closely identified with Apollo—who offered believers immortality of the soul.

Christianity had been tolerated during the early years of Diocletian's rule, but the emperor gradually grew concerned at reports of infiltration in high places (several governors' wives and a handful of army commanders had been baptized). The oracle of Apollo was consulted and recommended an all-out attack on the church; thousands were imprisoned, tortured, and slaughtered. Then, in the fourth year of the fourth century, Diocletian abdicated his throne, passed on rule of the empire to a pair of successors, and retired to his palace in what is now Split. The structure covers nine acres, a fortress with massive walls buttressed by towers. As the empire he once ruled fell into ruin before his eyes—its roads closed, its farms abandoned, its lands overrun by robber bands, its seas ruled by pirate ships—Diocletian was confronted at home by two even greater defeats, the conversion of first his wife, then his daughter, to Christianity. At the center of his palace, still intact, is the Peristyle, a collonaded square dominated by a domed building, octagonal on the outside, circular on the inside, that Diocletian designed as his mausoleum. Within a few hundred years of his death, it had become Split's cathedral; the former Temple of Jupiter was a bapistry.

Those who live in Split today are said to see Diocletian's Palace as commemorating a sequence of revenges, beginning with that of Dalmatia against its conquerors and ending with that of Christianity against its persecutors. What I saw, wandering through it on the evening my own country celebrated its birth, was the triumph of American popular culture, writ large in the posters for Stallone and Schwarzenegger outside the movie theaters along the narrow cobbled streets adjacent to the Peristyle, and printed small on the Marlboro hard packs that peeked out of every other shirt pocket. Through the open doors of each café, coffee bar, and disco on the square crashed the thudding synthesizers of what the rest of Europe calls "Yugo-rock," a form that seems to have married "In-A-Gadda-Da-Vida" to the theme song from *Miami Vice*.

In the eyes of the young people who loitered by the dozens outside the open doors along the square, I could see the price of America's victory, that insoluble mix of emulation and resentment, of wanting what we have and hating what we are. Passing a table where a woman was selling T-shirts that bore the logos of nonexistent sports teams—New York Lions, Chicago Tigers, Los Angeles Bears—I left the palace by the north gate, then found myself alone in front of an immense black statue that seventy years earlier had been the masterwork of the country's most famous modern artist, Ivan Meštrović. Meštrović had chosen as his subject a national hero, the tenth-century religious leader Gregorius of Nin, who won for priests here the right to say Mass in Croatian.

What was I—what was any American—to make of such a place and such a people?

In the steamy night air, I walked west of the old town, out past the yacht harbor where the seaport promenade becomes Setaliste Ivana Meštrovića. On this street, the most impressive building is the residence that the great sculptor built for his retirement. Meštrović never lived in it, having emigrated to the U.S. shortly after World War II.

Ratko and I left the next morning at nine. He was not pleased when I insisted upon taking the inland route, through the checkpoints at Grude and Vitina, and punished me with a shrug that was distinctly fatalistic. We encountered our first detachment of UN forces at Gorica, where a UNPROFOR tank had knocked over a fence; traffic was stopped while soldiers and the owner debated replacement costs. It was near the town where Father Milan lived, Imotski, that we began to see exploded houses. Serbs lived in them before the war: "Those who fled, a bomb was set off inside so they wouldn't come back. The ones who stayed, though," Ratko assured me, not convincingly, "weren't bothered."

Ratko was one of those—"and there are a lot of us"—who believed that the Muslims were his country's biggest problem, in the long term. "The only way this war will be settled is if we and the Serbs divide Bosnia between us and drive the Muslims all the way to Romania," he told me. But the Croats and the Muslims were allies, I observed, joined against the Serbs as a common enemy. Ratko shrugged again. "That is for now," he said.

Roads have no names in the former Yugoslavia, and this one, which was simply "the road to Split" or "the road to Mostar," depending upon which direction you were headed, snaked from precipice to precipice through hillsides that once had been thickly forested but now were utterly barren. "'No grass grows where the Turk trod' is what we say," Ratko advised me. I already knew, though, that it was the Venetians who had cut down most of the trees in these mountains, to build what for a time had been the largest fleet on earth, and that it was overforaging by the Croats' own goatherds that had left these slopes denuded.

As we approached the Bosnian border, I observed that all these little towns we were passing through as quickly as possible—"to avoid complications," Ratko said—appeared to be booming; the cafés and restaurants in Grude were so full that people waited in line for a seat. "Black market," Ratko explained. It was the biggest sector of the economy in Croatia and Bosnia these days, with control divided between the Zagreb Mafia and the UN soldiers. The Spanish regiment was here now, but the Dutch and Italians had taken their cuts earlier. Ratko spoke without rancor; it wouldn't last, and in the meantime everybody got a piece. Only a year earlier, armaments had been the most precious commodity, but the market in weapons had collapsed almost overnight. "Supply and demand," he observed with the shrug that so far had several dozen variations and punctuated every point he made. "So many guns around here these days that you can buy an Uzi for five hundred marks. In Amsterdam, you can sell the same weapon for five thousand marks, only you have to cross five borders to get there." Medical supplies had been hot for a while, Ratko said, but there was a glut of those on the market now also. What was the most sought-after item these days? I asked. "Ballantine scotch," he answered. "Definitely. More than anything else, people need to forget."

The highway between Vitina and Ljubuški was lined with walls built from calcite rocks that had been lifted from fields where not so long ago it had cost a month's labor to plow a single furrow through the *karst* (which as far as I could tell translated to "arid limestone waste"). The landscape on either side began to suggest some surreal and morbid archaeological calendar upon which wars that went back more than a thousand years were layered one upon the other: The ruins of Roman villas, Turkish castles, Hungarian forts, and Austrian barracks spill down hillsides all across Croatia, Bosnia, and Serbia.

Where Ratko and I were at the moment was, I knew, a matter not only of much debate but of considerable bloodshed as well. This was Bosnia, technically, but not a part of it even nominally administered by the government in Sarajevo. Most of the police and soldiers were Croatians whose uniforms identified them as representatives of a Zagreb-sponsored "protectorate" called Herzeg Bosna. In Belgrade, Slobodan Milošević insisted this was still a state of Yugoslavia; Karadžić and Mladić referred to it as part of "greater Serbia." The people who lived here had for centuries called the region Western Hercegovina. Before the war, Hercegovina was regarded generally as the least lovely province in all of Yugoslavia: "Dry," "stark," and "rugged" were the preferred adjectives of travel writers. Ground and sky are filled with rocks. To the west, the Roman-designed, Venetian-inspired ports of the Dalmatian Coast disappear behind a bulwark of mountains. East, the dark green Neretva River has carved perpetually shadowed gorges in the Dinaric Alps, famous for its outlaw heroes and poisonous black vipers. These mountains extend to a northern border marked by the forbidding but compelling Duvno Plains: "Petrified blue eternity," the region's most famous poet described the view in that direction.

For me, the dazzling light made startling silhouettes of every jutted outcropping or crumbling crag. What grew naturally in the red soil bristled with a survivor's intensity. Thornbush brambles—more gray than green and filled with needles so sharp they can slash to death a goat or cow that falls among them—were the most prolific indigenous vegetation. Everywhere I looked were tombstones: Illyrian tumuli, Roman stelae, Ottoman obelisks, in the weed-patch graveyards outside mosques, and among the flower-strewn crosses of crowded Catholic cemeteries.

In Ljubuški, the skyline was dominated by the ruin of a stone fortress on a hilltop just off the main road, built by the residents of this region six hundred years earlier to defend themselves against invading Turks. "Every child here grows up hearing the story," Ratko advised me.

As we coursed down out of the mountains onto the Brotnjo plateau and toward the parish of Medjugorje, I noticed at once a difference. The quality I saw in the faces of the people along the roadside I found difficult to name: "Defiant serenity" was the best I could do. It showed in the faces of two old women, wearing babushkas and starched skirts, who were using cottonwood switches to drive a herd of cattle across the road outside the UN barracks compound (a former communist "tourist camp" now encased in sandbags and razor wire). A convoy of trucks had stopped in the opposite lane, and soldiers in the powder-blue berets of UNPROFOR were shouting obscenities. The two old women were not oblivious, merely unperturbed: They weren't trying to get in the way or to get out; it was as if either effort would have been beneath their dignity.

When the road was clear, we passed through a grove of oak and hornbeam into a clearing where I got my first view of the Trtla Mountains, a small but dramatic range that divides Medjugorje (which means "Between the Mountains") from the rest of the Brotnjo. Curving east to west, the last of the Trtlas is also the tallest, a spectacularly rugged peak that has been known by at least four different names, each in its own way significant. Most commonly, it is called Križevac—Cross Mountain. The impact of the massive white edifice at the mountain's summit stunned me: The cross was clearly visible from five miles away and absolutely dominated the horizon. It had been constructed, I would learn, in the year 1933, and the events that ensued were regarded by the people in Medjugorje as prelude to the drama of the visions that had commenced nearly half a century later.

I noticed that Ratko never looked directly at the mountaintop, but rather flicked glances at it from the corners of his eyes. He was more interested in business than in religion, Ratko told me. "It's hard to worry about something you can't see," he explained with a raffish grin. He was a great disappointment to his uncle, Father Milan, Ratko observed a moment later, and did not smile this time.

Ratko steered his Opel onto Medjugorje's one paved road, which wound in a figure eight through the parish to the stretch of open-air cafés and tourist shops directly across from the twin bell towers of the huge ocher-colored church. We parked in front of a restaurant called Dubrovnik, where Ratko bought us lemonade and introduced me to Slavica, an attractive auburn-haired woman with the sharp features, blue eyes, and olive complexion that are typical of the region. She was about Ratko's age, and had kept her looks far better than most Croatian women, who tend to blossom early—statuesque creatures with spectacularly long legs and a proud, prancing carriage—then fade quickly after marriage. Slavica was still single and had become known, I would learn, as "Queen of the Guides," a status owing to both her longevity and her commanding presence.

She was from Mostar, Slavica told me, and I at once began to ask questions, mainly wanting to know what the risks might be of a trip to the battle-ravaged city, little more than ten miles away by car. Slavica reacted with alarm, almost angry: "Don't go there. And if you do, stay away from the east side." The Muslims, I knew, lived on the east bank of the Neretva, which ran through the middle of Mostar. From positions in the mountains that they had occupied for the past three years, Ratko explained, the Serbs were still shelling the Muslim section of the city. "You never know where the rockets will land, or when," Slavica said. "Yesterday they began at ten-thirty in the morning." What about the people who live there? I asked. Where do they go when the shelling starts? Slavica stared at me sadly for a few moments, then shook her head, aghast at my naïveté. "Underground, if they can," she said. A moment later, Slavica told us she had to meet someone. As she stood to leave, she placed a hand on my arm. "Please be careful," she said. "Don't be in a hurry to die."

Ratko's mood was somber after Slavica left. I felt responsible. We had better get going, he said, if he was going to make it back to Split before dark.

We followed the rutted one-lane road past fields planted with bulgur wheat and fig trees into a neighborhood of newer buildings, all white stucco with red tile roofs. As his little Opel passed through a gauntlet of dark cafés and dusty tourist shops, Ratko bemoaned yet again the war's ruination of his country's tourist economy. "In 1990, Medjugorje had more than three million visitors," he said. "Everyone here borrowed money to build. This year, we will be lucky to see ten thousand pilgrims. People can't pay their loans; some will lose everything."

I nodded, barely listening. Ratko got my attention, though, when he made a hard right off the paved surface onto a profoundly rutted clay lane that within the week I would be calling "Visionary Way." My driver pointed out the seer Vicka's house first, told me Marija's was just up the road, then bounced us past the large white stucco villa where Ivan lived with his wife, an American and former beauty-pageant winner known among the irreverent as Miss Massachusetts. "How does he afford such a place?" I asked. Ratko smiled cryptically. "That is the question," he said.

Next door was the more modest home of Medjugorje's youngest visionary, Jakov, surrounded by the tropical flowers he spent hours tending. Across the street was a gated compound of two new houses: Mirjana, her husband, Marco, and their two daughters lived in one, while her mother, father, brother, and sister occupied the lower floor of the other. Mirjana's mother, Milena, greeted us in the driveway with a smile that was missing half a dozen teeth. She seemed courteous but confused, as if my arrival, while not unexpected, was nevertheless a mystery. The older woman looked me over as if searching for clues at the same time she spoke to Ratko in Croatian, explaining that Mirjana and Marco were in Italy and would not be returning home until the next evening.

"In the meantime, you can explore," Ratko told me as he translated. "Cross Mountain is that way"—he pointed southwest—"and the church is over there"—he swung his arm north. "It is much shorter if you go through the fields. Just use the spires of the church to steer by." He shook my hand. "I hope you get what you need. Good-bye for now." Watching his Opel drive away, I felt as if I'd been marooned.

Milena, who spoke no English at all, handed me a key and pointed up a flight of tiled stairs. I opened the door to discover I would have an entire floor to myself. Set up as a sort of dormitory, the place normally housed prayer groups that included as many as thirty people. The largest and nicest room was in the front, where the window fit like a frame around the huge white cross atop Križevac. Overwhelmed by that view, I retreated to a smaller room in the rear with windows shaded by fig trees, dropped my bag on a bed in the corner, then went back outside into the heat and blinding light.

Ignoring the war and their own government's advice against traveling to Croatia or Bosnia, small groups of pilgrims from the U.S. continued to arrive in Medjugorje. One of these had assembled across the street in front of Jakov's house by the time I walked down Mirjana's driveway into the street. Jakov himself stepped outside a moment later, looking nothing at all like the photographs I had seen of a slim blond boy with fine features and huge wonderstruck eyes. This Jakov was, at twenty-four, a short and soft-bodied young man with a broad face and light brown hair who stood shyly in the sun, blinking as he faced the crowd with an expression that was more wary than warm.

Through their interpreter, the twelve American pilgrims asked a series of questions that were astoundingly inane—mostly about events that had taken place more than ten years earlier. I knew this young man must have given the same answers on thousands of earlier occasions. Several times, Jakov glanced over their heads to meet my eyes for a fraction of a second. The first time he looked at me, he nodded slightly; I was certain he knew I must be the American writer staying at Mirjana's. His eyes were easily Jakov's most compelling feature, and looking into them, I sensed that the young man was telling me something I did not want to hear: What he had to say already had been spoken; if I understood it, there was nothing more to talk about.

Whether or not this communication was all in my own mind, I felt touched by the sweet patience and sincerity with which Jakov replied to each and every tedious question put to him by the pilgrims. "It must have been very difficult; you were just ten," observed an elderly man in a whiny voice. Jakov nodded as he listened to the translator. "It was terrible and glorious," he said. "I have never been more frightened, and I have never been happier. Our Lady was with us; all else seemed unimportant."

PART II

BETWEEN THE MOUNTAINS

All mystics speak the same language, for they come from the same country.

—Saint-Martin

CHAPTER FIVE

In Hercegovina, holiness and horror have existed side by side for centuries. The aftermath of World War II, however, was a time when darkness seemed to extinguish the light. Serbian Četnik soldiers and Croatian Ustaše rebels were slaughtering one another pitilessly, only to be exceeded in savagery by the communist Partizan troops who "pacified" the region shortly before Germany's surrender in the north. As many as three thousand Ustaše retreated into the inaccessible passes of the Trtla and Dinaric ranges, living in small outlaw gangs that attacked government buildings and army depots. A huge network of secret police and local informers was utilized in what seemed an unending campaign to drive them out of the country. Local civilians suspected of supporting the Ustaše bands were punished terribly.

In Medjugorje, the church that had stood for fifty years was demolished in a few days, its rubble used to create a temporary crossing over the Lukoc River (where the Ustaše had blown up the bridge). Križevac was given a new name, Titovac, and the Orthodox church at the bottom of the mountain also was razed. Catholic priests were forced to join the work crews who carried the stones of the Serbian church to the summit and used them to construct a five-pointed star. The star was the new symbol of Yugoslavia, the villagers were informed, and Titovac was now a state shrine where "heroes of the people" would be annually commemorated under the supervision of Communist Party bosses. Failure to attend would mean a long jail sentence, at the very least. Spies were everywhere, and religious observation was a punishable offense. Even saying "God bless you" could land a person in prison.

In April 1945, at the same time Marshal Josip Broz Tito's Third Corps paraded through Sarajevo as liberators, the citizens of Medjugorje were being reminded of and punished for the slaying of Serbs by Croats on an almost daily basis. In time, every man in the village would be required to join the crews who worked at the edge of the ravine where the bodies had been tossed, using sledgehammers and chisels to carve steps into the face of the cliff that led to a monument honoring the "People's Martyrs."

Such abasements were part of a nationwide effort by the new communist government to suppress the animosities that had been fueling one war after another for nearly a thousand years. Serbs, almost fourteen million strong, were the largest group in Tito's "Yugoslav Federation," and wielded the greatest power in the Communist Party. However, Tito himself was the son of a Slovene mother and Croat father, and though he maintained his seat of government in Belgrade, the dictator continued to spend six months out of every year at his summer palace in Croatia. Croats and Slovenes were the second and third largest *narod*s (peoples) in the new Yugoslavia, and each was awarded its own republic, as were the Macedonians and Montenegrins. Eighteen other "national minorities," among them Albanians, Hungarians, and Jews, received official recognition, as did a total of fourteen languages and two alphabets (Roman and Cyrillic). The sixth and by far the most diverse republic in the Yugoslav Federation was Bosnia-Hercegovina, which Tito designated as "neither Serbian, Croatian, nor Muslim, but Serbian, Croatian, and Muslim."

Titoism was a canny, cold-blooded blend of terrorism and diplomacy that, for three and a half decades, successfully checked and balanced Yugoslavia's ethnic tensions but never came close to extinguishing them. Tito was a dictator who did his best to be all things to all people: In 1953, he divorced his second wife and married a young Serbian aide, symbolically uniting the country's two most antagonistic nationalities. After 1957, when the last of the Ustaše and Četnik guerrillas had been killed or driven from the country, the communist leader began to loosen his grip, instituting liberal economic reforms and decentralizing his government. Mixed marriages and integrated schools were encouraged all over Yugoslavia, but especially in Bosnia-Hercegovina. The strategy succeeded, at least superficially, in the cities, but made almost no impact at all on the villages of the countryside. Serb and Croat peasants who migrated to the cities of Bosnia and Hercegovina—most notably Sarajevo and Mostar—soon discovered that they were at a considerable disadvantage compared to the cosmopolitan Muslims, who assimilated easily and made excellent use of Tito's educational system. What the Muslims dismissed as merely an inferiority complex was for the Serb and Croat country folk a simmering resentment that would require only a slight increase in temperature to boil over.

Tito prevented this from happening, in part by increasing opportunities for personal expression that included even limited religious observation. In Medjugorje, the Franciscans were allowed to erect a new Catholic church (on sturdier ground), which opened in 1972. Constructed of concrete breezeblocks, the building was no thing of beauty, but its twin spires and unprecedented size gave it tremendous presence; the church in Medjugorje was by far the largest on the Brotnjo plateau, with seating for five times the congregation it drew for Sunday Mass.

Catholicism in Yugoslavia had emerged from World War II badly besmirched by its association with the Ustaše government. Only the Franciscans were free of taint in the eyes of their fellow citizens. During the Partizan pacification campaign, more than seventy Franciscans had been murdered in western Hercegovina, including seven friars at the monastary in Humac (among them Bernadine Smulyan, the priest who had supervised construction of the cross atop Križevac) who were shot in the head and thrown into the currents of the Neretva.

In 1956, the Vatican was permitted to address the controversy now known in the church as the "Hercegovina Case" by reasserting its command of the Catholic clergy throughout Yugoslavia. The Franciscans at this time still controlled sixty-three of the seventy-nine parishes in Bosnia and Hercegovina, and occupied a position of influence in the region that was unmatched by another order anywhere on earth. By the early 1960s, the friars' authority was under attack, not only from Rome but also from Mostar. In 1966, when Marshal Tito reinstated diplomatic relations with the Vatican, the bishop of Mostar (a man who had been sentenced to prison as a Nazi collaborator ten years earlier), praised Tito's government and argued that Christianity and Marxism were entirely compatible. At the same time, the bishop was persuading Rome to turn twenty-one Franciscan parishes over to the diocesan establishment; during the next two years, the bishop gained control of another eleven parishes.

To say that the diocesan priests—mostly young and from the cities— were not welcome in their new homes would understate the case; throughout western Hercegovina, parishioners barred the doors to their churches against the diocesan clergy and in several instances dealt with priests who tried to force entry by beating them unconscious. Tensions reached a peak in 1975, when the bishop of Mostar asked Rome for five more parishes— the five that had been the main Franciscan recruiting posts in Hercegovina for nearly nine centuries. When the Franciscan father superior in Rome sent the pope a letter explaining the importance of these parishes, he was promptly suspended.

In August 1980, when Pavao Žanić became the new bishop of Mostar, he immediately announced that the city's parish would be divided into two parts: Three quarters of Mostar's territory would become a new cathedral parish, while one quarter of the city would remain under the supervision of Franciscans. The uproar that ensued was described by the new bishop as "a revolt." On the following Sunday, nearly every Catholic in Mostar attended Mass at one of the four small chapels on the outskirts of a city where Franciscan monks continued to administer the sacraments, leaving the churches of the bishop's new cathedral parish virtually empty. On the Sunday after that, diocesan priests dispatched by Bishop Žanić showed up at the four Franciscan chapels to announce that the buildings had been reassigned to the cathedral parish. The diocesan priests withdrew only after their new congregations threatened them with violence. Žanić promptly accused the friars of inciting the people to riot and ordered that henceforth no Franciscans would be permitted to set foot inside Mostar's cathedral parish without his personal consent.

Even in the Yugoslavia of Josip Broz Tito, Medjugorje was as well known for its faith as for its poverty. And the symbol of that faith was the enormous whitewashed cross atop the mountain of many names. Though it bore two "official" designations, Sipovac and Titovac, the peak for centuries had been best known as Grmljavinac—Mountain of Thunder. Under the occupation of one invading army after another—Roman, Slav, Hungarian, Ottoman, Austrian, and Serb—the residents of this parish had conducted their rites of offering and sacrifice on the mountain's slopes. By tradition, the summit was believed to be the refuge of the most terrifying force known to the people of the Brotnjo, more powerful than the Romans and crueler than the Turks: Gromovnik, the spirit of thunder. For decade upon decade the people of the parish had been devastated by Gromovnik, who nearly every summer managed to summon up at least one awesome storm that blackened the sky and burst without warning. Most destructive were the hailstones as large as a child's fist, which could pound a crop to pulp in seconds. Equally dreaded were the torrid winds that screamed down out of the mountains, igniting spontaneous combustion fires that might burn out of control for hours.

The Catholic Church attributed construction of the cross atop Grmljavinac to a vision of Pope Pius XI, who in 1932 summoned Medjugorje's parish priest to Rome and said he had been told in a dream that an enormous cross should be erected on the highest mountain in Hercegovina, to commemorate the nineteen hundredth anniversary of Christ's crucifixion. During the next year, the people of Medjugorje would become the most famously devout Catholics in all of Bosnia and Hercegovina, carrying more than twenty tons of rock, sand, and water on their backs through giant boulders and thornbush thickets to the top of the mountain. When the cross was dedicated in September 1933, the ceremony served not only as the Catholic sacralization of a mountain but as a prayer for protection from Gromovnik, in whom the villagers had never stopped believing.

What ensued the mountain's transformation from Grmljavinac to Križevac was legendary throughout the Balkans: The summer hailstorms that for centuries had ravaged the crops of Medjugorje came to a virtual stop, as did the autumnal fires that seemed to start by magic. Hail still fell occasionally, but less than a tenth as often, according to the villagers, who reported that the stones were much, much smaller. As years passed, the dark clouds that gathered above the mountain, like the thunder and lightning that followed, came to be seen more as curious phenomena of nature than as the life-threatening rages of an angry spirit.

It was against this backdrop and in this context that the apparitions in Medjugorje would unfold.

Mirjana Dragičević was sixteen years old back in June 1981, a high school student from Sarajevo spending the summer at her uncle's home in Bijakovići, one of five villages that comprise the parish of Medjugorje. Like all others over the age of ten, Mirjana worked daily in the tobacco fields and grape vineyards that constituted the entire economic resource of the Brotnjo. In 1981, plants still were watered by hand from stone cisterns. Only a handful of families owned tractors, and more people traveled by donkey cart than by automobile. Nearly every house in the parish was constructed of "dry wall," which in Hercegovina means a house built of calcite rocks fitted together so snugly that no binding agent was needed, roofed with stone slabs and insulated with straw. Most of Medjugorje's men had worked at one time or another as contract laborers in Germany, and these earnings accounted for nearly everything in the village that had lifted people above subsistence level.

The violent storm that struck the village on the evening of June 23, 1981, stirred Medjugorje's most senior citizens to say they had seen nothing like it in half a century—since construction of the cross, several would insist. At dusk, the sky was streaked with bolts of lightning that spread in all directions, and the thunder was deafening. Armed with a crucifix that she brandished like a weapon, the wife of a local tobacco farmer walked from house to house, sprinkling holy water.

More than a dozen fires started by lightning strikes broke out in Medjugorje during the night; trees burned like torches. Fire trucks arrived from the municipal capital of Čitluk in time to save half the post office, but the old meeting hall that had been converted to a disco for teenagers burned to the ground. By morning, the fires were extinguished, and at sunrise the sky was blue clear to the horizon.

June 24 was the feast day of the last Old Testament prophet, John the Baptist, observed in Medjugorje with a morning Mass and the release of all children from their chores in the fields. Late that afternoon, Mirjana and her fifteen-year-old friend Ivanka Ivanković took advantage of the holiday to go for a walk, following the dirt track that was Bijakovići's main street, to the paved road leading west. Because she came from the most cosmopolitan city in all Yugoslavia, was a pretty blonde, and planned to attend university, Mirjana had a reputation among the locals for loose morals. Perhaps this was why she and Ivanka did not admit until much later that their intention that afternoon was to sneak cigarettes. The girls sang as they walked, not religious hymns, but pop songs they had learned by listening to the radio broadcasts from Zagreb.

The two traveled less than a half mile before reaching the austere mound known locally as Podbrdo (The Foothill). Mirjana barely noticed when Ivanka stopped at the base of the big rockslide on the foothill's south side, but herself halted when she heard the other girl call, "Look, the Madonna!" Mirjana stared not at the rockslide but at her friend, wondering if Ivanka was well. The girl's mother had died barely one month earlier, an event that shocked the entire parish: Mrs. Ivanković not only had been the most beautiful woman in Medjugorje but was considered by many the most religious. At the funeral, Ivanka, weeping hysterically, had thrown herself upon the coffin, refusing to let the gravediggers cover it. When Ivanka again insisted she should look at the rockslide, Mirjana found the tone of her friend's voice alarming. "Come on!" she called, waving Ivanka forward. "You think the Madonna would appear to us?"

Hesitating for a moment, Ivanka followed Mirjana. "I didn't believe what I thought I was seeing," she explained later. "I was confused. I couldn't tell what had happened, whether I was having a hallucination of some kind." What she thought she had seen, Ivanka said, was "a bright figure" or "outline" that for some reason she felt certain was the Virgin Mary.

Mirjana and Ivanka had not walked much past Podbrdo when they encountered a young shepherd girl, Milka Pavlović. Milka, thirteen, asked the two older girls to help gather her sheep and lead them back home. The three girls turned back toward the east. At the base of Podbrdo, Ivanka again said she saw a shining young woman who seemed more to hover than to stand, about two hundred yards away, near the top of the rockslide. This time, Ivanka's companions also looked toward Podbrdo.

Mirjana saw a luminous silhouette that gradually resolved into a beautiful young woman wearing a silver-gray dress and a white veil, holding a baby wrapped in a blanket. The girl knew that no one from the village ever went up Podbrdo, except to chase a stray goat, which meant climbing over huge boulders and through thornbush thickets. Even this was avoided in summer, when vipers were said to nest in the rocks.

The woman on the rockslide uncovered, then covered, then uncovered again the baby in her arms. Mirjana sensed she was being called, but without words or sounds.

Moments later, the three girls were joined by a fourth, sixteen-year-old Vicka Ivanković. Vicka was among the few girls in the parish to miss Mass that morning, instead taking the bus to Mostar to attend summer school; she had failed math during the spring term and was desperate to earn credit for the class before the regular school year started in September. The bus ride back to Medjugorje in the afternoon had been hot and miserable, and Vicka, sick to her stomach, had lain down for a nap shortly after returning home. She was awakened at about 5:30 P.M. by her younger sister, who told her that Mirjana and Ivanka had stopped by while she was napping and wanted Vicka to join them for a walk on the road to Cerno.

Vicka was in such a hurry to catch her friends that she went out wearing house slippers. As she approached Podbrdo, she spotted Mirjana, Ivanka, and Milka standing together at the base of the rockslide. "All three were staring at something," she remembered. "They seemed frightened." She thought her friends had seen a snake, Vicka said. "They beckoned me to come over. I hurried. Strange! What are they staring at with such attention? Then they all shouted, 'Vicka, look at the Virgin!'"

Suddenly terrified, Vicka kicked off her slippers and, barefoot, "fled like one who is mad." She ran all the way back to the village before collapsing against a stone wall, then burst into tears. The two Ivans, Dragičević and Ivanković, came up the road moments later, carrying freshly picked apples in plastic bags. For them, the sight of Vicka Ivanković sobbing uncontrollably was quite astounding. Vicka was the most fearless and outspoken girl the Medjugorje parish had produced, known for the defiant—some felt reckless—remarks that more than once had landed her in trouble with communist authorities. (The secret police were particularly unhappy with her at present, because Vicka insisted upon wearing a pair of blue jeans—the ultimate symbol of corrupt Western values—that her father had brought home from Germany.) Still sobbing, Vicka—between gasps for breath—persuaded the Ivans to accompany her back to the three girls who claimed they could see the Virgin.

When she reached her friends at the base of Podbrdo, Vicka, by her account, raised her eyes and saw a shining young woman standing near the top of the rockslide, holding a baby. At first, Vicka was struck dumb. When at last she could speak, Vicka asked the younger Ivan (Dragičević) to describe what he saw, but by then the boy was running off down the road in the opposite direction, spilling his apples as he leaped over a rock wall and sprinted across the fields. The older Ivan stayed, but said he could see only something "white and turning." After a few minutes, he collected the spilled apples and walked off after his friend.

All four girls remained. Each said she saw the woman on the rockslide continue to cover and uncover her baby. At one point she seemed to wave, as if motioning them forward. But none of the girls could move. Finally, the shining young woman and the baby in her arms began to fade, and in an instant they were gone. "I was shaking," Ivanka recalled. "I didn't know what the others saw or believed . . . I was afraid. We were all afraid."

Back at the village, the six young people "told everything," as Vicka put it. Few believed. Milka's older sister Marija, famous for her sympathetic nature—at sixteen already the confidante of nearly every woman in the village—laughed when the other girls said they had seen the Virgin, and "did not want to talk about it seriously," Vicka reported. Her uncle Simun rebuked Mirjana as "a clever city girl," and warned her to say no more. Ivanka's grandmother became irate: "What is the matter with you? Somebody puts a flashlight on their head and walks around." Vicka's claims were taken seriously at least by her own grandmother, who warned the girls that they might have seen the Devil: "Sometimes he disguises himself as an angel of light to fool people." By nightfall, nearly everyone in Bijakovići seemed to have an opinion about what the four girls had seen. "People say this was a flying saucer, or some strange light," Vicka's sister wrote in her diary, and went to bed.

Mirjana stayed up all night, alternately praying and shivering with fear, then went out at dawn to gather tobacco and tend the flocks. She and the three other girls were teased relentlessly by several young men, including one who kept threatening to climb Podbrdo and "catch the Virgin." By the time the sun was up, Mirjana, Ivanka, and Vicka all had decided to return to Podbrdo later in the day. "It was strange: We did not want to give up," Vicka recalled. "We agreed to go, at the same time, where we had seen the Madonna on the previous day. If it was really Our Lady, perhaps she would come back."

At mid-morning, Vicka and Marija Pavlović caught a ride with their neighbor Marinko Ivanković, an auto mechanic who drove them into Čitluk, where the girls caught the bus to Mostar for their summer school class. The normally vivacious Vicka seemed in a "dreamy, oblivious state," Marinko later said. It was Marija who told the mechanic that Vicka and three others claimed to have seen the Blessed Virgin on Podbrdo. "Fantasies of teenage girls," observed Marinko, who was thirty-nine. At this remark, Vicka burst from her reverie in a flare of indignation: "It was the Blessed Mother," she insisted. "And She held the baby Jesus, too. She was showing Him to us."

Marinko shook his head. Maybe he would believe if one of the Ivans said he had seen the Virgin, the mechanic allowed, but he was not about to take the word of some silly girl. Marija, though, was deeply affected by Vicka's mood. "If it happens again," she told her friend, "come and get me." "I will," Vicka promised.

Vicka was alone when she began walking toward Podbrdo just before six P.M. on June 25. She met Mirjana along the way, and when they arrived at the base of the rockslide, they found Ivanka waiting with a crowd of about twenty people from the village. At first, the three girls saw only flashes of luminescence. Vicka was certain the Virgin was coming again, and, as she had promised, ran back to the village for Marija, who was in the middle of preparing her family's evening meal. "Come!" called Vicka, who now was trailed by her ten-year-old cousin Jakov Čolo.

Marija left her house in such a rush that she put on a pair of her father's shoes, which were far too large for her. She lost one shoe before she was out of the village, and the other by the time she reached Podbrdo.

Barefoot, she stood with the three other girls and little Jakov at the base of the rockslide.

They were joined moments later by sixteen-year-old Ivan Dragičević. Ivan had insisted earlier that he would not return to Podbrdo; he was obliged to help his parents with their tobacco harvest. During the late afternoon, though, Ivan had become increasingly agitated and distracted. Finally, at about 5:30, he excused himself from his chores and made his way through the fields to the foothill.

The older Ivan, Ivanković, also had refused to return to Podbrdo that afternoon, saying that whatever happened the day before was "something for children." He, too, changed his mind at the last moment and came to the hill, but only in time to serve as one of fifteen eyewitnesses who would provide sworn statements about what happened next.

For Mirjana, Ivanka, and Vicka, the light on Podbrdo had become so intense that they began to imagine the hillside might melt. But then the shining young woman, wearing her silver-gray dress and white veil, seemed to pass through the light, and to stand—or float (for some reason the one part of her they couldn't see was her feet)—in the same spot where she had appeared the previous evening. This time she was not holding a baby.

Again it was Ivanka who claimed to see the Virgin first, Mirjana second, Vicka third. "They were saying, 'There she is!'" Marija recalled. "But I did not see her on the hill." Neither did Jakov. Ivan saw "something," but could not say what. The figure on the hill was beckoning them toward her, Mirjana, Ivanka, and Vicka told the others, but at first none of the six moved. Then, a few moments later, the children began to climb the narrow goat path that disappeared into the rockslide: Ivanka, Mirjana, and Vicka in front, followed by Ivan, with Marija and Jakov trailing.

Most astounding to the crowd that chased after them was the speed with which the six ascended the hillside. "We began to run as if we had wings," remembered Vicka, who, like Marija, had lost her shoes. "We went up straight through the brambles. We ran as if borne along. We felt neither stones nor brambles. Nothing. As if the ground were covered with sponge or rubber. Impossible to explain." Even the strongest and most agile young man from the village could not climb to the top of Podbrdo in less than ten minutes. All six of these children made it in less than two.

By the time they reached the spot where the shining young woman waited for them, in a clearing between three clumps of brambles, Ivan claimed to see her clearly. So did Jakov. Marija, though, saw just "blurred white contours." The five others knelt and made the sign of the cross, so Marija did as well. It was only when she joined the others in praying the Our Father, Marija said, that she saw the young woman: "First face, then hands. It was like a haze clearing."

The young woman smiled at each of them, Mirjana recalled, then said, in a voice more like singing than speech, "Praised be Jesus." Ivanka and Mirjana each fainted briefly. Jakov was so overwhelmed that he reeled and fell backward into a dense bramble of thornbushes, disappearing from sight. The others doubted he could get out without being slashed to ribbons, but a moment later Jakov scrambled out of the brambles without a scratch. All six children went to their knees again, and continued their recitation of the Our Father.

"We were praying because we did not know what else to do," said Vicka. "We were crying a little and praying a little." The young woman standing before them continued to smile, "glorious and gay," Vicka remembered, "wonderful beyond words." Then she began to pray the Our Father with them, the six said. After they finished the prayer, Ivanka was the first to speak. "Where is my mother?" she asked. "She is with me," the smiling young woman answered.

By then, their fright was becoming an ecstasy, explainded Vicka: "There are no words to tell it. It was as if we were not on earth. Nothing bothered us, heat or brambles. Our Lady was there, we forgot everything else." Mirjana, the one the others thought of as strongest and most mature, began to plead with the apparition: "No one will believe us. They will say that we are crazy. Give us a sign." The young woman responded with a smile, but for some reason, Mirjana looked at her watch and saw that the hands were turning backward.

All six then heard the apparition tell them, "Go in the Peace of God." "Will you come back?" Mirjana asked. The young woman nodded, then disappeared back into the misty light.

The six children made their way down the hill much more slowly than they had climbed it, all of them in tears. The crowd that waited for them on the rockslide seemed most impressed by the fact that none of the six bore even a single scratch or cut, despite having run straight through the thornbush brambles. Several people insisted upon looking at the soles of Marija's and Vicka's bare feet and were astounded to find them unmarked.

* * *

On the evening of June 25, mechanic Marinko Ivanković was arriving at Podbrdo just as the six children were returning to the base of the rockslide. The first words he heard were Ivanka's as the girl told her grandmother, through sobs, that the Virgin had said her mother was in Heaven. The tone of the girl's voice and the intensity of her tears affected him deeply, said Marinko, who decided at once that he should tell the clergymen at the church in Medjugorje.

The priest Marinko hoped to find was Father Jozo Zovko, the new pastor at St. James's. An impassioned preacher, Father Zovko's lengthy sermons had aroused—and exhausted—parishioners ever since his arrival in Medjugorje nine months earlier. The priest was away, however, ministering to a congress of Franciscan nuns in Zagreb. His first assistant, Father Zrinko Cuvalo, was an older man, simple and staid, who did not appreciate Marinko coming into the rectory smeared with sweat and dirt, wearing no shirt under his overalls. Father Cuvalo chuckled when the mechanic told him that the Virgin had appeared to a group of children in Bijakovići. "I took it as a joke," the elderly priest would explain, "because people used to talk about apparitions on windows and such things, here and there. I thought it was a child's game, and I told that to Marinko." The mechanic felt disappointed and confused: "Father Zrinko acted as if he couldn't care less if the Madonna had appeared. I couldn't understand it—it didn't seem possible."

Back in Bijakovići, the six young seers were no better met than Marinko, even by their own families. Ivanka's brother had seen her trying to touch this invisible woman she spoke to, and told his sister she was insane. The girl's grandmother wept, begging her to come to her senses. Mirjana's aunt and uncle were beside themselves as well, phoning Sarajevo to tell the girl's parents they believed she had suffered a nervous breakdown. Ivan's mother and father were furious with him, asking again and again how he was able to see what others were not. Of all the parents, only Vicka's mother was open to the possibility that the six children might be telling the truth. "My child, don't lie—that is a mortal sin," she told her daughter. "But if you have seen Her, say, 'I have seen Her.' Don't be afraid."

She and the other five hurried through their chores the next day, Vicka recalled, "impatient" as they awaited the evening. Late in the afternoon, the six set out from the village together, joining a crowd of nearly three thousand that had gathered at the base of Podbrdo, arriving in donkey carts and aboard tractors. The sun was still high at that time of year, and the sweltering heat of the Balkan summer became nearly unbearable amid the hundreds of perspiring bodies that encircled the seers.

Vicka again led first the other visionaries, then the assembled crowd, in the prayers of the Rosary: the Our Father, the Hail Mary, and the Glory Be. It was during their recitation of the Apostles' Creed that the six young seers began to shout, "See the light! See the Madonna!" A pure white light had "shot forth" three times, Vicka would explain later. She knew— and so did the others—that the Madonna had sent it "to show us the place where she would be standing."

Many in the crowd would say later that they, too, observed these flashes of light, though not the young woman whom the visionaries saw emerging from it. The spot where the light had flared was nearly four hundred meters higher up the hill than the location of the previous day's apparition. The six visionaries began to run toward it, trailed by a crowd that clambered over the boulders and through the thornbush thickets behind them.

Among those in the first group that followed was young Jozo Ostojić, only twelve at the time, but well known in the parish because he recently had set a regional record for the hundred-meter dash; people said he would be on the Olympic team someday. Jozo had heard about the alleged appearance of the Virgin earlier that afternoon from a hitchhiker he and his older brother picked up on the road from Čitluk to Medjugorje. He knew the alleged visionaries were six children from Bijakovići, Jozo later said, but no one had told him their names. Little Jakov Čolo was the one who astounded him: "Jakov was two years younger than me, and not really athletic; normally I can outrun him by a huge distance. But on this day, I can't come close to keeping up with him. He and the others seemed to be flying up that hill. There is no path, just rocks and thornbushes, but all six of them are moving at an incredible speed, bounding from rock to rock, taking enormous strides. I am running as fast as I can, but falling further and further behind, and so are the grown men running with me. We are gasping for breath, almost in tears, unable to believe what is happening."

Ivan was the first of the seers to reach the apparition site that day, Vicka recalled; one by one, she and the others arrived at the spot, sank to their knees beside him and began to pray. When the shining young woman appeared, the six later agreed, she spoke just the words "Praise Jesus" before Mirjana and Ivanka again fainted. The apparition disappeared for a minute or so, while Vicka and Marija revived their friends. When all six knelt together and resumed their prayer, "She returned," Vicka said, "as on the previous day, only still more joyous. Wonderful, smiling."

Jozo Ostojić was among the first few witnesses to reach the spot where the six young people knelt. "They all had red faces and damp eyes, staring at the same spot. Just by the way they looked, I knew at once it was true; I went to my knees and began to pray also."

Marinko the mechanic was in the next group to arrive at the apparition site. He carried a jar of holy water, which he pressed into Vicka's hands, urging her to sprinkle it on the figure of the woman she saw, "to see what she is, whether the Madonna or a devil." Those in the gathering crowd watched Vicka flick the water with her fingers at a spot just above her head, shouting, "If you are Our Lady, stay with us! If you are not, begone!"

In response, the young woman smiled, Vicka reported: "I think she was pleased."

Vicka and the other seers knelt again and began to pray the Apostles' Creed, over and over. Ten minutes passed before the apparition spoke another word, telling the children, "Stand. Do not kneel anymore."

"Why have you come here? What do you desire?" those in the crowd heard Ivanka ask.

"I have come to tell you that God exists," all six children reported hearing the apparition answer. "I am here because there are many true believers. I wish to be with you to convert and to reconcile the whole world."

"Did my mother say anything?" Ivanka then asked.

"Obey your grandmother and help her, because she is old," the six heard.

"How is my grandfather?" asked Mirjana, whose mother's father had died earlier that year.

"He is well," was the answer, audible to only the children.

Some in the crowd began to shout, asking for a sign. Several of the young visionaries joined in, pleading, "Give us a sign which will prove your presence."

The apparition smiled but remained silent for some time, the children said, then told them, "Blessed are those who have not seen, and who believe."

"Who are you?" inquired Mirjana.

"I am the Most Blessed Virgin Mary."

"Why are you appearing to us?" Mirjana asked. "We are not better than others."

In response, the Madonna smiled again, then told the seers, "I do not necessarily choose the best."

The six all knew then, but could not say how, that the vision was coming to an end. "Will you come back?" the crowd heard Mirjana ask.

"Yes, to the same place as yesterday," the children heard the apparition answer. "Go in God's peace." She disappeared then, the six said, just as she had the day before.

The entire event had lasted less than half an hour, though the six visionaries would say that to them it had seemed much longer. "Those six kids looked—I wouldn't know how to describe—lost," recalled the factory worker Grgo Kozina, who, with his brother Ante, had arrived at the apparition site almost the exact moment that the visionaries shouted, "*Ode!*" ("She's gone!"). In the suffocating heat, surrounded by the sticky bodies of the crowd that had followed them up the hill, the seers looked as if they were about to swoon, Grgo observed. Marinko was fanning the children and sprinkling them with water. Mirjana, Ivanka, and Vicka each needed help to walk back down the hill. Marija Pavlović, was for some reason able to go on ahead of the others. He and Grgo were about fifteen feet behind Marija, Ante Kozina recalled, when suddenly the girl turned right and looked at the sky: "She stretched her arms and she was moving very quickly—suddenly she knelt down." Those in the crowd behind her stopped, riveted. Ten minutes passed before Marija stood, her face bathed in tears. "Where are my friends?" she asked, then continued down the hill.

A crowd of people followed the girl, among them several who accused her and the other children of taking drugs brought from Sarajevo by the city girl, Mirjana. A larger group insisted that Marija halt and tell them why she had stopped halfway down the hill. Others demanded that the girl show them her feet, which again were bare. Marija lifted the soles of her feet to show that neither the rocks nor the brambles had cut them. Marija explained that she felt as if she had been carried up the hill, and then part of the way back down. Midway in her descent, however, she began to feel that she was being restrained. When she stopped, Marija said, the Madonna had reappeared to her: This time, above Her head was a cross that seemed formed from a rainbow in which the most vivid shades were blues. The Virgin then began to weep, Marija said, and called to her in a plaintive voice, "Peace, peace, peace. Be reconciled. Only peace. Make your peace with God, and among yourselves."

His heart felt as if it would burst in his chest as he listened to Marija speak, Ante Kozina later said: "I am one hundred percent sure that something supernatural happened to that girl."

It was after eight when Father Cuvalo returned from the monastary in Široki Brijeg, where he had spent the day at a Franciscan retreat. Outside the rectory in Medjugorje, he was met by four priests from neighboring towns, one of whom was the secretary to the bishop of Mostar, all begging to meet the six young seers. Escorted by this group, the elderly priest arrived minutes later in Bijakovići, but was overwhelmed by the crowd that still lingered in the village, tramping back and forth along its one dirt road, angling for a glimpse of the visionaries and an opportunity to hear what they claimed the Virgin had told them. The priests found their way to Marinko's house, where dozens of people stood pressed shoulder to shoulder, shouting questions at the visionaries. It was obvious that those who had been present during this supposed apparition were deeply moved, weeping and praying, begging the priests to hear their confessions. Exhausted and confused, Father Cuvalo was unable to determine even which were the children who claimed to have seen the Virgin. Too many people were talking at once, he said, it was too late, everyone was tired, they should all go home, rest and try to sort this out in the morning.

Even after Father Cuvalo returned to Medjugorje, hundreds remained in Bijakovići. Among these was the beekeeper Ivan Dugandzić. He had come to Podbrdo that evening as a skeptic, the beekeeper later explained, and to him what seemed most remarkable were the heat and the crowd. Unable to breach the press of humanity around the apparition site, he and his friends climbed on one another's shoulders to see, but were so far away that they couldn't distinguish the visionaries from those gathered around them. The entire spectacle had seemed to him an enormous lark, at once bizarre and amusing, the beekeeper said, until late that evening, after eleven, when he chanced upon the only one of the six visionaries he knew personally, Vicka Ivanković, as she returned from Marinko's house to her parents' home. The moment he looked at Vicka's face, the beekeeper recalled, "I knew it was true. From that moment, I have never doubted, the intensity of it was so enormous."

* * *

Early on June 27, Father Cuvalo asked the parents of the alleged visionaries to bring their children to church so that he might speak with them
privately. Four of the six arrived at St. James's that morning: Ivanka, Vicka,
Marija, and Ivan. He would speak only with the two who had seen fit to
make their confessions before Mass, the priest announced, then led Ivan
and Vicka into his office at the parish house. He kept the pair with him
until noon, a tape recorder running throughout the interview.

The old priest made little effort to conceal his annoyance with the
artless account provided by the two teenagers. "Did you lie?" he demanded of Ivan at one point. For the only time during the interview the
boy responded with vehemence: "I don't lie!" Finally, sounding more exasperated than intrigued, Father Cuvalo dismissed the teenagers, then
left the church himself for a meeting in nearby Capljina, determined not
to let this matter preoccupy him so completely as it had the rest of the
parish.

Father Zovko would arrive back in Medjugorje during his assistant's
absence. He was startled to find the church surrounded by cars, trucks,
tractors, donkey carts, and a huge crowd. Inside the rectory, the priest
saw the tape recorder sitting on the table in the meeting room, turned it
on and listened to Father Cuvalo's interviews with Ivan and Vicka. Father Zovko was chuckling when his elderly assistant arrived back at
St. James's a short time later. It was no joke, the latter said, but a serious
matter that must be dealt with at once, before this frenzy got out of hand.
All six of the children had promised to return to the church that afternoon, the older priest explained, so that Father Zovko could question
each of them.

Zovko was not nearly so conservative as his assistant. The claim that
the Virgin Mary had appeared to six children on Podbrdo was dubious
at best, he said, and at worst actually dangerous. Religious gatherings
outside a church were illegal in Yugoslavia, and those involved could be
arrested on criminal charges carrying significant penalties. He and Father
Cuvalo agreed that the most prudent course would be to question each
child individually, and to record every interview, so that their stories could
be compared and the discrepancies noted.

Father Zovko began with Mirjana. His tone at first was equally curious and skeptical. The priest's interest palled rather quickly, however;
like his assistant, he seemed infuriated that the six children described their
ecstatic experience in such simple, even pedestrian, language. His skepticism

had turned to irritation by the time he spoke to little Jakov: "You did not see her!" he sternly told the boy at one point. "I saw the Madonna," an adamant Jakov replied. "I saw Her as if She were in front of me. I saw Her like I see you."

Truthfulness was the one quality with which those who knew them would credit each of these six children. Otherwise, they seemed an unremarkable group. Only Mirjana was of above-average intelligence. It seemed to Father Zovko entirely unlikely that the Virgin Mary would select six such ordinary children to receive the blessing of a visitation. Still, there was something touching about the way these children bristled at any suggestion of dishonesty, yet seemed quite willing to accept the possibility that they had gone mad. Also, he was intrigued by the consistency in the physical descriptions of the Madonna offered by the six seers: She was a young woman about twenty years old, they said, with blue eyes, black hair, and a crown of stars around Her head; She wore a white veil and a bluish-gray robe. Each of the children said they had not been able to see the Virgin's feet, described Her as hovering just above the ground on a white cloud, and said She spoke in a singing voice.

It perplexed the priest that none of the six had used exactly the same words, even when they quoted the Virgin. Each of the seers had been asked what the Madonna said in reply to the question about why she was appearing in Medjugorje. Ivanka recalled the answer as "Because there are a lot of faithful." Mirjana remembered it as "Because all of us are the faithful." Ivan said he had heard "Because you are the best faithful." More disturbed than inspired, Father Zovko declined to join the crowd assembling at the base of Podbrdo, instead sending Father Cuvalo and his younger assistant, Father Viktor Kosir.

The visionaries had made it clear that they could not be persuaded to stay home that evening: "We would have gone [to Podbrdo] even if we had been told that we would be shot," Vicka recalled. "But one thing was puzzling us; we did not know where to go, where Our Lady would appear." Shortly after the priests arrived, the six seers decided to proceed up Podbrdo in two groups: Vicka, Ivanka, and Mirjana would go by one route; Marija, Ivan, and Jakov by a second. Whoever saw the Virgin first would alert the others. As it happened, each group began shouting at the same moment that they had seen the flashing light signaling the apparition site, and started up the hill from opposite sides.

Reporting back to Father Zovko later that evening, Father Kosir described himself as "awed" by what happened next: The six children had ascended the rugged hillside at "an incredible speed," said the priest, an athletic young man who reckoned that the seers climbed Podbrdo in considerably less than half the time it would have taken him. No person on earth was capable of such a feat, and certainly no child, he said: What he had witnessed was beyond explanation.

The visionaries stopped about twenty meters higher up the hill than the site of the apparition on the previous evening. The Virgin appeared to them for only a moment, remained silent, then disappeared, the six reported. The crowd that followed them up Podbrdo numbered about five thousand; again the visionaries were enclosed in a crush of sweaty bodies. For a few moments, the two groups lost each other in the crowd, then Jakov found Ivanka, Mirjana, and Vicka. Together, the four found Marija. Ivan joined them a moment later. Reunited, the six once again recited the prayers of the Rosary, then began to sing. Many from the crowd joined in the prayers and songs. The children seemed certain the Madonna would return. Then all at once the six went silent, staring at the same point just above their heads.

Some in the crowd said they saw light and pressed in toward the spot where they believed the Virgin had appeared. Many of those standing nearest to the visionaries lost control of both their emotions and their movements. The seers began to cry out that people were treading upon the Virgin's long white veil, and begged them not to, but by then the crowd could not contain itself, and surged forward. The Madonna had disappeared again, the visionaries began to shout; they all seemed near tears. Several respected men from the village pushed their way though the welter of thrashing bodies and forced the crowd back, insisting that people form a circle around the six children, giving them room to breathe.

The Madonna reappeared a moment later, the visionaries said, but then a small boy lunged forward out of the crowd. He had stepped on the Virgin's veil, the six cried, and She had disappeared again. (The Madonna was not upset with him, the seers later told the boy; in fact, She had never stopped smiling.) A few seconds after that, the Madonna reappeared to the visionaries. While the men in front held back the crowd, the apparition proceeded: "Praised be Jesus," the seers said they heard the Virgin sing. As instructed by Father Cuvalo, Jakov asked the first question: "What do you want from the Franciscans?"

"Have them persevere in the faith and protect the faith of others," the Virgin answered, according to all six children.

Then Jakov and Mirjana each asked for a sign, Jakov because "the people treat us as liars," Mirjana because "people say we are drug users and epileptics."

The Madonna answered at first only with a smile, then told them, the seers said, "My angels, do not be afraid of injustice. It has always existed."

Several of the visionaries asked how they should pray. "Continue to recite seven Our Fathers, seven Hail Marys, and seven Glory Bes," the Virgin answered, "but also add the Creed." She disappeared a moment later.

Among those who had helped control the crowd surrounding the visionaries that evening was Jozo Vasilj, better known as Postar (he had for years been the village postmaster). Postar commanded considerable regard in the Medjugorje parish, in part as patriarch of a clan so large that the neighborhood where they lived was identified on official maps as "Vasilj," but perhaps more significantly because of his reputation as a man who would speak on no subject unless absolutely certain that what he said was true. Postar had refused to go to Podbrdo for the first three evenings after the apparitions began. His wife and mother both went to the hill, and each said she thought the children were speaking the truth. "I was telling them, 'You crazy!'" he later said. "'Why is Lady coming here?' I felt nothing. I was against it."

On the fourth evening, Postar decided to see for himself, arriving nearly two hours before the apparition would begin. Already, there were more than a thousand people on the hill. He was preoccupied with controlling the crowd, battling the heat, and protecting the children, and barely noticed when the apparition began. "I saw nothing, I felt nothing," he remembered. "Seeing nothing did not bother me, but feeling nothing I was noticing more."

After the apparition had ended, the six children headed back down the hill. Postar sat down on a rock behind a large thornbush that grew along the edge of the goat path. The first seer he saw coming down the path was Mirjana: "She was walking as if half-drunk, reeling. She came right by me, but in such a crowd that nobody was interesting. So she did not see me sitting behind the bush. Ten meters behind her came Vicka and Jakov. And as those two came by, Jakov, being ten, was holding on to Vicka. I was eavesdropping behind the bush when Jakov looked down to Mirjana and said to Vicka, 'Look, now Our Lady is helping Mirjana.' I looked down at Mirjana, and at that moment she started walking properly. There was absolutely nothing I was watching that could be manipulated. And Jakov said it so softly, yet in the same moment Mirjana is walking normally.

"So I got up and followed those two, Vicka and Jakov, for twenty meters, perhaps a bit longer, until Vicka said, '*Ode!*' which in Croatian means, 'She's going!' And at that moment Mirjana raised her eyes to see, then sat down on a stone. There was no way Mirjana could have heard Vicka—she was too far away and there were too many people making too much noise; not possible.

"I find it difficult even now to describe what I felt. First I began to sweat very heavily, then I started crying. I actually burst into tears, and ran off into the bushes, so as not to be seen. I cried for more than an hour before coming back to my house. Since that day, I have never been with the children at an apparition. Because I know I won't see anything. But that day was such that I need no other proof. That feeling of being so certain, so close to Heaven, it has never left me."

On the morning of the fifth day, June 28, the six visionaries submitted to an exhaustive interrogation by Father Zovko, who spoke to each of the children separately. The priest was passing beyond skepticism and exasperation into outright hostility.

Fathers Zovko and Cuvalo had begun to recognize the various levels of threat posed by these gatherings on Podbrdo, and were tempted to take the danger personally. Both knew that the fervor Zovko had brought to the parish was not appreciated by many in Medjugorje. His impassioned homilies that ran two, three, four times the length of other priests' sermons had infuriated more than a few of the local parishioners, as did his private lectures and extra catechism classes that drew many of the young people away from their chores in the fields. Father Zovko even had formed a private prayer group of eight especially religious girls, appointing the elderly Cuvalo as its leader. That none of these girls were among the six supposed visionaries led the priests to wonder if some sort of subversion—a design either of resentment or of contempt—was at work here.

Beyond this, the priests were convinced the situation was "out of hand and coming to a head," Father Cuvalo recalled: "The hill was full of people. We were supposed to be available to help, but we ourselves were confused." The two priests agreed that the most likely explanation for the apparitions—if they were not fraudulent—would be the use of hallucinogenic drugs brought to Medjugorje by the outsider, Mirjana. The city girl "looked too pale to me," he explained, and concurred with Zovko that they should concentrate on questioning her. He was but one of many who believed "this is all nonsense," Father Zovko told Mirjana that morning. If these were real apparitions, the priest went on, the Madonna would have left some important message. Mirjana answered only by promising that she would again ask the Virgin for a sign.

Alone with Ivanka, Father Zovko stressed that these gatherings on Podbrdo were not only illegal but a detriment to true religious faith: "Why do people now have to go over the thornbushes and up there on the hillside, and not come here to the church?" he asked. At moments during his interrogations, however, it was obvious the priest had been touched, as when he asked Marija what she felt during the apparitions. "There is just no way I can describe my great joy when I see," the girl answered.

Vicka's terse defiance and her annoyance at the pestering questions made the priests chuckle in spite of themselves. When asked if the Virgin had been "vexed" by people stepping on her veil during the apparition on the previous evening, Vicka answered, "Look, Our Lady cannot be 'vexed.' She is not like us. She had no problem." When one of the priests asked why the Virgin wore such a long veil, her reply was "How should I know?" And when Father Zovko wanted to know what had caused the Madonna to disppear, Vicka told him, "Ask Her."

Late that afternoon, he again sent his two assistants to Podbrdo to observe the visionaries during these alleged visitations. The crowd gathered on and around the hill that day was the largest ever assembled in the Medjugorje parish; more than ten thousand—perhaps as many as fifteen thousand—were pressed together, dripping with perspiration and gasping for breath in the heat. Somehow, he and Father Kasir found Jakov and Marija just outside Bijakovići, and walked with them on the road leading to Podbrdo. Only moments after the priests had joined the children, Jakov and Marija began to cry out, pointing at a spot near the top of the hill. "Suddenly Marija's face turned bright red," Father Kosir recalled. "'Look! Look! Look!' she shouted. Jakov did not say anything, but together they ran ahead with what seemed incredible speed. Marija wore a white blouse and a red skirt, so I could see her distinctly as she ran far ahead of me, almost seeming to fly. It was impossible for me to keep up with her."

Among those at the front of the crowd that surged up the hill behind the children was Grgo Kozina, carrying the tape recorder that would provide the first record of the apparitions other than personal diaries. The tape he made that evening begins with Grgo's own voice whispering, "It's Sunday, six-twenty-nine—six-thirty. The wind is blowing and the bushes are moving. The six of them were kneeling and are now getting up—now they are kneeling again."

"Did She come?" Grgo can be heard asking in a louder voice.

"Yes. Yes. She came," the visionaries reply.

The six then can be heard whispering among themselves, trying to decide what questions they should put to the Madonna. "'Let's ask Our Lady what does She want from us," one of the girls suggested, then the others joined in: "Our Lady, what do You want from us? Let's all ask. Our Lady, what do You want from us?"

"Where is She?" Grgo asked, whispering again. "Here," Jakov whispered back, then joined in with the others, repeating the Virgin's answer to their question: "'Let the people pray and persevere in the faith.'"

The visionaries then repeated three times the question they had been given by Father Zovko: "Our Lady, what do You want from our priests?" A moment later the six seers called out the Virgin's reply: "'Let the priests be strong in faith and help you.'" Grgo shouted to the crowd, "They asked what did She want from our priests, and She replied, 'Firm faith.'"

The voices of the visionaries speaking among themselves are heard next: "Let's ask, as Father Jozo was wondering, why She is appearing here and not in the church," Ivanka suggested.

"Our Lady, why don't You appear in the church, so everyone can see You?" the voices of the six called out. Mirjana alone repeated the Virgin's answer: "'Blessed are those who do not see, but believe.'"

"'Blessed are those who do not see, but believe,'" Grgo shouted to the crowd.

"Will You come to us again? Will You come back?" the six asked. A moment later they conveyed her answer: "Yes, She will, at the same place. She will come again, here at the same place."

Several moments later Vicka's voice can be heard again: "Look, there She is!"

"Where is She?" Grgo asked. "On the bush, or on the rock?"

"Here," Vicka said. "Here. She is disappearing slowly. She is disappearing slowly. She has gone! She has gone! We shall pray again."

"She has gone; they are praying again," Grgo's voice whispered into the recorder. "Nineteen minutes before seven." Vicka and Marija began to lead the crowd in a hymn. Suddenly, though, the visionaries cried out again: "Here She is! She is here!"

"Seven," Grgo whispered. "They have just seen Her again."

Vicka called out another question: "Dear Madonna, what do You expect of these people?" A moment later Vicka relayed the reply: "'Let those who do not see believe as those who do.'"

"Will You leave us a sign so that people believe that we are not liars or comedians?" Vicka asked.

The Madonna's only reply, the visionaries told Grgo a moment later, had been a smile, followed by the words that had been Her last at each apparition—"Go in the peace of God"—and Her slow, sparkling fade into the pearly light from which She had emerged less than an hour earlier.

On the morning of June 29, Father Zovko again questioned the children. Pressure on the six was mounting hour by hour. Their families remained far from supportive. Ivan's parents told him repeatedly that the apparitions were happening only in his mind. Whether real or imagined, Ivan said, he found the Madonna's appearances "difficult to experience." The apparitions were "a terrible shock," he explained, "and we asked ourselves what was happening to us, if we were on earth, in Heaven, if we were alive or dead. We no longer knew anything of where we were." Marija told Father Zovko that for the first two days after she first saw the Holy Virgin, "I was scared and not able to eat. My hands were completely white; when I saw Her the first time my hands were cold like ice."

Mirjana's parents had arrived from Sarajevo, alarmed by relatives in Bijakovići who "thought I had become insane," as the girl put it. The city girl had seemed from the start more concerned than any of the others with doubts about her mental health. She was reassured when her parents, after questioning her until midnight, announced that she seemed well to them, and that they were returning to Sarajevo the next day: "My mother [told] my uncle, 'Something must be happening.' My family knows I do not lie."

Ivanka again admitted that, on the evening of June 24, she had convinced herself she was "hallucinating" her vision of the Madonna. Like each of the others, however, she clearly was growing more confident and more certain. To Father Zovko, the soft-spoken girl expressed not only disappointment in the local clergy and the civil authorities but also a hint of disdain for them. "The majority don't believe," she told the priest, including him by implication.

Each of the visionaries was adamant that the Madonna would appear again that evening. "She's never deceived us," Ivanka noted. Mirjana said she believed the Virgin would appear "even if we were placed in jail." Vicka told Father Zovko that the Madonna would find them "even in America."

The priest's position seemed to have hardened. He confronted the children with reports from witnesses that, while they appeared to be in a state of bliss during the apparitions, several were seen weeping afterward. Each of the visionaries agreed this was true; not one of the six, though, offered an explanation. For the first time, he attempted to shake them with warnings and threats. "Stop deceiving people!" he ordered Ivanka. When the girl continued to insist she was telling the truth, the priest lost his temper: "We are here in front of God and the cross. It is terrible to play with religion. God cannot leave it unpunished."

"But I've seen," Ivanka answered. "It is not a lie. I see Her as I am seeing you." Breathing deeply to keep his composure, Father Zovko asked if the Madonna intended to leave a sign. "I don't know," Ivanka replied. "Do you realize the crowd is terribly disturbed?" the priest asked. "They see no sign, you don't change. The people feel terribly deceived by you, taken advantage of. How can you do it?"

"I believe I see Her. What can I do?"

At that afternoon's Mass, the pews were filled to overflowing. Zovko used the homily to make his initial public statement regarding the apparitions, insisting his own mind was open, but urging parishioners to put their faith foremost in Scripture. Even as he spoke in church, the six seers were being subjected to the first in a series of interrogations by the civil authorities of Yugoslavia's communist regime. Municipal police from the Ministry of Interior office in Čitluk arrived in Medjugorje that afternoon with two vehicles—one an ambulance—and ordered the purported visionaries aboard. The police claimed to be concerned about the children's mental health; their apprehensions, however, were mainly political.

Catholic devotions were the last overt vestige of Croatian identity, and those who had inherited Tito's power feared that any nationalist uprising would emanate from the Church. News that Croats by the thousands were gathering on a hill in Hercegovina already had been received with alarm in the Bosnian capital of Sarajevo; orders were issued to Mostar, then to Čitluk, that this entire spectacle must be contained before matters got out of hand.

The young seers first were taken to the police station in Čitluk and interrogated. Stymied by the children's insistence that they had seen the Madonna, the police ordered the six back into the ambulance and escorted them to the regional medical center. A pediatric specialist there examined the children and reported that they were physically healthy and did not seem to be under the influence of drugs. Police officials responded by sending the six to the city hospital in Mostar. There, the children were subjected to a crude form of shock therapy—led into the hospital's morgue to view corpses in various stages of autopsy. Mirjana was most visibly disturbed, but all admitted they were frightened—except Vicka: "Why should I be afraid?" she asked. "Everyone dies. It is the common lot."

Even Vicka seemed shaken, however, by the hour the six spent waiting with an assortment of the mentally ill in the lobby of the hospital's psychiatric wing. The psychiatrist who saw the six described her examination as "basically a conversation." "I thought it was a matter of hallucination, and wanted to calm them down, to reason with them," she would explain. Vicka's recollection differed: "[The doctor] attempted to make us some kind of sickies. She suggested that we were imagining things; that we were some kind of addicts; that we were fooling the people."

They were living in their imaginations, the doctor told the six seers, to avoid real life; if they persisted, they would end up in a mental hospital with the sort of people they had seen waiting outside. This especially frightened Mirjana, who had heard of many instances in Sarajevo where opponents of party officials were locked up in psychiatric wards, never to be heard from again. The doctor's threat was followed by another attempt at reason. "You have lost your mother," she told Ivanka. "You had the impression that she was appearing to you." "But I did not lose my mother," Mirjana interjected, "and I saw the apparition also." After two hours with the children, the psychiatrist dismissed them, then wrote a report in which she admitted being impressed by how "collected and well-balanced" they seemed.

The seers then were driven back to Čitluk to be examined by yet another physician. He had been ordered by the police to look for the influence of hallucinogenic drugs, Dr. Ante Bijević explained. The six arrived at the doctor's office just before 4 P.M., and Dr. Bijević spoke with them individually. "Normal, balanced, well-situated in time and in space, no hallucinations," were the conclusions he reached in each instance. His examination was cut short at five-thirty when the children began to fidget,

worried about getting back to Bijakovići in time for that evening's apparition. It was Vicka, inevitably, who brought things to a head, marching
into the doctor's office to demand, "Is it over?" "It is not your turn yet,
but you can take a seat," he answered. "I am, thank God, young and
healthy," Vicka responded. "I can remain standing. And when I need a
medical examination, I shall come of my own accord. Now is it finished?"
Flustered, the doctor asked the girl to hold out her hands. Vicka did.
"Look, these are my two hands, with ten fingers," she said, wiggling them
under the doctor's nose. "If you don't believe me, count them." She turned
on her heel and walked out the door. This girl seemed so sensible, Dr.
Bijević would explain later, that he saw no point in proceeding further,
and let the children go.

At a quarter to six, the seers piled into a taxi and rode back to Bijakovići,
stopping at home for a glass of water, then heading straight to Podbrdo.
Ivan did not join them at the foothill that evening, yielding to the pleas
of his parents, who were terrified by the secret police stationed outside
their front door. By the time the other five visionaries arrived at Podbrdo,
the crowd awaiting them had swelled to at least fifteen thousand, more
than five times the population of the entire Medjugorje parish. In their
number were an assortment of civil and clerical authorities who had been
sent to observe.

Fathers Cuvalo and Kosir once again had been dispatched to watch
the visionaries; the former was "undercover," wearing civilian clothes and
carrying a camera. He arrived at the previous day's apparition site well
ahead of the visionaries. The spot was surrounded by a small crowd standing in a circle around a clearing perhaps twenty-five meters wide; at the
clearing's center were a large thornbush and a stone. Pretending he had
no idea of the site's significance, he walked into the circle and sat down
on the stone. When some in the crowd began to object, Father Cuvalo
told them he was a priest, then added, joking, "When She comes, I will
give Her my place."

Also on hand were three doctors sent by the chief of police to stand
with the children during the apparition. One of them was the young
pediatrics specialist who had examined the seers that morning, Darinka
Glamuzina, an ardent apparatchik who had boasted to the children of
her atheism, describing how, as a teenager, she refused the sacraments
whenever her parents forced her to attend Mass.

Again, it was sunny and hot, and the visionaries led the sweaty crowd
first in songs, then in prayers, until, at 6:26 by Grgo Kozina's watch, the

five went silent and began to stare at a point just above their heads. "They just knelt," Grgo whispered into his tape recorder.

The voices of several seers can be heard on the tape next, asking, "Dear Madonna! Are You glad that the people are here?" A moment later they called out, "She is smiling. She is glad."

"Dear Madonna!" they asked next. "How many days will You stay with us?"

"As long as you wish," was the Madonna's answer, the seers reported a moment later.

"Will You leave a sign?" one of the seers asked next.

"I will come again tomorrow," was the Virgin's only answer, according to the children, who began to repeat more or less the same questions they had asked the day before: "What wish do You have for us here?" ("That you have a solid faith and that you maintain confidence.") "What do You expect of the people who have come in spite of the brambles and the heat?" ("Let the people believe firmly and not fear anything.")

"Will we be able to endure all this?" one of the seers asked. "Many people persecute us because we 'see,'" explained another.

"You will be able to endure, my angels," the Madonna answered, according to the children. "Do not fear. You will be able to endure everything. You must believe and have confidence in Me."

The seers then made a startling request. Motioning to Dr. Glamuzina, they asked, "Could this lady touch You?"

"There have always been unfaithful Judases," the Madonna answered. "Let her come." While the breathless crowd watched, Vicka helped the young doctor place her hand on the Madonna's long veil. "She is touching Her," the seers began shouting a moment later, then, "She left! She left!"

Dr. Glamuzina reacted visibly, wearing an expression that thrilled some but frightened others: She had seemed to experience a sort of electrical shock, those closest to her said. The doctor herself described what she felt as "a shudder." She stood awestruck for a moment, then turned and began to stagger back down the hill. At the base of Podbrdo, Dr. Glamuzina told the waiting police she would have nothing further to do with their investigation, then refused to say another word about what she had experienced.

Back at the apparition site, the children stood in silence, seemingly bewildered, then began to sing again, joined within moments by the crowd. Several minutes would pass on Grgo Kozina's tape before the voices of the seers could be heard again, shouting, "The light! The light! Here She is!"

Moments later, the visionaries brought forth another person from the crowd, a pathetically ill three-year-old boy named Daniel Setka. "Dear Madonna!" the seers called. "Will this little boy, Daniel, ever be able to speak? Please make a miracle so that everyone will believe us. These people love You very much. Dear Madonna! Make one miracle."

"She is looking at him!" several seers informed the crowd. "Dear Madonna, say something!"

"Is She still looking at the boy?" Grgo asked.

"She is still looking!" several of the children said, then began to call out again: "Dear Madonna, say something, we ask You! Say something, we ask You! Say something, dear Madonna!"

Nearly a minute passed, the visionaries would report, before the Virgin answered: "Let [Daniel's parents] firmly believe that he will be healed."

"Go in God's peace," she told them a moment later, according to the children, who began to shout again: "She has left!" "Look, the light!" They then began to sing, joined by the crowd.

Father Kosir had positioned himself much closer to the visionaries than Father Cuvalo, standing just ten feet from the five when they ceased their singing and began to stare fixedly, their expressions rapt. The younger priest could not entirely conceal how deeply the experience had affected him: "As I looked at their faces, I felt the apparition—as they called it—had begun. I watched Jakov very carefully; he was looking downward and in front of him. After their 'conversation' with the Madonna ended, I approached Jakov and asked him where the Madonna had come from—above, or the left or the right. 'I saw her right in front of me,' he said. If he had said he had seen her elsewhere, he would have had to move his head, and I would know he was lying. But he did not." Shortly after the apparition ended, Marinko came to the children, carrying a stone with a cross painted on it, Father Kozina recalled; when Marinko asked where the Madonna had appeared, all five pointed to the same spot.

The priests led the children back to the rectory and interviewed each individually, asking them to describe the Madonna's appearance and what she had said in response to their questions. The consistency of their answers convinced him the seers were telling the truth, the younger priest said. "My intention had been to demonstrate that their versions contradicted each other and thereby to discredit their allegations, and preserve the parish from credulity and from becoming a public laughingstock," he explained. "But they passed every test."

Father Cuvalo later sought out Ivan, the visionary who had not come to the hill that evening, to see if perhaps he had broken ranks and was prepared to admit deception. Such was not the case. The decision to obey his parents and to stay away from Podbrdo had made him sick to his stomach, Ivan said. Through waves of nausea, he walked halfway from his parents' house to the hill and stood by the side of the road, watching the crowd gathered at the apparition site. He made a silent vow that he would never be absent again, Ivan said, and at that moment the Madonna appeared to him. "Be in peace, and take courage," was all she said, according to the boy.

When Ivan returned to his family, he discovered that armed guards from the state security police, commonly referred to as "*milicija*," had been assigned to the home of each visionary. Instructed to follow the seers' movements and to prevent them from returning to what was now known as "Apparition Hill," the guards barred doors, peered in windows, even stationed themselves on rooftops, warning the children and their families that "serious consequences" would result if they went again to Podbrdo. One senior police official attempted to persuade the six that they were equally endangered by the enormous and increasingly unruly crowds drawn to the apparitions on the hillside. "Keep out of sight," he told Vicka. "The people are walking off their jobs. Nobody wants to do anything. Everyone thinks only of seeing you."

Father Zovko met with his two assistants on the morning of June 30 to discuss a situation that now threatened the entire parish. He and Father Cuvalo still were skeptical, but also increasingly confused; the two agreed they could not be sure if the children were fabricating the apparitions, or were experiencing some profound adventure of the imagination. Father Zovko was at once irritated and shaken when Father Kosir confessed how deeply moved he had been by what took place on Podbrdo during the previous evening, and that he now felt the claims of the six children should be taken seriously.

Further complicating matters, a fourth priest who had been dispatched to the parish, Father Tomas Pervan, announced that he too believed the children's experiences were genuine; Father Pervan was convinced, however, that the apparitions had resulted from a diabolical possession, and insisted that the six be subjected at once to an exorcism.

The parish priest summoned the visionaries for yet another round of interrogations immediately after morning Mass. He began with Ivanka, who still was badly shaken by the previous day's visit to the psychiatric wing of the hospital in Mostar. Moments after the girl admitted how frightened she was, the priest suggested that the apparitions were the work of the Devil. "Can't you see that Satan is here, and not the Madonna?" Father Zovko asked at one point. Ivanka shook her head, absolutely adamant: "It is Her. I know it." Abruptly, the priest changed his tack, attempting to draw Ivanka into an admission that it was all a hoax: "How long did it take Marinko to write up those questions, the answers, and what you should say?" he asked. "He did not write the answers, only the questions," Ivanka replied. A moment later he suggested it would be better if he, a priest, supplied the answers. "What answers?" Ivanka asked, no longer hiding her exasperation. "The Madonna answers, not us."

The priest next summoned Mirjana, the seer most obviously distracted by her apprehensions. "I am not afraid of the *milicija*," she told Jozo, "but I am petrified that they might put me in the hospital." He moved at once to exploit the girl's fear, hoping to force a confession of fraud. "God terribly punishes anyone who misleads people," he reminded Mirjana. "Do you know that?" She did, the girl answered. "Those who are misleading people, those who are transmitting the wrong messages," the priest went on, "they are severely punished. . . . How is it that you are going to get out of this?"

"What can I do," Mirjana asked, "when I see Her and other people can't?" The priest continued to make threats: "It may be tomorrow that God terribly punishes you six," he warned. "I don't think He will," Mirjana replied. "Why won't He?" Father Zovko probed. "Because we are not lying," Mirjana said.

Did she feel sorry for those who could not see the Madonna? the priest asked suddenly. She felt "a terrible sorrow," the girl responded. But perhaps she enjoyed the attention of those for whom she had become a special person, one of the blessed, Father Zovko suggested. Mirjana shook her head: "That disturbs us. We would rather be by ourselves."

Mirjana and each of the other seers did reveal one significant area of vulnerability, in their preoccupation with when the apparitions would end; it was a question that each of the six put to the priest. Mirjana said she had resolved to ask the Virgin "to tell us exactly how many days She is going to be with us." What did she herself think? the priest asked. "Something keeps telling me two or three more days," the girl answered.

Before ending the interrogations, Father Zovko pressured each of the visionaries to ask if the apparitions might be moved from the hill to the church, then gave the six a list of questions they were to ask when they next saw the Virgin. The children were barely out the door when he received a call from the local chairman of the Communist Party, demanding that he appear in Čitluk that afternoon to offer an "explanation" of recent events in his parish. He and Father Cuvalo departed for the municipal capital at once, well aware how perilous their situation had become.

At almost that same moment, a pair of social workers—one from the Council of the Republic in Sarajevo—arrived in Bijakovići and summoned the seers and their families to a meeting at Vicka's. There, the two social workers informed the parents of the six that they had been instructed to take the children on an "outing" in order to discuss their experiences during the past week. It was either them, the two young women explained, or the secret police, who were headed for Medjugorje from Čitluk at that moment. Seconds later, the seers piled into a large sedan and were driven south.

In Čitluk, Fathers Zovko and Cuvalo were discovering just how seriously the civil authorities took the events in Medjugorje. The local chairman of the Communist League began the meeting by warning the priests that they must immediately "extinguish this charade." The two Franciscans attempted to explain that the events in question were beyond their control, but the chairman cut them off: These gatherings on the hill in Medjugorje were religious in character, he observed, which meant that responsibility for the restoration of order must fall on the local clergy. A moment later the chairman confided that, like the priests, he could expect "dire consequences" if the situation were not brought under control: His superiors in Sarajevo wanted these "demonstrations" stopped and promised that heads would roll if they continued. The most the two of them could do, the Franciscans said, was attempt to move the crowds from the hillside into the church. That would be satisfactory, said the chairman: "They can pray all day, and all night too, so long as they don't do it on the hill."

For the six young seers, what at first had seemed either a rescue or an abduction was turning into an adventure. The two young social workers drove them, touring style, to the magnificent waterfall at Kravica, then in Capljina treated the children to the first really expensive restaurant meal of their lives. The social workers stopped for ice cream in Cerno, and suggested continuing on to a resort along the Dalmatian Coast. Completely caught up, the seers did not grasp what was happening until almost six o'clock: Driving west through grain fields, they could see Cross Mountain, and moments later the huge crowd gathering on Podbrdo. The six immediately demanded that the social workers stop the car and let them out. More than ten kilometers from Bijakovići, the two women knew the children had no chance of reaching the foothill in time for the evening apparition and did as they were asked.

The children realized their situation only after they climbed out of the long sedan and ran into the field along the side of the road. They stopped, looked at one another, then knelt in a group and began to pray. Moments later, all six said, they saw a luminous cloud that began to assemble above the crowd—nearly twenty thousand strong that evening—gathered on Podbrdo. They knew at once it was the Madonna, recalled Vicka, and began to weep: All six saw her clearly a moment later, gliding toward them through the air, her long veil streaming behind her. The visionaries began to sing.

The social workers, who a moment earlier had been cracking jokes ("Ask the Virgin what She's going to do to me for stealing you this way," the social worker from Sarajevo), now said they too saw something ("a light" was all they would allow later). Terrified, the two young women jumped back into the sedan and sped away, leaving the children beside the road.

As always, the Virgin greeted them that evening with "Praised be Jesus," the seers said, then joined them in reciting their respective Our Fathers, which her voice made more song than prayer.

Mirjana spoke first: "Are You angry that we were not on the hill?" The Virgin answered that it did not matter. "Would You be angry if we did not return any longer to the hill, but waited in the church?" Mirjana then asked. The Virgin, Mirjana and the others would agree, responded with a curious smile, then said, "Always at the same time." Again the seers asked that the Virgin leave a sign. She responded by moving slowly away from them, according to the six, until the light shone once more on the people assembled at Podbrdo. They heard her parting words, "Go in the peace of God," and the light was gone a moment later.

The seers stood and began to walk across the fields toward Medjugorje, arriving nearly an hour later. At Podbrdo, the crowd that streamed back down the hillside rumbled with disappointment, passing stories that the children had run away, that they were in jail, that they were in a mental hospital, that they had admitted it was all a game that got out of hand.

Before going home, the seers stopped at the church of St. James, where Father Zovko hustled them at once into the rectory. The priest was delighted when the seers told him they had asked if future apparitions could take place in the church, rather than at Podbrdo. "Somehow, She seemed undecided when we asked Her this," Mirjana reported. "Even so, She said that She will not mind." Zovko thought it might be a good idea if the visionaries went to the people still waiting at Podbrdo. "Mirjana, what would you say?" he asked. Mirjana again seemed to believe that her wish to please the priest was divinely inspired: "Something urges me to go on the hill—something seems to be telling me to say, 'The Madonna has appeared in another place. She told us to go to the church for visions.' We should say that all true Christians should go to church."

"Then go and tell the people!" Father Zovko urged.

Vicka objected, fearful that the crowd would not let the children alone if they appeared publicly. The others agreed, suggesting they simply tell friends and family members that the next evening's apparition would take place in the church, and allow word to spread.

"What if the people do not come to the church?" asked the priest.

"That will be okay," Vicka told him. "It would be better if the six of us were alone. We would prefer that."

"Does the Madonna come because of you, or because of the people?" the priest asked.

This questioned silenced the seers for several moments. "Because of us," Ivanka said, then paused. "Why did She choose us?" she asked. Marija shook her head: "I think because of us and because of the people, equally," she said. Mirjana agreed: "Because of us, and because of the people, to strengthen the faith of the people." Vicka said it was true that they had an obligation to the people, but she still felt it was unnecessary to address the crowd that evening: "Those who believe in God know what is of God, and will learn everything that they need to know."

Father Zovko conceded the point, finally, and sent the children home at nine that evening. The seers would arrive in Bijakovići, just in time to learn that the security police had taken Marinko to Čitluk for questioning. The six immediately called for a taxi and rode to Čitluk. With Vicka in the lead, they walked into police headquarters, demanding Marinko's release.

They were confronted by the local chief of police, who told them the mechanic was accused of encouraging religious gatherings in a public space. Vicka answered with defiance, insisting that Marinko had encouraged nothing: "Arrest us if necessary, but leave this man alone." Sputtering, the chief turned his wrath on Vicka's mother, who had accompanied the visionaries: "What an education you are giving your children!" he said. "This country of Tito which we have freed with much blood, you are going to destroy it!"

"You keep your Tito," Vicka told the chief. "We have Our Lady."

The children waited at police headquarters several hours, until Marinko was released. It was nearly two A.M. by the time they returned to Bijakovići.

Early on the morning of July 1, Father Zovko heard about the three-year-old boy, Daniel Setka, who had been commended to the Madonna by the visionaries at the apparition on the evening of June 28. The priest at once summoned Mirjana and asked her to describe the Virgin's response. "She looked at the child for two or three minutes," Mirjana replied. "The look was full of mercy . . . there was a strong faith that the child would get well."

"Then why didn't he?" Zovko demanded.

"She said to believe strongly and the child will get well."

"How can the child believe when he is so little?"

"She said, 'Let us strongly believe that he will get cured,'" said Mirjana. "I think it meant for the child and his parents to have strong faith."

"Do you think the boy will ever get well?" the priest asked.

"I think he will, because She looked at him with such mercy."

"When will the boy get well?" he demanded.

"In a year or so, I think," she guessed.

What neither the priest nor the visionary knew was that the boy's healing already had taken place.

Daniel Setka had become seriously ill—"stiff and blue"—when he was four days old. Unable to determine a cause, his pediatrician sent the infant to the Children's Hospital in Mostar. One month later, his condition remained undiagnosed; doctors said the baby would not live a year. His parents responded by sending Daniel to a series of clinics for testing:

Electroencephalogram scans showed the child experienced "paroxysms" at the rate of three to five per second, but no doctor could offer an explanation until a professor at the medical school in Sarajevo diagnosed the boy as suffering from a combination of spastic hemiparesis and epilepsy. At the age of two and a half, Daniel was a pathetic figure; unable to speak or walk, he could barely hold his head up.

His family was religious, and made pilgrimages to various shrines in Yugoslavia, but nothing changed. The Setkas continued to seek a miracle, however, and rushed to Medjugorje when they heard about the apparitions on Podbrdo. A neighbor in Bijakovići introduced the family to the six seers. "The little boy looked half-dead," remembered Vicka, who met him at her parents' home on the afternoon of June 28. Daniel's father had carried him up Podbrdo that evening. At the seers' urging, the crowd permitted the child to stand near them during the songs and prayers; it was Vicka who presented the boy to the Madonna during the apparition.

He had a vague but immediate feeling that his son was stronger, Daniel's father said, though he saw no real indication of this until the family stopped at the café near the church in Medjugorje. Moments after they ordered dinner, in the presence of assorted witnesses, the boy slapped the table and in a voice everyone nearby could hear said, "Give me a drink." These were, claimed his parents, the first words he had ever spoken. Daniel's mother and grandmother began to shout and weep; his father cried out, "This is a healing."

Daniel's parents brought him back to Podbrdo the next day. Though far from spry, he managed to take two steps on his own power before falling. He still could not hold his head up for more than a few seconds and had not spoken another word since his exclamation in the café. His parents carried him most of the way up the hill, stopping every twenty meters or so to let the boy wobble for a moment before his legs collapsed beneath him. At a level spot little more than halfway up, his parents put Daniel down and watched him stand steadily for a few seconds, then begin to walk with apparent ease. Moments later, he began to speak, though witnesses said the words came out in such a jumble that it was impossible to understand what he was saying. All at once, the boy began to climb over the rocks. Standing atop one, he turned and called, in a voice that was both loud and clear, "Mama, look, I'm walking!"

As his sobbing parents knelt to pray, those who had been present spread the story through the village. Word of the boy's healing had reached Sarajevo by that afternoon; TV crews and newspaper reporters began to arrive from all over Yugoslavia—there even were calls from reporters in Italy. This influx further agitated the civil authorities in Mostar and Sarajevo, who had been stunned once already that day, when the two young social workers assigned to keep the six seers from going to Podbrdo on the previous evening both submitted their resignations, insisting that they could not continue after what they had witnessed in the field outside Cerno.

More militia officers arrived in Medjugorje during the afternoon, doubling in number within a few hours. Meanwhile, in Čitluk, officers continued to direct their threats toward Father Zovko, warning that the priest would face criminal charges if he was unable to control the "demonstrators" who assembled at Podbrdo each evening.

The Medjugorje pastor felt not only powerless but increasingly isolated; now *both* of his assistants seemed to believe that these apparitions might be real. It was the power of the confessions he was taking and the conversions he was witnessing that persuaded him, Father Cuvalo explained. Most affecting was a local woman who had made a public scene at Podbrdo on the evening of June 29, scoffing loudly at these so-called seers and at all who believed such fairy tales. "God exists, but only in your imaginations, idiots!" she had shouted at one point. Something had happened to the woman that evening, however, and the confession she made to him the next morning was the most moving he had heard during the thirty years of his priesthood, Cuvalo said.

The leadership of the Communist League was more determined than ever to quash the devotions that surrounded these alleged apparitions. Teams from the security police summoned the families of the visionaries to a meeting at the elementary school and warned them that, unless this entire spectacle came to a stop at once, their children would be committed to mental hospitals and they would be sent to prison. Villagers who wished to court favor with the communists visited the seers' homes and warned their parents that they should fear for the children's very lives. That afternoon, the families arranged a meeting with Father Zovko, begging the priest to intervene. "In anguish," as he described it, the priest locked himself alone in the huge church and knelt at the altar to ask for guidance.

While he prayed, two officers of the *milicija* attempted a ruse, offering four of the visionaries a ride in a police van from Bijakovići to the church in Medjugorje. This way both sides would get what they wanted, the officers explained: The police would keep the seers away from

Podbrdo and the seers would not have to pass through the frighteningly large crowd that already filled the village streets. Ivanka, Marija, and Vicka accepted, but began to bang on the van's windows—shouting for help—when the officers drove past the church toward Čitluk.

All three girls would say later that the Madonna appeared to them briefly, offering encouragement, but that her unexpected appearance terrified them, and "we went rigid with fear," as Vicka put it. The two officers, alarmed by the expressions on the girls' faces, shouted that they were witches and stopped the van. The three girls immediately flung open a door and ran into a tobacco field, heading back toward Medjugorje. The *milicija* officers abandoned the van and gave chase on foot.

For Father Zovko, what happened next was "decisive." He was still in the church, on his knees at the altar, the priest recalled, when he distinctly heard a voice tell him, "Come out and protect the children." He obeyed without thought or delay and went straight to the center door at the church's main entrance. The moment he opened the door, the priest said, he saw the girls running toward him from out of the fields. "They told me, 'The police are chasing us! Hide us!'" he recalled. "They had gathered around me and were crying. . . . I embraced the children and took them to the rectory, locking them in an unoccupied room." The police began banging at the door a moment later. "They asked me, 'Did you see the children?' 'I did,' I answered. The police nodded and began running fast toward the village of Bijakovići to catch them."

By four that afternoon, the other three seers all had arrived at the church. Word spread among the pilgrims headed toward Podbrdo that there would be a special service in St. James's that evening. At around 5 P.M., Father Cuvalo led the assembly in the prayers of the Rosary, and at six Father Zovko began the celebration of Mass. "There is nothing to which I could compare the number of people in the church," the latter remembered. "It was so crowded that I found it impossible to extend my hands."

It was during Father Jozo's homily that the Madonna came to them in the small room at the rectory where they still were hiding, the six seers said. The Virgin remained silent, they told the priest afterward, offering only a smile, then vanished a moment later.

The morning of July 2, 1981, began with yet another round of threats from the security police. Pressure on local authorities was being exerted not only out of Sarajevo but now from as far away as Belgrade. The militia officers posted outside the visionaries' houses shouted through the windows, cursing the children, their parents, their Madonna, and their God. The officers kept pointing to the holsters on their belts, warning that the revolvers inside were not "ornaments."

After breakfast, the six seers again gathered at Vicka's house, then in the afternoon walked together through the tobacco fields to the church. At that evening's Mass, Father Zovko for the first time presented the visionaries to his congregation. Jakov described to the crowd an apparition that had taken place in the rectory ten minutes earlier: This time the Madonna had spoken just three words, the boy said—her greeting, "Praised be Jesus." Jakov had been the one who again asked for a sign. In reply, the Madonna smiled but remained silent, the boy told the crowd, though he and all of the other seers agreed that she had seemed to nod.

The service that followed Jakov's brief speech would be compared by one critic to a Pentecostal revival. The crowd stood packed together in the stifling heat of St. James's interior, sweating, sobbing, shouting, moaning. For most present, the atmosphere of spiritual rebirth had become palpable, something they could taste and see. Nearly every man, woman, and child in the church joined Father Zovko in vowing to fast for three days as a sign of penance and conversion.

The next morning, July 3, the bishop of Mostar, Pavao Žanić, arrived in Čitluk, where he questioned the priests from the Brotnjo region about their respective impressions of events in Medjugorje. Afterward, the bishop instructed them to be prudent in all they said or did, then asked that at least one priest be present at all apparitions from this day forward, and that each session be tape-recorded.

The visionaries, however, believed that this evening's apparition would be the last. The seed of that idea had been planted in the seers' minds as early as June 25, when a cousin of Vicka's gave Mirjana a book about the visions of Bernadette at Lourdes. None of the six had known previously about Lourdes, but by June 27, Mirjana and the others were reading the book aloud to one another. After learning that the Virgin had appeared to Bernadette on a total of nineteen occasions, the Medjugorje seers agreed among themselves that it was likely they also would see the Madonna nineteen times. They began counting each appearance, tallying up as many as three or four on some days.

Mirjana in particular had become preoccupied with when the apparitions would end. She put this question to the Madonna at the apparition on June 30, and afterward reported, "Something told me, 'Three days.'" None of the other seers had heard this answer; it was the sole occasion on which one visionary claimed to have heard the Virgin say something the others present did not. Nevertheless, all six seemed to accept that the apparition on the evening of July 3 would be their last.

The crowd that assembled in Medjugorje during the afternoon of the third was so large that estimates of its size varied from twenty-five thousand to more than fifty thousand. People again packed the church, then surrounded it, standing between parked cars, police vans, and tall weeds, singing to the accompaniment of the cicadas. The prayers of the Rosary began around five P.M. An hour later five of the seers gathered in the room at the rectory set aside for them (Mirjana had left that morning for Sarajevo, wanting to experience her final apparition at home). "The children looked very restless and frightened, like chickens hiding from the hawk," noted a priest who was keeping a detailed journal of each apparition. Ivanka, still dressed in mourner's black, asked the priests who followed the seers into the room to please leave, because she and the others intended to use this occasion to ask the Madonna some questions of a private nature. The priests replied that they had been instructed by their bishop to be present, but promised to maintain strict confidentiality.

The children did not look happy about it, but conceded. Marija told the others, "Let's pray; it is the hour of the apparition." The five recited the Rosary, then began to sing. They went silent at exactly 6:25, according to the priests, kneeling and staring at a point just above their heads. "We all knelt down too, observing intently," one of the Franciscans reported later, "but neither saw nor heard anything."

Something had changed: Jakov seemed to be speaking to the Virgin, but whatever he said was not audible to the priests in the room. The others moved their lips also, but again made no sound the witnesses could hear, until, all at once, they uttered, "*Ode!*" Still on her knees, Ivanka turned to Jakov and demanded, "Why are you asking for that?" Jakov had again asked for a sign, the others explained.

The visionaries were led into the church a short time later, to stand at the altar with Father Zovko. Vicka and Jakov addressed the crowd, again speaking into both a microphone and a tape recorder. "The Madonna really appears to us," Jakov said. "It is a fact. I swear it on my life. I asked for a sign. And She lowered Her head as if She approved. Then She disappeared."

"This evening the Madonna gave messages for us, and not for the world," Vicka said. "When She appeared for the last time this evening, She said, 'My angels! I bless you, you will be happy, and you will go into the bosom of your Father. Keep your faith.'

"Go in peace," Vicka then told the crowd. "Good-bye to everyone." She and the others exited to loud applause, both saddened and relieved, they would say, that it was over.

News of an end to the apparitions had not yet reached Sarajevo, where the president of the Communist Republic of Bosnia-Hercegovina announced on the morning of July 4 that the "demonstrations" in Medjugorje were officially declared "counterrevolutionary." Oblivious, the seers went their separate ways that evening. Vicka was picking flowers with some friends at 6:25 P.M. when she complained that her fingers had gone suddenly numb, then fell to her knees a moment later and began to stare fixedly at a spot just above her head. The Madonna had appeared to her, she told her companions a few minutes later, sounding, they said, at once frightened and joyous. Each of the others made a similar report. Ivan said that he had seen the Virgin while washing up after a day spent helping his family with the tobacco harvest; Marija's apparition had taken place in her bedroom at home in Bijakovići. Mirjana was the most emotional, phoning from Sarajevo to say that the Madonna had come to her during a grueling police interrogation that had lasted from early that morning until well into the night.

On Sunday evening, July 5, the five still in Bijakovići gathered at the church, and again, they said, the Madonna appeared to them. "We realized then that this was not like Lourdes," Marija recalled.

CHAPTER SIX

In the Vatican, those who knew the histories of Bosnia and Hercegovina were filled with dread at the thought of an incursion into that murderously complex land of religious ecstatics and ancient enmities. To them, the notion that the Virgin Mary had come to Medjugorje as a messenger of peace seemed not only outlandish but frightening, given all that might come to light before an investigation of the claimed apparitions was completed.

Western Hercegovina is some of the most blood-soaked ground on earth. Invaders bent on conquest or pillage have been pouring into the region for twenty-five hundred years, and each passing horde has left behind at least a little that is part of the people who live there now. The Illyrians were the first to settle Hercegovina and the Brotnjo plateau, moving in from the Dalmatian Coast during the Iron Age. Greeks and Celts soon followed, invading from different directions—the same ones they left by when driven out by Roman legions under the command of Augustus Caesar. In the village that would become Medjugorje, the Romans constructed a small basilica, with altars dedicated to Sylvanus and Diana.

When the empire of Augustus was divided in A.D. 395, Croatia, Slovenia, Bosnia, and Hercegovina remained with the Western Roman Empire, while Serbia, Kosovo, and Macedonia went to the Eastern Roman Empire. This was the beginning of a historical dialectic that would synthesize into one bloodbath after another for the next sixteen hundred years.

Early in the fifth century, the Romans were being felled by successive Visigoth, Hun, and Lombard invasions. Slavic tribes from eastern Poland and the mid-Russian plains, who would become the core bloodstock of Yugoslavia (which means "South Slavs") arrived in the company of marauding Huns during the seventh century. Taller and more fair-haired than their cohorts, with higher cheekbones and bluer eyes, the Slavs were civilized by the Byzantine emperor Heraclius, who promised that if they drove out the Huns, he would give them Illyria. The only condition was that the Slavs convert to Christianity. Neither side could have imagined then that this marriage of convenience would produce perhaps the most devout and mystically inclined Catholics on earth.

There were no Catholics in the Illyria of that day: Not until the latter years of the eighth century was the religion of the Roman Church imported by Charlemagne's Frankish armies. The crescent shape of the present-day border between Croatia and Bosnia outlines with haunting exactitude the eastern frontier of Charlemagne's empire, which in time would become the western frontier of the Ottoman Empire. Knowing this, it is not difficult to understand why Croatian Catholics have for centuries conceived themselves the sentinels of western Christendom, guardians at the gate against both Byzantine perversion and Ottoman infidelity. Hercegovina in particular has been both battleground and buffer: The magnificent Stari Most (Old Bridge) spanning the Neretva in Mostar would serve as a symbol of passage from East to West for countless poets, historians, painters, and photographers.

What authorities in the Vatican understood better than perhaps anyone outside Yugoslavia was the lasting impact upon the region of the first major historical development of the second millennium, one that had its roots in the greatest heresy ever to afflict the Christian Church. The Gnostics (Knowers) had emerged as an esoteric religious movement during the late first or early second century, promising a secret knowledge of the divine that drew adherents from every corner of the known world. Whether Gnosticism arose in response to the early Church or preceded it has been argued persuasively by both sides. The origins of the heresy have been attributed variously to the pagan mythologies of Mesopotamia, to the visions of an Indo-Iranian priest, to the intellectual rebellion of sectarian Jews, to the metaphysics of Plato, to the dualistic religions of the Orient, and to a combination of all these elements.

What can be said with some confidence is that the two most propulsive human forces in the history of Gnosticism were a pair of Persian sages, Zoroaster and Mani. It was Zoroaster, nearly two thousand years before the birth of Christ, who reported a vision in which the god Ormazd revealed that he was the Supreme Being. And it was Zoroaster as well who first described the universe as a cosmic battleground between forces of light and darkness engaged in eternal conflict.

Mani was born more than two hundred years after Jesus to an aristocratic family of southern Babylonia and raised as a member of their austere baptist sect. At age twelve, however, Mani began reporting visions in which an angel of God had told him he would be the prophet of a new and ultimate revelation. These visions lasted until Mani turned twenty-four and journeyed east as a Christian missionary. In India, the young man was profoundly influenced by his introduction to Buddhism. Upon returning to Persia, he proclaimed himself the last prophet in a succession that included Zoroaster, Buddha, and Jesus, whose partial revelations, Mani explained, were subsumed by his own teachings. With the protection of the Persian emperor, Mani preached throughout the Middle East and sent missionaries to the Roman Empire. The prophet's immediate and enormous success as a religious teacher was at first less of a threat to Christianity than to orthodox Zoroastrianism, whose leaders sought to silence him. They would succeed when a new emperor took the Persian throne in the year 274; soon after, Mani was executed as a heretic.

Before his death, Mani had contributed significantly to the doctrines of Gnosticism. While a majority of Western Gnostics professed to be Christians, their cosmology more resembled that of Hindus: From the original, uncreated God, a series of lesser divinities had been generated by what the Gnostics called "emanation." The last of these was the goddess of wisdom, Sophia, who could not suppress her yearning to know the unknowable Supreme Being. This corrupt desire had produced a sort of evil twin to God who in turn created the physical universe. While the Gnostics believed this universe of matter to be wholly wicked, they also believed that "sparks" of the Divine Being had entered it, imprisoned in human bodies; reawakened by knowledge, these divine sparks that dwelled in humanity could return home to the transcendent spiritual realm.

Especially disturbing to the early Christian Church was that many Gnostics identified their evil deity with the Jehovah of the Old Testament, a book they interpreted as an account of this cruel god's determination to keep human beings captive in the material world. The eviction of Adam and Eve from Paradise, the Great Flood, and the destruction of Sodom and Gomorrah all were understood as efforts by this evil god to punish the attempts of humans to acquire knowledge.

Even more offensive to orthodox Christians (the word "orthodox" was coined in the second century to distinguish straight and true followers of Christ from false and twisted "heterodox" believers) was the Gnostic rejection not only of Jesus' atonement through suffering and death but also of his resurrection. Christ, the divine spirit, was not born into but rather had inhabited or "overshadowed" the body of the man Jesus, the Gnostics taught, and did not die on the cross but instead had ascended by choice into the divine realm from which he came. (Alternative Gnostic accounts had Jesus substituting a scapegoat who was crucified in his stead, or being taken down from the cross while still alive and smuggled out of Jerusalem to live as a monk among the Essenes on the shore of the Dead Sea, or to die of old age in Kashmir, or to be killed by the Romans at Masada, or to travel to Europe and sire the future French royal dynasty.) Whatever they believed, most Gnostic Christian sects rejected the cross as a religious symbol, saying it was wrong to worship an instrument of death and torture. They also challenged the authority of priests and rejected all sacraments, including baptism and the Eucharist, instead practicing rites that involved sacred hymns and magic formulas.

Mani, like Zoroaster, had divided existence into contending realms of good and evil: The realm of Light (or spirit) was ruled by God, while the realm of Darkness (or matter) was ruled by Satan. The two realms had been entirely separate, until a primal catastrophe in which the realm of Darkness invaded the realm of Light. This event had pitted the forces of good and evil in a perpetual struggle that eventually produced its consummate battleground—the human race. The human body was material and therefore evil, while the human soul was a fragment of the divine light that must be redeemed and released from the prison of earth.

Manichaeans were divided according to the degree of their spiritual perfection into two distinct classes: The Elect practiced strict celibacy and vegetarianism, refused wine, shunned labor, and devoted themselves to preaching; the much more numerous Auditors were permitted to marry, but were discourged from procreation, required to observe weekly fasts, and obliged to serve the Elect. The best an Auditor could hope for was to be reborn as a member of the Elect. (Mani had accepted the Buddhist doctrine of reincarnation.)

While earlier forms of Gnosticism had been suppressed by the end of the third century, Manichaeism flourished during the fourth, spreading into China and attracting followers throughout the Roman Empire, most notably in North Africa. St. Augustine was a Manichaean for nine years before his conversion to Christianity, and later wrote the most important early polemics against the heresy.

By the Middle Ages, Manichaeism had all but faded from existence in the West. It lingered on in Eastern Europe, to enjoy a bloody revival and breathtaking expansion in the Balkans during the last years of the tenth century, guided by a previously obscure Bulgarian Orthodox priest who called himself Bogomil (Dear to God). Bogomil at once accepted and adapted the cosmology of Mani and earlier Gnostic teachers. God had sired two sons, Bogomil preached: The eldest, Satanel, first rebelled against his father's authority, then attempted to usurp God's role as Creator. What that son fashioned, however, were grotesque parodies of his father's work. Instead of Heaven, Satanel produced earth; instead of angels, men. Even then, Satanel's creatures could not move or breathe, until he had stolen a flame of divine fire and hidden a spark inside each human heart. This very act would prove Satanel's undoing when God responded by sending His second son, Logos—Christ—down from heaven to assume a phantom body and break the power of the Evil One over His creation, the human race.

Like earlier Gnostics, followers of the Bulgarian prophet (who called themselves Bogomils) despised images and rejected the sacraments. They accepted the whole of the New Testament, but only the Psalms and the Prophets from the Old Testament. The personal practices of Bogomils ranged widely, from dour asceticism to debauched hedonism, each approach rooted in the belief that the physical body was not only evil but irrelevant. The ascetics fasted and prayed virtually without ceasing. They were literalists who regarded human excrement as the ultimate symbol of material evil and regularly took huge doses of purgatives. The hedonists assumed the position that since the human body was irredeemable, it was unimportant what one did with it. Thus did the sexual promiscuity and perversity of the Bogomils become notorious throughout Europe. (The English slang word for sodomy, "bugger," derives from "Bulgar.")

It was not Bogomil's religious preaching, but rather his calls to insurrection, that made the Bulgarian an enemy of the great powers who surrounded him on all sides. Early in the eleventh century, Bogomil began his political career by exhorting Macedonian peasants to rise under the banner of his faith against the rule of Constantinople. The great Bosnian prince Kulin was an early convert to Bogomilism, and through him the new religion became closely identified with Bosnian independence. Confronted by a threat that now was not only spiritual but also temporal, both the Roman Catholic and the Greek Orthodox Churches persecuted the Bogomils relentlessly for the next 250 years. The council of Constantinople decreed that all the heretics must be burned alive. Rome held equal sway in the region, however, and insisted upon attempting to "reconvert" the Bogomils, killing them if they refused. The first Franciscan monks to enter Bosnia were sent by the Church to save the heretics from themselves.

The urgency of this mission increased when the Gnostic revival spread into Western Europe, moving from the Balkans into Italy, from there to the Swiss Alps, and then finally to southern France, where a group called the Albigenses became a hub of heresy, posing a threat to its primacy that the Christian Church had not seen in nearly a thousand years. When repeated attempts to reconvert the heretics by peaceful means failed, Pope Innocent III launched the Albigensian Crusade that desolated the French countryside. Charging the Albigenses with devil worship, human sacrifice, cannibalism, incest, sexual perversion, and practice of the Black Mass, soldiers of the church slaughtered them by the thousands. Early on, the knight leading the crusade was asked by his men who among the heretics should be put to the sword. He answered with a line that has been refrained for more than seven centuries: "Kill them all. God will know His own." The final defeat of the Albigenses came in March 1244 at Monsegur in the foothills of the Pyrenees, where more than two hundred heretic priests were massacred.

The Gnostic movement in the Balkans would not be so swiftly suppressed. Bogomil himself had been executed by the Byzantine emperor, but his religious vision lived on, even under a murderous onslaught from both East and West, from the Greek Orthodox Church on one side and from the Roman Catholic on the other. The heresy sank its deepest roots in Bosnia and Hercegovina, the one part of Europe where it had become the faith of not only rebellious peasants but ruling lords as well.

Among its strongholds was a village called Medjugorje.

If the apparitions at Medjugorje were not like those at Lourdes, what they *were* like was being revealed slowly—too slowly, some would complain—and seemed subject to almost constant change. For most of that first July, the five children in Medjugorje (Mirjana had remained in Sarajevo) gathered each evening at the church, meeting for their group apparition in a small room opposite the sacristy.

In the opinion of most observers, the seers' visions appeared, paradoxically, to deepen even as they took on a more ritualistic quality: Late in the afternoon, the five would enter what was now known as the "apparition room" together, usually accompanied by several priests and assorted invited guests who would deposit religious medals, rosaries, and other objects on a table in front of the visionaries, so that the Virgin might bless them. Still standing, the children would begin praying the seven Our Fathers, seven Hail Marys, and seven Glorias that they said the Madonna had requested.

It is clear that what happened next profoundly affected everyone admitted to the apparition room as a witness, including scientific skeptics and avowed atheists: As they began their third Our Father, the visionaries would fall to their knees—as if electrocuted, more than one observer would say. Their lips continued to move, mouthing the words of the Rosary prayers, but no sounds could be heard. The seers' eyes fixed always on the same spot, next to a crucifix about eight feet in front of them. Their expressions remained enraptured, even as a full range of emotions passed across their faces, from tears of grief to smiles of ecstasy. The apparitions generally lasted between two and fifteen minutes, although some had gone on as long as forty-five minutes. The five seemed to speak to their vision throughout the experience, but no sound could be heard, until they began to pray the Our Father again, and all their voices became audible in the same instant, on the words "who art in heaven."

As the visionaries explained it, what they experienced as the apparitions began was a splendor of light, brilliant but gentle, from which the Madonna seemed to emerge; in the instant of Her appearance, they began to lose all awareness of the material world and entered a separation from time and space that deepened to the point of utter removal as the apparitions continued into August and September. When asked to describe the Madonna, the children all spoke of Her beauty, but in general lacked more descriptive language. Their failure to achieve eloquence frustrated many of the priests who questioned them. The Virgin "glowed with holiness," they said, draped by a long gown that flowed straight down, unbound at Her waist, to cover Her lower extremities (they still hadn't seen the Virgin's feet). The color of Her gown was described as "a luminous gray," but the seers seemed unsatisfied with this, because the gown seemed not of a color but of a quality. On the other hand, they agreed that Her complexion was olive, and Her cheeks rosy red. The long white veil covered the Virgin's hair entirely, they said, except for one small black curl visible on the left side of Her face.

The Madonna, the seers added, spoke to them in perfect Croatian: "I hear Her voice and words in the normal way," Ivanka would tell an inquiring priest, "as well as what the others say."

It pleased Father Zovko that, when their vision was ended, the seers participated in the Mass as ordinary worshippers, singing with the choir and congregation; occasionally Jakov asked to serve as an altar boy. When the service was over, the children met with pilgrims, answering their questions "very humbly, very piously," as one skeptical priest from a neighboring parish noted. This absence of grandiosity on the part of the visionaries was immensely reassuring to all of the clergy who came to investigate their claims. Vicka, asked by a priest if she experienced the Virgin "as one who gives graces or as one who prays to God," replied instantly, "As one who prays to God." When the same priest asked her if a prayer in the church at Medjugorje carried more power than a prayer in another church, the girl said she would ask at the next apparition. The Madonna had told her that the power of a prayer varies only according to a person's faith, Vicka reported back the next day.

In mid-July, there were five evenings in a row when the seers reported that the Virgin had failed to appear to them. It seemed the apparitions might be at an end after all, but the visionaries were not nearly so serene as they had been two weeks earlier. All of them, in fact, grew despondent, unable to comprehend that the Madonna would abandon them without warning. They continued to meet at the church during the evening Mass, however, and on the sixth night reported that the Virgin had returned, thanking them for remaining faithful and promising not to leave again without advising them in advance.

The visionaries said they continued to ask the Madonna for a sign. "Even if I were to leave the sign, many people would not believe it," the Virgin told them on July 21, according to the seers. "Many people will only come here and bow down. But people must be converted and do penance." They asked again for a sign at a special apparition just before midnight on July 27, Vicka said, and the Madonna answered with symbols that they alone could see—a heart and a cross that appeared in the sky as She disappeared. Two days later, Jakov asked the Madonna if he and the others could embrace Her. She answered that they could, one at a time. Those present as witnesses would report that after they "touched the Virgin," the seers' hands were astonishingly cold—"literally like blocks of ice," one said.

Both the police and officials of the Communist League by now were demanding that Father Zovko discontinue the evening Mass. He asked the children to consult the Virgin; Her reply, they told the priest, was "Continue to celebrate the Mass." After this, the Medjugorje priests were summoned for interrogations on a daily basis. Officers of the federal police followed the pilgrims and the priests who came from other regions of the country, demanding to know the nature of their conversations with the visionaries and with Father Zovko. The Čitluk communists spread a rumor that the Franciscans had fabricated the apparitions in Medjugorje in order to raise money to build a new extension to the church, then in late July demanded that St. James's be closed "pending further investigation."

Father Zovko refused, driving to Sarajevo to argue his case before the Commission of Religious Affairs. The commission chairman confronted the priest at a meeting that evening, complaining that the people of his parish had abandoned their work in the fields and factories, that crops in Medjugorje not only were going untended but had been trampled underfoot by the crush of pilgrims, and that instead of irrigating the fields, the local water supply was being used up by pilgrims. When Father Zovko appeared unmoved, the chairman began to shout, charging that the assemblies in Medjugorje were more political than religious, that furtherance of Croatian nationalism was their true purpose, and that the mastermind behind it all would be prosecuted as "an enemy of the people."

To protect the church, the seers announced that they again would meet each evening for their apparition in the open air on Podbrdo. This return of huge crowds to the hillside enraged Communist League officials in Sarajevo and Belgrade, and their threats grew increasingly violent. On August 11, Father Zovko was summoned to the Communist Party headquarters in Mostar, given a final warning to stop the crowds from assembling on Podbrdo, and ordered to abolish the evening Mass at St. James's. He would continue to celebrate Mass, the priest responded, as long as people came to the church. That evening, he delivered a sermon on Moses' forty years in the desert; the authorities interpreted this as a veiled reference to forty years of communist rule.

The next afternoon, two army helicopters flew over the summit of Križevac and dove straight at the crowd gathered on Podbrdo. Alternately swooping and hovering, the helicopters raised huge clouds of red dust with their whirling blades. Roaring engines drowned the screams of those on the ground below, creating a virtual stampede. Dozens were injured, though no one was killed. Moments later, an army of militia officers stormed Podbrdo from below, waving guns and ordering an evacuation of the hill. That night, the security police erected rope barriers blocking all paths to Podbrdo, and stationed armed guards along the entire base of the hill.

On the afternoon of August 13, two squads of militia officers arrived from Mostar with a team of police dogs and took up positions at the entrance to St. James's. An elderly priest who objected was arrested and taken away in handcuffs.

Forbidden from meeting in public, the seers began to gather each evening for their apparitions in the fields and orchards surrounding Bijakovići. The sense of danger escalated enormously on August 17 when Father Zovko was arrested on charges of sedition. The next day, a team of secret police dispatched by the Ministry of Interior arrived in Medjugorje to search St. James's. The officers seized not only the church collection box (containing about four thousand dollars in total currency) but all documents and letters pertaining to the alleged apparitions, as well as audiocassettes of the priest's early interviews with the visionaries. The assistant pastors were confined to quarters under armed guard, and the church doors were locked from inside.

That evening, and each evening after, the seers gathered—in the fields and orchards, or at Vicka's house—for their apparition. According to Vicka, the Virgin told them on the evening of the parish priest's arrest: "Do not be afraid. I wish that you would be filled with joy, and that the joy could be seen on your faces. I will protect Father Zovko." During this fugitive period, the children said, the Virgin came to them for the first time clothed other than in Her white veil and silver-gray dress, appearing on the Feast of the Assumption in garments of gold that covered Her from head to toe.

August was also the month when people other than the seers began to report witnessing miraculous sights. Such claims were especially abundant during the three-day period of August 2, 3, and 4. At the apparition on August 2, the Feast of Our Lady of Angels, a crowd of more than 150 reported seeing the sun spin in orbit, descend toward the crowd, then retreat. All present either wept, prayed, or fled. The hundred or so who remained said they had been able to stare at the sun without discomfort, let alone damage, to their eyes, and that they had seen "figures" materialize out of the orb and arrange themselves into the shape of a cross. Moments later, six small hearts appeared in the sky, these witnesses would insist, centered around a large heart. Then a white cloud formed and covered Podbrdo; gradually it dissipated, and the sky was clear, the sun once again in its normal place.

On the afternoon of August 24, Vicka was at Ivan's house when she heard an uproar in the street and dashed outside to find a crowd of people staring toward Križevac. She looked also, Vicka said, and, like the other visionaries, saw the Virgin in the place of the cross at the top of the mountain. More than a dozen people in the crowd said they saw not the Virgin Herself but what they described as a "statue" of the Madonna where the cross should have been, and reported that when the statue disappeared, they again saw the cross. Vicka and the other visionaries reported seeing at that moment the word "*mir*" (Croatian for "peace") written in letters of gold across the sky above the mountain. More than a hundred witnesses claimed to have seen the same phenomenon.

Father Cuvalo was most prominent among a group of priests who did their best to discourage such "gullibility," regularly confronting the crowds of pilgrims who gathered in the street hoping to see the sun "perform its antics." "It's your heads that are spinning, not the sun," he scolded one group. Still, dozens of witnesses continued to report observing a pulsating and spinning of the sun that threw off giant red, purple, and blue bubbles, or seeing crosses that appeared and disappeared, or being dazzled by brilliant surges of light before and during the apparitions. More than a score of miraculous healings were claimed during the month of August alone. The priests spent little time investigating these cures, increasingly preoccupied by their concern for Father Zovko, who now faced trial on a charge of treasonous conspiracy and had been advised to expect a long prison term.

The Mostar communists scheduled Father Zovko's trial for the last week of October. On October 19, the Medjugorje visionaries reported that the Virgin had asked them to fast for a solid week on bread and water, and to pray as often as they could for Zovko. They then were permitted a vision of the priest in his prison cell. During their apparition on the following evening, Vicka pleaded with the Madonna to intervene on the priest's behalf: "Paralyze someone; strike someone on the head. I know it is a sin to speak so, but what can we do?" The Madonna replied only with a smile, the children said, then led them in a song, "Jesus Christ, in Your Name."

Father Zovko's trial began and ended on the same day, October 21. He was convicted of sedition, a crime that could carry a sentence of death. At that evening's apparition in Medjugorje, it again was Vicka who spoke out: "Dear Madonna, I know You do not have the spirit of vengeance, but try anyway to bring certain people to reason."

"Do not fear for Jozo," the Virgin answered, according to the seers. Would the priest be condemned to death? Vicka asked. His sentence would not be pronounced until the next day, the Virgin answered, according to the seers, and his punishment would not be "severe."

Indeed, Father Zovko was not sentenced until the next morning, when he was given a reduced term of three and a half years in prison. During that evening's apparition, Vicka told the Virgin that she and the others were sad. "You should rejoice!" the Madonna responded.

That evening's apparition would mark a turning point for two of the more skeptical priests in Medjugorje, the first being Father Cuvalo, whose scolding of the credulous had grown increasingly vehement. He himself had witnessed what could only be described as a supernatural phenomenon, the elderly priest would admit the next day, this being a "blazing whiteness" that emanated from the cross atop Križevac at the moment the visionaries said the Virgin had come to them. The second priest was Father Luka Susac, who had arrived in Medjugorje that afternoon from Humac to take confessions. During the seers' apparition, he glanced through a window toward Križevac and saw, instead of the cross, a white pillar of bright light that gradually became the "outline" of a woman who stood with her arms extended, gazing toward the church. He summoned three other priests, who all would testify that for half an hour they had witnessed the same phenomenon.

Many in the crowd of pilgrims who milled about in the churchyard reported observing this "figure" or "statue" or "outline" of a woman on the mountaintop at that same moment. Soon hundreds were kneeling on the lawn outside the church, praying, singing, gasping, and weeping until the cross reappeared and the sky began to darken.

The events of that evening were eclipsed on the afternoon of October 28, one week after the trial of Father Zovko, when a strange fire erupted on Podbrdo at the site of the first apparition. More than five hundred persons would swear they had observed the flames; among these were nearly a dozen armed guards from the militia who had been posted at the base of the hill. The fire burned for fifteen minutes, growing steadily brighter, without apparent fuel. The guards insisted that someone had doused a thornbush with gasoline and set it ablaze. They hiked up the hill to investigate, but could find no remains of the fire whatsoever: no embers, no ashes, nothing.

After their apparition that evening, the seers reported the Virgin had told them the fire on Podbrdo was "a herald of the Great Sign" to come. What that Great Sign would be and when it would appear, only they six were permitted to know in advance.

"How could it be us? And why?" Vicka wondered. "We could not begin to imagine."

By November 1981, Father Zovko had disappeared into the limbic maze of Yugoslavia's vast and notorious prison system, his duties in Medjugorje assumed by Father Cuvalo. The elderly priest's administration already had been eclipsed, however, by the leadership of his most junior assistant, Father Tomislav Vlasić.

Previously pastor of the large congregation at St. Francis of Assisi in Capljina, Father Vlasić was a noted scholar—also regarded as the region's foremost liturgist—who had visited Medjugorje for the first time on June 29, the fifth day of the apparitions in the parish. He had arrived late that morning, just as the seers were returning from an interrogation at the police station in Čitluk. Jakov was the first of the children he spoke to, recalled Father Vlasić, who found the boy remarkably frank and open: "I soon became convinced that he was undergoing some unusual experience, but I had no idea what it was." Mirjana was the one who most deeply affected him, Tomislav said. When he spoke to her that morning, the girl from Sarajevo told him she would not go back to Podbrdo that evening: "If they take me back to question me, I'll have a nervous breakdown," Mirjana had explained. Yet that evening he saw Mirjana with the others on the hillside, and asked her after the apparition why she had changed her mind. "She said, 'When it came time, no one could have stopped me; there was no longer any question of going or not going.'"

He had questioned five of the six visionaries at the home of Marinko, the mechanic, following that evening's apparition, and after that, "For me, there was no doubt. Except for Mirjana, these were normal peasant children, of modest scholastic ability, limited imagination, and not even particularly devout. They were having a genuine religious experience."

Within weeks Father Vlasić had asked to be replaced at the prestigious post he held in Capljina, the largest city between Split and Mostar, so that he might be assigned as an assistant pastor in tiny Medjugorje. During early August, Father Zovko sent him this message: "I shall be going away soon. Be ready to take my place." Father Vlasić arrived in

Medjugorje on August 18, the day after Father Zovko's arrest, and by October had assumed the role of "spiritual adviser" to the visionaries.

This was the period during which the messages reported by the children increased in scope and portent. At the same time many matters the seers claimed to have discussed with the Virgin sounded quite personal, some even slightly inane. Mirjana especially seemed to experience the Virgin as dispenser of motherly advice, one who warned her to break off a relationship with a girl who was using drugs or instructed her to avoid arguments at school. The others reported that the Madonna again encouraged them to fast on bread and water, and suggested as well that they give up television, alcohol, and cigarettes. The Virgin always added, however, that they themselves knew what was necessary. "You are free," the Blessed Mother reminded them again and again, the seers said. "It is up to you to choose."

During the apparitions, the seers said, they were invited to ask questions on any subject, and the Madonna rarely failed to answer, though her replies could be cryptic and on several occasions gave offense to those who styled themselves as guardians of Catholic dogma. "Are all religions good?" the children asked at the apparition on October 1. "All religions are similar before God," said the Virgin, a statement that more than a few priests found shocking. More reassuring was Her response to a question the seers posed six days later: "Are there, outside of Jesus, other intermediaries between God and man, and what is their role?" "There is only one mediator between God and man, and that is Jesus Christ," the Virgin answered.

The Virgin's reply to a question about reincarnation had been unusually lengthy and detailed: "We go to Heaven in full conscience; that which we have now. At the moment of death, we are conscious of the separation of body and soul. It is false to teach people that we are reborn many times and that we pass to different bodies. One is born only once. The body, drawn from the earth, decomposes after death. It never comes back to life again. Man receives a transfigured body. Whoever has done very much evil during his life can go straight to Heaven if he confesses, is sorry for what he has done, and receives communion at the end of his life."

The priests were both disturbed and intrigued that the seers seemed not to realize the magnitude of certain statements they attributed to the Madonna, especially those concerning the purpose of the apparitions in Medjugorje. Nothing was nearly so auspicious as the Virgin's announcement that these would be Her last appearances on earth, and that they were intended to provide humankind with a final opportunity to repent and convert. The Madonna then explained that She had come to Medjugorje in Her ultimate aspect, according to the seers, telling them at the apparition of October 12, "I am the Queen of Peace."

By the fall of 1981, the devotions in Medjugorje were opposed by a foe who would prove far more formidable and intransigent than the communist state. This was the bishop of Mostar, Pavao Žanić. Bishop Žanić had seemed an enthusiastic supporter during his first trip to Medjugorje in July 1981. After interviewing all six seers, the bishop announced, "I am firmly convinced that no one has influenced them . . . Six innocent simple children like these would have told all in half an hour if anybody had been manipulating them . . . And I am equally convinced that the children are not lying." Father Zovko had actually had to dissuade Žanić from proclaiming the apparitions authentic then and there, arguing that the bishop should permit the Church to conduct a formal investigation before making any pronouncement.

In August, the bishop had been summoned to Sarajevo for an interview with officials of the State Security Police. When he returned to Mostar, Žanić seemed more solicitous of skeptics. On August 16, the bishop issued his first public statement, repeating that he did not believe the children were lying or being manipulated. "However," he added, "the most difficult question remains: Are [the six] undergoing subjective supernatural experiences?"

Father Zovko was arrested the next day, and the bishop went silent on the subject of Medjugorje for the next five months. That his position had been reversed was not revealed until January 1982, when Bishop Žanić formed the first episcopal commission assigned to investigate the apparitions in Mejugorje; all four theologians selected by the bishop to sit on his commission had announced earlier that they believed the young seers were frauds. Just one of those four would visit Medjugorje to meet the visionaries, and when this theologian changed his mind and concluded that the apparitions were authentic, Žanić berated the man for permitting himself to be "brainwashed," then dismissed him from his position.

The moment I met Mirjana, I knew she was neither a liar nor a lunatic, at least not of any sort I knew about. The young woman's eyes were the blue of alpine lakes, luminous with clarity, unnerving in their repose. Her gaze was penetrating but did not probe. She struck me as quite sure of herself yet entirely unassuming. She also was prettier than in the pictures I'd seen, and much more stylish than I had imagined, slim and tanned in a silk travel suit.

I got the feeling I wasn't what she expected either, and our brief conversation had an awkward, tenuous quality. Standing in the driveway outside her front door, we mostly discussed logistics. Mirjana seemed pleased to hear that I preferred to dine at the cafés in Medjugorje rather than to continue eating the huge meals her mother had been preparing for me. She suggested walking routes, proposed a time when the two of us could sit down together, asked who else I intended to interview, and advised me how to make contact with them. Mirjana's English seemed to me quite good, but she insisted we would need a translator to speak of "important matters," and said she had someone in mind. She suggested I use the same person when I spoke to Vicka, whose English was quite limited.

I apologized for my Serbo-Croatian vocabulary, which consisted of no more than a half-dozen words. A look of genuine concern appeared on Mirjana's face. "Here, say simply 'Croatian,' not 'Serbo-Croatian,'" she advised me. "I am not a nationalist, but many are. If you speak to Serbs, say 'Serbian.' If you speak to Muslims, say simply 'your language.'" I smiled, thinking how different this conversation was from what I'd imagined. Mirjana arched her eyebrows. "It is serious," she said. "You are in a country where people are killed for saying the wrong word at the wrong time."

I attempted to project a chastened demeanor, but apparently was not convincing. Mirjana shook her head and smiled. "How long do you stay?" she asked.

"I'm not sure," I replied.

This answer also appeared to amuse her. "Some who say that never leave," she observed.

"I won't be one of those," I assured her.

"You have only just arrived in Medjugorje," she told me. "You do not know yet what you will be."

The next morning, I again trudged off into the dusty labyrinth of footpaths that divided fields from vineyards and linked the villages of the Medjugorje parish. I had walked about a half mile without seeing another soul, when I stopped in the shade of an immense fig tree to catch a cooling breeze. For perhaps the fifth or sixth time since setting out, I looked over my shoulder at that immense white cross atop Križevac; it so completely dominated the southern horizon that one constantly felt either inspired or oppressed by—but never indifferent to—its looming presence.

A small company of Irish pilgrims appeared suddenly, marching toward me in single file from the opposite direction. They were praying in loud, strident voices, eyes cast down, blue-beaded rosaries clasped tight in front of them. The sweat-streaked, ruddy face of the woman in the lead was drawn into an expression that another might have seen as sober piety, or perhaps as grim determination. To me, the lady looked half-mad, and when she joined the others in pleading to be saved from the fires of hell, I recoiled into a shudder that shook me at intervals for the next fifteen minutes.

Easy opportunities to mock Medjugorje offered themselves again and again as I hiked the last half mile to the square surrounding the church. The first commercial building I came to, on the very edge of the fields, was a bookstore called Devotions, its windows bright with the reds, greens, and oranges of Coke, Sprite, and Fanta logos; only when I approached to within a few feet did I see the smaller, less colorful images of Jesus and Mary interspersed among the soft-drink signs. The stalls of assorted trinket dealers lined the main road when I finally came to it, jam-packed with acrylic rosaries and plaster Madonnas. It was another bad day for business, and the owners wore dull expressions as they sat in small pockets of shade, surrounded on all sides by hot pavement and glaring sunlight, except for one woman who waved a shiny cross on a chain at me and shouted, "Fourteen carat."

I glanced once more toward Križevac, thinking that it was my third day in Medjugorje and I still hadn't visited either Cross Mountain or Apparition Hill. Half a dozen taxis, mostly old-model Mercedeses, were parked along the curb outside the church; for five dollars they would drop their fares off at the base of either site. I kept walking, and moments later was again in the church square. I hadn't gone back inside St. James's again either. I sat on a bench near the front entrance for a few minutes, watching people fill plastic containers from the hand-cranked water pump, thought about getting breakfast at Café Colombo, but instead walked across the street to a sidewalk café called Mira's, an establishment favored by locals, Croatian soldiers, and religious pilgrims.

I hadn't been seated long before my attention fixed on a patron at a nearby table. He was about my age, perhaps a few years older, with longish hair that was very neatly combed, and a bushy mustache that was exceedingly well maintained. The fellow exuded sophistication, wealth, and breeding: His slacks and striped shirt were of the finest combed cotton and looked custom-made; there was a monogram on the pocket of his shirt, and tassels on the calfskin loafers he wore. He had an Apple PowerBook set up on the table in front of him, connected to a cord that ran from the café's enclosed kitchen space. The owner was extremely solicitous, as were the numerous visitors who stopped by the mustached man's table. In the space of twenty minutes I heard him conversing in German, Italian, French, Croatian, and, finally, English, which he spoke like an American.

To me, the most interesting thing about him was the copy of *Time* that sat folded on the table next to his computer. I heard him tell a young woman who spoke English with a Spanish accent that he had picked it up yesterday in Split. Ever since arriving in Medjugorje I had been aching for news of the world. Finally, I asked if I could borrow the magazine. He handed it over without hesitation, adding only that he wanted it back when I was done. I was halfway through the international section when the two of us struck up a conversation about reports that all three armies—Serb, Muslim, and Croatian—were massing in the north, near Bihać, for what many thought might be the decisive battle of the war. That led to an inquiry about what I was doing in Medjugorje. When I told him, the fellow asked to see some identification. I still had no idea what his role might be, but complied, sensing that this was a person of influence. Also, despite his peremptory tone, I liked him.

I opened the sheaf of papers I was carrying; on top was my credential from *Rolling Stone*, with an attached letter written by the managing editor. He broke into a delighted grin. "*Rolling Stone* in Medjugorje," he chortled. "This is too rich." He introduced himself then, did Nicholas Maria Johannes Alexander Graf zu Eltz, by his familiar name, Nicky Eltz. "Where are you staying?" he asked. When I told him I was at Mirjana's, Nicky's eyes bulged with wonder. "You're from *Rolling Stone* and you're staying at Mirjana's," he said, then shook his head and laughed thunderously. "Oh dear boy, what a position you're in."

I met Vicka on the morning of my fourth day in Medjugorje. The meeting, like the interpreter, had been arranged through Mirjana, who was to sit down with me that afternoon.

I knew from reading about Vicka that during the past seven years, she had been afflicted by an astonishing variety of life-threatening ailments, the best known being a brain tumor. I was aware as well that Vicka was the only one of the six visionaries who remained unmarried, and had been told how admired she was for keeping her commitment to a life of service and sacrifice. All this had predisposed me to imagine a rather dour young woman, pious but dry and difficult. Face-to-face, however, Vicka would prove perhaps the most radiant human being I had ever encountered.

Each morning, she blessed the pilgrims who formed a line outside her little blue house, and was in the midst of this ritual when I arrived. I was immediately moved, watching the way she gazed into each visitor's eyes, offering not just warmth and welcome but a depth of feeling—of love— I could have given only my closest friends. The enthusiasm of her response varied from person to person, but she never once glazed over, not even for an instant.

After the pilgrims had gone, we retired to a small, bare room upstairs, furnished with four simple wooden chairs, decorated by a crucifix and a painting of the Virgin. This was where she experienced the Blessed Mother's apparitions each evening, Vicka explained. In her dress, her speech, and her manner, Vicka was a peasant, utterly unaffected. Openness was the most attractive quality of her broad and blemished face, except for those dark, lustrous eyes that, like Mirjana's, seemed never to blink.

"Now what do you want to ask me?" she demanded, and smiled. There was amusement in her expression, and a hint, perhaps, of mockery. I began by inquiring about the extensive medical and scientific testing to which Vicka and the other visionaries had submitted themselves: Why had she agreed to it, and what had it meant to her? Vicka shrugged, as if she found this an odd and largely irrelevant line of inquiry, but answered each question. She and the others agreed to the testing because the Madonna had told them it was their choice, and because the priests had pleaded with them to cooperate. As for what it meant to her—nothing. "God cannot be proven," she told me. "Finally, we all must believe. Or not."

Vicka had promised me an hour, but we were only about fifteen minutes into our interview when I began struggling to get words out, barely able to ask even the briefest of questions. Later, I would try to think of who else had affected me similarly, and couldn't come up with a single name. I recalled my interview with the Dalai Lama twelve years earlier:

I had found the exiled Tibetan leader delightful—no one I've met before or since has described his own foibles with such genuine amusement—but the Dalai Lama had not reached me at the level Vicka did. Staring into the eyes of this plain young woman, with her close-cropped dark hair and pockmarked pale skin, I wasn't sure if I felt awed or unnerved, or whether I would know the difference. I managed to stammer out that I had read about her illnesses and sufferings. Vicka responded with a nod but no change of expression. I was trying to think why I had brought that up, then found myself blurting, "Vicka, are you ever unhappy?" For several moments, she regarded me in silence. There was a twinkle in her eye; I knew that she knew I would never believe her if she answered no. She smiled. "No," she told me. "Never."

"When you had the brain tumor," I persisted, "weren't there ever moments when you became angry or afraid?"

Vicka looked at me as though she enjoyed the comic relief but really didn't need it. "I am with Our Lady every day," she answered at last. "How can I be unhappy, even for one moment?"

I met her gaze, took a breath, and felt myself go silent. It wasn't a case of being unable to think what I wanted to ask; I had become literally incapable of speech.

Vicka smiled again, more kindly, it seemed, then said she had promised me an hour, and that if we sat together in silence she would consider the time well spent. The interpreter, though, felt obliged to earn her money, and kept bringing up this or that interesting point, hoping to prompt discussion. Each time I would nod and Vicka would smile. For the next forty minutes, neither of us said a word.

Then Vicka stood up and so did I. "What you need to know," she told me, "is that Lord Jesus and Our Lady both love you very much. They have brought you here for a reason, and it is up to you to understand what that reason is. The answer is in your heart."

She walked out the door without looking back.

Little more than an hour after walking away from Vicka's in a state that was somewhere between dazed and entranced, I sat down with Mirjana, determined to snap out of it. The smooth tile floor and thick stucco walls of the subterranean room where Mirjana's own apparitions took place helped, holding the temperature a good twenty degrees below the searing ninety-eight outside.

Mirjana at first seemed either not to notice or not to mind my aggressive tone. I began by asking her also about being tested, not by scientists, in her case, but by the persecution of the communist authorities during the fifteen months she spent in Sarajevo after her departure from Medjugorje on July 3, 1981.

Because of her easy availability and her separation from the other "subversives," Mirjana had been singled out by Interior Ministry officials as a prime target of the state's investigation into the "antigovernment demonstrations" that had continued to take place eighty miles south in Medjugorje. Each morning of that subsequent school year had begun with the arrival of two secret police officers at the front door of her parents' apartment. For the next hour or two or three, she would be subjected to an interrogation that was no less exhausting for its familiarity: Sitting opposite her across a table piled with documents, the officers played a relentless game of good cop/bad cop, one posing threats while the other offered temptations.

"First they say I will not be allowed to finish school or attend university," Mirjana recalled. "Then they say I will go to prison, or spend the rest of my life in a mental hospital. They say there are people who want to have me shot. After some time they know that I would not be frightened by anything they would do to me, so they began to say what they will do to my parents, that they would lose their jobs, that we will lose our home, that my father would go to prison. Then they say that if I tell it is all a lie I can go to best school or university, and will have any job I want, that my family can have better home—many things they offer."

Eventually, Mirjana found the police interrogations easier to take than what happened after she was dropped off at school. There, her teachers—as instructed—mocked and taunted her relentlessly, encouraging the other students to join in. "I was cut off by all friends, every one," she remembered. "During day I am totally alone."

Mirjana's father, watching his sixteen-year-old daughter be led away in handcuffs each morning only to arrive home each afternoon in tears, suffered terribly. "His hair turn white in that one year," she said. "But my mother always say I must tell truth, and that if Holy Mother appear to me it is most important thing. "

I was taken aback when Mirjana added that she considered those fifteen months in Sarajevo the most blessed period of her life. "What?" I asked. She nodded. "The others had to share the apparitions, but my time with Holy Mother was very intense and very private. She come to me in my room every day, and help me understand what is God's plan."

Could Mirjana help me to understand also? "I can tell only little," she answered. "In time, all will be revealed." I knew it was pointless, yet I began to badger her, demanding to know why God's plan should be kept secret, observing that to say she knew but couldn't tell was bound to arouse suspicions. Mirjana took it all in, then nodded again. "I know now why you come first to me—you are unbeliever."

"I wouldn't say that," I replied.

"Then you believe?" Mirjana asked.

I wouldn't say that either.

"We should stop for now," Mirjana then told me.

"Why?" I demanded.

"It is impossible to go further until you know what you believe," Mirjana replied. Her tone changed abruptly, becoming much more peremptory. "Have you been to Križevac?" she asked.

I confessed that I hadn't climbed the mountain yet, but intended to soon. "You must go," Mirjana said. "Go to cross, find out what you believe."

I tried to change the subject with a question about her return to Medjugorje from Sarajevo: Was it because of the war?

She shook her head, refusing to let me lead. "You must go," she told me.

Wearing only a tank top and shorts with my hiking boots, I could feel the sun cooking the skin on my neck and shoulders as I walked west. The road climbed, and soon I was looking down through grape arbors into the yards of the little stone houses below. I had gone perhaps a half mile, steadily uphill, before I saw a hand-painted sign that read "Cross Mountain" and realized I was headed toward Križevac. This was as good a time as any, I decided, and continued in that direction. The grade grew steeper as I threaded my way through the neighborhood of Vasilji, and I was clambering across the boulders and through the thornbush brambles at the bottom of the mountain almost before I knew it. I climbed quickly past the first station of the cross, where an elderly couple knelt in prayer beneath the pounded copper image of Jesus standing in his crown of thorns before Pontius Pilate.

By the time I reached the fourth station of the cross, where Mary was watching Her son carry His cross to Calvary, the chirr of the cicadas in the fields had faded. For a few minutes the only sounds I could hear were those I made: heavy breathing, dripping sweat, sliding rocks; my heartbeat seemed thunderous. Somewhere around the seventh station, I thought I heard voices above me and wondered if I was imagining them. It was a relief to discover they were real, when I came upon a group of nuns at the eighth station, singing in French as they knelt before a rough wooden cross that looked as though it had been set into solid rock. I went past without slowing, but as I did, I noticed for the first time that the sky was changing. When I'd started up the mountain thirty minutes earlier, there hadn't been even the trace of a cloud. Now a dense bank of dark, purplish gray was moving my way at astonishing speed. As the sun disappeared, the temperature on Križevac dropped twenty degrees in ten minutes. Yet to the east the sky remained a clear and perfect blue; sunlight still gleamed off the white stucco walls and red-tiled roofs of the village in that direction.

I began to grow uneasy when I realized how localized the massing of clouds had become; they were gathering in a black knot directly above the peak of Križevac. My knees buckled when a bolt of lightning fell out of the sky straight toward me; for a moment everything I could see appeared in silhouette, backlit by the bright white flash. The clap of thunder that came a moment later seemed to shake the whole hillside. The clouds burst in an instant and rain fell in sheets. I was soaked within seconds, but trembled more from fear than from cold. Never had I believed more in a God of wrath than I did at that moment. This paroxysm in the sky was aimed at me, I felt certain, as a rebuke to my heedlessness. The storm gathered force with each step I took. Yet it seemed futile to turn back, so I continued to climb, expecting to be struck dead at any instant, numb with terror, yet at the same time anxious to complete the journey. Judgment was at hand, and I admitted guilt on all counts.

At the ninth station, where the copper image was of Jesus falling for the third and final time, I stopped and knelt on the wet rocks to pray for forgiveness. I went to my knees also at the tenth station ("He Is Stripped of His Garments"), and at the eleventh ("Jesus Is Nailed to the Cross"). The singing nuns caught up with me at the twelfth station, where the image was of Jesus dying on the cross. When I stood up, a dark-haired and dimpled young woman dressed in an ankle-length gray skirt, a blue sweatshirt, and a white cap with a long bill approached me. She was with the nuns, I thought. The young woman smiled but wore an expression of concern—apparently because what little clothing I wore was soaked through. She removed her hat and handed it to me, gesturing that I should put it on. I tried to refuse, but she nodded insistently, covering her own head with the hood of her sweatshirt.

So on went the cap as I hiked up the last and steepest leg of trail to the top of the mountain. I was astounded by the white cross when I finally saw it up close; from a distance I had imagined it as a towering object, at least two hundred feet tall. The cross atop Križevac was, in fact, only about forty feet high, massive but not really immense. This discrepancy struck me for some reason as an epitome of my vainglory; I needed the cross to be two hundred feet tall to justify the effect it had on me. I knelt about twenty feet from the broad concrete base of the monument, and at the moment I did, the young woman in the blue sweatshirt appeared again, this time carrying a small white towel. I didn't bother to resist as she laid the towel across my shoulders, like a miniature shawl.

On my knees in the mud and stones, staring up at a cross that was only forty feet tall, not two hundred, realizing how ridiculous I must look in this young lady's long-billed cap, with her little towel draped across my shoulders, I broke into a laugh that was unlike any I'd ever produced. I'd laughed at myself before, of course, many times, but never with so much joy. I tried to stop, out of respect for the seven or eight others on the mountaintop, all with their heads bowed in prayer, but couldn't. When it struck me that what was perhaps the first real religious experience of my life had culminated in a giggle, I laughed even louder, laughed until tears began to stream down my cheeks, utterly convinced that the same God I had believed just moments earlier to be planning my obliteration now was joined with me in some sacred guffaw. I wouldn't have believed it was in me to delight so completely in my own absurdity. What I felt was more than relief; it was liberation.

By the time my laughter ended, I was alone on the mountaintop. I stood up and wondered what had happened; I hadn't noticed the nuns leaving, and didn't realize even that it had stopped raining until I hiked perhaps a hundred yards or so back down the mountain. The clouds were breaking up and blowing away almost as rapidly as they had appeared. The sun was burning my back again before I reached the tenth station of the cross. I went down the mountain from that point as rapidly as I could without serious risk of injury. My speed on the rocks would be much remarked upon before I left Medjugorje—several people from the village said they had never seen anyone travel faster—yet I never caught up with the singing nuns or the young woman who had accompanied them. At the base of Križevac, I decided that somehow I had passed the group without knowing it. I climbed back up the mountain all the way to the sixth station, but still saw no sign of them.

I hurried back to the bottom again, waited for another half hour, then laid the hat and the towel on a boulder beside the trail at the first station of the cross. When I came back the next day they were gone, but I never again saw the young woman who had given them to me.

CHAPTER SEVEN

My clothes and hair were almost dry by the time I reached the church square. I sought the shade on the stone steps below the front entrance to the church, and for some time sat eavesdropping on the conversations all around me. These were mainly about the thunderstorm I just had experienced at much closer range than had the Canadian pilgrims who were talking about how "awesome" it had been. Their tour guide, a local, noted that there had been no hail. "I have seen other storms that lasted longer," he told his group, "but few if any that were so sudden or so loud." That the guide sounded truly impressed by the fury of the tempest ressured me somehow. I felt utterly drained and slightly ridiculous, yet deeply happy.

I found Nicky Eltz a few minutes later at Mira's, parked in front of his PowerBook. He at once brought me down a notch by saying of the storm, "There's one or two like it every summer," but became excited himself upon learning where I had been when it hit. "It was your first time up Križevac?" he asked. I nodded. "Marvelous," he said, and chuckled. My account of what had happened at the summit made him even happier. He chortled, slapping the table with his palm. "Everyone who climbs Križevac for the first time comes back down with a story," he told me, "but yours will be one of my favorites. God showed you His sense of humor. There's exceptional grace in that."

During the next hour, Nicky regaled at least a dozen passersby with the tale of my assault on Cross Mountain. I felt incapable of saying another word on the subject, but Herr Eltz seemed pleased to do my talking for me, and made the story a bit more amusing each time he told it. What surprised me was how genuinely person after person enjoyed the comedy of my climb up Križevac; I had expected that the pious might view me as irreverent.

Between visitors to our table, I probed for Nicky's own story. What he told came in fragments so out of sequence that I wasn't sure at moments if he was talking about last week or ten years ago. The technique seemed purposeful, as if it was his intention to disorient me. Nicky proved most forthcoming on the subject of his family background. His airs were not an affectation, I learned, but an inheritance; the records of the Eltz family went back at least as far as the tenth century in the Rhineland, along what is today the border between Germany and Austria. The Dvořác (Castle) Eltz in Bavaria is considered a classic of medieval architecture and has for decades been among Germany's top tourist attractions. Nicky's branch of the family had ventured rather far afield, beginning in the early eighteenth century, when they accepted the invitation of Archduke Karl VI to settle with three other aristocrat families along the south bank of the Danube. Their stated mission was to "tame and industrialize" the Croatians; their unstated purpose was to fortify the eastern border of the Holy Roman Empire against the expansionist aggression of the Turks. In both regards the venture was successful: By the early nineteenth century, the Eltz estate in Vukovar covered 167,000 acres, and the family had built the region's first shipping port, its first weaving factory, its first Catholic high school, and its first Lipizzaner horse farm.

The reforms that ensued the collapse of the Hapsburg Empire at the end of World War I had by 1918 reduced the Eltz estate to less than one-third its former size. The Eltzes remained, nevertheless, the richest and most influential family in the region. Nicky showed me what had been the family's main residence in Vukovar by pulling out a Croatian twenty-kuna banknote, which pictures the Dvořác Eltz on its front side. His grandfather was the younger of two brothers, and lived in what was known as the Mali Dvor (Little Castle) nearby. As early as 1921, it had mattered little which brother resided in either castle, because by then the family was losing its holdings in regular increments as one property after another was "federalized" by the government of the newly created Yugoslavia. Recognizing the inevitable, the Eltzes returned to Austria in 1923.

The family history Nicky told became increasingly vague at this point. There was not, however, any sordid involvement in the Third Reich to cover up: Nicky's father, after earning doctorates in art history and archaeology in Vienna and Berlin, had spent the years 1934 and 1935 supervising excavation sites in Kurdistan, and in 1937 avoided conscription as an officer in the German army by emigrating to Switzerland, then moving to the United States a few months later. Nicky would not say so, but it was evident that by this point his family's fortune had been nearly exhausted. Surrendering some rather lofty career ambitions, Nicky's father took a nominal but remunerative position with an American corporation based in Newark, New Jersey. Nicky's esteem for the man, dead some twenty years now, clearly was enormous. He seemed to have a more ambiguous relationship with his mother, who had grown up in a house with more than thirty servants and found it rather difficult to make do with the 160-acre Essex County estate her husband purchased shortly after their marriage. Mrs. Eltz now maintained an apartment in Salzburg and a cottage on Martha's Vineyard.

All Nicky would say of his youth was that he had been raised in a comfortable but by no means sybaritic fashion, that his family spoke German at home and English outside it, and that he had graduated with a degree in architecture from the University of Pennsylvania.

Nicky managed to be at once evasive and loquacious on the subject of what he had done after college. He told me a long and entertaining story about driving his new Peugeot from Paris to Dakar with two "school chums" during the summer after graduating from Penn, and described in colorful detail the months he spent working for his father's old hunting guide in Alaska, but said hardly a word about how he ended up in Eugene, Oregon, the college town where he spent most of his young adulthood. I knew already that in Eugene, Nicky had operated a gallery called Near Eastern Tribal and Village Rugs and Trappings, which generated a short-lived international sensation by selling a Caucasian rug for a then record price of $161,000, but I was startled when he mentioned that he still had a wife and two teenage daughters living in Oregon.

Nicky went cold and dark when I asked why he wasn't with them anymore. What little he would say suggested that something terrible had attended the family's disintegration: There was a fleeting reference to a court judgment totaling hundreds of thousands of dollars that his wife had won against him, and another to his arrest on unspecified charges at the airport in Eugene. Then, the next thing I knew, Nicky was talking about arriving in Medjugorje for the first time back in 1987, accompanied by the queen of Liechtenstein.

When I asked again about his family, Nicky warned me not to push it. A moment later he informed me that his wife was "under attack" by demonic forces, then got up from the table and walked away.

* * *

I went back to Križevac on the day after my initial ascent. The climb was much slower this time, because I stopped at each station of the cross. I couldn't find it in me to recite the litany of Our Fathers, Hail Marys, and Glorias that were suggested by the signs posted at each station. Instead, I simply knelt on the rocks and tried to stay with the sensations of clarity and conviction that had moved within me almost constantly during the past twenty-four hours.

With a strange sort of detachment, I marveled at how like a radio my mind worked, scanning restlessly from station to station, tuning in to this entertainment or that one, drawn equally to bad ideas and to good ones. At moments I felt certain I could hear the God station signaling through the static, but I always lost it, unable to hold my dial steady for more than a few seconds at a time, and afterward wondered if it was all in my imagination. That wondering was weightless, because the deepest part of me kept insisting that it knew what it knew. Happiness and awe seemed conjoined in a way I couldn't recall ever having experienced. My sense of time was altered as well. I felt surrounded by eternity and saturated in history. "This is what the world felt like two thousand years ago," I thought.

At the summit of the mountain I found myself alone. I sat on the broad concrete base of the cross and looked out for miles in all directions. The past that in my own country scarcely seemed to exist was here not just present but visible. Behind the Hill of Apparitions, near the summit of the mountain called Crnica, I could see the ruins of the fort the Illyrians had built here seven hundred years before the birth of Christ. Illyrian tumuli—graves covered by mounds of rocks—made odd bumps on pockets of flat ground all through the hills that surrounded Medjugorje. Facing toward Capljina, I could see the cypress trees surrounding the large Roman estate that was laid to waste by Goths in the early fifth century. Most of the centurians' tombstones had been removed, however, to the Regional Museum in Sarajevo.

Gravemarkers have been the principal instrument of historical studies in Hercegovina. The most ornate necropoles found in the region are those that were carved between the twelfth and fifteenth centuries. Floral motifs, reliefs of hunting and dueling scenes, and assorted symbolic designs cover the tombstones of this period. For most of the past two centuries, this sepulchral art has been attributed to the Bogomils, but in recent years scholars have determined that some of the carving was done by Catholics, or perhaps by Bogomils who chose to celebrate the Catholic sacraments. These discoveries have had the troubling effect of blurring the boundaries between one system of belief and another, leaving academics to argue at length about who was who and what was what.

The earliest written records of this region were produced by the Franciscan monks who arrived on the Brotnjo in the mid-thirteenth century, marching in columns out of Austria and Hungary. Tenacity and inventiveness were the hallmarks of the Franciscans, not only in their battle against Bogomilism but also in their struggle to survive the waves of conquering armies that swarmed over the Balkans for the next six hundred years. In the village they were the first outsiders to identify as Medjugorje, the friars encountered a people whose embrace of Bogomilism was in large part an expression of how successfully Gnostic heresies had incorporated the traditional pagan religions of animism and ancestor worship in Eastern Europe. On the Brotnjo Plateau, the important rituals practiced by the people were those intended to appease the fearful Gromovnik: In what was called "the dangerous season," the clan elders of Medjugorje would climb the thunder god's mountain, chanting and sprinkling water, strewing young plants and green fruit as they went. At the summit, they would sacrifice a young goat, then conclude by lighting fires that ringed the mountain's peak.

The Franciscans (who believed the ceremony had been introduced to the area by the Bogomils) countered by teaching the people of Medjugorje practical methods for fighting back against the power of Gromovnik: how to build their houses of stone rather than wood, so they wouldn't burn or blow over so easily; how to create windbreaks by planting rows of cypress along the edges of their fields; how to dig deeper wells; how to save their water in cisterns. The friars even helped the villagers form firefighting crews. Then, gradually, the monks undertook to turn the pagan ceremonies conducted on the slopes of Grmljavinac into Christian rites. On Catholic holidays, for example, the priests led a lighted procession up the Mountain of Thunder to venerate Christ and the Virgin Mary.

It was the fifteenth-century conquest of Bosnia and Hercegovina by the Ottoman Empire that cemented the bond between the people of this region and their Franciscans. Traditionally, the Church in Rome had used the monks as missionaries who forged a parochial infrastructure that would in time be taken over by diocesan priests. After the Turkish conquest of Hercegovina, however, the diocesan clergy fled, while the

Franciscans remained to struggle and suffer alongside their flocks. Every Catholic church in Bosnia and Hercegovina was either burned to the ground or converted to a mosque, and Christian religious observations were forbidden under penalty of death. The friars took to the hills, conducting masses in caves and in the remnant forests of the Dinaric Alps.

Even then, the Franciscans persisted in returning to their villages, ministering to the outlaw bands called Ustaše (Rebels) who, from their mountain hideouts, staged repeated attacks on Turkish tax collectors and trade caravans. The most famous Ustaše leader, the bandit-prince Mijat Tomić (a heroic figure still eulogized in countless Croatian folk songs), maintained his principal encampment in a complex of caves near Medjugorje at Lake Blidi. The Turks replied with brutal reprisals on those who offered aid and comfort to the rebels, organizing village-by-village hunts for Ustaše leaders: When the rebels were captured, first they, then their blood relatives, were executed on the spot, either beheaded or impaled alive on spikes. If the rebels escaped, villagers selected at random would be tortured until they revealed the nearest Ustaše hideout.

The assorted vendettas such tactics inspired were lethal but localized, and can seem almost insignificant when compared to the darkest and most enduring legacy of the Turkish reign over Bosnia and Hercegovina, the ethnic hatred that was generated when the Bogomils became Muslims. The Islam practiced by the Ottoman Empire, with its strong mystical strain and syncretic elements, seemed to many Balkan heretics a far more accommodating religion than Christianity. Like Muslims, the Bogomils did not recognize the authority of priests, or even of popes. And like Muslims, the Bogomils regarded Jesus as a great prophet but not as a divine being, rejecting both the symbol of the cross and the practice of communion.

More significantly in the eyes of their neighbors, conversion to Islam would provide the Bogomils numerous material advantages. The Turks promised any Bosnians who became Muslims not only protection from persecution by the Roman and Orthodox Churches but an array of opportunities that they would enjoy for the next three hundred years: education at the best schools, access to the professions, appointments to administrative positions, and claims to disputed lands. In time, the new Slavic Muslims would consider themselves a separate race—"Bosnjaks," they called one another. To Croatian Catholics and Orthodox Serbs, however, the Muslims were nothing but betrayers who had sold out their neighbors to a hated enemy.

The Serbian Orthodox Church worked more easily with the Turks than did the Roman Catholic, and at one point the Serbs even were authorized to collect tithes from Catholic worshippers. Franciscan monks led the resistance to this practice, generating a tradition of militant Catholicism and of warrior priests that spread throughout Bosnia and Hercegovina. The Turks answered by encouraging Serbian clans to occupy or settle in Catholic villages. In Medjugorje, the Ottomans first closed off Mount Grmljavinac (or Sipovac, as the Turks wanted it called), then converted it to a military fortress. Shortly after this, a Serbian family was invited by the Ottomans to take possession of land near the base of the mountain. Even when the Serbs became Catholics, they continued to be regarded as interlopers, and blood feuds between them and neighboring Croatian clans resulted in outbreaks of violence that littered the landscape with dead bodies until well into the sixteenth century.

Eventually, the Franciscans managed to interpose themselves, first between the Serbs and their neighbors, then between the Turks and the conquered people of Hercegovina. Promising to promote peace and to encourage cooperation (including the regular payment of tribute to the Turks), the friars won protection for their parishioners and a measure of freedom for themselves. They were especially successful on the Brotnjo Plateau, where the Ottoman governor gave the Franciscans free lodgings and tax exemptions, but as well the right to construct six small chapels in Catholic cemeteries.

The success of the Franciscans in quelling disputes among the clans and in providing a predictable payment of tribute pleased the Turks, and the friars soon were able to reward their parishioners by negotiating a reduced tax on the peasant farmers of Medjugorje. Their role as mediators between conquerers and conquered eventually would permit the friars a freedom from the rule of Rome that few monastic orders in Europe have known. Soon, for the people of Bosnia and Hercegovina, the friars *were* the Catholic Church. Franciscan freedom and the authority that went with it would not be seriously threatened until the nineteenth century, when the Turks were driven out of Bosnia by the armies of the Hapsburgs and their Austro-Hungarian Empire.

I panicked on the morning of my seventh day in Medjugorje. Over breakfast at Mira's, I informed Nicky that I was leaving. He knew why without being told: I had realized the change taking place inside me might be irreversible. Desperate to get away before it came to that, I decided to find a seat on the next bus out.

Nicky received all this with a smile and advised me to wait a day or two. "You're not the first to feel this way," he said. "It will pass if you let it." His patronizing tone infuriated me. "I'm not even Catholic" was all I could think to say. This annoyed Nicky. "What does that have to do with anything?" he asked. "You think Our Lady is here only for Catholics?"

"I don't know if She's here or not, but I wish *I* wasn't."

"You've got so much to protect, don't you?" he asked after a few moments. "And you're so afraid that if you give it up, you'll have nothing."

"Maybe what scares me is that I'll end up like you, in a retreat that never ends."

He reddened, but held his tongue for several moments. I felt the anger draining out of me.

"The one thing I didn't expect," Nicky said finally, "was to see you run away with your tail between your legs."

"Sorry to disappoint you, Nicky, but I wasn't prepared for this place. I think I overstepped."

"Overstepping is probably the only way you have of getting anywhere." That had the ring of truth. "I'll make you a deal," he told me. "Stick around for another forty-eight hours, and if you still want to leave, I'll drive you to the airport in Split myself."

After a moment's hesitation, I nodded. "I'll just hang out," I said, speaking more to myself than to him, "and watch the show. "

"Right," Nicky agreed, smiling. "Watch the show."

Strangely, knowing I'd be gone in two days not only helped me relax but also made me more interested in the people around me. Through Nicky, I had by then met most of the other Westerners who owned ready access to the visionaries, the priests, and the parish office in Medjugorje. "Permanent pilgrims," I called them, though they were better known as "Loopers," a coin termed by a British humanitarian worker to describe those who were "in the loop."

Nicky was the senior Looper, clearly, but the one who occupied the most demanding position at present was the other American among them, Rita Falsetto. Tall and tan with bright blue eyes and a tangle of true blond curls that she refused to brush or comb, Rita was a former all-American college basketball player whose unself-conscious radiance had distracted any number of young men from the village. Without pay, she worked twelve hours a day as the principal assistant to the priests in the parish office, living on her limited savings and whatever money she could beg or borrow from relatives back home in Colorado. The remainder of her waking hours she devoted to prayer and penance. After college, Rita told me, she had spent her days mostly on an assortment of athletic endeavors (becoming, among other things, a world-class bodybuilder), by night picking up men in bars. What had transformed her previously feckless existence into the life of perpetual worship she led at present was rooted, as I understood it, in the unusual relationship between her parents. Rita and her Catholic mother had been abandoned by her Jewish father when she was a small child, and the two women had struggled to stay afloat for years afterward. Rita had grown up despising her father and adoring her mother, whose faith was the guiding light of family life. Rita fell away from the Church as an adolescent, then as a young woman was confronted by an astounding development: Her father, who had seen neither his wife nor his daughter in more than twenty years, showed up at Rita's mother's front door one day to announce that he was dying of cancer and had nowhere else to go. Without hesitation, his long-estranged wife took the man in, nursing him tenderly during the last months of his life. Observing, mostly from afar, her mother's capacity for forgiveness and self-sacrifice had been for Rita a wrenching experience. Torn between simmering rage at one parent and awestruck admiration of the other, Rita had nearly come apart before choosing the Christian sentiments that were inspired by her mother. She returned to her religion with a fervor that resulted in her first pilgrimmage to Medjugorje. As soon as she arrived, Rita said, she knew that this was "the holiest place on earth" and committed herself to remaining for as long as possible. After exhausting her funds during her first stay in Bosnia, she went back to the U.S., worked two jobs to save money, then returned as quickly as she could. She had lived here for slightly more than a year this time on less than four thousand dollars, and wouldn't leave, Rita said, as long as she could feed herself.

Included among the Loopers by association was Karen, the young woman who had given them their name. She was a reclamation project to whom Nicky and especially Rita were devoting many hours. Grossly overweight, with bad skin and broken teeth, Karen was at least slightly drunk every time I saw her. Loud, profane, rude, and snobbish, she showed up at Mira's each evening, quickly downed two or three water glasses filled with red wine, then began to hold forth on the shortcomings of assorted colonials. Loutish Yanks became a favorite target soon after my arrival. "When you're as rich as I am, you can say whatever you damn well like," she advised me on the evening we met. It was a consolation of sorts that Karen didn't like Huns either, or Frenchies, or Eyetals, and wasn't for that matter terribly impressed by Croats. She reserved a special disdain for namby-pamby priests and nicey-nasty nuns of every nationality. And these doltish pilgrims one saw everywhere, fingering their bloody beads—they were a sorry lot. The individual Karen detested above all others, was Jesus Christ. At the end of each evening, completely wasted yet curiously coherent, she not only took the Lord's name in vain but cursed Him as a liar and a fraud. "Fuck you, Jesus!" I heard her shout on several occasions as she staggered across the paving stones of the church square.

Karen did have her good points, of course, principally a keen wit and a lively intelligence. She was also courageous, one of the relatively few humanitarians willing to carry medical supplies into any part of Bosnia where they might be needed, including those that lay under the siege of Serb artillery. "Risking your life's nothing special if you don't care about living," she cheerfully informed me.

The family into which Karen had been adopted as an infant owned one of the oldest and best-known businesses in England. They were also, Karen maintained, the leaders of the largest Satanic circle in London and had subjected her to horrific abuse from the time she was a young girl. She hated Jesus in particular, she explained, because all during her childhood she had prayed to Him, begging to be rescued from the hell of her life, but the bastard never did a thing to help her.

Karen didn't hate everyone. She admired Nicky, adored Rita, and like them was eagerly anticipating the imminent arrival in Medjugorje of the most esteemed Looper, Milona Hapsburg. Monika Ilona von Hapsburg Erzherzogin von Osterreich was her full name, daughter of the archduke of Austria, Jozsef Arpad Erzherzog von Osterreich, and his wife, the Prinzessen zu Lowenstein. Since her first visit to Medjugorje in 1984, Milona had played a role in the devotions here that made her a figure of enormous significance for both pilgrims and the people of the village. Two years earlier, however, she had become involved in her first romantic relationship in more than a decade, with a fellow ten years her junior whose blue-blood pretensions Nicky mocked by calling him Charles the Fifth. I wasn't yet privy to the details, but apparently some very odd things had occurred when Charles visited Medjugorje during the previous summer. As a result of Charles's "fits," everything about Milona's place in the iconography of the parish was being called into question. That she would be returning in a few days, alone, was a subject of wide interest and high anxiety.

"Can you comprehend what it has meant for the people here, these simple peasants, to have a Hapsburg kneeling next to them in their church?" Nicky asked me.

"I'm a real American, Nicky," I answered. "I haven't got a clue."

It helped to know that the Hapsburgs, whose Holy Roman Empire included not only Austria and Hungary but also much of Germany, Spain, Italy, Belgium, Holland, and the future Czech Republic, had control of Croatia for nearly two hundred years before they ousted the Ottoman Empire from Bosnia and Hercegovina. For Austria, the Krajina (Military Frontier) between eastern Croatia and western Bosnia served as the front line in a century-long battle that blocked the Turks from their ultimate goal, Vienna. Reluctantly, Croatia had become part of the Hapsburg Empire's "military confines," those regions where the entire male population between ages sixteen and sixty were considered a standing army.

"The Croats have always been superb soldiers," Rebecca West wrote in her 1941 magnum opus, *Black Lamb and Grey Falcon*, but then so have the Serbs, who settled in the Krajina at the invitation of the Hapsburgs, assigned both to fortify the borders of the empire and to subdue the nationalist yearnings of Croatia. Thus was the tripartite collision of ethnic identities and animosities in the region guaranteed.

Until late in the nineteenth century, Hercegovina remained in the hands of the Turks, though the Ottoman grip was loosened, while the Croats continued to serve, more and more unhappily, under the Austrians. The Serbs, meanwhile, applauded the emergence of Russia as a world power and the czars as champions of the Orthodox faith. Ethnic unrest and attempts by assorted claimants to this title or that one became footnotes to the Ottoman Empire's slow deterioration.

In 1878, the Congress of Berlin gave the Hapsburgs control over Bosnia and Hercegovina. Though not as cruel as the Turks, the Austrians were no less domineering. For all they contributed to the region—roads, rail lines, and construction projects that stitched the countryside—they exacted payment through tolls and taxes. They also fought with the Franciscans for control of Catholicism in Hercegovina. Allied with those in Rome who regarded the friars as obstinate and unorthodox, the

Hapsburgs encouraged the Vatican to create a diocesan system for the Church in Bosnia and Hercegovina that would force the Franciscans to accept an enormously reduced role throughout the region.

In Medjugorje, the Hungarian and Slovene priests assigned to the village by the bishop of Mostar announced soon after their arrival that they intended to build a new parish church. The people of the village fought them every step of the way. When the diocesan priests went door-to-door collecting funds, they were chased away with pitchforks and scythes. The locals not only refused to help with construction of the new church, they refused to sell food to foreign workers when they arrived. The villagers' most effective subversion was to encourage the Hungarian and Slovene priests to build their new church on a former marsh where the ground was so soft that the first wall began to collapse before the second one was completed. After four years, the new church finally was finished, but the people of the parish refused to set foot in it. At the end of the nineteenth century, despite being backed by both the the Hapsburgs and the Vatican, the bishop of Mostar admitted defeat and commanded the diocesan priests to return home. Most did, though a significant number stayed to join the Franciscan order.

By then the Austro-Hungarian Empire had begun to crumble. Bosnia and Hercegovina in particular were breeding grounds for the ethnic tensions and insurrectionist agitation that eventually would topple the Hapsburgs, especially after the rest of Europe began taking sides: While Germany adamantly opposed the mounting nationalism of the Serbs, Russia and Great Britain enthusiastically supported it. This was the period when the Balkans became known in the Western press as a "hotbed of dark passions and blood revenge." The image hardly was dispelled when the king of Serbia and his wife were murdered in the palace at Belgrade in June 1903, their naked bodies thrown from a bedroom window.

In June 1914, Austria, increasingly concerned about the alliance of Serbia with the Russians, dispatched its imperial heir, Archduke Franz Ferdinand, to Bosnia to oversee military maneuvers on the Serbian frontier. In Sarajevo, on St. Vitus's Day, the archduke was assassinated by Gavrilo Princip, a member of a Serbian nationalist group called the Order of the Black Hand (the seal of the order was a clenched fist holding a skull and crossbones, surrounded by a knife, a bomb, and a bottle of poison). When it was revealed that eight thousand rubles had been paid to the leaders of the Black Hand by a Russian military attaché in Belgrade, World War I was set in motion, though not before the Austrians arrested everyone in Bosnia and Hercegovina harboring anti-Hapsburg sentiments, then hanged most of them, women as well as men. Photographs of the dangling dead still are displayed in public buildings all over Hercegovina, and are treated as icons in Serbian communities.

After the Great War ended the reign of the Hapsburgs, Hercegovina became part of the new nation known as the Kingdom of Serbs, Croats, and Slovenes. Its king, Alexander, was simply a Serb, one whose policies wreaked havoc upon the Catholic and Muslim populations. On the east bank of the Neretva River, all along the ancient trade route from the Dalmatian Coast to Mostar, Ottoman garrisons were converted to villages of Serb "gatekeepers" who imposed crushing tolls on the traffic in people and goods. The Serbian population of a town called Zitomislići not only controlled access to the Brotnjo Plateau but maintained the only winepress in the region, charging an exorbitant fee on the grapes used to make the famed Zilavka and Blatina wines that were the principal commercial products of western Hercegovina.

In Medjugorje, a Serb merchant acquired an exclusive right to purchase grape juice and grain from local farmers, and soon became the most powerful man in the parish. The merchant's plan to create an Orthodox monastery at the foot of Sipovac was the last straw; soon after, rebel bands of Ustaše reappeared, destroying Serb property and attacking Serb officals. King Alexander responded by abolishing democratic institutions and ruling with military units of Serb royalists known as Četniks.

Throughout Hercegovina, the Četniks plundered Croat and Muslim villages with impunity, suppressing local resistance and seizing whatever property they desired. Zitomislići became the main staging area for Četnik assaults on the Brotnjo plateau. Eight miles from Medjugorje, in Capljina, Četnik units practiced for battle by tossing Catholic babies in the air, then catching them on the tips of their swords. Several buildings were constructed in the city for the sole purpose of hanging rebellious Croats; the Četniks also borrowed the Turk custom of publicly impaling rebels on spikes. (Muslim suffering was no less; more than three thousand Bosnjaks were killed by Četnik units in eastern Hercegovina during 1924 alone.)

Many Croats fled Hercegovina. Those young men who stayed nearly all joined units of the Ustaše, which by then had adopted tactics nearly as brutal as those of the Četniks. Motives became more and more mixed, even in the practice of religion; when construction of the cross atop the mountain now known as Križevac was completed in 1933, many celebrated the event as a victory for Croatian nationalism. What had been a series of

isolated skirmishes became all-out war in 1934, when Ustaše leaders organized the assasination of King Alexander at a meeting with the French
president (who was killed also) in Marseilles. Though their grip was loosened, the Serbs retained control of Yugoslavia until 1941, when the Axis
powers invaded the country and dismembered it. In Zagreb, the commanding German general proclaimed the "Independent State of Croatia," and
appointed Ustaše leader Ante Pavelić as its president. For the next four
years, while the rest of the world was consumed by the Allied/Axis struggle,
the Yugoslavs fought mainly among themselves in what may have been
the most convoluted civil war in human history.

Ante Pavelić had been living in Italy and was a protégé of Benito
Mussolini, who had helped him build the clandestine organization responsible for the assassination of King Alexander in Marseilles. The Pavelić
government, supported at the beginning by the Catholic Church, soon
adopted not only fascist policies but also fascist tactics, determined to
deal with the Serbs in much the same way that the German Nazis were
disposing of Jews. The official Ustaše program called for "one-third of
Serbs killed, one-third expelled, and one-third converted to Catholicism."
However, when the Church renounced its earlier endorsement of Pavelić,
those plans for expulsion and conversion were abandoned, so that the
Croatian Nationalist forces could concentrate on collecting Serbs behind
barbed wire and executing them. In the Ustaše concentration camp at
Jasenovac, near the Bosnian border, as many as half a million Serbs,
Muslims, Gypsies, Jews, and dissident Croats were exterminated. The
camp had no gas chambers; instead, the killing was done mainly with
bullets, axes, and knives (there is also a famous photograph of three Ustaše
militants posing with a chainsaw against the throat of a Serb prisoner just
before decapitating him).

Among the assorted armies at large in the countryside, Bosnia and
Hercegovina were the principal battlegrounds. The Ustaše formed its most
rabid columns from the militant nationalists of Hercegovina, while the
most vicious Četnik militias assembled in Bosnia. Month after month,
Serbs and Croats attacked each other's villages, murdering, raping, and
looting, until they were joined by a third force, the communist Partizans,
led by Josip Broz Tito, who eventually would surpass in brutality both
the Ustaše and the Četniks.

The ultrarightist Četniks at first fought side by side with the Partizans, then turned on the communists and joined the fascist Italian forces.
Most of those the Četniks killed, however, were Muslims. Some Bosnian

Muslims formed their own Ustaše column to join Croatia's war against the Četniks, while others enlisted in the "Muslim Brigades" of Tito's Partizans. And after the Četniks began slaughtering whole villages in Bosnia and Hercegovina, virtually every antifascist Croat was forced to join the Partizan forces. At the same time, layered above, below, and all through this tangle of terror were the localized but long-standing blood feuds of assorted clans.

"Until the Partizans came, the main problem in Medjugorje was no food," recalled Postar's uncle Pero Vasilj. "Everybody was hungry. We had no real Partizans among our people here, just a few working as spies, telling the others who had sent their sons to fight against them. The men of this part of Hercegovina were known as the toughest in the whole country, but when the soldiers came, they had weapons and we had none."

"For most of us, it was a very confusing time," Iva Vasilj, the maternal grandmother of the visionary Ivanka, would tell me. "So many sides, all fighting. The people of this area didn't know which was the right army. Every one that came said they are the right one. We are afraid of them all. We don't know who to trust. Many, when they hear the soldiers are coming, just run away to hide somewhere." Iva's husband was among the 1.7 million—more than a tenth of Yugoslavia's prewar population—who had been killed by the time the fighting was finished. In Hercegovina, more than half the homes were destroyed and nearly two-thirds of the villages abandoned. Medjugorje had paid a high price for being one of the communities that endured.

The war first had reached the parish in May 1941, when a band of Ustaše led by a member of a Croat clan slaughtered the entire herds of cows, goats, and poultry belonging to a Serbian family. Ethnic tensions bubbled, with occasional outbreaks of violence, until the late summer of 1942, when the Medjugorje parish was marked by an incident so shameful that the people there would spend the next fifty years trying to forget about it.

Within forty-eight hours of cutting my deal with Nicky, I had realized that one did not escape from a place like Medjugorje by running away. In the alternative, I began to explore. I soon discovered a community that was full of hidden paths and secret entrances. They led to cemeteries, often, or to abandoned sentry posts set back in the hills. I always felt vaguely intrusive and surreptitious when I followed one for more than a few steps.

My curiosity generally won out over my discretion, however, putting me in a variety of awkward situations, and one that was actually dangerous.

Walking one afternoon where the figure eight of Medjugorje's main street curved around Crnica, the second highest mountain of the Trtla Range, I stumbled upon an offshoot of broken pavement that led eventually to a rough, rubble-strewn one-lane road. Winding as it sank then rose again, the road was a river of gravel interrupted by islands of asphalt that disappeared into an ominous landscape of red cinders and pale gray rocks. Little more than a mile along the road, sheer cliffs began to rise on one side, while deep ravines fell away on the other. The shoulders of the road turned into shallow trenches filled with garbage, and the stench in spots was sickening. In the distance, a vortex of carrion birds swirled above a dead animal. I kept walking but did not get much farther before a group of four young men drove toward me in a late-model Mercedes convertible, all wearing camo T-shirts with cutoff sleeves, accoutred with bits and pieces of military uniforms. Except for the driver, each carried either a rifle or a machine gun, barrels pointed straight at the sky. I knew they must be members of the dreaded HOS (Home Defense Force).

The four looked at least as startled to see me as I was to see them. Braking to a halt in a huge cloud of red dust, they stared at me in wonder for a few moments, then began to motion me away with the barrels of their guns. "Not for pilgrims," one of them said in English, then pointed past me toward the main road. I wasn't going to argue. Masking my fright behind an expression of confusion, I turned on my heel and headed back the way I had come.

Half an hour later, I was again on asphalt and surrounded by houses. What had just happened seemed too surreal to be true. The effect was amplified when I asked several locals where the road led and they replied that no such road existed. One young man acknowledged that the road was there, but said it went nowhere. It was Nicky who told me, several days later, that the road led to the hamlet of Surmanci. I could not go to Surmanci, Nicky added after a pause. It was too far to walk and no taxi would take me. Neither would any other local. Neither, for that matter, would he. When I asked why, all he would tell me was "It's not necessary."

Some time would pass before I learned even a little about why the people of the Medjugorje parish seemed so determined to keep Surmanci a secret. The story went back to August 1942, when Ustaše officers decided that the Brotnjo plateau must be "swept clean" of Serbs. That month, the entire population of Serb "gatekeepers" at Zitomislići had been taken prisoner and herded into a huge bunker built into the side of a cliff by German engineers. The Ustaše plan was to seal the entrance and leave the Serbs inside to starve. This plan changed when a convoy of Nazi trucks packed with Serb prisoners arrived in Zitomislići. Under orders to report back to their own units as quickly as possible, the Germans turned their prisoners and their trucks over to the Ustaše and promptly departed. After brief deliberation, the Ustaše pulled their own prisoners from the bunker, packed them on the trucks with the other Serbs, and drove toward the isolated hamlet of Surmanci. There, on the road just outside the village, the trucks stopped. The Serbs were unloaded and ordered to stand along the shoulder. Minutes later, every one of them—men, women, and children—were slaughtered and thrown into a ravine. How many exactly were killed that day is not known, but the victims numbered at least several hundred.

Medjugorje, identified as Ustaše headquarters, was singled out by the Partizans for special attention in the reprisals that ensued; scarcely a family escaped the cycle of incarceration, torture, rape, and confiscation that went on for twelve years. The "Liberation Committees" set up by the Partizans to administer the territories swiftly became oligarchies that ruled with a barbarity not matched by even the Ottomans. In villages all across Bosnia and Hercegovina, Partizan units led by Serbs and Montenegrins forced Croats and Muslims to rape and murder neighbors while their children watched. More than a quarter of the Brotnjo's population was killed.

I found any number of people who were willing to talk about the savagery that had engulfed the Brotnjo plateau after 1945, but not a single soul who would so much as acknowledge the massacre at Surmanci. Even on the big tablet map in the church square, I could find no indication of Surmanci or of the road leading to the little village. It was as if, for the rest of its parish, the place didn't exist. But Surmanci was out there, hidden from view behind the Hill of Apparitions.

CHAPTER EIGHT

By the spring of 1982, both church and state were growing increasingly interested in the backgrounds and the experiences of Medjugorje's six young seers. Secular and religious authorities seemed equally perturbed that the visionaries were such ordinary teenagers. Ivan made a particularly poor impression. "Talking with him, one gets the impression that he has little initiative and is almost inarticulate," observed a Croatian priest who was in Medjugorje to question the children. "Darkly taciturn and rather dullwitted," a second investigator wrote of Ivan, who had announced in the fall of 1981 that he intended to study for the priesthood. After enrolling at a junior seminary near Dubrovnik, Ivan lasted only a few months before withdrawing in frustration, unable to achieve a passing grade in even a single course.

Vicka was no scholar either, having dropped out of high school that fall, while Marija was forced to repeat her junior year. The two girls were of "at best average intelligence," as one investigator put it, yet inspired praise from nearly everyone who met them. Vicka, "the natural leader, full of energy, courageous, and outspoken," was also the most emotionally expressive of the seers. Words like "natural" and "unaffected" were used again and again to describe Vicka, whose calloused hands gave evidence that she continued to work daily in the fields with the rest of her family. Most who sat with the visionaries during their apparitions found Vicka irresistible to watch: "She simply radiates delight," said one investigator.

Marija was regarded as "the most serene and deeply spiritual" of the six. Wrote a newspaper reporter (and avowed athiest) who had come from Belgrade to interview the visionaries: "If there is nothing authentic in Medjugorje but Marija, it is enough. I observed her closely, and I would put my hand into fire to testify that this girl is not play-acting."

While many visitors noted Ivanka's beauty, most found conversation with her a disappointment. "She seems to be more superficial, and thus typical of modern teenagers, than the other girls in the group," one investigator observed.

"Fidgety" was the adjective most often applied to young Jakov. At the same time, a number of investigators described the boy as perhaps the most persuasive proof that the apparitions were authentic: "Any normal child his age—and he is one—would soon rebel against going every day to make a show," noted a priest who had interviewed all six children. "In fact, Jakov is the most regular of the six in church attendance; he has never missed even one service."

Mirjana remained the favorite of those frustrated by the thick tongues of the others: "She is the brightest and best-educated of the group," one investigator noted, "and gives the clearest and most descriptive accounts of apparitions and messages." Though not in Medjugorje to greet visitors or speak to reporters, Mirjana continued to attract the greatest share of attention from civil authorities, in large part because of her vulnerabilities: She lived with her family in a state-owned apartment, planned to attend university, hoped to enter the professional class, and was the daughter not of a farmer but of a hospital radiographer who could be threatened with the loss of his job. Unyielding, Mirjana was expelled from her high school in early 1982 because she had missed too many classes while undergoing police interrogations. Her parents enrolled her in a new school where nearly all the other students were Muslims or Serbs. "They didn't know me and weren't interested," she would tell me thirteen years later, "so in some ways school was easier." It was easier at least until her last semester, when the secret police contacted officials at the school and told them Mirjana should not be permitted to graduate. She got her diploma despite this, aided by a sympathetic teacher who helped the girl conceal the date she would sit for her final exams.

Back in Mostar, Bishop Žanić was whispering privately that the Medjugorje visionaries were either hysterics or frauds. The enthusiasm of those sympathetic to the apparitions, meanwhile, was dampened by a political atmosphere that seemed to grow more dangerous with each passing day. Shortly after Father Zovko's criminal conviction, two more Franciscans who had moved to Medjugorje were charged with sedition and sentenced to prison with him. In the city of Duvno, the editorial staff of a newspaper that had published an innocuous article about the prosecution of the priests was angrily attacked by the secretary of the Religious Commission of the Republic; within a month the newspaper ceased publication.

While he seemed reluctant to convene the second and much larger commission that was to conduct the Church's official inquiry, Bishop Žanić had begun to encourage a number of independent investigators he believed might discredit the apparitions in Medjugorje. Among the first to visit the village at the bishop's behest was Father Radagost Grafenauer, a "specialist in the discernment of spirits" who had been presented to Žanić by a member of his original commission in late 1982. After listening to twenty cassettes of interviews with the visionaries, Father Grafenauer announced that he saw no point in going to Medjugorje, "since the Madonna is not appearing there." Only at the bishop's insistence did he agree to travel the twelve miles to the village. There, he spent two days reviewing the parish "chronicle" of the apparitions, speaking with the local priests, and interviewing the seers. Grafenauer returned to Mostar not only convinced the apparitions were genuine but an ardent champion of the Medjugorje visionaries.

When the priest submitted his report to the bishop, the latter became enraged and dismissed Father Grafenauer as an investigator, charging that he had been "converted" by the lies of the Franciscans. Nothing upset Žanić more, though, than Grafenauer's report that the six young seers were praying for him daily—at the Madonna's urging, they said. "You pray for me as a sinner?" Žanić demanded of Marija after summoning her to Mostar. "No," the girl answered. "We pray for you as our bishop."

The next "expert" invited by Žanić to investigate the apparitions in Medjugorje was Dr. Ludvik Stopar, a professor of psychiatry at the University of Maribor and a member of the prestigious International Commission of Doctors. Dr. Stopar had been permitted to examine the six young seers over a period of weeks during late 1982, conducting a battery of neurological, psychological, intelligence, and personality tests on each of them. Without exception, he wrote in the report he submitted one month later, his results "show the children to be absolutely normal and free from all psycho-pathological reactions." The visionaries had given him permission to observe them during their apparitions on a number of occasions, Dr. Stopar reported, and the only word he could use to describe the state they entered into during these sessions was "inexplicable": At the same time that their perception of and sensitivity to the outside world became profoundly diminished, the brain waves of the six indicated tremendously heightened mental activity. "I know of no technical term to cover that particular state," the doctor admitted.

Like many of the scientists who would follow him, Dr. Stopar was flabbergasted by the way the visionaries went absolutely silent in the same instant at the beginning of the apparitions, even though they all still appeared to be speaking normally. Even more incredible, he added, was the way all their voices became audible again at exactly the same moment as they uttered the words "who art in Heaven." Knowing it would subject him to scathing professional ridicule, not to mention the scorn of Bishop Žanić, the professor nevertheless ended his report thusly: "I had the impression of coming into contact with a supernatural reality in Medjugorje."

The state of Yugoslavia found itself in much the same position as Bishop Žanić. After dispatching one of the most respected child psychologists in Sarajevo to examine the Medjugorje visionaries, the government received a report in which all six seers were described as enjoying exceptionally good mental health. Only a few weeks passed before both the bishop and the communist state were provided with the best opportunity to ridicule the devotions in Medjugorje that had presented itself so far: First Vicka and Jakov, then Mirjana, claimed that the Virgin Mary had taken them physically to visit Heaven, Hell, and Purgatory.

I took an immediate dislike to Ivan, and the feeling was mutual. "Stupid and surly," I would call him afterward, a description that brought suppressed smiles to the faces of several people who knew Ivan better than I did. Nicky warned me I was being unfair: "Ivan is simple and shy. That gruff exterior is something he puts on to deal with people who confuse or threaten him. You, I imagine, do both."

As near as I could tell, the problem between Ivan and me had started when his wife, Lureen, the former Miss Massachusetts, learned that I wrote for *Rolling Stone* magazine and promptly advised her husband that this publication was dedicated to corrupting the morals of youth. And youth, I would discover, was Ivan's special ministry. "You are not here for truth. You are here to make joke of us," Ivan said accusingly during our brief encounter on his front porch.

Would Mirjana permit me to stay with her if that was so? I asked. Ivan's house was right across the street; I knew he had seen me coming and going. "Mirjana and I are not same people," he answered. "She make her choice, I make mine. But you think we are all alike." How did he know what was in my mind? I asked. The question stopped him for a moment. "You do not need me," Ivan said finally. "If others are speaking to you, you will get what you want." Ivan's wife was eavesdropping over his shoulder. The blankly bemused expression on her face infuriated me. "Your choice," I told Ivan, then turned and walked away, astonished to discover myself trembling with rage.

It was some consolation to learn that Ivan was by far the most un-popular of the visionaries, especially with people from the U.S. and Western Europe, among whom he was notorious for his rude behavior. He seemed to be well liked by his fellow Croats, except for a few who complained that he was less careful than the other visionaries about ac-cepting gifts and favors. After my anger cooled, I found myself more perplexed than offended by Ivan's attitude.

"Remember that everyone here is watching you," Nicky advised me later that morning over cappuccinos at Mira's. "When they see that you're sincere, old boy, that's when they'll warm up to you. Try to keep in mind that they've had their trust abused again and again by reporters, writers and so-called intellectuals from the West." I nodded, only half-listening, thinking about Mirjana. Being on the outs with her had become much more difficult to bear since the miserable failure of my meeting with Ivan.

An opportunity for reconciliation presented itself that very afternoon, when I spotted Mirjana sitting with her four-year-old daughter, Maria, in the flower garden next to their house. She was cordial but wary when I strolled over, said hello, and sat down. I knew a resumption of our ear-lier conversation (the one that had triggered my ascent of Križevac) would be a mistake, and instead made small talk about feeding dahlias and fight-ing slugs back in Oregon. Mirjana seemed relieved that I wanted only to share her company for a few minutes.

Maria, dark-haired and vivacious, at once began to show off for me, kicking over a watering can and snatching a rattle away from her baby sis-ter. In Croatian, Mirjana admonished her daughter to behave, but the girl was enjoying the attention and turned away from her mother, glancing back at me with an expression of perfect insouciance. Mirjana seemed em-barrassed, blushing slightly as she looked at me and shrugged. "Maria is what we call back home a 'pistol,'" I told Mirjana, who smiled gratefully.

"Some people expect visionary to be more than human," she said. We sat in silence for a few moments. As she watched her daughter, Mirjana's expression grew sad. "It is difficult to be visionary and mother at same time," she said suddenly. "I love my children, my husband, my family.

But there is nothing that compares to my time with Blessed Mother. That is greatest love I know, and in every other moment of my life, even with children and husband, I wish more to be with Our Lady."

There was a poignancy in Mirjana's voice that disarmed me utterly. I felt closer to her in that moment than I ever would again.

"People envy us, that we see the Blessed Mother and speak to Her, but I would not wish it for anyone else," Mirjana told me. "To know Heaven and live on earth is pain no one else can imagine."

She had left earth for the first time on All Souls' Day (November 12) in 1981, Vicka recalled, when the Virgin appeared unannounced to her and Jakov, explaining that She wished to take the two of them to visit Heaven, Hell, and Purgatory. Jakov, barely eleven, began to sob, pleading with the Virgin to leave him behind. Later, Jakov would admit: "I said, 'Our Lady, take Vicka. She has seven brothers and sisters; I am an only son.' But Our Lady said that we should not be afraid, because She was with us. And after that we went."

Heaven was "so far beyond description," Vicka said, that she felt foolish speaking about it. Paradise had appeared to her as a "huge endless tunnel filled with an unearthly kind of light." She could see countless people who seemed to wear robes of a luminous yellow and gray, "all as if filled with some indescribable joy. Your heart stands still when you look at it." All he could remember of Heaven, Jakov said, was "many people praying, all speaking together."

"Did Heaven have boundaries?" Vicka was asked by a Croatian priest. "Yes and no," the girl answered. She was reminded of how it was at the edge of Adriatic Sea: "Where you stand there are boundaries, but up ahead there are none." Vicka would be mocked relentlessly for saying that Heaven had "a kind of door" at its entrance, yet continued to insist this was true: The Virgin had explained that "a narrow passage" awaited everyone who attempted to enter Paradise.

They had been shown Purgatory next, the two said. Jakov saw only "a cloud" with people moving inside. Vicka's description again was much more detailed. She had viewed Purgatory as a "dark chasm," suspended between Heaven and Hell. The atmosphere suggested a mist filled with ashes; she was reminded of how it felt to enter a fog-shrouded cemetery on a winter day. She heard "moanings and lamentations, and the sound of countless fingers knocking, as though they want to get out." The Virgin had told them that Purgatory was "the place where souls are purified, and that much prayer is needed for the people there," Vicka said. To her, it had seemed a place of suffering.

Hell, of course, had been far worse. "I do not want to speak about Hell," Jakov said. "Hell exists; I have seen it. Perhaps before, I had some doubts, but now I know it really exists." Vicka described Hell as a vast pit with "an ocean of raging flames" at its center. She had watched the damned approach the fire naked, then hurl themselves willingly into it: "Before they went into the fire, they looked like normal people. The more they are against God's will, the deeper they enter into the fire, and the deeper they go, the more they rage against Him." Each of these souls emerged from the fire with hideously blackened skin, Vicka said: "They don't have human shapes anymore; they are more like grotesque animals, but unlike anything on earth."

She and Jakov had been in her friend Jakisa's house that day when the Virgin took them, Vicka recalled. They "returned to earth" feeling as if they had been physically absent, a belief that was confirmed when Jakisa's mother asked where they had been hiding, then said she had spent the past twenty minutes looking for them.

It was just a short time after this that Mirjana reported she too had been offered the opportunity see Heaven, Hell, and Purgatory, but accepted only the Virgin's offer of a trip to Paradise. She would not attempt to describe Heaven, Mirjana said, because no words could convey the beauty of it. Eventually, at the Virgin's urging, Mirjana said, she had accepted a glimpse of Purgatory, a place where she could see only "people shivering, thrashing, writhing in pain." The Madonna explained to her why such a place was necessary: "Since nothing can live in the sight of God but pure love, God's justice cleanses." The Virgin described Purgatory as a series of "levels" that stretched all the way from the gates of Hell to the portal of Paradise. Souls in Purgatory who prayed frequently were permitted occasionally to communicate with the living, the Madonna said; because the dead no longer have free will, they cannot atone for their sins and are completely dependent upon the prayers of those still living.

Terribly frightened by what she had seen, Mirjana found it difficult to accept that a place of even greater torment could exist: "I asked Our Lady how God can be so unmerciful as to throw people into Hell to suffer forever." The Virgin then explained that the souls in Hell had gone there of their own free will, Mirjana recalled. What about those who wanted out? Mirjana asked. How could God ignore their prayers? "Then the Madonna explained it to me: People in Hell do not pray at all; instead they blame God for everything. In effect, they become one with Hell, and they get used to it. They rage against God, and they suffer, but they always refuse to pray to God. In Hell, they hate Him even more."

She asked the Madonna if many people went to Hell, Mirjana said, and was told, "Today, most people go to Purgatory, the next greatest number go to Hell, and only a few go directly to Heaven."

For Bishop Žanić, reports of these visits to the beyond were conclusive evidence of how preposterous the claims of the Medjugorje visionaries had become. What astonished the bishop was the number of people inclined to believe such nonsense. More than fifty thousand people from all over Yugoslavia had gathered in Medjugorje to celebrate the first anniversary of the apparitions in June 1982, and nearly twice that number were expected to assemble in the village for the second anniversary in 1983.

Insisting that something must be done to shatter this mass hysteria, Žanić stepped up his campaign of denunciation. His opening salvo was perhaps the most plausible explanation of the apparitions that he would ever offer. Indulging in a bit of Jungian analysis, the bishop observed that it had been Ivanka, "whose mother died a few months earlier, and who was much interested in knowing where her mother went," who first claimed to see the Virgin Mary. The girl's grief obviously had been the "psychic catalyst" of the events that followed, the bishop observed.

Soon after his pronouncement, however, Žanić was stymied by the reports of Dr. Stopar and the child psychologist from Sarajevo, each of whom had agreed that the apparitions in Medjugorje, whatever they might be, were not hallucinations. But for Žanić, debunking the apparitions and defending his personal reputation had become inseparable goals. This was clear to all after the leading Catholic theologian in Yugoslavia charged publicly that the bishop's attacks on the Medjugorje visionaries were motivated by the need "to assuage the guilt of his own cowardice." Determined to offer a devastating reply, the bishop returned to his claim that the apparitions were fraudulent and became intent on obtaining evidence to prove it.

Probing for inconsistencies in the statements of the visionaries, Bishop Žanić had sent the members of his first commission to Medjugorje late in 1981 to demand that the seers confide when this "Great Sign" promised by the Madonna would manifest itself. All four of the visionaries living in the village at that time refused to speak on the subject, as did

Mirjana when the commission members followed her to Sarajevo. Finally, the bishop's investigators cornered Ivan at the seminary, where he had enrolled a few months earlier, demanding that he describe the Sign and give the date of its appearance. Overwhelmed, Ivan complied with a written statement in which he revealed that the Sign would appear on Podbrdo at the site of the first apparition, and that it would be formed of a flame that burned continuously but without consuming. Ivan also wrote that the Sign would appear in the month of June, but then became aware—"within myself," as the boy would put it—that he should not reveal the year, and dropped his pen on the tablet in front of him. Bishop Žanić would claim that Ivan had written that the Sign would appear in June 1982, only to be himself discredited when the "document" was produced for public inspection.

The bishop did not wait long to bring new charges, alleging the Medjugorje seers had made promises of miraculous healings that contributed to the deaths of at least three people. First, he named a child from Grude whose parents had been promised that the Virgin would cure her of leukemia; the girl died only a few months later, Žanić noted. The girl's parents, however, testified that the visionaries had made no such promise, but rather advised them simply to pray and fast. Žanić next cited the case of a teenage girl who had died after the children told her the Madonna counseled against an operation that might have saved her. The girl's older sister promptly answered that the remarks attributed by the bishop to the visionaries were "totally inaccurate." Žanić tried one more time, charging that a man from Belgrade had died after the seers assured him that a scheduled operation would succeed "as long as he prayed." It was the dead man's daughter who came forward in this instance, testifying that her father had spoken to just one of the Medjugorje six, Ivan, who had promised only that he would recommend the man to the Madonna at his next apparition.

The Franciscans went on the offensive themselves at this point, observing that more than a year had passed since the Yugoslav Bishops' Conference had ordered Žanić to convene a new investigative commission; they demanded to know why the bishop of Mostar refused to act. The pressure on Žanić increased tremendously in December 1983, when the widely respected archbishop of Split, Frane Franić, issued a public statement in support of both the Franciscans and the visionaries. Simply in terms of conversions, the archbishop observed, "Medjugorje has accomplished more in two years than all our pastoral action has done in forty."

Six weeks later, Bishop Žanić announced the members of his new investigative commission, appearing on television to boast that the fourteen appointees were "all doctors of doctrine, morals, pastoral theology, and psychology." The Franciscans responded by observing that one of these "doctors of doctrine" was a man who specialized in cataloging dogs. The main qualification for appointment to the bishop's new commission, the friars charged, seemed to be an open hostility toward the apparitions in Medjugorje. The Franciscans were affirmed when the commission issued its first press statement, asking that all pilgrimages to Medjugorje cease at once, then announced it would not be meeting again for some time. "The Holy See suggests we not hurry the investigation and the bringing of a final judgment," it was explained.

The priests in Medjugorje were offered at least a little encouragement when Father Nicholas Bulat, a professor of dogma at the seminary in Split, came to Medjugorje shortly after being named to the bishop's new commission. Father Bulat asked if he might observe an apparition, and was given a seat in the rectory directly behind the seers. Wearing dark glasses and a long cassock, Bulat appeared to be praying along with the visionaries as their ecstasy began. Suddenly, though, the professor lunged forward and plunged a long leatherworking needle into Vicka's left shoulder blade. The force of the blow pushed the girl forward and to one side. She showed no reaction at all to the pain, however, and continued to pray, even as blood soaked her blouse. Bulat then stabbed Vicka a second time, and again there was no reaction. The priest departed moments later, silent and trembling, refusing to speak to anyone. Although it was deplored publicly, Bulat's "assault" on Vicka would be celebrated among some Franciscans as one more piece of compelling evidence that the children were neither frauds nor hysterics.

The attention of both those who supported the devotions in the village and those who opposed them was almost immediately diverted by the arrival on the scene of the first investigators from outside Yugoslavia. These were a team of Italian doctors who arrived in the village early that spring and announced that they had received permission from the Vatican to conduct the first serious medical and scientific study of the Medjugorje visionaries.

I had been in Medjugorje for a little more than a week before my introduction to Father Slavko Barbarić. Best known these days as the "spiritual director" to the visionaries, Father Slavko had been perceived as a potential fifth columnist when he joined the parish staff in 1983, nearly two years after the apparitions began. Slavko had grown up about twenty miles away, in the village of Rasno, and was well known in the area, having been regarded during his youth as perhaps the most brilliant scholar ever produced by the region. It was a considerable disappointment to his government when the young man joined the Franciscan order in the early 1970s, shortly after completing his two years of service in the Yugoslav army. During his twenties, Slavko had seemed the sort of priest destined to spend more time in libraries than in sacristies. A polyglot intellectual, he had by the age of thirty earned an assortment of degrees from several European universities. Bishop Žanić personally had approved his transfer to the Medjugorje parish. This was a priest with a Ph.D. in psychology (from the University of Freiburg in Switzerland), the bishop observed, a scientific skeptic who betrayed none of the emotional excesses nor charismatic tendencies that were the hallmarks of men like Jozo Zovko and Tomislav Vlasić. A friar himself, Slavko might well be the perfect man to infiltrate the Franciscan hoax in Medjugorje and expose it to the outside world.

I had heard a great deal about Father Slavko before meeting him, and was rather overawed by the effect this man seemed to have on people; the love and respect he inspired was of a different order than anything I had encountered previously. "The most convincing protagonist," Nicky called the priest. At first glance, though, I found Slavko unimpressive, a slender, wiry, middle-aged man of medium height, with a long face and a beaked nose. There was a twinkle in his eyes, but even that was obscured by the thick lenses of his horn-rimmed glasses. He had only one really remarkable physical feature. "I can't stop looking at his hands," Nicky would remark to me a few days later. "Neither can I," I admitted. They were unusually large, with long, thick fingers that did not taper at all, perfectly blunt at the tips. Father Slavko's seemed the sort of hands a man might have in a dream, but not in real life.

The priest began our first meeting by debunking his own myth. He was never so hardheaded as he had been made out to be, Slavko said: "I accepted from the beginning that apparitions were possible. If in Lourdes and Guadaloupe, why not in Medjugorje? But I admit I had more doubt than belief. When I first met the visionaries, I was expecting them to try to convince me. But they made no effort to do so. This was what made me want to look at them more closely."

The first possibility he entertained was that the apparitions had been orchestrated by overzealous priests. "Now, what do you need to organize a group of young people?" he asked. "First, you need an organizer, a leader. Then you need a motivation, maybe national interest, maybe attention, maybe money. Something that can make these young people more interested than soccer, basketball, music, fashion, whatever. Okay, maybe, as communists and bishop both believe, organizer is the parish priest, Father Zovko. Maybe he convinces these young people that they need to do something big here. Maybe he says, 'People will come, you will have money, you will have good life,' and so on.

"But I see problems with this theory right away. For example, when the group first comes together, the organizer is not here. Okay, maybe the group chooses the organizer later. It is possible. But when police come and put the organizer in prison, what happens? Nothing changes. And when the group itself begins to suffer, all of them suffer together. No one tries to escape. Eleven police stations in this district, each with three officers on duty at any time. And they change shift every eight hours, so these children are being questioned, watched, followed, by a hundred officers every day, for months and months. In Sarajevo, Mirjana is taken to police station every day for six months. All her friends are brought to police station also, to be asked what she has told them. There is all this persecution and suffering, the organizer is in prison, the children and their families are under pressure, being threatened and ridiculed. And yet it is still going on. Psychologically, you cannot explain how that could be."

The second theory he had considered was that of religious fanaticism, Slavko said. "But they do not act like fanatics. These are children, aged ten to sixteen, but when you tell them, 'I do not believe,' they do not attack you, they do not try to convince you, they do not argue with you. Like the postman, they deliver a message and they go home. They do not worry at all about what people expect of them. Looking at them, you see very soon that they are not the most intelligent, they are not the most strong, they certainly are not the most devout. I told them early on, 'If I was going to organize something like this, I would never pick any of you.' You cannot find the answer by looking at this group, so the answer must be outside of them.

"Then I think, 'Perhaps there is a parapsychological explanation.' For me, there are two main kinds of parapsychologists. If one is believer, he will see that the members of this group are not hysterics, or schizophrenics, or psychotics, and he will say it is possible that this is the work of God. If the observer is atheist, he will say, 'Okay, we do not know how to explain this now, but perhaps in a hundred or a thousand years, when science is more advanced, we can know.'

"There is yet another interpretation, that of the materialist, the Marxist. For the Marxist, religion is the opiate of the people, and God is a projection: 'We poor people cannot solve our problems here on earth, so we are inventing somebody beyond the clouds to help us.' We must consider this hypothesis. I mean, look at us. We are suffering here for a thousand years, always wars, always blood, like now. So perhaps people begin to say, 'Somebody will come to save us.' It is possible. Maybe these children absorbed all this desire and began projecting to the people, to give them peace and hope. But again, you only have to meet the visionaries. Mirjana could care less about Croatian nationalism. Jakov can barely wait to finish school and prayers so he has time to play soccer. These are not people sitting in a corner and waiting for the next apparition, living for the attention it brings them. They are normal children in every way. Even more than if pretending, they would be consumed by this if it was a projection. And these are not children who have a natural gift for such a thing. They are not depressive. They are not children with overactive imaginations. Far from it.

"So, after I try all these various theories, I find that none works. It is by process of elimination that I come to this point."

Slavko had been the main liaison for the parish with the team of Italian doctors who showed up in Medjugorje during early 1984. "If they have an explanation for this, I want to hear it," he explained.

The Italian doctors all would focus on observations of the visionaries during their apparitions. Dr. Enzo Gabrici, a neuropsychiatrist, spent four days in Medjugorje examining Ivan, Jakov, Marija, and Vicka, then filed a report in which he excluded any possibility of "hallucinatory phenomena, epilepsy or post-hypnotic suggestion." He found Vicka particularly impressive; the girl's ease and spontaneity mitigated strongly against an interpretation of hysteria. He saw no indication of neurosis or psychosis in any of the other three seers he tested either, Dr. Gabrici wrote, making special note of the fact that the Medjugorje visionaries, unlike spirit mediums, "retain perfect conscious of their identity." It fascinated him that "Vicka shows no signs of emotional hardship." After one of her visions, Dr. Gabrici wrote: "The apparition does not tire her as is the case with hysterical trances; on the contrary she feels more invigorated." Jakov, Gabrici noted, would run outside to play soccer immediately after his apparitions; such normal behavior simply was not an aspect of hysterical or hallucinatory visions.

Dr. Lucia Capello, a neurologist, observed an almost complete lack of agitation in the children during the apparitions. Dr. Capello wrote that she had been not only impressed but deeply shaken by "the three synchronizations" in the seers' behavior: First, the visionaries dropped to their knees and their voices became inaudible in the same instant, without even a split second of separation; second, without any observable awareness of one another, their voices again became audible at exactly the same moment, on the third word of the Our Father; finally, the head and eyes of each visionary were raised in the same instant at the end of the apparition (when the Madonna ascended), as all five uttered the word "*Ode*." There was "no natural explanation" that could account for such perfect simultaneity, Dr. Capello wrote, particularly in the second and third instances.

Heart surgeon Mario Botta harnessed Ivan to an electrocardiogram to observe that the boy's heartbeat maintained a perfect rhythm of eighty to ninety-nine pulsations a minute during an apparition, exactly what it had been before and after his ecstasy. Given the extraordinary level of activity indicated by Ivan's brain waves, Dr. Botta reported, he was inclined to believe that whatever happened to the seers during the apparitions "transcends normal physiology." (Ivan would report later that the Virgin had smiled at seeing him attached to the electrocardiogram, and that he had asked what She thought. "It is not necessary" was Her only reply.)

The most aggressive tests performed on the visionaries were conducted by Dr. M. Frederica Magatti, who tried shouting at, jabbing, and pinching the seers during an apparition, without obtaining "any observable reaction." Finally, after noting that the eyes of each child had become "hugely dilated" during their apparition, Dr. Magatti used a film projector with a 1,000-watt bulb to blast their pupils with light. None of the five had reacted, Dr. Magatti wrote; not only did their pupils remain unusually dilated, but the eyelids of each seer continued to blink at a normal rate. Her tests were merely "preliminary," Dr. Magatti noted; nevertheless, she was prepared to assert that the Medjugorje visionaries, during their apparitions, were demonstrating the most complete "suspension of consciousness of their relationship with the exterior world" she had ever observed in a subject.

Father Slavko regarded the imperviousness of the children to pain, whether it be a needle jabbed into their flesh or a blinding light played across their eyes, as far less significant than the context in which this was demonstrated. "Look at the fakirs of India, who after long hours of meditation can block all sensation of pain, who can even cut themselves without bleeding," he told me during our first meeting. "Then look at Jakov, who comes running in from school, throws down his books in the corner, sits to pray the Rosary, has his apparition, then five minutes later is outside playing with the other children. The doctors examine these visionaries and say that everything is normal, except during the five or ten or fifteen minutes of the apparition; no one can explain what is happening to them during that time.

"I recommend this to you: Look at what is happening here from every point of view, listen to the critics, ask every question, investigate all possibilities. But if you cannot offer any better explanation than the one the seers themselves provide, consider that what they say may be true. When you have done all you can with your mind, submit the question to your heart and see what is answer."

Slavko had made his own decision by the the summer of 1984, when he sent Bishop Žanić the "methodical analysis" of the Medjugorje visionaries that had been requested almost one year earlier. Slavko began his report by stating straight off that the psychological tests he conducted showed no signs of psychosis or hallucination, then gave a summary of the results. What struck him as far more profound, the priest went on, was that "ecstasy has not diminished but rather enhanced the identity and freedom of the visionaries. They understand the desire of the Virgin, but She has left them free, and they in turn feel absolutely free to make their own decisions."

During one of their earliest apparitions, the seers had reported that they had asked the Madonna if She wanted them to join religious orders. The Virgin replied that this was Her wish, but that each of them must make his or her own decision. However, by 1983, Ivanka was involved with the young man she later would marry. Mirjana was an economics major at the University of Sarajevo. After dropping out of the seminary, Ivan had said he still might join the Franciscan order, but gradually abandoned the idea and passed a waiter's course in Mostar so that he could be licensed to work in Yugoslavia's state-controlled restaurants. Jakov said he was too young to think about his future. Marija told the priests that she thought a great deal about becoming a nun, but for now was taking a course as a hairdresser at a commercial school in Mostar. Vicka said that entering a convent was something she considered, but the girl continued to work with her family in the fields.

Ultimately, not one of the six would become a priest or a nun. Father Slavko sighed when I asked if the seers had disappointed the Virgin in this regard. "Probably," he said. "In the end, they all decide for themselves. I am called 'spiritual director,' but I do very little directing. They listen to what I say. Sometimes they agree, often they do not. Always they do what they want. As I told you earlier, these are not the six I would have chosen. When I came here, the youngest was eleven and the oldest was eighteen. The two 'leaders,' Vicka and Mirjana, were so individualistic that it became evident to me very soon that no one could control this group. It would have been impossible to 'produce' what was happening in Medjugorje, because these were not children inclined to take orders from anyone."

He felt it was quite significant that the apparitions had never been even slightly disrupted by the comings and goings of the visionaries or of the priests who advised them, Slavko said. Furthermore, the experiences of the seers had seemed to grow more rather than less individualized over time. Vicka alone claimed she had been instructed to buy "three notebooks" in which she was to chronicle the Madonna's life story. It was Ivan who reported that Jesus had been presented by His mother on four separate occasions, twice as a baby and twice as a man, while Marija reported that the Madonna had given her a message for Pope John Paul II, and that "I wrote to the Holy Father, as She told me to." Ivanka said she had seen her dead mother four times since the start of the apparitions, during which her mother said it was not necessary to pray for her, because she was in Heaven: "She said that she will pray for us." When Mirjana was asked about the light that surrounded the Madonna during Her apparitions, the girl paused a moment, then replied, "Maybe there is light around Her. I don't know. I don't ever focus on the light. Her presence is so personal to me that I am not aware of any other thing except Her immense love, Her immense beauty, Her immense presence."

Nothing that any of the children said about their visions of the Virgin made anything remotely like the impact of Mirjana's announcement in January 1983 that her apparitions had ended on the previous Christmas Day, shortly after she was given the last of ten "secrets" describing a series of impending events that would end the world as we know it.

CHAPTER NINE

Apparitions of the Virgin Mary, especially the "major" ones, are viewed by those who believe in them as both a promise of salvation and a prelude to apocalypse. However, even most Catholics are unaware that reported visitations of the Madonna go back at least to the third century, when St. Gregory the Wonderworker testified that Mary had appeared one evening, accompanied by John the Baptist, to instruct him in "the mystery of piety." Another eleven hundred years would pass before the first claimed apparition to generate sustained interest (and the endorsement of a pope). That event occurred in 1491, when a group of Alsatian villagers swore the Virgin had warned that God's wrath was about to come down on them like a hailstorm.

Perhaps the most impactful reported apparition of the Virgin in all of history took place in 1531 on a hill just outside Mexico City. There, an Aztec Indian peasant named Juan Diego claimed he had met a beautiful young woman who identified herself as the "eternal Virgin, holy Mother of the true God." This vision instructed him to go straight to the bishop of Mexico and inform him that She wanted a church built at the spot of their encounter, said Juan Diego. The bishop demanded a sign, and Juan Diego was provided with one, a bunch of roses that bloomed in midwinter. The Virgin told him to bundle these roses tightly in his cloak, Juan Diego said, and not to open the garment until he was in the bishop's presence. When Juan Diego unwrapped his cloak, however, he—and the bishop—discovered that the image of the Virgin had been infused into the cloth. The fabric of this Indian garment was cactus fiber, a material that usually decomposes after twenty or thirty years. However, Juan Diego's cloak, and the image of the Madonna that it bears, have lasted nearly five centuries. Even at the end of the twentieth century, more than ten million people go to the church of Guadaloupe each year to view the image on Juan Diego's cloak, and the object may be the single greatest reason for the success of the Catholic Church in Latin America.

"Modern" Marian apparitions are popularly thought to have commenced with the visions of Bernadette at Lourdes in 1858. In fact, they began twenty-eight years earlier, at the Sisters of Charity novitiate on the rue de Bac in Paris. There, a nun named Catherine Laboure reported that the Virgin had appeared to her as a luminous figure who stood with one foot on a white globe while the other pressed down upon a green serpent with yellow spots. In Her hands, Catherine said, the Virgin held a golden ball that represented the world. These images were believed to be from the Book of Revelations, in which a "woman clothed with the sun" does battle with Satan for the fate of human souls. Catherine Laboure did nothing to discourage this idea, reporting that the Virgin had warned her the world was about to be overcome by "evils of all kinds." Mary also instructed her to strike a medal of the pose in which she had presented herself, Catherine said. The "Miraculous Medal," as the holy object became known, was a phenomenal success with Catholics; millions had been distributed worldwide by the time of Catherine's death in 1876, and that number today is well into the billions.

The first Marian apparition in which prophetic "secrets" allegedly were given to the visionaries took place in 1846 at a village called La Salette, in the French Alps. The La Salette seers were a pair of shepherd children, fourteen-year-old Melanie Calvat and eleven-year-old Maximin Giraud. The two reported that the Virgin had appeared to them while they were watering cattle at a spring, weeping as She told them of Her suffering on behalf of humankind, then warning of terrible things that were to come. A series of what were regarded as miraculous healings at the spring soon caught the interest of Church authorities, who removed Melanie and Max from their parents and enrolled them at the Sisters of Providence school in Corps. French priests who questioned the two were largely unimpressed by Melanie and Max, describing the children as "unrefined." Even the most skeptical clerics would concede, however, that when the pair spoke of their experiences with "the Lady," they seemed transformed, discussing these events with an eloquence and sobriety that neither could demonstrate at any other time.

Word that the Virgin had given each of the La Salette seers a "secret" began to spread throughout France during 1847. Other than disclosing that such secrets existed, the two children refused to say more about them, explaining that the Lady had warned them to tell no one. Offers of rewards, threats of imprisonment and death, assorted tricks and ruses all failed to convince the children to reveal their secrets. Their interrogators would admit to being quite impressed with the resolve of the youngsters. Max was considered rather dull-witted, yet in his refusal to disclose the secrets showed "a precision, a reserve, and a firmness entirely strange to his age and condition," one priest observed. When informed that he was obligated to tell his confessor, Max thought for a moment, then answered that since the secret was not a sin, he need not confess it.

By 1848, the secrets of La Salette had become a subject of great interest to those who hoped to restore the French monarchy. Counterfeit prophecies circulated widely. At the same time, officials of the Church renewed their efforts to convince Melanie and Max that they should reveal what they had been told. The interrogators concentrated their energies on Max, working on the boy all during 1849 and 1850, at one point even attempting to scare the secret out of him with a man said to be possessed by a demon. It was the archbishop of Lyon who finally persuaded Max in 1851 that he must confide his secret to "God's representative on earth," Pope Pius IX. After Max wrote what he claimed to have been told by the Virgin in a letter to the pope, the boy seemed to rejoice, throwing the paper into the air and shouting, "I am unburdened! I no longer have a secret! I am as others!"

Melanie was a harder case, but eventually agreed also to write her secret in a letter to the pope, though only if she could personally seal and address the envelope. While she wrote her letter, Melanie asked the priests in the room what "infallibly" meant and also how she should spell the words "soiled" and "anti-Christ." Pope Pius IX read the letters in the presence of two priests. "Here is all the candor and simplicity of a child," the pope remarked after reading Max's letter, to which he had seemed to respond with modest enthusiasm. The pope wept openly, however, while reading Melanie's letter. A friend in whom Pius confided would say only that Max's letter announced "mercy and the rehabilitation of things," while Melanie's much longer composition had warned of "great chastisements."

Within three years, pamphlets purporting to reveal the Secrets of La Salette began to circulate across Europe, nearly all of them attributed by their authors to Max. Only one of these is considered authentic, a booklet published in 1871 that addressed mostly the subjects of conversion and peace, except for a warning near the end about a monster who would appear on earth at the beginning of the twentieth century. Max personally did not enjoy anything like success as an adult, attempting an assortment of careers, from liquor dealer to priest, and failing at them all. In 1874, he moved into the new sanctuary at La Salette, living there on charity until his death ten months later.

It is nearly certain that Melanie was the author of a brochure entitled "The Secret of La Salette," published in 1879. The text was an unrelenting account of the evils that would beset the world in the end, notable for its excoriation of unfaithful priests and for a description of how the righteous would be vindicated in the period of peace when Jesus commanded His angels to execute all men addicted to sin. Melanie's opus ended on a note of triumph that was straight from Revelations, describing the defeat of the Beast by the archangel Michael, the purification of the earth, the consumption of the works of pride, and the renewal of all that is good. After this work was published, Melanie spent the rest of her life attempting to establish what she called the "Order of the Mother of God" (its male counterpart was to be called "Apostles of the Last Times"), but found herself in a conflict with Church authorities that did not end until her death in 1904.

The apparitions at Lourdes began twelve years after those at La Salette, and were in the beginning no less controversial. Fourteen-year-old Bernadette Soubirous, in fact, was held in even greater contempt by local authorities than Melanie and Max had been. Her parents were day laborers whose rented lodgings were described in a report made soon after the apparitions began as a "foul, somber hovel" in a building that once had been the town jail, before being abandoned as too unsanitary even for criminals. The Lourdes prosecutor described the Soubirous as "miserable people" whose language, habits, and reputations inspired "not only doubt, but disgust."

In interviews with the local police commissioner, Bernadette reported that her apparitions had begun on the morning of February 11, 1858. She was gathering bones along the shore of the nearby Gave de Pau River, the girl said, when she heard a rustling noise in a hedge above the grotto known as Massabeille, looked up, saw the hedge moving, then spotted "something white" behind it that resolved into the shape of a young girl. Bernadette called her apparition *aquero*, a local dialect term meaning "that one." She stared at *aquero* for a moment, then knelt and prayed, Bernadette said. In response *aquero* smiled, the girl said, then disappeared into the grotto. Her mother told her the vision was a dream, Bernadette recalled, while her aunt called it an illusion.

Her next apparition had come three days later, on February 14, immediately after Sunday Mass, when she returned to the grotto with several other girls, carrying a bottle of holy water taken from their church. They knelt and had begun to say the Rosary when *aquero* appeared again (to Bernadette alone), just above the grotto's entrance. She intended to ask *aquero* if she was present on behalf of God or the Devil, Bernadette said, but at that moment a girl who had been trailing her group threw a stone that frightened the other girls so completely that they bolted upright and scampered back toward town. *Aquero* immediately disappeared.

Four days after that, Bernadette came to the grotto with a lady from a prominent local family who had become intrigued by her story. Together, they knelt and recited the Rosary. *Aquero* appeared to her then, Bernadette said, and signaled that she should approach. When she drew near, the girl said, *aquero* asked her to "have the grace" to return to the grotto for the next fifteen days.

Some of her neighbors suggested to Bernadette that *aquero* might be the ghost of an especially pious teenage girl who had died the previous October. Bernadette said only that *aquero* appeared to her as a girl about her own age, who wore a white dress with a blue waistband and carried a rosary on her arm. As instructed, Bernadette returned to the grotto each morning between February 18 and March 4, and reported apparitions on all but three of these days. By February 22, when an article about her apparitions appeared in a local newspaper, many of her neighbors believed Bernadette was seeing the Virgin Mary. The girl herself never made that claim, but did report that *aquero* had referred to herself as "the Immaculate Conception."

People in the crowds at the grotto described Bernadette as stiff and motionless during her ecstasies, eyes open and fixed on a spot just above the grotto. The girl became very pale during the apparitions, they said. At moments her lips moved as if speaking. Bernadette smiled occasionally, but at other times her eyes filled with tears. Whatever it was, something about the girl's bearing made a profound impression on those present.

The crowd in the grotto had grown to more than a thousand by the morning of February 25, when Bernadette startled her witnesses by crawling on hands and knees to the back of the grotto, where she began to dig with her bare hands until the hole she had made filled with muddy water. After several attempts, Bernadette managed to drink some of the water, smearing her face with mud. Afterward, when people demanded to know what she was doing, Bernadette said that *aquero* had ordered her to drink at "the spring" and to wash in it. Later that day, a group of local people dug with shovels at the same spot, and discovered that there actually was a spring beneath the ground there. They carried bottles of water from the spring back to town, and within a week as many as a dozen people swore that they had been cured of assorted ailments by drinking this water.

By the morning of Bernadette's final apparition on March 4, the crowd at the grotto was estimated at between five thousand and twenty thousand. A reporter from Paris wrote that all the streets, paths, mounds, and fields surrounding the grotto were filled with people. The din was deafening, he observed, filled not only with prayers and invocations but also with insults and dares. Street urchins hung from the tree limbs like monkeys, and the wealthy snarled at peasants not to soil their clothes. Bernadette appeared, carrying a candle as usual, but stopped to embrace a partially blind child named Eugenie Troy. The girl's apparition that morning was a brief one; *aquero* had been angered by the disbelief of those present, and declined to speak, Bernadette explained. Though the girl herself seemed not to have noticed, a number of observers reported that a dove had hovered above Bernadette's head during her ecstasy. Whatever had taken place, one result was the healing of Eugenie Troy's eyes.

After her apparitions ended, Bernadette, who had suffered from asthma for years, was removed from Lourdes to convalesce at the waters of Cauterets. From there, she moved to the hospice school operated by the Sisters of Charity at Nevers. She testified twice before the episcopal commission investigating her apparitions, once in 1858 and again in 1860, and in 1862, her local bishop declared that her apparitions were worthy of the assent, and issued a decree sanctioning a cult of devotion at the Lourdes shrine.

Bernadette joined the Sisters of Charity as a nun in 1866, and remained in residence at the order's motherhouse until her death in 1879. She was beatified by the Church in 1925, and canonized in 1933, on the basis of four miraculous cures that had been proved to the Vatican's satisfaction. To this day, she remains the standard by which other Catholic mystics are judged.

Bernadette had not yet been fully recognized at the time of the apparitions in Fátima, Portugal, a phenomenon that would "touch the Church at the level of the papacy more than any other event of its kind," as the theologian Michael O'Carroll has observed. Extraordinary interest has been shown not only by a succession of pontiffs, however, but also by millions of Catholic faithful in the three Secrets that seer Lucia dos Santos claims were given to her by the Virgin.

The determination of authorities to wrest from Lucia what she purported to know about the future of mankind was even more implacable than that experienced by the La Salette seers. Immediately after learning of these supposed Secrets, the antireligious mayor of Fátima's county had the nine-year-old shepherdess Lucia, along with her two younger cousins, Francisco and Jacinta Marto, brought before him, ordering the three to reveal all and to promise that they would not return to the apparition site. When neither bribes nor threats worked on the children, the mayor warned Lucia he would get what he wanted, even if it meant taking her life. The mayor then ordered the three removed from their families and taken to nearby Ourem for further questioning. All efforts at intimidation failed. Finally, the mayor ordered that the three children be locked into a jail cell and told they were being kept there while a cauldron of boiling oil was prepared. Lucia and her cousins waited behind bars for several hours, then were led out one at a time and informed that they were being given one last chance to confide what they knew. If they refused, police told each of them, they would be thrown alive into the oil. None of the three said a word. Defeated, the mayor turned the children over to a team of theologians and priests who interrogated them for two months. In all that time, the only information about the Secrets they got was Francisco's agreement that people would be sad if they heard them. This was all that Lucia had told him, the boy explained.

Lucia clearly was the central figure in the events at Fátima. The first apparition in the sheep pasture known as Cova da Iria had taken place on May 13, 1917. As Lucia would describe it, "a lady dressed all in white, more brilliant than the sun, shedding rays of light clearer and stronger than a crystal glass filled with the most sparkling water and pierced by the burning rays of the sun," had appeared to the three children as they rested in the shade of an oak tree. Francisco and Jacinta would agree they heard the woman in white say, "I am from Heaven. I come to ask you to be with me here for six months in succession, on the thirteenth day at the same hour. Then I will tell you who I am and what I want." The lady had said other things, the two younger children added, that only Lucia could remember. Afterwards, their older cousin warned Jacinta and Francisco not to tell anyone what had happened, but Francisco could not contain himself, exclaiming, "Oh, what a beautiful lady," over and over after the three returned home. It was Jacinta who told their parents that she and her brother had seen "Our Lady." Lucia, when questioned about her demands that the other two keep quiet, explained she had not been sure the "pretty little woman" they saw really was the Virgin Mary, and wanted to avoid ridicule.

The youngest of seven children, Lucia long had been regarded in her village as an exceptional child, renowned for her phenomenal memory and ability to entertain. At festivals, her sisters would dress and groom the girl, then place her on a crate to sing and dance. She was widely admired. Lucia had learned the catechism by the age of five and was permitted to take her first communion at six, even though ten was the usual age. Lucia lost her special status at age seven when her mother insisted that the girl be sent to tend the family's flock of sheep. When Lucia's sisters objected to this, their mother answered that her youngest daughter was "just like all the rest."

Within one year, the other shepherd girls who joined Lucia in tending flocks among the hills above the village began to report extraordinary experiences. In 1915, one group of girls reported seeing a figure like "a statue made of snow" in the air above a grove of trees. Lucia told them not to tell anyone, but the girls did anyway and were mocked by the other villagers. Lucia's own mother dismissed such claims as "childish nonsense," and the girl became a figure of derision for many in her village.

The second apparition at Cova da Iria took place on June 13, the Feast of St. Anthony. Lucia was distressed to find a crowd waiting when she arrived that morning at the Cova da Iria with Jacinta and Francisco. While her two cousins ate lunch and played with the other children, Lucia sat in silence, wearing a serious expression. It was just after noon when the older girl called to her cousins, "Our Lady is coming." All three ran under the oak tree, where they said the woman in white had appeared before. Lucia raised her clasped hands and called, "You asked me to come here; please tell me what You want." Immediately afterwards, many in the crowd heard what they described as a sound like "the buzzing of a bee." Moments later they heard a noise "like a rocket, a long way off," as one witness put it, but could see only a tiny cloud a few inches from the oak tree that rose slowly and moved away toward the east. The three seers stared in that direction, until Lucia shouted, "She has gone back to Heaven! The doors are shut!" Several witnesses said the shoots of new growth at the top of the tree that had been standing straight up before the apparition now were bent toward the east.

People began to climb the tree, pulling twigs and leaves from its top branches. Lucia shouted at them to take only from the bottom of the tree, where the Virgin had not touched it.

A much larger crowd awaited Lucia and her cousins at Cova da Iria on July 13. Two men held back those in front, to keep Jacinta and Francisco from being crushed. Lucia knelt a short distance away, praying the Rosary, then stood up quickly, looked to the east, and called to the people to close their sun umbrellas because Our Lady was coming. Francisco and Jacinta's father, Manuel Marto, a skeptic, said he looked hard and could see nothing, but then noticed a small grayish cloud resting on the top of the oak tree and all at once felt cooled by "a delicious fresh breeze." He also heard a buzzing sound, Manuel said, like a mosquito in an empty bottle. At one point Lucia became "pale as death," Manuel recalled, and began repeating "Our Lady" in a frightened voice, again and again. (It was during this time that she was given her Secrets, Lucia would explain later.) He then heard a sound like a clap of thunder, Manuel said. Lucia rose to her feet, pointed to the sky, and shouted, "There she goes!"

Manuel Marto was a believer in the apparitions after that day, as were many others from the village. The three seers still were mocked by a majority of their neighbors, but a substantial minority now treated them as saints; grown men from the countryside would prostrate themselves at the children's feet, begging them to ask the Virgin for a favor. Lucia's mother only became more determined to force her daughter's admission that it was all a lie, and resorted eventually to beatings with a broomstick. Lucia continued to insist she was telling the truth, and the crowds at Cova da Iria grew each month.

Nearly seventy thousand people, including reporters from newspapers in Lisbon, Madrid, and Paris, were present to witness the last apparition on October 13. Most in the crowd were soaking wet; a storm of monumental proportions had struck the area on the evening of the twelfth, and it continued to rain all during the following morning. Lucia and Jacinta, wearing new dresses and white wreaths in their hair, were led under umbrellas to the apparition site, followed by Francisco. A priest who had been praying there all night asked when the Virgin would appear. At midday, said Lucia. The priest looked at his watch, said it was midday already, then added that the Virgin does not lie. Just minutes later, the priest began to shout that the time was past, that the apparition was all a delusion, and that the children should go home. Lucia, near tears, said the others could leave, but she was staying. Only a few more minutes passed before the crowd saw the girl turn to look east, then heard her tell Jacinta to kneel, that she had seen lightning and knew the Virgin was coming.

Lucia called to the crowd to be quiet, then told them to close their umbrellas. At that very moment, according to witnesses (including every one of the newspaper reporters present), the rain stopped and the clouds opened. Lucia raised her head and cried, "Look at the sun!" Her command was taken up by the crowd, many of whom began to weep and ask what they were watching. Even a majority of the reporters at Cova da Iria would say that they had seen the sun tremble and dance, streaming with colors more brilliant than any rainbow's. Many in the crowd claimed they had seen the sun whirl like a giant wheel, then plunge toward the earth as if to burn it up. A handful of skeptics, nearly all newspapermen, would concede only that the sun had seemed to radiate an unusual heat, and that within minutes their sopping clothes were completely dry.

The Virgin had again come dressed in white, Lucia would say afterwards, accompanied by St. Joseph, who held the baby Jesus. Suddenly Mary appeared sorrowful, and beside her an adult Jesus looked with pity on the crowd, then raised His hand to bless them. At the very end of her ecstasy, Lucia said, she had seen the Virgin as Our Lady of Mount Carmel, dressed in dark brown. Jacinta and Francisco said they saw only Mary with St. Joseph and the Holy Child: Jacinta claimed she heard some of what the Virgin said; Francisco reported that he could not hear the Virgin at all, but only saw Her.

The widespread interest in the apparitions did little to help Lucia at home. Most of her village shunned the girl after Fátima's popular priest abandoned his parish to avoid any assocation with what was happening there. And Lucia's own mother still refused to believe her daughter. Less than a year after the apparitions, a flu epidemic swept through the area, and Mrs. dos Santos was among those afflicted. Convinced their mother was on her deathbed, Lucia's sisters urged the girl to pray to the Virgin. Mrs. dos Santos did get well, yet refused to change her opinion. "How strange!" Lucia's mother told her. "Our Lady cured me and somehow I still don't believe!" Later, when she was told that some people from the village were ready to kill her daughter, Lucia's mother said that would be fine, "so long as they force her to confess the truth."

Francisco and Jacinta both caught the same flu during that epidemic, and neither ever fully recovered. Francisco died in April 1919 at the age of eleven. Ten months later, nine-year-old Jacinta was dead as well.

Lucia was fourteen when she entered the College of the Sisters of St. Dorothy at Vilar do Porto in 1921. She joined the order in 1925 and served her postulancy at Ponteverda. There, alone in her cell, she received the first in a series of visions that eventually would convince her to reveal what earlier she vowed to keep secret. On Christmas Day, Lucia said, the Virgin appeared to her accompanied by a child who was elevated on a luminous cloud. The Virgin showed a heart encircled by thorns, and the child asked that she have compassion on her Most Holy Mother. Less than two months later, while she was working in the convent garden, Jesus appeared to her as a child and asked if she had told the world what the Virgin wanted. In late 1927, after her spiritual director asked for a written account of her experiences, Lucia went into the tabernacle to place the matter before God. While praying, she did not see Jesus, but heard Him tell her that she should write what the priest asked, except for the last of her three Secrets, about which she must keep silent. The final appearance of the Virgin that Lucia would acknowledge occurred on June 13, 1929, in the chapel at the convent in Tuy, where she had lived for the past seventy years. She was asked, Lucia said, to sacrifice herself for those who sinned against the Holy Mother's Immaculate Heart.

The apparitions at Fátima were declared "worthy of assent" by the bishop of Leira in 1930, but did not become well known outside Portugal until the early 1940s, when Lucia's *Memoirs* began to appear. Lucia's descriptions of her first two Secrets were quite detailed: The Virgin began by showing her and Jacinta a vision of Hell as an oceanlike inferno: "Plunged into this fire were demons and souls in human form, like transparent burning embers, all blackened or burnished bronze, floating about in the conflagration, now raised into the air by the flames that issued from within themselves together with great clouds of smoke, now falling back on every side like sparks in a huge fire, without weight or equilibrium, and amid shrieks and groans of pain and despair, which horrified us and made us tremble with fear." The second Secret involved the means by which devotion to the Immaculate Heart of Mary might save the souls of sinners, Lucia wrote: The Virgin had told her that what she knew as the Great War was going to end, but that an even worse one would break out during the pontificate of Pius XII if people did not cease offending God.

After the final volume of Lucia's *Memoirs* was published, demands that she reveal the still-undisclosed "Third Secret of Fátima" grew much louder. The bishop of Leira held authority over the woman now known as "Sister Lucy," but was reluctant to order that she reveal her last Secret. During the summer of 1943, however, Lucia became seriously ill. Finally, in September of that year, the bishop met with Lucia in the infirmary at Tuy and asked if she might write down the third Secret so that it would be recorded. A month later, he ordered her to do so. Lucia's superior at the convent reported that, on January 2, 1944, the Virgin had appeared to Sister Lucy for the first time in fifteen years, and during this encounter had authorized her to record the third Secret. On June 17, 1944, a letter in Lucia's handwriting was delivered to the bishop of Leira. Although Lucia had given him permission to read it, the bishop declined, then did everything in his power to persuade higher Church authorities they should take possession of the document. An opportunity to unburden himself did not present itself to the bishop until early 1957, when the Vatican's Congregation for the Doctrine of the Faith asked for photocopies of all of Lucia's writings. The bishop responded by delivering the original and only copy of the third Secret to Rome, in a sealed envelope.

"Sister Lucy" by then had become a kind of living treasure of the Church. Hidden behind the walls of her convent at Tuy, Lucia was a figure of enormous mystery and importance for many Catholics. In 1954, she gave her first interview for publication to the founder of the Better World Movement, who asked if his organization was the Church's response to Mary's message. Lucia said that, given humanity's present condition, only a limited number could be saved. Was she saying that many would go to Hell? the man asked. Yes, Lucia answered: "Many are lost." Lucia's second interview was given in 1957 to the Mexican priest who had been appointed as advocate for the beatification of Jacinta and Francisco. During this conversation, Lucia confirmed a report that had surfaced ten years earlier, stating that the third Secret of Fátima would be revealed in 1960. She then gave her first and only indication of what the third Secret might involve, explaining that the Holy Virgin was engaged in a decisive battle with Satan, who knew his time was growing short and was determined to steal as many souls as possible. By the time this struggle was finished, Lucia said, people would be "either of God or the Evil One." She added that, if Russia were not converted, the country would be an instrument of God's chastisement for the entire world, and that many nations would be annihiliated.

Observing the impact on Catholics of Lucia's remarks, many in positions of authority objected. It was extremely dangerous, one Church theologian wrote, when "the claims of an individual, even of a woman as sincere and holy as Sister Lucy, are treated as the word of God."

The only copy of the third Secret of Fátima in existence was now kept in a wooden chest bearing the inscription *Secretum Sancti Offici* that sat on a table in the private apartment of Pope Pius XII. The significance accorded by the Holy See to the apparitions at Cova da Iria was formally acknowledged on October 29, 1950, when, amid much fanfare, the "Pilgrim Statue" of the Fátima Virgin arrived in Rome after traveling through Europe for almost three years. The very next day, at a meeting with more than four hundred bishops, Pope Pius XII announced his intention to define the dogma of the Assumption, holding that the Virgin Mary had been assumed not only spiritually into Heaven but bodily as well. Later that same day, Pius took a walk alone in the gardens behind the Vatican where the Fátima statue had been installed. He was strolling up the esplanade of Lourdes, the pope reported, when suddenly he saw the sun transformed into "a pale yellow opaque globe completely surrounded by a luminous halo." The halo seemed to be formed by a very light cloud that covered the globe, Pius said, which somehow permitted him to stare directly into its light without discomfort. The globe began moving outward, slowly turning over on itself, moving first from left to right, then from right to left, before once again becoming the sun as he knew it.

After the death of Pope Pius XII in 1959, the box containing the third Secret of Fátima was delivered to the new pope, John XXIII, who read Lucia's letter but issued no public statement. Close friends of John reported the pope had told them that since the text did not pertain to his times, he preferred to leave its disposition to his successors. Pope Paul VI read the third Secret shortly after his coronation in 1963, but issued no public statement on the subject. It is not known if John Paul I read the third Secret during the few weeks of his doomed papacy, but immediately before his election, the short-lived pope had made a pilgrimage to Fátima, meeting privately with Lucia afterwards.

Published reports stated that John Paul II had read the third Secret shortly before his visit to Fátima in 1982, but the pope declined to comment. In 1984, though, Cardinal Ratzinger confirmed that the pope had read the third Secret, then added that John Paul would not make it public. There the matter rested, except for two brief assertions by the pope, one in 1982, that "Fátima is more relevant and more urgent than ever," and another in 1991, that "Fátima is the Marian capital of the world."

Between Fátima and Medjugorje, only one reported apparition of the Virgin would produce apocalyptic prophecies of comparable influence. The alleged visitations of the Madonna in Garabandal, Spain, that began during the summer of 1961 are steeped in mystery and controversy. The seers again were children, four girls aged twelve and eleven. As at Fátima, one visionary was more central than the others.

This was Conchita Gonzalez, who, on the morning of June 18, 1961, had persuaded her companions to join her in taking some apples from a tree in the yard of the local schoolmaster. The girls were eating their apples in the rocky lane leading from the village to a group of nine trees known as "the Pines," when they heard a noise like thunder. Suddenly overcome by remorse, the girls began to pick up stones and throw them to their left (where the Devil lurked, according to local legend). Tiring of this, they began to play marbles, until Conchita cried out, claiming that she was seeing a beautiful figure that shone brilliantly but did not hurt her eyes. It was an angel, she said. Believing their friend was having a fit, the other girls began to lead Conchita home, but then saw the shining figure also. Terrified, all four girls ran to the village church.

The story spread through the village, half scandal, half farce. The next afternoon, when the girls went back up the lane leading toward the Pines, they were taunted by neighbors and chased by a group of young boys who threw rocks at them. The girls admitted they did not see the angel that day or the next. People jeered at them as they went back toward the Pines on the fourth day, shouting that they would rather pray in an alley than in the church. A group of adults from the village, led by an especially skeptical woman named Clemintina, followed the girls all the way to the spot where they stopped to pray the Rosary. Little more than an hour passed before the girls began to cry out that they could see the angel again. Clemintina was convinced by the state of ecstasy the girls entered, and her belief swayed many other villagers.

The four girls reported seeing the angel on five of the next seven days. The angel neither spoke nor signaled, the girls said, but merely smiled. On June 24, the angel floated in the air above what the girls described as "a sign" printed with text. Only Conchita could recall any of the words, and this was just a fragment of the first sentence. On the evening of July 1, the girls reported that the angel had appeared again with the sign, and that this time he spoke, telling them that the Virgin Mary would explain what it meant.

The Virgin appeared to them the next evening as our Lady of Mount Carmel, clothed in a white robe with a blue mantle and a crown of golden stars. She looked about eighteen, wore her dark brown hair parted in the middle, and had a long face and a delicate mouth. She was very pretty, the seers said, yet surprisingly frail. The Virgin was accompanied by two angels, according to the seers, one of whom was St. Michael. Next to the other angel, whose name she did not know, Conchita said, was a large eye that she believed was the Eye of God. During this first apparition, the Virgin spoke to the girls about small matters, such as working in the fields, stacking hay, and watching their skin darken under the summer sun. The Virgin laughed with sweet amusement at their responses, the girls said, taught them the proper way to recite the Rosary, promised to return the next day, then disappeared. The girls reported regular appearances of the Virgin after this, and interest in their apparitions spread to surrounding villages. The crowds in Garabandal soon became so large that a corral was built around the apparition site to protect the girls.

Many qualities of the reported apparitions in Garabandal were unique and therefore disturbing to Church officials. The Virgin's appearances were made known to them in advance by three "interior calls," the girls said. The first call was a "weaker feeling of joy," as Conchita described it, and often came well before they heard the second call, which was much stronger and seemed to alter them dramatically. The girls always left for the corral after the second call, and became very excited and happy after reporting that they had heard the third call, because the Virgin invariably appeared a few moments later. Suspicious neighbors suggested separating the girls to test their claim of these "interior calls." One evening after the four reported hearing the first call, two girls were taken to a house at one end of the village, while the others were taken to a house at the opposite end. Half an hour later, the girls in both houses said they had received the second call, and all four arrived at the corral in the same moment. Eventually civil guards would be put in charge of separating the girls, keeping them under lock and key in four different houses. Yet the girls continued to report that they had heard the second call and to arrive at the corral with unfailing simultaneity.

The same "paranormal abilities" that so troubled Church officials were what convinced a growing crowd of spectators that the seers were experiencing genuine apparitions. The faces of the four girls were transformed during their ecstasies, those who watched them said; the expressions of serenity and delight they wore made each of them exquisitely beautiful. Also, the speed with which the girls reached the apparition site after they heard the second call amazed those who watched them. While their legs did not seem to be moving any faster than normal, witnesses said, the girls took impossibly long strides and covered ground at three times their normal rate; athletic young men in their teens and twenties, who ran mountain paths, could not keep up with these girls half their size. And not one of those who came to Garabandal to debunk the apparitions could imitate the girls' manner of returning from the corral: Usually they ran backward, often on their knees, and at an incredible speed; many witnesses were overwhelmed by emotion when they saw that not one of the girls showed even the slightest scratch or bruise on her legs. Perhaps most peculiar of all was the way the force of gravity seemed to increase around the girls whenever they saw the Virgin. They became so heavy that even the largest man in the village could not lift them an inch off the ground. Basque laborers who prided themselves on their strength were brought in to give it a try, and witnesses watched man after man fail in attempts to raise the girls during their ecstasies, then walk away trembling with fright.

During one apparition, witnesses heard the four girls all speaking in different languages: One prayed in Greek, another in German, and another in English, while the fourth girl sang a hymn in French. Soon after this, the four girls reported that the Virgin had kissed some pebbles they were holding, and wanted these stones distributed to people in the crowd. Immediately, people began to bring pebbles by the dozens to the apparition site for the Virgin to bless, piling the stones in a heap at the knees of the seers as they prayed. During their ecstasies, the girls would hold pebbles up, then drop them, scattering the stones in front of them. Yet afterwards, they always returned each pebble to the same person who had offered it, and were unfailing in making the right match. When their apparitions ended, the seers also were consistently able to identify any priests who had come to Garabandal in secular garb, even naming the order to which each man belonged.

The bishop of Santander was hostile to the apparitions at Garabandal, however, and the investigative commission he appointed took an unusually aggressive attitude. This was most evident in the medical "examinations" conducted by the commission's doctors, a majority of which involved testing the seers' sensitivity to pain. During the apparitions, they were repeatedly pinched or scratched by the doctors, who on a number of occasions also pricked the girls' legs with needles. During one apparition, physicians directed the beams of a powerful electric light into the seers' eyes while other doctors jabbed their flesh with needles. The girls smiled, according to witnesses, and spoke to their vision, saying, "They are? . . . But we don't feel anything."

Suspicious that Conchita somehow dominated and influenced the other girls, the bishop's commission asked if they might remove the girl to Santander. Only after the team of doctors and priests who examined Conchita reported that she was physically and mentally healthy was the girl returned to her mother. But Conchita's absence had permanently altered the nature of the apparitions. After the girl's return, the ecstasies of all four seers became increasingly individualized, occuring at different times and in different places, sometimes on two or three separate occasions during the same day. It was in this period also that the girls exhibited the most dramatic of their paranormal abilities. A number of priests who witnessed these phenomena were unnerved, and warned that the apparitions might be the work of the Devil.

This second phase of the apparitions was when the seers began to report they were receiving "messages" from the Virgin. Many of these messages were confidential communications to people in the crowd, the girls said, but the Virgin also was giving them information that She warned must be kept secret. Conchita had been told the most, according to the other girls. She was permitted to reveal only that the Virgin had told her of three future events that would change life on earth forever, Conchita said. The first of these would be "the Warning," an opportunity to repent and convert that Conchita described as a brilliant illumination of conscience, one that would permit all humans on earth to see themselves as they appeared to God. Within twelve months of the Warning would come "the Great Miracle," as Conchita called it, an event she could not describe at all except to say it would take place among the Pines in Garabandal and would be the greatest manifestation of the supernatural in the history of the world, an all but irresistible sign of God's presence. She was permitted as well to tell people that the Great Miracle would happen at eight-thirty on a Thursday evening, Conchita said, and that it would fall on the feast day of a Eucharistic martyr. Those who responded to the Warning and the Miracle with disbelief or ingratitude, Conchita went on, would bring upon themselves a third event, "the Chastisement." She and the other girls all were given a brief glimpse of the Chastisement, Conchita said, and had been stricken with a horror so intense that they could find no words to describe the magnitude of it.

While neither she nor any of the other girls were permitted a preview of the Great Miracle, a priest who came to Garabandal for the apparition in early August 1961 had been shown it in a vision. This was during a time of intense questioning by Church officials, a period in which the four girls were pleading insistently to the Virgin for a sign that would prove them to doubters. At an apparition in front of the church altar at noon on August 8, Conchita was heard crying out, "At Lourdes and Fátima you gave them proof!" That same evening, all four girls fell into an ecstasy and walked toward the Pines. During the subsequent apparition, a Jesuit priest who stood nearby, Father Luis Maria Andreu, raised his head in an expression of transport and shouted, "Miracle!" four times so loudly that everyone in the crowd heard him. Ordinarily, Conchita said, she and the other seers were completely unaware of the people around them. On this one occasion, they all had seen Father Andreu. And at the moment he became visible to them, the girls said, the Virgin told them this priest was seeing both Her and the Great Miracle.

It was about ten P.M. when the apparition ended. Father Andreu left Garabandal in a Jeep and rode to neighboring Cosio to meet with the pastor there. The handsome young Jesuit said that he now believed the children, according to the pastor, who cautioned Father Andreu not to repeat this publicly. From Cosio, Father Andreu rode in a caravan of four cars headed for Reinosa. The young priest "radiated happiness," said the driver of his car. After waking from a brief nap, the Jesuit began to tell his traveling companions how happy he was, and how grateful for the "favor" that the Virgin had bestowed upon him. They were all fortunate to have such a mother in Heaven and should have no fear of the afterlife, he told the others, then announced in a loud voice, "This is the happiest day of my life!" A moment later, Father Andreu raised his head and went silent. Another passenger asked if anything was wrong. He answered that he was sleepy, then lowered his head, coughed faintly, rolled his eyes, and died.

The event that would generate both the widest interest and the deepest controversy at Garabandal took place almost one year later, on July 18, 1962. This was the "Miracle of the Visible Host." On May 1 of that year, the Garabandal seers began to say they had been receiving communion from an angel. (A similar claim had been made forty-five years earlier by Lucia dos Santos at Fátima.) During the appearance of an angel on June 22, Conchita said, she had pleaded yet again for a miracle. On June 30, the angel told her that he would make the communion host he gave her visible to all who were in her presence, and that this miracle would take place on July 18.

Church officials warned the girl of the humiliation she would bring upon herself if the miracle did not occur, but Conchita continued to insist it would happen. On the morning of July 18, several thousand people had assembled in Garabandal. The crowd grew increasingly restless as evening came and no apparition had taken place. It was nearly two in the morning when Conchita's ecstasy finally began. The hundreds who still waited on the girl swarmed around her as she stepped out of the house where she had spent the evening and fell to her knees in the street. A villager named Pepe Diaz, who had been with Conchita since early that morning, had to fight through the surging crowd to stay close to the girl. People began to scream as they were knocked to the ground, or tripped over those already fallen. Men and women both grabbed at him to try to take his place next to Conchita, Diaz recalled, tearing at his clothing, stripping off his shirt and belt. Struggling to keep his balance, surrounded by the noise of the crowd, he could not hear Conchita but saw her clearly under the beam of his flashlight.

As he watched Conchita stick her tongue out of her mouth, "a terrible feeling of disaster" overcame him, said Diaz, whose face was only about eighteen inches from the girl's. When Conchita's tongue remained bare, he was consumed by a sense of failure, but then, as he watched, a "neat, precise, and well-formed host" appeared on the girl's tongue. The object he saw increased steadily in volume and remained visible for three minutes. "I saw in that Host a live force which reminded me of sea waves, sparkling and moving under the sun, when we see them from a distance," he would write.

Dozens of others in the crowd swore that they had seen the host also. One witness said he saw a "white shadow." Another said the object on Conchita's tongue had been like "a snowflake upon which the sun's rays were striking." One man in the crowd managed to aim a motion picture camera at Conchita, and there is a single frame of the film he shot that many people believe shows the host forming on the girl's tongue. Investigators would later conclude only that the film was not doctored; what it shows, they added, must remain a matter of personal opinion.

Many people have interpreted the Miracle of the Visible Host as proof that the Garabandal apparitions were a trick of Satan. Conchita's own mother was for some time among those who subscribed to this theory. The five members appointed to the bishop of Santander's investigative commission continued to insist that the apparitions were merely a hoax.

According to the four girls, the Virgin warned them early on during the apparitions that they would suffer because of Her gift to them, and told Conchita that she, like the others, would at one point deny what they had seen. Exactly this began to happen during the spring of 1963. The first disavowal (and the only one that endured) was made that March by a girl named Maria Cruz. Many in the crowd had noticed that during the ecstasies of the seers, Maria seemed to be looking in a different direction than the other girls. Finally, someone asked her directly after an apparition if she had seen the Madonna. Maria answered in a monotone that many found frightening, as if it were a voice other than her own: "No, I did not see the Virgin."

The ecstasies of the other girls ended soon after this, and within a month or two all four seers were admitting doubts. The girls seemed to be "in a trance," Conchita's mother would say. Gradually, each of the others joined Maria Cruz in stating that the apparitions had not been real. Their denials were oddly ambiguous, however. The girls told their parents, for example, that they had never seen the Virgin Mary nor any angels, yet insisted they had never tried to deceive anyone, and maintained that what they said about the three "interior calls" and the Miracle of the Visible Host was true.

Most interesting, as Conchita would later observe, was that she and the other girls all knew they had seen the Virgin even as they denied it. The pressure of the crowds and the opposition of the Church, she said, were inadequate to explain her disavowal; she did not know why she had done it.

The antagonism of Church officials was very real. One commission member warned Conchita that people would think she was crazy if she did not deny the apparitions and that she might spend the rest of her life in an asylum. If she cooperated with the commission and admitted the apparitions were false, Conchita was told, she would be considered a *señorita* and might even attend college. All the girls were informed by their confessor that he would refuse them absolution if they failed to make a public retraction of their claims. During September and October, the four girls were interviewed by the bishop, and each signed a document stating that the apparitions had been false.

Before the end of that year, Conchita had "returned to reality," as she put it, along with two other seers, and once again was saying that the apparitions were genuine. Her ecstasies had resumed (and would continue for nearly two more years), she said. The other two girls said they no longer saw the Virgin, but were certain that earlier they had, and did not know why they denied it.

Conchita obtained an audience with Pope Paul VI in January 1966, about six months after the cessation of her apparitions, and was reported to have confided the date of the Great Miracle. Her own doubts would overcome her again only one month later, after she entered a Carmelite Mission in Pamplona. She wanted to join the sisters, Conchita said, but had been told during an interior locution that she was not called to be a nun and that God wanted her to remain in the world. Her new confessor refused to give Conchita absolution unless she made a second public retraction. Soon after this, another of the seers, Mari Loli, visited Conchita at Pamplona and questioned their experiences. A number of priests encouraged Conchita's own doubts, and the girl's distress increased day by day until, finally, she signed a second retraction. That retraction too was withdrawn only a short time later, but by then the bishop of Santander had the document in hand and was using it as the basis for a negative judgment on the events at Garabandal that he issued in March 1966.

Conchita had married an American and was living in New York State by the time the Vatican ordered the creation of a new ecclesiastical commission to investigate the apparitions at Garabandal. Based mainly on interviews with witnesses, this commission produced a positive finding and delivered it to the Vatican in October 1991. No judgment of the Church would be issued, it was reported, until the Great Miracle foretold at Garabandal had taken place.

Conchita, though withdrawn into private life, has continued to insist that the Warning, the Great Miracle, and the Chastisement all will occur during her lifetime (she was born in 1949). Maria Cruz maintains her disavowal of the apparitions, while the other two seers seem to exist in a limbo of equivocation. When he interviewed Mari Loli during the early 1990s, journalist Michael Brown found her "giggling and semi-amnesiac." He asked Loli if she had any doubts about seeing the Virgin, and received this answer: "Well, I don't remember very clear, and it seems like it happened to somebody else sometimes . . . I don't know. I don't think too often about it, and my life is not based on what happened to me."

Nevertheless, she remained a devout Christian, attending Mass every day, Loli said, and was horrified by the descent of the modern world into decadence. When Brown asked her about the warnings and punishments prophesied at Garabandal, she became vague, if not evasive: "With the Warning, I know what year it's supposed to happen. About chastisement, I—I was so young." She admitted she was frightened of what might happen, Loli added a moment later, yet said, "I hope God does something soon. Actually I look forward to it, even a punishment . . . It's going to take something directly from God for the world to change."

"To fear God is to know God," I would hear several times during my stay in Medjugorje. This scriptural wisdom was quoted on each occasion by someone determined to help me understand the necessity of the Secrets or the purpose of the Warning-Miracle-Chastisement scenario. They were the same people who saw it as enormously significant (and often as sub-limely ironic) that I was staying in the home of the woman they believed knew more about this part of God's plan than any other person on earth.

"I don't understand loving God and fearing God at the same time," I told Mirjana one broiling afternoon when we met in the cool recess of her basement. "Those who truly love God do not need to fear Him," she told me. Her words sent a thrill of terror through me. Mirjana saw this and nodded gravely. "Very few of us truly love God," she said. "And because of this we fear Him."

It seemed to me that Mirjana had said a great deal to encourage this fear. "I am frightened myself," she told me, "each time I meet an unbeliever."

"Because of what you know about the Secrets?" I asked. Mirjana began to nod, then caught herself and looked at me as if I had tried to lure her onto forbidden ground. "I have told you I can say nothing about the Se-crets," she reminded me.

"You have spoken about the Secrets before," I said. Mirjana shook her head. "Never," she said. "Whatever you hear or read, people have made it up."

This wasn't entirely true, though I wouldn't have the confidence to say so until later, after verifying that Mirjana had spoken at length on the subject of the Secrets during two separate tape-recorded interviews with Croatian priests in Medjugorje.

The first of these interviews was conducted in January 1983 by Father Tomislav Vlasić, who revealed soon afterwards that Mirjana's apparitions had ended in December 1982. On Christmas Eve, she had been given the last of the ten Secrets she was to receive. Her final apparition on the evening of the twenty-fifth was unusually long, lasting about forty-five minutes. She and the Virgin "summarized everything that had been said between us." The Virgin told her she would cease appearing to the others as well, when they had received all ten Secrets. "I asked her why—why I had to be the first," Mirjana told the priest. "She said that she had stayed with us a long time, longer than is necessary, but that this is the last apparition on earth."

Father Vlasić demanded to know if she meant that "this is the last apparition in this period of Church history, or whether it means the end of the world or that Mary will never appear again." Mirjana admitted she was unsure, but did know that both the apparitions and the Secrets were related to an ancient agreement that God had made with Satan. "The Virgin told me God and the Devil conversed, and the Devil said that people believe in God only when life is good for them. When things turn bad, they cease to believe in God. Then people blame God, or act as if He does not exist. God therefore allowed the Devil one century in which to exercise an extended power over the world, and the Devil chose the twentieth century."

During that apparition on Christmas Day, the Virgin had consoled her by promising to appear each year on her birthday, Mirjana said, and at times of "grievous difficulty," but made it clear that "I will have to live without Her daily personal visits." After the Madonna had gone, "I just sat there, like a statue. I felt very strange. I thought to myself, 'This can't be true—She will come again. I will pray at the same times, and She will return.'" Evening after evening, "I would pray, long and hard, as if I were in a trance," Mirjana told the priest. "I would ask myself, 'Why has this happened? Why is She not here? She will not come again.' Oh, it was terrible, terrible!"

Mirjana had said a great deal more about the Secrets during an inteview with a priest she had grown close to in Sarajevo, Father Petar Ljubičić, during the late summer of 1985. On September 4 of that year, Father Ljubičić reported that Mirjana had seen and spoken to the Virgin Mary on her birthday (March 18) during each of the past three years, then he issued this public statement:

"Sometime previously Mirjana had told me that I would be the priest to whom she would entrust the secrets . . . On June 1, she told me definitely that she would confide the Secrets to me. She told me that ten days before each occurrence of the Secret she would give me a paper similar to a parchment. Three days before the event I am to make the Secret in question known to the public. When the event takes place, I will give the paper back to Mirjana and wait for the next Secret.

"Mirjana emphasizes that the time is at hand when the first Secret will be revealed," the priest added. "That is why she urges vigilance and prayer in the name of Our Lady."

Soon after, Father Ljubičić released the transcript of his interview with Mirjana. In it, Mirjana said she had been shown the first Secret "like a film running before my eyes." Of all her experiences with the Virgin, Mirjana told the priest, this had been "the worst": "I became sad and asked Her if it had to take place just like that," Mirjana recalled. "She said, 'Yes.'"

Was this first Secret "the Sign"? Father Ljubičić asked. In her answer, Mirjana revealed more about her Secrets than she ever would again: The Sign would "appear after the first two Secrets have happened," Mirjana said. "The first Secrets are not as horrible as the rest," she explained. "They will serve as a warning to shake up and wake up the world . . . to make people acknowledge that God really exists." The first Secret, though not "a catastrophe in a huge sense," would be an occurrence of sufficient magnitude to convince a majority of people on earth that it represented a divine intervention. Between the first Secret and the second would be an intense period of grace in which many people would convert. Many more would convert after the second Secret, Mirjana added, but a great number of people, particularly in the countries of the West, would insist that there was "a natural explanation" for each of these events. The Sign—"permanent, indestructible, and beautiful"—was the third Secret, Mirjana said, and after it appeared, conversion would be difficult if not impossible.

The fourth, fifth, and sixth Secrets Mirjana referred to obliquely as affirmations of some sort: "For those who have converted, it will be a time of great joy." The last four Secrets were a series of events so terrible that she could barely live with the knowledge of them. She had wept for hours upon learning the eighth Secret. "I begged for it to be made less severe. Every day, I beseeched the Madonna to get it mitigated, and at last She said that if everyone prayed it might be averted. But then She told me the ninth Secret and it was even worse. As for the Tenth, it is terrible and nothing can alter it. It will happen."

When asked if mankind had entered the end times, or whether the Second Coming and the Apocalypse were part of what she had been told, Mirjana answered, "That is part of the Secrets."

Several years later, Mirjana had very briefly discussed the Secrets during an interview with a Vatican investigator, who said he could not believe that the events described in the Secrets were inevitable. "If all of us are converted and become saints," the priest asked, "will the ten Secrets still come to pass?" "It is not possible for everyone to become a saint," she replied. "Even when Jesus came to earth, many did not believe." What about the report that prayer had "softened" the eighth

Secret? the interviewer asked. That report was somewhat inaccurate, said Mirjana. It was the seventh Secret, not the eighth, that had been mitigated, she explained. And at the same time she learned this, Mirjana said, the Virgin had informed her that no part of the last three Secrets could be altered in any way. Yet nothing was certain, Marija said on several occasions when asked about the Secrets; the situation had been created by human behavior, and if people changed—through prayer and penance—the situation might also change.

The second of the visionaries to report receiving all ten Secrets was Ivanka, who on May 6, 1985, shared an unusually bifurcated apparition with Marija, Jakov, and Ivan. While the Madonna appeared to them for only two minutes that day, the other three seers said, Ivanka's vision had gone on for another six minutes. During that time, Ivanka said, the Virgin gave her the tenth Secret, then asked that she wait alone the next evening. After her private apparition on May 7, Ivanka handed Father Slavko a sheet of paper on which she had written: "As on every day, Our Lady came with the greeting, 'Praised be Jesus.' I responded, 'May Jesus and Mary always be praised.' I never saw Mary so beautiful as on this evening. She was so beautiful and gentle. Today She wore the most beautiful gown I have ever seen in my life. Her gown and also Her veil and crown had gold and silver sequins of light. There were two angels with her. They had the same clothes. Our Lady and the angels were so beautiful. I don't have words to describe it; one can only experience it. Our Lady asked me what I would wish and I asked to see my earthly mother. Then Our Lady smiled, nodded Her head and at once my mother appeared. She was smiling. Our Lady told me to stand up. I stood up, my mother embraced me and kissed me and she said, 'My child, I am proud of you.' She kissed me and disappeared."

The Virgin told her that this was her final daily apparition, Ivanka wrote, "then said not to be sad, because She would come on every anniversary [of the first apparition] except this year. She told me, 'Do not think you have done anything wrong. With all your heart you have accepted the plans which my Son and I had . . . What I have spoken to you these years about the Secrets, speak to no one until I tell you.' Before She left, I asked Our Lady if I could kiss Her, and She nodded. I kissed Her and asked Her to bless me, and She did."

Vicka had reported just three weeks earlier, on April 17, 1985, that now she too was receiving the Secrets, which were revealed to her almost as rapidly as they had been to Mirjana. The normally effervescent young woman stirred a considerable apprehension in Medjugorje on April 22, 1986, when she wept copiously during her regular evening apparition, then reported that the Virgin had just given her the ninth Secret. Nearly a decade later, Vicka still was waiting to hear the tenth Secret. The only one of the Secrets that Vicka had been willing to discuss during that time was the Third, that of the Sign. The Sign would appear on Podbrdo, Vicka said, at the site of the first apparition. It would be "on the ground" and would appear suddenly. Will everyone be able to see it? Vicka was asked. "All who come," she answered, adding, "The Sign will be both permanent and unalterable." During that same interview, Vicka stated that she and the other visionaries had not discussed the Secrets with one another, and said she did not know what the others had been told.

For many in Medjugorje, the greatest evidence both of the prophetic power of the apparitions and of the scale of the events described in the Secrets was a report Mirjana had made after an apparition back in 1982. This was during the period when the seers still were submitting to the Madonna questions that had been written by Franciscan priests. One friar had asked Mirjana to inquire if Croatia would ever be free. The Virgin's answer, Mirjana reported, was: "Yes, after a small war."

"Three hundred thousand dead already," Slavko observed during one of our earliest conversations in 1995. "If that is 'a small war,' what would a large one be?"

When I met her, it was nearly ten years since Mirjana last had spoken publicly of the Secrets. I knew already that these privately held prophecies had been by far the greatest source of controversy among the priests and theologians who believed the apparitions in Medjugorje to be genuine. Father Slavko told me that he had advised Mirjana to say nothing further on the subject. He felt that a fascination with the Secrets either encouraged "a kind of fatalism" in people, the priest explained, or caused them to "live for the future, rather than in the present."

Father Vlasić had not been so circumspect in his remarks. Asked once by an interviewer, "Do you personally think that we are in the times prophesied by John's Apocalypse?" he had answered, "Yes, certainly." He had qualified his response slightly a moment later, explaining, "One can never know what 'last times' means . . . but we must really be aware that we are now in the time of great events when God wants to work a change for us, and thus the visionaries say that these apparitions are the last for humanity and that with these events the time of Satan is finished."

Archbishop Franić compared the Medjugorje visionaries to biblical prophets who passed along messages they could only incompletely understand. A phrase like "the time is near," he noted, might mean it would come in five thousand years.

When I asked Slavko why he thought God would find it necessary to give the visionaries secrets in the first place, the priest answered with a shrug, "I can only say that secrets would not be secrets if people knew about them."

I repeated the question during my meeting with Mirjana in her basement. Her reply was even more opaque than the priest's: "What makes secrets necessary is part of the Secrets." The ultimate catch-22, I remarked to myself. Mirjana looked at me with a curious expression, then said, "Even we visionaries do not know all of God's plan. We, too, are required to have faith."

Oddly, the one subject connected to the Secrets on which Mirjana would speak was this "parchment-like" paper she claimed to have been given, the one on which all ten Secrets were written. Why was that necessary? I asked. "So that I can live or not live," she said, "and the Secrets are still there." Hadn't she said earlier that the Secrets would come to pass during her lifetime? I asked. "It was reported that I said it," she answered, with a slight smile, then added, "What God plans for me is something I can never know with absolute certainty. If I did, I would not need faith."

I asked again about the parchment, and Mirjana said it was a material unlike anything else on earth. Her expression was earnest but also quite matter-of-fact, betraying not the slightest hesitation or discomfort. Had she showed it to anyone? I asked. "Two people," she answered, "a cousin and a friend. My cousin read it as a prayer. My friend saw it as a letter in which somebody is asking somebody else for help. Our Lady later told me that everyone who sees it will see something different." Mirjana gave me an odd smile. "You could be sitting in the same room with it right now," she said, "and you would not know what it was."

CHAPTER TEN

One morning near the end of my second week in Medjugorje, I was awakened by a large tour group of Tahitian pilgrims in matching floral outfits, who were singing religious hymns in French, hoping this might persuade Mirjana to come outside and meet with them. (It did.) Six hours later, I was sitting not fifty yards from a group of Algonquin Indians decked out in braids and ribbon shirts. The Indians had assembled under the poplar tree, where they prayed each afternoon to the beat of tribal drums. After fifteen minutes or so, the Indians were joined by a chorus of white-legged Czech teenagers who wore Bermuda shorts with steel-toed brogues and black socks.

Earlier in the week, the square had been overrun by a collective of Australian feminists who were stopping in Medjugorje to seek blessings from Father Slavko before continuing on to Sarajevo, where they intended to stage a demonstration for peace in Sniper Alley. The priest tried to talk them out of it, but to no avail. "Good luck to the ones who get out alive," Nicky remarked. Now the Franciscans were mobilizing against an "attack" by a busload of recruiters from the Children of God cult who enticed local Catholic youth with the delights of promiscuous sex. "Wherever Our Lady is, the great good she brings inevitably attracts great evil," Father Slavko told me.

My favorite snapshot of the fortnight was the biker gang from Berlin, who thundered into town one afternoon arrayed in wardrobes of black leather and chrome chain, then parked their flame-painted BMWs along the edge of the courtyard directly across from Mira's. Medjugorje's pastor, Father Ivan Lindeca, hustled outside armed with his Polaroid camera to minister to this motley crew. After a half hour of verbal jousting and badass poses, several of the bikers clomped into the church to confess. This success had the friars beaming for days.

Among the assortment of characters who came and went, only a hand-ful managed to attach themselves to the Loopers. Most affecting was Father Francis, a Ugandan priest who had come to Medjugorje in civil-ian clothes, explaining that he felt unfit to wear his clerical collar. The horrors he had witnessed since the reign of Idi Amin had revealed him as a coward who lacked true faith, Father Francis explained. Only after sev-eral stern lectures from Nicky did the African priest agree to wear his vestments and to assist with communion at the evening Mass. Soon he was wearing his collar even during daylight hours. Shortly before he was to depart, Francis sat down next to me at Mira's with a radiant smile and announced that he felt renewed: He had been taking confessions, he ex-plained, and nearly every one he heard moved him to tears. The atmo-sphere of holiness in Medjugorje was something he had not found even in Rome, Francis said. "Here, it is like the time of Christ."

More ambiguous were the motives of a former drug and weapons dealer from Rotterdam, who had hitchhiked to Medjugorje all the way from Marseille after his release from a five-year term in a French prison. He was here to celebrate the first anniversary of his conversion to Catholicism, the man announced to me at least half a dozen times. He was a troubling com-bination of sincerity and insinuation, mooching meals and bumming beers from the other pilgrims even as he instructed them in the Glorious Mys-teries. Wearing the same clothes day after day, unwashed, with teeth that looked as if he hadn't cleaned them in years, the man spoke the patois of a hustler in several languages, and was watched with a wary eye by the locals as he moved about the village carrying all his worldly possessons in the pockets of his cargo pants, encumbered only by a cruel nickname I had given him, "the Frying Dutchman." Father Slavko said his heart was true, however, and to atone, I had taken to buying the Dutchman a Tuborg each afternoon, listening solemnly as he confessed the terrible sins he had com-mitted in half the cities of Western Europe.

Deeply held convictions that the last shall be first and the prodigal must be welcomed had made Medjugorje a magnet for lost souls who sought refuge in the expatriate community of the parish. "Everyone who comes here is a sick person hoping to be healed," I was advised by Nicky. I found it easier to listen when my new friend stepped out of character one evening to join Rita and Michelle in a hilarious recitation of some memorable recent cases. These ranged from a former porn star—"Miss Quadruple X," Nicky called her—convinced that every man who looked upon her would be consumed by the fires of lust, to a virginal Irishwoman who conceived a romantic interest in Father Slavko and lurked outside the sacristy after Mass to insist that the two of them were meant for each other, like St. Francis and St. Clare.

Perhaps the most notorious permanent pilgrim in Medjugorje—and certainly the best-known American—was David Hoepp, owner of the Devotions bookstore. Hoepp had been held up to ridicule in an infamous *Harper's* article as a Texas goofball whose shop peddled the most morbidly absurd collection of fabricated miracle photographs in all of Medjugorje. Had the magazine's writer looked beyond this mere nougat of sarcasm, she would have found a veritable feast of scandal. Hoepp's last stop before Medjugorje had indeed been Texas, but the man's roots were in Massachusetts. This the people of the village had learned during the previous Easter week, when an American pilgrim showed up with an article about Hoepp clipped from the *Boston Globe*. The newspaper report not only detailed the numerous counts of sexual molestation that had been filed against the bookstore owner back in his home state, but described the efforts to avoid extradition on those charges that apparently had led him to Medjugorje. Word of Hoepp's past spread rapidly through the parish, setting off a spirited debate on the nature of Christian duty. The local civil authorities wanted Hoepp to receive the traditional treatment of a pedophile: Throw him in jail, they said, and let the other inmates beat him to death. "If not that, at least drag him out into the bushes and castrate him," one café owner suggested. The priests insisted it was possible that the man's repentance was sincere, and said he must be given an opportunity to reconcile with Christ's mercy. The argument of the priests prevailed, but only on the condition that Hoepp promise never to be alone with a child under the age of eighteen. Shortly after I arrived in Medjugorje, several local people reported seeing the bookstore owner in the company of two young boys. The military promptly informed the American he had two weeks to get out of the country. Hoepp pleaded innocence and swore his conversion was genuine, but the Franciscans, after no small amount of agonizing, had concluded that he should go.

If nothing else, Hoepp's case illustrated how complex the process of governance had become in Medjugorje. These days, the parish operated as both a fledgling democracy and a de facto theocracy, but also as a military dictatorship, an outlaw hideout, and a community under foreign occupation. The UN troops and European Union police officers comported themselves as if they had taken charge, but never seemed to be around when anything important happened. Croatian president Franjo

Tudjman clearly had more influence over the region than did the Bosnian head of state, Alija Izebegović. Like me, most people took orders from whoever happened to be pointing a gun at them. What I found remarkable was that the Franciscans seemed to have the final say on almost any matter other than military action.

The authority of the priests appeared most tenuous anytime a band of HOS "guerrillas" rolled into town. Sporting either shaved heads or ponytails, the HOS were almost uniformly thugs who dressed in cutoff camos and got quite a kick out of noisily stacking their Uzis and AKs on the table whenever they stopped in Medjugorje for a restaurant meal. The sense of menace that surrounded these flat-eyed men was considerably enhanced by the knowledge that they almost certainly could get away with killing you if they felt like it. The HOS generally drove big brand-new Mercedes or BMW sedans, stolen and smuggled into the country across the Austrian and Slovenian borders. What would most irritate me most about news coverage of the war when I returned to the U.S. was how little mention I could find of the role played by organized crime. Half the HOS, at least, was affiliated with one crime gang or another, and this was no less true of the Serb and Muslim irregulars; the tunnel that provided the only remaining access to Sarajevo was being kept open these days entirely because none of the three sides wanted to cut off the flow of smuggled goods.

Though the national leadership was in Zagreb, local bosses ran their gangs out of small-town discotheques. Nearby Ljubuški, with a population of just six thousand, had tallied a total of twelve murders in the month prior to my arrival, a figure that was not unusual. The soldiers of these disco armies claimed to be fighting against Četniks and Bosnian paramilitaries called Mujahadin, and no doubt shot their share of Serbs and Muslims. One always had the feeling, though, that they were looking mainly for an opportunity to turn a buck. Encountering them on the open road and catching a glimpse of the men in the backseat as they peered past the barrels of their weapons through the tinted glass of a 700-series BMW never failed to knot my stomach.

The good citizens of Medjugorje seemed at once to tolerate and disdain this riffraff: Whenever a unit of guerrillas took an outside table at the Restaurant Dubrovnik, the Muslim waiter stayed indoors; instead, the HOS were served by a Croatian refugee from Tuzla who once had been the manager of a shoe factory. The people here had been accommodating strangers and strangeness, both sacred and profane, for so long that very little could faze them. "Twenty million people already have been here," Postar observed, when I asked if he wanted to visit the U.S. "I need not to see world, because world will come to Medjugorje."

The first foreign pilgrims, said Postar, had arrived in the village during the summer of 1983. His earliest houseguests were a pair of Austrian students whom he had hidden in a back bedroom. "The code was that if either of them heard me speak word '*milicija*,' they were to jump out window and run up mountain," he recalled. "And two days after I took them in, that happened." At that time, the apparitions in Medjugorje still were depicted by the communist press as part of a "fascist" movement of Ustaše extremists, and a Yugoslav citizen caught harboring uninvited foreign visitors faced a choice between one hundred days in jail or a fine of nearly one year's income. Podbrdo was closed for two solid years, ringing the church bell was prohibited as "provocative," and the rectory was searched scores of times by militia officers searching for "propaganda literature hostile to the state." Sermons inside the church often were drowned out by low-flying helicopters, and the collection box at St. James's was seized on nearly a dozen occasions.

The anti-Medjugorje campaign in the state-owned media not only failed but actually increased interest in the apparitions by publicizing them. Pilgrims from inside the country and out continued to make their way to the village, their numbers increasing month by month; during the summer of 1983, as many as forty Franciscans were in Medjugorje to take confessions.

The communists had seemed to recognize that they were fighting a losing battle as early as the previous Feburary, when they reduced the prison sentence of Father Zovko and released the priest on the condition that he not return to Medjugorje. Father Zovko's forced absence only made him a more honored martyr, one who had emerged from prison gaunt, ashen, and nearly deaf in one ear. Late in the summer of 1983, the communists opened Podbrdo, made the grounds near the church available for religious services, and began to relax the ban on foreign visitors. Officially, this "lenience" was explained as a reward to Church leaders who had cooperated with the authorities. Everyone in Yugoslavia knew that money was the real reason for the change in government policy: Pilgrimages to Medjugorje were the source of much-needed foreign currencies, and the communists intended to rake in as much of that cash as they could.

Predictably, many of the earliest and most aggressive profiteers were local government officials. The same militia officers who for months had beaten, arrested, and interrogated the people of Medjugorje now showed up at church on Sunday, posing as worshippers while they angled for an opportunity to buy land where they could build hotels or boardinghouses. Many locals who refused to sell were punished with the loss of jobs and pensions; some families lost even their medical benefits. Nevertheless, almost no one in Medjugorje, no matter how poor, would accept an offer for their land. "Those who did cooperate with the communists are considered the biggest traitors in Medjugorje," Postar told me. "Nobody will look at them. They are the ones who got rich from that time, though, and they have the most. It is a big joke here that the biggest communists are now the biggest capitalists."

By the summer of 1984, two government-owned travel agencies had obtained exclusive licenses to arrange "tourist excursions" from Medjugorje, while a third state-run agency secured a monopoly on the transport of pilgrims to and from the village. At that time, the people of Medjugorje still were so removed from the outside world that they imagined all foreign visitors came from Germany or Austria. "When the first group of pilgrims arrived from Italy," Postar recalled, "they were called 'the Italian Germans.'"

The number of pilgrims continued to swell, especially after the 1984 Winter Olympics in Sarajevo. A number of correspondents who were covering the Games got wind of events in Medjugorje and arranged surreptitious visits to the village. Among the articles that resulted was an exceptionally generous and insightful piece written by Richard West and published in the London *Spectator*. Despite warnings that accommodations in Medjugorje amounted to "no hotel, one pub, one hot-dog stall and one public lavatory consisting of three sheds with doors that do not shut, enclosing three holes in the ground covered with excrement," as West described it, groups of pilgrims soon were arriving in the village from all across the European continent. Encouraged by the Franciscans, the seers did what they could to accommodate these early arrivals, receiving the pilgrims in their family homes at intervals all during the day. Foreigners who waited outside for admission soon were approached by enterprising villagers selling bread, fruit, and drinks. The police tried to stamp out this incipient capitalism, fining the pilgrims for breaking the peace and the villagers for selling food without a license, but both sides persisted.

The visionaries and their families conspired to circumvent the government and its spies by sending trusted associates (*zajednici*, as they were called in Medjugorje) to the private homes where the pilgrims were staying, and arranging a schedule of prayer services. Assembling in small groups at the church, the pilgrims then would be escorted to the children's homes. When the secret police got wind of this, they imposed heavy fines on those who organized "illegal religous processions." Soon, every one of the *zajednici* had lost his job, and many were forced to travel abroad to earn a living.

The two licensed travel agencies took a more pragmatic approach, offering the *zajednici* jobs in exchange for a steady supply of pilgrims. The seers and the priests in Medjugorje reacted with horror, announcing that they would permit no further contact with either government travel agency. The government intervened at this point, forcing a compromise: In exchange for a regular supply of pilgrims for their excursions, the travel agencies would transport pilgrims to and from the homes of the visionaries, accompanied by *zajednici* who would oversee the entire operation. While this provided the children and their families with a measure of freedom from persecution, it also forced them to participate in the organization of what the government called its "religious tourist economy." The Bijakovići-based prayer group known as Emmanuel soon became the headquarters of what critics described as a "patronage network," arranging food and housing for the pilgrims, providing tour guides and translators, answering phone calls and letters, even hiring a bookkeeper. Those from the parish who were not included took to referring to them as the "Sindikat."

The village of Medjugorje soon had its own prayer group, called Maria. The central figures of Maria were a pair of eleven-year-old girls who would become known as "the seers of the second generation," distant cousins Jelena and Marijana Vasilj. The experiences reported by Jelena and Marijana were quite distinct from the apparitions of the original six children. They saw (and more often heard) the Madonna "in an interior way, through the heart," as Jelena would explain, with eyes closed and only during "deep prayer." Such ecstasies are not unknown in the Catholic Church, which refers to them as "inner locutions."

These had begun first for Jelena, who would emerge eventually as an enormously important figure in Medjugorje, no less significant for many villagers than Mirjana or Vicka. Church investigators expressed unqualified admiration for the girl's "spiritual maturity" and intellectual sophistication. "Determined, decisive, with no hint of anxiety or desire to please" was the description of the girl offered by an Irish priest who had been quite disconcerted by her. Theologians found Jelena far more intriguing than any of the original six seers. Her emergence troubled some in the Medjugorje parish, however. Initially, the priests were disturbed by Jelena's announcement that the Virgin wanted to form a prayer group, wondering why the six original visionaries had not been told this. Only a short time later, the original seers reported that the Virgin had confirmed Her desire for a prayer group, and said She wanted it to be called Maria.

Jelena's locutions had the endorsement of the seers, apparently, but soon after this a new controversy erupted. When Podbrdo was reopened, the original six began gathering on the hill for their apparitions. Almost immediately, a message attributed to the Virgin appeared on the community board at St. James's, urging everyone to return to the church. The seers were furious, and for the next two weeks left their seats in church empty, meeting each evening on Podbrdo and receiving visitors in their homes. A number of people in Bijakovići accused the Franciscans of "inventing" Jelena and Marijana to shift the focus of devotions in the parish from their village to Medjugorje, just as they had diverted attention from Podbrdo by exalting Križevac. The original visionaries deplored such pettiness, accepting Jelena and Marijana as genuine, but clearly believed the friars saw their influence over the two girls as an opportunity to take control.

Jelena would become even more problematic as she passed through her teens and grew into an astoundingly beautiful young woman. There simply had been nothing like her before in Medjugorje. The young men of the parish in particular were alternately distracted and intimidated by Jelena, and the feeling that no one was worthy of her contributed to a growing sense of isolation around the girl.

Faced with her intelligence, her beauty, and her "special graces," many in Medjugorje found it a relief to learn that Jelena, unlike Mirjana and the others, did not claim to know the future. During her locutions, she asked a number of times to hear the Secrets, Jelena said, and had been informed on each occasion that she was not intended to have this knowledge. All she had been told, Jelena said, was that "the future of the world depends somehow on what happens at Medjugorje."

The earliest indication of the importance that Medjugorje would take on—at least within the Catholic Church—may have been the arrival in the village at Christmas in 1983 of the elderly French theologian, Father René Laurentin. Silver-haired and elegant in his matching ensembles of soutanes and skullcaps, Father Laurentin was a small man with a large presence. The French priest's *Short Treatise on Marian Theology* was regarded within the Church as the seminal work on the subject. Also well known for his six-volume study of the apparitions at Lourdes and his biography of Bernadette Soubirous, Father Laurentin was enchanted by the Medjugorje visionaries from the moment he met them and made little effort to conceal this in the short book he published after his return to France in 1984, *Is the Virgin Mary Appearing at Medjugorje?* For him, the answer was yes.

Anticipating the outcry that would ensue, the venerable priest promptly took a step back and made a bow to Church dogma, explaining that the apparitions should be interpreted as "a sign from heaven," but not "an absolute communication." "There is always an element of the relative in the apparitions," Laurentin wrote: "This relativity is due to the manner in which God and the Virgin, or any other Saint or servant of God, adapts to the one who beholds them and to the local situation. The relativity is also due to the living and normal interpretation of the communication made to each person."

The book (based in large part on the research of the Croatian theologian Ljudevit Rupčić) made an immediate impact on French Catholics, who began to organize pilgrimages to Medjugorje during the summer of 1984. And by the time of his second visit to Yugoslavia in December 1984, Father Laurentin's success had made him some powerful enemies. Bishop Žanić was infuriated by the Frenchman's assertion that any "contrary indications" to the authenticity of the apparitions "derive from unfortunate interferences and insufficient appreciation." It was the communists, though, who arrested Father Laurentin at the airport in Mostar shortly after his arrival in Hercegovina and charged him with illegally distributing religious literature. After a humiliating strip search, the priest was hauled before a judge, found guilty, heavily fined, ordered to leave the country, and forbidden to return for at least a year.

The communists would have been better served by expelling Laurentin's traveling companions. These were a team of physicians from the University of Montpelier who were about to conduct the most complete scientific study of an alleged supernatural event in the history of Catholicism. The leader of the French doctors (and Laurentin's partner in the project) was Dr. Henri Joyeux, an internationally renowned cancer researcher. Six months earlier, Joyeux had come to Medjugorje on his first trip to the village accompanied by only an electronics engineer. The two men had made video- and audiotapes of the visionaries during thirty-five apparitions, hoping to determine whether the "synchronizations" of the seers might have been orchestrated. Back in France, after several weeks of studying the tapes at the slowest speeds possible, Dr. Joyeux became convinced that "definitive" tests were warranted and organized a team of other doctors from the university. He could not, of course, prove that these six children were actually seeing the Virgin Mary, Dr. Joyeux told Father Laurentin. However, the doctor felt certain that he would be able to confirm or eliminate an entire range of medical and psychological explanations.

The problem was that the seers refused to cooperate, citing the Virgin's statement to Ivan during the tests by the Italian doctors nearly a year earlier: "It is not necessary." Only after several days' delay and a series of strenuous arguments were Dr. Joyeux and Father Laurentin able to convince young Jakov that the children should ask the Virgin for permission to be tested during their next apparition. This they had done, the six reported that evening, and the Madonna's reply was succinct: "You are free." After another day of discussion, all six visionaries agreed to be tested.

The most eminent of the physicians on Dr. Joyeux's team was the ear, nose, and throat specialist Dr. François Rouquerol. He had been able to demonstrate a clear "disconnection of the auditory pathways during the ecstasy" of each visionary, Dr. Rouquerol reported. He had proven that most convincingly, the doctor explained, by blaring ninety decibels of engine noise into the ears of the seers during their apparitions; none had reacted. He also reported that, while his instruments showed the visionaries' voices had become completely silent during the apparitions, their lips, tongues, and facial muscles had continued to function exactly as when speech was audible. Somehow, completely separate from the rest of their physical faculties, the larynx of each seer had ceased to operate during the period of silence. This anomaly was singular in his experience and could not be accounted for by any condition known to medical science, Dr. Roquerol concluded.

The opthalmologist on the French team, Dr. Jacques Philippot, not only confirmed the profoundly inhibited eyelid reflex to dazzling light observed earlier by the Italian doctors, but also demonstrated that from the beginning to the end of their apparitions, the gaze of all the children remained fixed on exactly the same point several feet above their heads. Even when he tried to block their vision with an opaque screen, Philippot noted, the seers' eyes had not reacted. What Philippot considered most compelling was that he had measured a simultaneity of eyeball movement among the visionaries of less than one-fifth of a second at both the beginning and the end of their apparitions; this was so far beyond the capacity of normal human functioning that no form of collusion or manipulation could account for it.

Heart specialist Dr. Bernard Hoarau reported that his electrocardiogram, blood pressure, and heart rhythm examinations of the seers during their ecstasies "allow us to exclude totally the existence of the phenomena of dreams, sleep or epilepsy." Neurologist Dr. Jean Cadhilac added that the tests he had conducted on the visionaries "eliminate formally all clinical signs comparable to those observed during individual or collective hallucination, hysteria, neurosis or pathological ecstasy."

Like nearly everyone else who studied the results obtained by the French team, Dr. Joyeux was most impressed by the electroencephalogram tests that had measured activity in eight distinct areas of the seers' brains during their ecstasies. All states of consciousness known to neuroscience involved some admixture of alpha (receptive) and beta (reactive) impulses. Dr. Joyeux observed that the ratio of activity in the seers' brains prior to an apparition was exactly normal: ten alpha cycles to twenty beta cycles each second. Falling asleep or into a trance state would have increased the beta cycles while reducing the number of alpha cycles. During their apparitions, exactly the opposite occurred: Their beta impulses stopped completely. The six young people were not simply awake during their apparitions, but hyper-awake, in a state of pure meditation that previously had been observed in just a handful of Trappist or Buddhist monks while deeply in prayer. And those monks had achieved this "generalized alpha rhythm," Dr. Joyeux noted, only when their eyes were closed, whereas the Medjugorje visionaries had kept their eyes wide open during the entire time of their apparitions.

In the spring of 1985, Dr. Joyeux submitted a report that concluded: "The ecstasies are not pathological, nor is there any element of deceit. No scientific discipline seems able to describe these phenomena." Concurrent with the publication of his work, Dr. Joyeux agreed to an interview with *Paris Match*. "The phenomena of the apparitions at Medjugorje cannot be explained scientifically," the doctor told the magazine's interviewer. "In one word, these young people are healthy and there is no sign of epilepsy, nor is it a sleep or dream state. It is neither a case of pathological hallucination nor hallucination in the hearing or sight faculties . . . It cannot be a cataleptic state, for during the ecstasy the facial muscles are operating in a normal way." The ecstasies of the seers at Medjugorje "do not belong to any scientific denominations," the doctor added. "It is more like a state of deep, active prayer, in which they are partially disconnected from the physical world, in a state of contemplation and sane encounter with a person whom they alone can see, hear and touch. We cannot reach the transmitter, but we can ascertain that the receivers are in a state of sane and good working order."

In September 1985, shortly after Dr. Joyeux left Medjugorje for the last time, the Italians dispatched their own all-star team of doctors from Milan's Mangiagalli Clinic to the village. The most intriguing results obtained by the Italian team were reported by Dr. Michael Sabatini, a psychopharmacologist fresh from the faculty of Columbia University, where he had spent years studying "the problem of pain." At Columbia, Dr. Sabatini had developed an instrument he called the algometer, designed to measure the intensity of pain created by applying pressure to particularly sensitive areas of the body. He had used his algometer on each of the Medjugorje seers, and the results showed that the six entered a state of "complete analgesis" during their ecstasies; that is, they were unable to feel pain. This proved beyond any doubt, Dr. Sabatini wrote, that the seers "do not fake and do not deceive." The doctor who supervised the Mangiagalli Clinic team, Dr. Luigi Frigero, stated that the results obtained by Dr. Sabatini and the neurological tests that demonstrated the seers were not simply awake but hyper-awake during their ecstasies had created a contradiction that "cannot be explained naturally, and thus can be only preternatural or supernatural."

Over the next several years, this claim would be tested by fresh teams of Italian, Polish, Austrian, English, and American scientists; but for many Catholics, Medjugorje already had been validated. While it was correct to report that the state of consciousness observed in the children during their apparitions existed outside any scientific category, René Laurentin would write, "the best explanation is that the visionaries are in living, personal, normal contact with a person from another world."

Laurentin made no dent in the Catholic whom he most hoped to convince: Bishop Pavao Žanić. In June 1984, nearly a year before Joyeux's report was published, the bishop was notified that medical tests already conducted on the visionaries "ruled out hallucination." Nevertheless, in October 1984, Žanić issued a report—distributed to episcopal conferences worldwide—announcing: "The Bishop of Mostar, after mature reflection, has arrived at the conclusion that it is morally certain that the events at Medjugorje are a case of collective hallucination." In early 1985, after Laurentin had "conveyed his astonishment," the bishop wrote a personal letter to the French priest stating that he was withdrawing his hypothesis of hallucination and now inclined once again toward the theory that the apparitions were an elaborate hoax.

By this time Žanić had demoted Father Jozo Zovko to a subordinate role in the imagined intrigue against the Mostar diocese, replacing him at the top with "the mystifier and charismatic magician," Father Tomislav Vlasić. That Vlasić had not learned of the apparitions until four days after they began and made only two visits to Medjugorje before August 18, 1981, Žanić dismissed as irrelevant. The "evangelical nature" of the Madonna's purported messages had betrayed Vlasić's involvement, the bishop insisted. Žanić also believed that Father Slavko had become Vlasić's principal collaborator in the fraud, and during 1984 transferred both priests out of the Medjugorje parish. That their absence made no appreciable impact on either the seers or their apparitions confounded the bishop, who came to the conclusion that the conspiracy must be a massive one involving any number of Franciscans, as well as the visionaries themselves, and their families.

Shortly before the third anniversary of the apparitions, Bishop Žanić arranged a meeting in Mostar that was attended by three priests and a nun from Medjugorje, as well as the visionaries Ivan, Marija, and Jakov. He only recently had received scandalous information concerning Father Vlasić, the bishop told the group: Apparently the priest had fathered a son by a former nun who now was living with her illegitimate child in West Germany. When one of priests told the bishop that this was slander, Žanić replied (according to Franciscans): "Things have come to the point that somebody must perish. Either I must perish, or Medjugorje." One month later Father Vlasić himself was summoned to Mostar for a meeting with the bishop, who had attempted "blackmail," the priest reported to the other friars afterwards, threatening to publish the case against him if Vlasić refused to admit the apparitions were a fabrication. Vlasić refused, and fully expected Bishop Žanić to follow through on his threat.

In time Žanić would, but first he stepped up his media campaign against Medjugorje: "What is behind all this are charismatics and Pentecostals," he told a German reporter, "and above all a large group of fanatical Franciscans who wish to justify their disobedience to their bishop and to Rome." Convinced that the results of the tests by Dr. Joyeux's team of doctors would be published before the end of the year, the bishop pushed his commission to deliver its report. In late 1985, the results of the episcopal commission's final vote were announced: Only two of fourteen members were prepared to say they believed the apparitions were genuine. Archbishop Franić promptly answered with an open letter to Cardinal Ratzinger in which he noted that separate teams of Yugoslav, Italian, and French doctors had examined the Medjugorje seers, finding no evidence of fakery or hysteria. Bishop Žanić arrived in Rome during April 1986 to submit his findings. Summoned to a meeting with Cardinal Ratzinger, the bishop was stunned when the cardinal asked that he suspend his negative judgment, dissolve his episcopal commission, and place the entire matter in the hands of the Holy See. Before Žanić returned to Mostar, the Congregation for the Doctrine of the Faith announced that it had "freed" the bishop and his commission from further investigative duties and was ordering the Yugoslav Bishops' Conference to appoint a new commission under its direction.

By the end of 1985, René Laurentin would note, tests conducted on the seers of Medjugorje by teams of doctors from assorted European nations had demonstrated that the state into which all six entered during their apparitions could not be explained by any known medical diagnosis. From the strictly scientific point of view, that left some explanation that would be found on the hazy periphery of psychiatry, in some previously undetected kind of "religious hysteria."

Naturally, that possibility excited those who proposed it, and was most thoroughly explored by a pair of Italian doctors who would be given an unusual degree of personal access to the seers. Dr. Giorgio Sanguinetti, a professor of psychiatry at the University of Milan, specialized in the study of delirium—religious delirium in particular. Dr. Sanguinetti was less interested in studying the ecstasies of the seers than in observing the six during the course of their daily lives. Certain patterns were observed again and again in "delirious people with a mystical bent," he explained: Most telling was a sense of omnipotence "not necessarily expressed with noisy insistence or displayed fanatically, but coming across with a quiet, complacent silence. This hides the sense of triumph through a privileged relationship with the transcendant." Such persons have little genuine interest in other people and lack the capacity for spontaneous communication, Dr. Sanguinetti wrote; if criticized or questioned, "they react resentfully and without restraint, intolerant of any contradiction." Extravagant behavior and theatrical gestures were common to such individuals, even when alone.

Therefore, the doctor concluded, "I consider it of fundamental importance to emphasize that in all my conversations with the young 'visionaries' of Medjugorje I have never discovered, on any occasion, any thought, look, conversation, attitude or behavior similar to these pathological states which I have listed. First of all it must be made clear that the 'visionaries' live a normal life; they are integrated in their community and in their families and are treated by others as if they were not 'visionaries'; they themselves relate to others as if they were no different from other people, or from themselves before they became 'visionaries' . . . they differ from others only in the time they give to the practice of religion and to the visions; all this is done in a very natural way without piousity or complacency; their behavior is by preference discreet and, politely, they try to shield themselves from the overpowering pressure of pilgrims, when this is possible. They are quite open to conversation and seem patiently resigned to having to answer the same questions; in this they are not effusive, nor are they withdrawn or exhibitionist. On the contrary they look calm and peaceful and gentle. They do not try to convince one, and they do not exceed what is asked of them; their smile is not smug or malicious, and it is not artificial. Their movements reflect only kindness and good will. They certainly are not looking for attention or for an audience; they do not offer interpretations or personal opinions about their mystical experiences; all they want to do is report the facts and admit that they are happy."

As I read Sanguinetti's observations of the seers, I felt as if the words had been pulled from my own head. The physician who spoke to me most personally, however, was Dr. Marco Margnelli, a neurophysiologist who came to Yugoslavia during the summer of 1988 convinced that previous charts of the seers' brain functions during their visions had been faulty. A specialist in altered states of consciousness and an avowed atheist, Dr. Margnelli arrived in Medjugorje, he admitted, looking for "any evidence that would contradict it or expose it as a fake." The doctor conducted an array of medical tests on the visionaries, but seemed almost uninterested in the results by the time he returned home and granted an interview in which he described the seers' visions as "a genuine state of ecstasy."

"As a scientist, I can only declare that the children really pass into another state of consciousness—a condition that one can also reach through meditation techniques, such as auto-training, though not as profoundly," Dr. Margnelli explained. He would not presume to describe this state the seers entered, "but we were certainly in the presence of an extraordinary phenomenon. Whether we are dealing with an authentic apparition or something else we cannot explain and I cannot say. It is a question I prefer not to put to myself."

Only a moment later, though, Margnelli added a statement that would startle his colleagues: "Since returning from Yugoslavia, I have been thinking about it continually and I confess, I also ask myself *nonscientific* questions, such as what the meaning of the whole thing can be." Dr. Margnelli then described a series of events to which he had been witness, from the "synchronous movements" of the visionaries to the apparently miraculous healing of a woman with leukemia. What had affected him most deeply were the birds: During the late afternoon, they would gather in the trees outside the rectory where the seers shared their apparitions, chirping and cooing and calling by the hundreds, at times deafeningly loud, until "they suddenly and simultaneously all go silent as soon as the apparition begins." This "absolute silence of the birds" haunted him, the doctor admitted.

A few months after returning to Milan, Dr. Margnelli became a practicing Catholic.

CHAPTER ELEVEN

Depending upon what—and whom—one believed, by 1986 René Laurentin had become either the great chronicler of the most important Marian apparition in Church history, or the great apologist for the most outrageous hoax ever perpetrated upon Catholics. The most significant negative opinion of both Medjugorje and Father Laurentin still was the one held by Bishop Žanić, who by now had accused the French theologian of, among other things, lining his own pockets through sales of his annual reports on developments in the village. The bishop also charged the priest with participating in an organized cover-up of certain statements attributed by the visionaries to the Madonna, particularly those that questioned the bishop's judgment. As Laurentin would observe, "The principal argument of Bishop Žanić is reduced to the following: The apparition criticized the bishop. Therefore it is not the Virgin."

The bishop was beginning to find allies drawn from both the extreme left and right wings of the Church. The most notable voices on the left were that of a French-Canadian parapsychologist named Louis Belanger, and his partner, Father Ivo Sivrić, a Franciscan from the U.S. who had been born in Medjugorje. In an interview published by a Quebec newspaper during June 1985, Belanger had laid out a premise at least as far-fetched as any put forth by Medjugorje's supporters: "Tectonic movements of mountains and rocks, which move in cycles, can set off piezo-electric and geomagnetic effects, which are visible in the form of columns of light and can influence the behavior of a living organism. This electromagnetic light, as it passes through the temporal lobe . . . gives rise to visions which are interpreted according to their culture . . . The children in Medjugorje really saw a luminous phenomenon, which they interpreted, in accord with their culture, as being the Madonna. What else could they possibly see, these young people brought up in the faith and cult of Mary?"

Father Sivrić, who had accompanied Belanger during the parapsychol-ogist's one brief stay in Medjugorje, produced a book he titled *The Hidden Face of Medjugorje*. The volume was an astonishingly shoddy compendium of rumor, gossip, and outright falsehoods that concluded the apparitions had been produced by a combination of imagination and fabrication, and clearly were "a copy of Lourdes." This opinion was based mainly upon the fact that Mirjana had been given a book about the visions of Bernadette a few days after the apparitions in Medjugorje began. The villagers in Medjugorje were quick to point out that the American priest's relatives were local pariahs. Shortly before the apparitions began, it seemed, one of Sivrić's nephews had been appointed to set up the communist cell of Medjugorje, a project that was aborted when virtually the entire parish converted to active Catholicism.

Nevertheless, any number of "modernist" Catholic publications and organizations spread both the accusations of Sivrić and the assertions of Belanger. The large leftist French Catholic daily, *La Croix*, deemed the apparitions at Medjugorje to be both a hallucination and a manipulation. Most of the opposition to Medjugorje from the far right wing of the Church argued that "Medjugorje is a perverse and incoherent work of the Devil," as one ultraconservative priest put it. Especially disturbing to these critics was the "indifferent ecumenism" of the messages attributed to the Virgin: The Virgin's insistence that true Christians must "respect" other religions, in particular Islam, was an affront to Catholic orthodoxy, several anti-Medjugorje theologians contended. These writers were par-ticularly offended by Mirjana's report that the Virgin had instructed her to respect the Islamic faith of her neighbors in Sarajevo, saying, "In God, there are neither divisions nor religions. It is you in the world who have created divisions." Clearly such ideas were intended to undermine the primacy of the Catholic Church, it was argued.

René Laurentin countered that the Virgin had asked the faithful to respect Mulsim peoples, not Muslim doctrines. He then noted with some amusement that the Madonna of Medjugorje had managed simulta-neously to offend both liberal progressives and reactionary traditional-ists, further evidence for him that the apparitions must be genuine.

The most notable subscriber to Father Laurentin's reports on events in Medjugorje was Pope John Paul II. The French theologian had met privately with John Paul to discuss the situation in Yugoslavia on at least three occasions, and while he was obliged to respect the confidentiality of the pope's remarks, Father Laurentin felt equally compelled to report both the high level of the Holy See's interest in Medjugorje and John Paul's personal enthusiasm for the devotions there. The Vatican's decision to block a negative judgment of the apparitions in the village was unprecedented, noted the priest, and was itself proof of the importance that the pope placed on what was happening in Medjugorje. By 1987, John Paul was increasingly candid about his belief that Medjugorje was an apparition event on a par with Lourdes and Fátima. At a meeting with a group of Italian bishops in June of that year, in response to an inquiry about how the subject of Medjugorje should be handled, the pope said, "I'm astonished at this question. Aren't you aware of the marvelous fruits it is producing?"

Early in 1988, the pope learned that a group of thirty-three priests from Brazil had stopped in Rome on their way to a retreat in Medjugorje, and invited the entire company to a private concelebration of Mass in the Papal Chapel. Afterwards, John Paul blessed the retreat and asked the priests for their prayers. One of three bishops in this group reported that the pope had described Medjugorje to him as "a world center of spirituality." In April 1989, Paul Hnilica, the exiled Czech prelate who now served as the auxiliary bishop of Rome (and also as one of the pope's closest confidants), traveled to Russia to represent John Paul at a meeting in Moscow and afterwards reported that the pope had admonished him for not stopping in Medjugorje on his way home. "If I wasn't a pope," John Paul told Hnilica, "I'd have been in Medjugorje long ago."

Distressing as such remarks must have been to Bishop Žanić, they were even more offensive to some on the extreme right wing of the Church. A group called the Catholic Counter-Reformation, whose intellectual leader, Michel le Trinite, the abbott of Nantes, was a vehement opponent of Medjugorje's ecumenism, went so far as to announce it had excommunicated John Paul for his support of the apparitions in Yugoslavia.

Many moderately conservative Church members observed that Hans Urs von Balthasar, the Swiss archbishop widely regarded as the most influential Catholic theologian of the late twentieth century, had remained silent on the subject of Medjugorje. Some even suggested that Balthasar was keeping quiet because he did not share the pope's enthusiasm for the claimed apparitions in Yugoslavia. Shortly after Bishop Žanić published his first Posizione on Medjugorje, however, the archbishop replied with an open letter that began, "My Lord, what a sorry document you have

sent throughout the world!" A short time after this, in London, Archbishop
Balthasar issued a second public statement: "Medjugorje's theology rings
true. I am convinced of its truth. And everything about Medjugorje is authentic in a Catholic sense. What is happening there is so evident, so convincing." In his masterwork, *Gloria*, the archbishop had written at length
about a concept he called Theodramatik, "the drama of love being played
out between God and the world." What was taking place in Medjugorje
was the greatest example of Theodramatik he had witnessed during his
lifetime, said Archbishop Balthasar, who referred to the village several times
as "a theater of holiness."

In July 1987, Bishop Žanić encouraged those who hoped he had been
chastened by agreeing to address a large confirmation ceremony at
St. James's Church. Virtually the entire parish turned out to hear his sermon, hoping that at last the bishop might seek a peaceful resolution of
the ongoing conflict between the Mostar diocese and the Medjugorje
Franciscans. The crowd was stunned when Žanić began by announcing
that he was banning priests who led pilgrimages to Medjugorje from saying Mass in his diocese, that priests who insisted upon attributing a supernatural character to the ecstasies of the seers were not to celebrate
Mass in Medjugorje, and that the visionaries themselves were no longer
welcome to hold their claimed apparitions in the church rectory. Satan
had taken charge in Medjugorje, he continued, and what was happening
in the village constituted the greatest deception in the history of Christianity. The complicity of the Franciscans in this deception "merits the
depths of Hell," Žanić declared, then prayed aloud that the Virgin Mary
expose the fraud being perpetrated in Her name.

Within a few weeks, the Catholic News Service had spread Bishop
Žanić's remarks worldwide, and the subject of Medjugorje was more
controversial than ever. In September 1987, the Yugoslav Bishops' Conference attempted to undo some of the damage by issuing a "Directive
on Medjugorje" that corrected Žanić on a number of points. While it
was improper to endorse the messages of the Madonna reported by the
Medjugorje visionaries from the altar of the church, said the directive, it
was equally wrong to attack the apparitions as "mendacious and diabolical." And no individual priest had the right to condemn the devotions in
Medjugorje, but must submit to the judgment of the commission appointed by order of the Holy See.

Whatever Bishop Žanić said about Medjugorje or the Bishops' Conference concluded seemed increasingly irrelevant, given the escalation

of international interest: From fewer than 50,000 in 1983, the number of pilgrims who visited Medjugorje would grow to 462,000 in 1985, to 857,000 in 1987, and then to 1.1 million in 1989, the first year in which the number of visitors was greater than at Fátima. By 1990, more than three hundred bishops, archbishops, and cardinals had made pilgrimages to Medjugorje, and some of the most influential members of the magisterium had endorsed the apparitions. Among these was the esteemed archbishop of Prague, Cardinal Frantisek Tomasek, who issued a public statement that he was "profoundly grateful to God for Medjugorje." Said Cardinal Joseph Siri of Genoa, "I can only say that I see many atheists leaving Genoa for Medjugorje who return with a rosary in their hands." Judging simply by its fruits, any number of bishops and cardinals observed, the apparitions in Medjugorje ranked among the most important religious events of the millennium. Healings and conversions were the fruits most highly prized by the Catholic Church, it was noted, and Medjugorje had produced both in astonishing numbers.

Among the Franciscans, conversions were at least as valued as cures, and in many cases were understood as inseparable from physical recovery. I found the parish archives filled with the testimonies of those who believed their lives had been fundamentally altered by an encounter with the Madonna of Medjugorje. So many were so affecting that any attempt to winnow out the worthy seemed presumptuous beyond bearing. None moved me more, though, than the story of a former IRA member named Marc Lenaghan who in 1982 had been sentenced to twelve years in prison for shooting a British soldier on Falls Road in Belfast. He and the other IRA inmates had scorned Christians as cowards and traitors, but nevertheless attended each and every Mass in the prison chapel, because it was the only opportunity they had to share news of plots and conspiracies. He first heard about Medjugorje during Easter week in 1984, from a chaplain who was recently returned from a pilgrimage to Yugoslavia. He was astonished that a man who seemed generally sensible could believe in such a fairy tale, but for some reason permitted the chaplain to put him into contact with other Irishmen who had visited Medjugorje, and eventually even accepted a book of the Madonna's "messages." He could not say how, or even when, but "the love of God entered me." In 1988, with time off for good behavior, Lenaghan was released after serving only six years of his sentence, and went directly from prison to Medjugorje. He had hoped to see the spinning sun or to experience an apparition, Lenaghan admitted somewhat sheepishly, but nothing of this sort happened. What might be described as a miracle did occur, however: At the foot of the cross on Križevac, he had been approached by a man who introduced himself as a British soldier, then a few moments later revealed that he had been patrolling Falls Road in Belfast on February 15, 1982, the day that Lenaghan had shot his compatriot. At the end of this conversation, Lenaghan and the Brit had prayed a Rosary together for peace in Northern Ireland.

Many other testmonies I read that day would linger in my mind for months afterwards, memories that surfaced with what seemed an unwarranted immediacy. I thought a number of times about the Italian photo model who at nineteen had discovered she could triple her income by working also as a call girl, then became a drunk and a drug addict in order to deal with what she called her "workload." Her first contact with Medjugorje had been to pick up a booklet about the apparitions at the train station in Milan. To comfort herself, the young woman recalled, she began to recite the prayers in the book, most often after returning home to her apartment at three or four in the morning. Months passed before she made her way to Medjugorje, where she spent three days without eating or sleeping, and on her last morning made confession to Father Zovko. Upon returning home, she immediately gave away all her clothes, all her jewelry, and eventually all the money in her savings account. For some, this might have been excessive, she acknowledged, but for her, "earthly consolations had become bitterness."

I was humbled by the lengthy and eloquent account of a heroin addict from Zimbabwe who had come to Medjugorje to kick cold turkey in a tiny room with a view of Križevac; and unsettled by the story of an unfaithful Austrian housewife whose conversion had coincided precisely with the physical healing of her sickly husband. The testimony that most disturbed me, because it reminded me of everything I hated in myself, was that of a haughty, humorless German intellectual who wrote that she believed only in "freedom and self-determination," "regarded God as an invention," and, as an apostle of Sartre, had learned to "resent the human condition as fundamentally absurd." I winced especially at one passage in the long narrative the woman had written: "To me, people seemed naive, manipulated, repugnant, and superficial . . . My habitual reactions were aversion, disdain, criticism, and self-destruction." She agreed to come to Medjugorje with her family in 1986, mainly because she appreciated the change in her parents when they returned home from an earlier trip: "They reproached me less," she wrote, "even when I was disagreeable." On her first day in Medjugorje, she met a priest named Father Pero and told him straight out that she did not believe in God. "Father Pero's face lit up and he said, 'I am happy that you are here; the Mother of God will do the rest.' I was totally upset." She hated being in Medjugorje, and said so to anybody who would listen. Then one afternoon, simply to amuse herself, she had joined a German-language group in singing the *Sanctus* of Schubert. "And suddenly I believed. I do not see how to better describe this moment. Between the moments before and later, I began to believe that God existed." A few months later she joined a religious community.

I was alone while I read these testimonies, and a good thing, because I spent a lot of that time blinking back tears. At the same time, I kept asking myself what all this proved, other than that religious feelings existed. It was simpler somehow to read about the healings. The events described might be more fantastic, but the reports had an opaque quality, couched as they were in the dispassionate vernaculars of science and medicine. The parish kept a list of more than five hundred allegedly miraculous healings in the church rectory, under the supervision of the stern-faced former policewoman Marija Dugandzić. Dr. Luigi Frigero had been the first to review these files at length, back in 1986, and admitted his amazement at the level of documentation the Franciscans had maintained. It would take at least four years, he predicted, to study and verify the Italian cases alone. In 1987, another Italian doctor, Antonino Antonacci, arrived in Medjugorje to establish the Bureau of Verification of Extraordinary Healings. This was modeled on the Bureau Médicale at Lourdes, said to impose standards of proof even more rigorous than those applied by the Vatican's Consulta Medica.

This determination to validate Marian miracles by medical science went back to the first year of the twentieth century, when a virtual regiment of prominent physicians examined the case of a man named Gabriel Gargan. Two years earlier, Gargan had been a post office clerk who was working in the mail car of an express train bound from Bordeaux to Paris when it hit an object on the tracks and derailed. Gargan was left paralyzed from the waist down, consigned to spend the rest of his life in a hospital bed. Within eight months, the man's feet had become gangrenous and his body weight had dropped by more than half, to just seventy-eight pounds. Gargan's pitiful condition was proved to the satisfaction of several French courts, which awarded him a considerable sum to pay for the nurses he needed night and day. An aunt who was a nun of the Order of the Sacred

Heart pleaded with him to visit Lourdes, but for fifteen months he refused. Finally, hounded by his mother, the man agreed to make the trip, carried by stretcher the entire way. When he was bathed in the waters of the spring that Bernadette Soubirous had discovered half a century earlier, Gargan went unconscious and could not be revived. Assuming he was dead, the man's devastated family wheeled him by carriage back to their hotel, stopping on the way for the procession of the Blessed Sacrament. A priest carrying the host passed by and blessed both the covered body and the company of mourners. A moment later there was movement under the cloth that covered Gargan, and then he sat up. As the crowd watched in wonder, Gargan announced that he wanted to walk. His relatives tried to restrain him, but he pushed them off, stood up, walked several paces, and announced that he was cured. The sixty doctors who subsequently examined Gargan agreed, though none could explain how his health had been restored. For the next fifteen years, he worked at Lourdes in the service of invalids. A handful of those to whom he ministered were healed; many more were not. The mystery of divine intervention only deepened.

At Medjugorje, the most well-documented healing was that of an Italian woman named Diana Basile, from the town of Ferro. The facts of the case had been compiled by the University of Milan's Specialist Clinical Institute, where Basile once worked as a secretary. In 1972, Basile was a thirty-two-year-old married mother of three who began to show the first symptoms of a profound multiple sclerosis: uncontrollable shaking in her right hand and complete blindness in her right eye. Gradually, she lost nearly all use of her right hand, and her right knee became so rigid that walking was nearly impossible. Treatment with the hormone ACTH slowed the disease, but by the summer of 1983, Basile had become completely incontinent, unable to lift her right arm, and capable of a shuffling walk only when assisted by an adult who could support her weight. She became seriously depressed during early 1984 as her physical condition deteriorated; former colleagues doubted she would live another five years.

During May of that year, the woman accepted the invitation of a nurse at the clinic to join a pilgrimage to Medjugorje. On the afternoon of May 23, Basile, helped by two members of her tour group, made it to the steps below the altar of St. James's Church, but was unable to reach the sacristy in time to be admitted with those who would observe that evening's apparition. A French priest who guarded the vestibule warned her not to move, lest she disturb those inside, but at that moment the door to the room opened and she was able to step inside and kneel. The young visionaries went to *their* knees in that same moment, Basile said; suddenly she heard a loud noise, and became completely unaware of her surroundings. Obscure episodes from her life, nearly forgotten, began to flash before her eyes, and she lost all sense of time and place. At the end of their apparition, the young seers walked out of the sacristy to stand before the main altar of the church. Without thinking, Basile stood and followed them, walking normally. When she returned to her hotel in Ljubuški, the other members of her group told Basile she seemed like a different person. During the night, Basile discovered that she was no longer incontinent; by morning she was able to see with her right eye. That afternoon, in thanksgiving, Basile walked barefoot from Ljubuški to Medjugorje, a distance of six miles, and climbed Podbrdo. By the time she returned home, every sign of her illness had disappeared.

Reading through the other cases, I could not help but notice how many of them involved either MS or some other disease that attacked the nervous system. Difficult to diagnose and impossible to cure, such illnesses also are remarkably resistant to scientific study, making it very difficult to prove that a healing has been miraculous. The most famous person to claim she had been healed by the Madonna of Medjugorje was entertainer Lola Falana, who, like Diana Basile, had been diagnosed with multiple sclerosis. In 1989, Falana was living in Las Vegas, confined to either her bed or a wheelchair. Watching television one day, she began to flip through the channels, stopping on a religious station that was showing a documentary about Medjugorie. In her own words, "When the television showed the crowd of pilgrims which ascend the Hill of Apparitions, I experienced a great desire to go there, to walk with them, but my legs were inert, dead. Then, with tears in my eyes, I prayed to the Blessed Mother to heal me, promising Her that if one day I would be able to walk again, I would go there." Within a month, all the symptoms of Falana's illness had disappeared, and, as promised, she came to Medjugorje, announcing upon her arrival that she would devote the rest of her life to witnessing her faith.

Many of the cases in the files at Medjugorje involved injuries and diseases more suitable to scientific certification. At least two of those who claimed miraculous healings were themselves medical doctors. One was a general practitioner from the Philippines whose breast cancer had only recently metastasized; when she came to Medjugorje, she reported receiving a spiritual healing at the twelfth and thirteenth stations of the cross on Križevac; by the time she reached her home in Cebu, all traces of her cancer had disappeared. The other was an Italian pediatrician with an ulcerated colon that had abscessed into a life-threatening fistula. Two resections of the doctor's colon had failed to stop the seepage of intestinal contents into his bloodstream, and during the fall of 1984, the man's family came to Medjugorje to pray for a cure. For the first time in years, he also prayed, the doctor said, promising the Virgin that if he were healed he would go to Medjugorje in person. Overnight, according to both the patient and the physician who was treating him, the man's fistula closed.

A case I found especially difficult to dismiss involved Charlene Vance, a woman from New Orleans. In 1986 on Halloween, Vance had thrown a party at her home on the north shore of Lake Pontchartrain; it included a hayride. As the group was riding in a wagon pulled by a tractor, they noticed that a barn had caught fire. The driver of the tractor sped up, but not fast enough for Charlene Vance, who jumped out of the wagon to race ahead, only to be pulled under the wheels and dragged twenty feet. The other riders screamed at the driver to stop, but the panicked man instead put the tractor in reverse and ran over Vance's leg. The tibia and fibula each were broken in two places. Far worse was Vance's ankle, which had been crushed to a pulp. She had no firm bone left in the ankle to which they might attach a rod or pin, doctors told her; even if her leg bones healed properly, she would walk with a severe limp for the rest of her life.

Though not a Catholic, the despondent Vance had been persuaded by a friend to join a pilgrimage to Medjugorje. Her doctor objected, but in the end agreed to equip Vance with a special heavy-duty cast that would give her the support her ankle couldn't. The trip was miserable, and she felt even worse after arriving in Medjugorje, recalled Vance, who found the village terrifying. On her first day there she created an enormous scene outside the church, shouting, "I hate this place." There was no escape, however, and out of boredom Vance agreed to join her friends on a hike up Podbrdo. The heat was terrible; her leg began to swell, and huge blisters formed under her cast. Her friends were relentless, though, and somehow managed to convince Vance to try Križevac the next day. At the fourth station of the cross, she was approached by a monk in a white habit, who began to tell her about someone named Therese Newman, a German stigmatic apparently well known to European Catholics. His rosary had been placed on the stigma of Therese Newman's right hand, the monk said, as he took the beads from his pocket and touched Vance's forehead and leg with them.

She was moved in some mysterious way, Vance said, and spent the entire night at the summit of Križevac, praying. As she descended the mountain the next morning, she noticed that the pain in her ankle was gone, but assumed this had resulted from the peace that had come over her during the night. One day after returning to New Orleans, she went to her doctor to have the cast removed and have her ankle x-rayed. The X rays showed that the bones in her ankle had been completely restored. Her flabbergasted doctor warned her she would need crutches for a while, because the muscles around her ankle were badly atrophied. Vance responded by jumping off the examining table and walking across the room. Almost a year later Charlene Vance purchased a book about the life of Therese Newman and discovered all that she had in common with the German woman: Both had been born on April 8, both had suffered severe leg injuries while trying to put out a barn fire, and both had been miraculously healed one year later.

It was another American, however, a woman named Rita Klaus, whose healing had become the most widely publicized of all those associated with the alleged apparitions in Medjugorje. The media attention given Klaus perhaps had less to do with her nationality than with the fact that she was a former nun, one who had fallen from the faith nearly three decades earlier. Even before arriving in Medjugorje, I knew a good deal about the case: A few days before leaving home, I had received an envelope with a return address I did not recognize, from a person I had never met; inside was a seven-year-old article clipped from the *Pittsburgh Press* that chronicled Klaus's recovery in considerable detail. I read it on the plane to Rome.

Her name had been Rita McLaughlin thirty years earlier, when she had rejected religion in favor of science and left the convent to enroll in college as a biology major. She was diagnosed with multiple sclerosis not long after her graduation, and because of her disease had been unable to find a teaching job. The young woman eventually obtained a position in western Pennsylvania, but could pass her physical examination only by concocting the story that she had been stricken with polio as a teenager, so as to explain her muscle weakness. She married a fellow atheist and bore the first of their three children. The oldest child was just a few months old when its mother lost her grip and dropped the infant. Rita's disease continued to progress. The degree of her physical debilitation was what made the Klaus case so compelling: By 1986, she was suffering not only blurred vision and periodic incontinence, but spent nearly all her waking hours in a wheelchair. She was not a small woman, and it took three people twenty minutes to help her upstairs into her bed at night. As the muscles degenerated, her legs began to warp—inward at the knee, outward at the ankle. She could not even sit in her wheelchair without buckling her lower limbs into steel braces.

According to the *Pittsburgh Press* article, Rita heard about Medjugorje in early 1986, and began praying to the Virgin Mary. On the evening of June 18 that year, she heard a voice she believed to be the Virgin's. A prayer welled up inside her, followed by an electric jolt that ran through her entire body. She awoke the next morning and, for the first time in years, felt sensation in her legs; the feeling increased all day long. During the afternoon, Rita unbuckled the keeper on her right leg brace and discovered that her twisted limb was perfectly straight. A moment later, she took off her left leg brace and stood up. That evening, without assistance, she walked up the stairs to her bedroom. The next morning, she ran down those stairs, then ran back up. Later that day, she walked more than a mile to the home of the friend who first had told her about Medjugorje.

Rita Klaus had seen any number of doctors at an assortment of clinics during the years of her illness, creating a large body of medical documentation. What astounded the succession of doctors who had examined her both before and after her healing was not that her recovery had been total but that it had been immediate. A spontaneous remission of multiple sclerosis was not inconceivable, the physicians agreed, but the degeneration of the muscles in Rita's legs had been so extreme that months of physical therapy would have been required for her to even walk across a room, let alone run up and down stairs.

When I looked through the Rita Klaus file in Medjugorje, I found the remarks of the various physicians who had examined her to be more perplexing than enlightening. One after another, they seemed to conclude that what had occurred was a miracle, and then in the next breath to insist that it couldn't be. One doctor had felt certain that there was a scientific explanation, though he couldn't offer even an implausible theory of what this might be. The same man revealed a moment later that his sister, who suffered from multiple sclerosis, had spent the past seventeen years in a wheelchair. "Tell me how this happened," the doctor told his interviewer, "and I'll use it again."

I closed the file with a sigh and stepped out of the dark room back into the light of day. What does it take, I wondered, to become convinced? I'd never have asked if I'd known that Rita Klaus was in Medjugorje to answer me.

I sat with Father Slavko in a small room just off the parish office, sipping orange soda through a grimace as the priest tried to explain how the Catholic Church could hold that God created everything that exists, while at the same time insisting God did not create evil. "Augustine explains that evil is not a presence but an absence," he said. "It is to good as darkness is to light. What God created was the free will that permits not only men, but also angels and spirits, to refuse the highest good in favor of a lesser good. It was by their choice, Augustine tells us, that God's creatures, on earth and in Heaven, introduced evil into the world."

I had been nodding along as if I understood, but as soon as the priest stopped talking, I began to shake my head. He suppressed a smile. "Someone is waiting outside to speak to you," Slavko said after a long pause.

My heart nearly stopped when he stood up and opened the door. I had no idea who or what to expect. A moment later a large, handsome, white-haired woman stepped into the room. I recognized her at once as Rita Klaus. "I will leave you two alone," Slavko said, and closed the door behind him. Rita sat down in the chair the priest had just vacated and smiled at me kindly. There was an urgency in her eyes, though, that caused me to hold my breath. I assumed this woman wanted to tell me of her healing, and was about to say that I had read her story when she leaned forward, laid one hand across the top of mine, and said, "Satan exists." I gasped slightly. "The evil inside you comes from temptation," she added a moment later. "You have to make a decision, either for the good or for the bad. So the evil *is* inside us, as you believe, but it's also out there, and believe me, it is very real and very pervasive. The best thing the Devil can do is convince you that he doesn't exist, because if he doesn't exist, we don't have any responsibility."

I still hadn't said a word, half-wondering if this woman before me was a hallucination. Yet she appeared so steady and so sure. "Wherever God is present, good is present," she continued, "and wherever good is present, evil also is present. That comes from the very basis of existence. Even in science, you have positive and negative charges." I managed to nod.

"God created the Devil as an angel of light," she explained. "He also created freedom of choice, and the Devil made a very bad choice. It came from pride. Pride is the root of all sins. It's the very essence." She smiled again. "You know a lot about pride. But we're all guilty of it. That's why we needed the Savior. We do wrong because it looks good.

"Let me tell you my story. I don't want to scare you, but I think you need to hear." Rita had such a grip on me that I would have listened until I fainted from exhaustion. "Now, my story really starts after my healing," she said, "but I'm going to back up anyway, because I want you to understand that my spiritual healing came first, about five years earlier, and was much more significant. A friend of mine called and asked if I'd go to a healing service in the neighboring parish. I didn't want to go. I said, 'I don't believe in it.' I thought of it all as so medieval and out there: 'Healings don't happen anymore. I'm a scientist, a trained biologist, and I don't believe in any religion.'

"She called me several times, and each time I got angrier. This is an educated woman. I wanted to know how she could believe in such nonsense. She asked, 'Have you ever seen him on TV?' The priest who was conducting the service, she meant. And I told her my brother, who's an investigative reporter on TV, exposed these charlatans all the time. How these people are planted in the audience and the whole thing was a fraud. My husband happened to be listening to this last conversation. And he asked me, 'Why are you acting like this? I want you to go.' Now, my husband isn't Catholic, and he isn't religious. I said, 'Are you serious?' And he told me what I was becoming, how nasty and ornery I was: 'Even our own children are afraid to talk to you, because you're always so angry about what's happened to you.' I said, 'How do you think I feel?' We went back and forth, and finally I said, 'Okay, I'll go.' Still very defiant. I asked my friend, 'When is this so-called healing?' She said, 'After the Mass.' I said, 'Okay, but I'm not going to make a spectacle of myself, dragging myself up on the stage on my crutches.'

"That day the church was packed; everybody who had a pimple on his nose was there to get healed, and I was ha-haing about it all. They crammed me into this pew with everybody else, and put my crutches on the floor. All these priests are walking up the aisle, and everyone is standing up to say the Our Father. So I tried to stand up. I had braces that when I stood up, they would lock my legs into a stiff position. That was the only way I could walk, using crutches. So I tried to stand and the braces locked. I grabbed the back of the pew in front of me, and all that did was make me start to slide under the pew. People were grabbing me, pulling me up, trying to get me back on my feet. Talk about making a spectacle of yourself.

"I just wanted out of there, but this priest grabs me from behind and starts pushing me up to the altar. I can't get away, because he's got me in this bear hug. I was so angry. 'How dare you touch me without my permission?' I was red-faced, but the priest was praying and so were all these other priests, and they were coming up and putting their hands all over me. I was just mortified.

"Then all of a sudden something happened. It was like I wasn't there. Everybody was gone. There was just white light all around me. And I felt so incredibly loved. I can't describe to you what it was like. I felt such peace and I was absolutely loved and nothing else seemed to matter. Suddenly I found myself praying. Saying that it was okay, that whatever God wanted was right. There was no physical change, but I was healed on the inside. I literally went home a different person. I was someone who had been a nun, but I had never been truly religious. Now, though, I was.

"Physically, I actually got much worse over the next five years. I couldn't even walk with crutches anymore. But I never asked God for a healing. One day, though, I was just so tired of it all, thinking, 'When will this end?' And then I heard a voice say, 'Just ask.' I knew as soon as I heard it that the voice was the Blessed Mother's. So I asked, and within the next twenty-four hours I was healed, healed completely, as if nothing had ever been wrong with me.

"People think that after you have a healing, everything is wonderful. And it is wonderful. But when God allows something very good to happen to you, it's for a reason, and there's a responsibility that goes with that. So my life didn't get easier after I was healed, it got more difficult. After my healing, I got so much attention that I couldn't go anywhere. I'd have people all around me if I just tried to go to the grocery store. This one girl actually passed out when she saw me walk for the first time, just keeled over in a dead faint. That's the kind of effect it had on people.

"My husband, though, he was scared. He didn't know why, didn't know what to do with it. He wondered if it was permanent: 'Is she going to wake up tomorrow and she'll be sick again? If we don't act just perfect, is God going to take it away?'

"So here is where the story I want to tell you really starts, about a year after my physical healing, one night when we were in bed. I was asleep and I woke up feeling this terrible pressure on my arm. It was my husband. He was practically cutting off the circulation, he was squeezing so hard. And he was breathing really strangely. Gasping. Desperate. I said, 'Ron, what's the matter?' No answer. So I turned on the lights and the sight of him terrified me. His eyeballs were literally coming out of his head. It was like he had seen something so horrible that he was exploding from inside. He kept gasping, like it was getting more and more difficult to breathe. And so I just started to pray, begging God to save him. After about five minutes he just jumped out of bed and rushed into the bathroom.

"He stood in front of the mirror, absolutely gray. I wanted to call the doctor, but he said, 'No, just give me a few minutes.' He was still breathing very hoarse, and had a hard time talking. Finally he said, 'You aren't going to believe me if I tell you what happened.' I said, 'Yes, I will. Tell me.'

"He said, 'I woke up and I felt a terrible pressure on my chest. I thought I was having a heart attack, and then I opened my eyes. And there was a huge black dog sitting on my chest, with red eyes, like fire.' He said, 'This wasn't a dream. Believe me, I was not sleeping. I was awake. I've never been more wide awake in my life.' He said, 'I've never felt afraid like that in my life. Never.' He said, 'Did you pray for me?' And I said, 'Yes.' He said, 'It seemed like forever.'

"Then the next night, the same thing again. And the next night. The fourth night, he refused to go to bed. He said he just wasn't going to fall asleep. I couldn't understand what was happening. I kept praying, but I thought it might be all the stress of the attention and the change and being afraid I would get sick again. The only thing was he said as soon as I started to pray, he could feel it leaving.

"So I called a priest who's a good friend of mine and told him what had happened. He said, 'When you go to bed, put holy water all around the mattress. I'll get you some.' But it took almost a week before my husband would come back upstairs to go to bed. He stayed on the couch, but whenever he fell asleep, it happened again.

"My husband finally said, 'I know what it is. It is the Devil. He really exists. I doubted. I doubted everything. I even doubted your healing. But now I don't doubt anything. Because what else could possibly make the Devil so angry?' My husband said he thought the Devil was trying to use him against me. The truly amazing thing was that as soon as my husband accepted that it was Satan, Satan left him alone. He didn't go away, though—he started on my children. My youngest, Ellen, who was then seven years old, told me, 'Mommy, there's this strange dog that runs down the steps after me.' I thought it was our dog, Matty, but she said, 'No, it's not Matty. It's a big dog. And it's got red eyes.'

"We had been very careful never to tell the children about any of this, because we were not going to frighten them. I questioned my daughter about when she saw this dog and where she saw it. She said, 'Sometimes I see it staring at me from the other room.' And she says, 'When that dog's in there, Matty won't go in.' And Matty *was* acting strange, growling and whimpering.

"This was all happening in the last week of October of 1992. At this time I was getting ready to go to Boston to work on my book. People had asked me and asked me, 'Please write your story. You can't talk to everybody.' Finally I said, 'Okay, the next publisher that calls, I'll say yes.' So I did. I put as much as I could on tape, but then I was supposed to go to Boston and start working with the editor.

"That week was Halloween, and my two oldest girls wanted a party on the Saturday before. I said okay, but one of the girls they invited brought a Ouija board. My girls sneaked it upstairs, because they knew I wouldn't allow it in the house. They also took this oil candle of mine up with them, one of those things with a glass globe. They turned off all the lights and were asking questions like 'Who am I going to marry? How many kids am I going to have?'

"But then my daughter Ellen, who is very bright, asked, 'Am I going to have a happy life?' And she put the pointer down and it started to move all by itself. First it went over and touched 'Yes,' then it swung back and touched 'No.' They were all, 'Whoaaa.' Not touching it. Finally my daughter asked, 'Who are you?' And it went over to the question mark. So they got an idea. They picked the pointer up and used a piece of masking tape to attach a pencil. And then they put it down on top of a blank sheet of paper. And then they said, 'Identify yourself.' And the pointer started to move again. They thought it was writing, but it was drawing. And then all of a sudden, the oil candle exploded—flame shot straight up into the air, until it actually burned the ceiling. And the kids ran downstairs screaming, every one of them. We heard this absolutely terrified screaming, and then this thundering down the stairs, and the front door opening, and all this shrieking as they ran outside. We thought they were just having a good time, but then we heard crying and sobbing.

"So we went out the front door, and they were all standing in the front yard. I said, 'What did you do, scare yourselves with ghost stories?' I told them to come in, but they wouldn't. My daughters told me, 'Mommy, don't go upstairs.' Finally I coaxed them all back into the house, but they were still crying and shaking. After a while they told me what happened, but it came out very broken. My husband tried to convince them they were just imagining it. Finally Ellen said, 'I know what. Go up and get the piece of paper off the Ouija board.' My husband went up alone, and came back down with the Ouija board and the pointer and the paper. And he said, 'Is this what scared you kids? Who drew this?' And they said, 'Drew? Isn't there a name on it?' And Ron said, 'No, there's a picture on here. But it's very faint.' So we turned on the lamp and held it under the light and could see it clearly. It was a picture of Satan, but not the Satan a kid would draw. This thing was so elaborate: Beard, horns, a figure of a man sitting on a huge rock, legs crossed, with cloven hooves and the most horrible grin on his face.

"Ron took the Ouija boad and the pointer and the paper outside, and burned everything in their presence. My daughters' friends were still in hysterics, though. And they called their parents and asked them to pick them up. They said, 'We're not spending the night here. This is a weird house. And we think your mom is really weird too.' They left in tears, and my daughters were in tears.

"The next couple of days were sheer hell. This thing was *in* the house. We all slept downstairs on the couches. The next night, two A.M., we hear this huge thud, this bang so loud it seemed impossible. And then this crying. Ron goes in and finds our daughter Heidi, who was fifteen then, pressed up against the wall, unable to move. Heidi said, 'Mom, this thing. First it was in the doorway. And it just kept looking at me.' I said, 'Was it the dog again?' And she said, 'No, this was like a man, but not.' She said it was dark, and had red eyes like the dog, but it was a person. She said, 'I was so scared I couldn't even scream. Then it came over to the bed and it climbed on my chest. And it started saying really awful words, but I didn't know what they meant.' My daughter said, 'Then he told me he was going to bury my soul in Hell.' Heidi said she was able to speak to him without using her voice. And she told him, 'I don't want to go to Hell.' And he said, 'When I'm finished with you, you'll want to go to Hell.' She said, 'Then he picked me up by my heels and swung me around the room and threw me against the wall.' And she was hurt, hurt bad.

"I thought, 'This can't be happening.' It was like out of the Middle Ages. I got on the phone to my priest. And he kind of pooh-poohed it at first: 'Why don't you just downplay it for now, and I'm sure it will stop.'

So I tried that. The next night, though, it was the same type of stuff again. So I called Father Glenn and I said, 'I really need some help.' He came out and questioned the girls. Then Ron told him about his experience. And Father Glenn said, 'I believe.' Then he asked, 'What are you doing that is upsetting Satan?' I said, 'I'm supposed to go to Boston to work on the book.' He said, 'That's why this is happening!' He said, 'You need to make Satan understand that you can't be scared off. Once he understands that, he'll leave you alone.'

"My husband told me, 'You have to go do the book.' So I went, with a lot of trepidation and after a great deal of praying to Jesus to see us through. I left Father Glenn at the house, and we put St. Benedict's medals everywhere. We even custom-made slips for the mattresses and stuck the medals inside those. My husband had thought this sort of stuff was pure superstition, but now he was all for it.

"I got to Boston and then up the Cape, where my editor lives. I called home and they said everything was peaceful. From that day, we've never had any problems. The only bad outcome is that the two girls who were there that night both went and told everybody. So we had all these people gossiping. Even teachers at their public school told my daughters, 'You know, your mom's probably not all right. We've heard stories about what happened at your house. Does your mom have psychic abilities?' What can you say? We live with it."

I had listened for more than an hour without saying a word. For most of that time I was shivering uncontrollably, the muscles in my back clenched so tight that they ached for days afterwards. I knew that Rita Klaus traveled throughout the U.S. speaking to Catholic groups, and assumed she had given this testimony on numerous occasions. "No, never," she said. "This is the first time. My confessor said I shouldn't. But Father Slavko is my spiritual director, so when I came here and he said to talk to you, I felt I should. He said, 'It's not a coincidence that you're here at the same time that Randall is here.'"

She studied me for a few moments with a very tender expression. "You're wearing a medal," she said finally. "What is it?" I pulled the object out of my shirt. It was a religious medal that my mother had given me years ago, the only object of its kind that had ever been in our family; more than fifty years earlier, my mother's eldest sister had pressed it into her hand at the hospital before dying at the age of sixteen. I'd kept the thing in a box for years. Shortly before my flight to Rome, I had removed it from storage and placed it around my neck. I had no idea why I'd done this, I told Rita, then admitted that I didn't even know what kind of medal it was.

"It's a scapular," she informed me. "The first one was given to St. Simon by Our Lady when She appeared to him in the thirteenth century. Those who wear it now do so to identify themselves as Mary's people. It's supposed to provide protection from death and evil."

I stood up, suddenly ready to leave. She stood too, stepped forward, and gave me a hug. "Our Lady has brought you here for a purpose, Randall," she told me. "I'll pray that you find strength and courage."

CHAPTER TWELVE

By 1990, the strangest and perhaps most dubious quality of the apparitions in Medjugorje, at least in the opinion of those assigned to investigate them, was how long they had gone on. During the past nine years, more than three thousand apparitions had been reported by the six Bosnian Croat seers, compared to a total of twenty-four at Lourdes and Fátima combined. Yet, among the priests of the parish, there was a sense of constant change and continuous adaptation. The Franciscans, for example, had consented to at least one of the decrees issued by Bishop Žanić at the open-air Mass in 1987, promising that the seers no longer would meet in the rectory for their daily apparitions. Instead, the group gathered in the choir loft of St. James's each afternoon before evening Mass (no one could prevent the children from coming to church to pray, the friars explained). Nearly everyone in Medjugorje agreed that what was intended by the bishop as a punishment had turned out to be a great improvement: The crowds of pilgrims who once clamored for admission to the tiny apparition room now sat in church and prayed the Rosary.

It was during this period that villagers and visitors alike began to remark upon the change in Vicka. The once husky farm girl had taken on a distinctly emaciated look; "gaunt" and "fragile" were the words most often used to describe her. Even more striking was that the vivacious and outspoken young woman had become increasingly deliberate—at times even labored—in both movement and manner, climbing the stairs to the choir loft in short, mincing steps, then speaking in what many disappointed observers called a monotone. Vicka had dropped out of the Textile School in Mostar, and was reported to once again be working with her family in the fields. However, the young woman's neighbors said they rarely saw her outdoors anymore.

It was her confessor, Father Bubalo, who eventually revealed that Vicka had been suffering terrible headaches and frequent blackouts, falling into a state of unconsciousness for hours at a time. "Comatose" was the word used by those who attempted, unsuccessfully, to wake her. Early in 1988, tearful family members reported that she was unconscious for as many as sixteen hours a day, often waking early each evening just before her apparition, then afterwards lapsing at once back into her coma. During her increasingly abbreviated waking periods, Vicka would offer no explanation for her condition. When her mother pleaded with her to ask the Virgin for a healing, Vicka only shook her head and said, "Many souls benefit from this." Finally, Vicka confided to several priests (among them the pope's confidant, Archbishop Hnilica) that her illness was part of an "assignment" she had accepted from the Virgin. Though she would not divulge the nature of her duty, she did say that she would be required to make certain sacrifices; among these would be a period of fifty days without an apparition.

For the first time since June 1981, Vicka's neighbors whispered that she was possessed. Such gossip was fueled by her behavior that winter, when Medjugorje was visited by an American boy who was dying of AIDS. This was at a time when even most Americans were uncertain and anxious about how the disease could be transmitted; in Yugoslavia, the spread of the AIDS virus was a subject fraught with frightening rumors and morbid superstitions. Even members of her own family were disturbed when the dying boy came to visit Vicka and she awakened at once to greet him. The boy asked for a kiss, and she promptly complied, placing her lips directly on his. Shocked and alarmed, several neighbors warned the young woman that she might now have AIDS herself. Vicka did little to reassure them, dismissing such concerns with a wave of her hand.

In February 1988, Vicka at last agreed to a medical examination. Doctors in Zagreb took X rays that showed a small cyst exactly at the point where the brain and its stem meet. However, the cyst was too tiny to account for Vicka's periods of unconsciousness, doctors said. Furthermore, its location made removal—or, for that matter, even a biopsy—impossible.

Two weeks later a pair of priests assigned to the Commission of Inquiry formed by the Yugoslav Bishops' Conference arrived in Medjugorje to ask Vicka if it was true that she knew the date when her suffering would cease. Yes, she replied. Would she be willing to write that date on a piece of paper and place it in a sealed envelope? the priests asked. That would be permissible, said Vicka, who then wrote brief notes on two pieces of paper and placed them in separate envelopes, one to be kept by the Commission of Inquiry, the other by the Franciscans in Medjugorje.

One month after this, Vicka confided the nature of her "assignment" to Father Bubalo: Following their visit to Purgatory, the Virgin had said that many souls were stranded there without anyone on earth to pray for them, and "invited me to suffer for these abandoned souls." Since accepting this assignment, Vicka explained, during what appeared to be periods of unconsciousness, she had been "traveling" with the Virgin.

Just days later, on the basis of these statements and a set of symptoms that seemed to have no clear basis, an Italian doctor assigned by the ARPA medical association to investigate the seers of Medjugorje diagnosed Vicka's condition as one of "hysterical conversion." Two of the doctor's colleagues, an Austrian and a Pole, signed the diagnosis, but the three were confronted by more than twenty of their peers at a meeting in Milan on March 25. The reports of assorted psychologists and psychiatrists who had examined Vicka at greater length (only one of the three doctors who said she was hysterical had spent even a few minutes with her) and had found her in good mental health were deemed to be more reliable, and the ARPA panel voted overwhelmingly to reject the diagnosis of the Italian doctor and his two associates.

The neurologist from Split who headed the scientific section of the Yugoslav Bishops' Commission of Inquiry announced that he would abide by the diagnosis of hysteria, but only if the three doctors who had signed it went back to Medjugorje and examined Vicka more thoroughly. They agreed, and one week later arrived in the village to spend several hours interviewing her in the rectory at St. James's. Immediately afterwards, all three signed a document stating that she was in good physical and mental health, free from any form of pathology.

Vicka's crippling headaches and long periods of unconsciousness continued. Then on Sunday, September 18, she informed those who had received the two sealed envelopes back in February that she wanted them opened in one week. The bishop of Banja Luka (appointed to preside over the Commission of Inquiry) arrived in Medjugorje on September 25 accompanied by three priests who were to serve as witnesses. In their presence, both envelopes were opened and two identical letters were removed. The purpose of her illness, Vicka had written, was the salvation of souls; the Virgin had promised that her sacrifice would be completed on September 25, 1988, and that on this date her suffering would cease. Upon reading the letters, the bishop of Banja Luka asked that she submit to another medical examination: X rays taken a few days later showed that the cyst at the base of her brain was gone. The seer said only that she no longer felt ill and had suffered neither headaches nor black-outs since September 25.

The people of her village, however, would report that they had noticed an indelible change in Vicka's personality: The tart-tongued irascibility that had been her hallmark was gone. Though not nearly so subdued as she had been during her illness, she was now much more serene and soft-spoken. When an interviewer from Rome arrived in the village to ask what purpose she was serving, she replied: "We are the mouthpieces for the salvation of all. My role is to be a witness for the words of the Madonna, and to receive the pilgrims who come to my home. It is the vocation of my life."

While Vicka appeared to be choosing the life of a secular nun, Ivanka had become the first of the Medjugorje visionaries to marry and start a family. Her husband was a local man, Branko Elez, with whom she had been involved before the apparitions began. Nevertheless, many in the village were shocked and disappointed by the announcement of her wedding: Both Bernadette Soubirous and Lucia dos Santos had entered convents; and for these neighbors, it was inconceivable that Ivanka could maintain both a spiritual dialogue with the Holy Virgin and a sexual re-lationship with her husband.

Ivanka acknowledged that the Blessed Mother had said She would "very much like" for all six visionaries to become priests or nuns; at the same time, the Virgin had added, as always, "That is for you to choose." The couple had tested themselves with separations of as long as a month at a time, Ivanka admitted when she announced her engagement, yet she and Branko still were drawn to each other. At that time, she said she would delay her wedding until after her annual apparition in June, and proceed with the marriage only if she received the Madonna's blessing. That ap-parently was forthcoming; though Ivanka would not reveal what words were exchanged, she emerged from the apparition in a "happy and light-hearted mood," as one observer put it, and said she now felt free to marry. All five of the other seers were in attendance at Ivanka's wedding on De-cember 28, 1986, the Feast of the Holy Family. Afterwards, they joined in reminding their neighbors that marriage was a sacrament, not a sin.

Ten months after the marriage, Ivanka gave birth to a daughter, Krystina. Already the most secluded of the visionaries, she withdrew ever deeper into her private life, moving to a house that was more than a mile from the neighborhood where the other seers maintained their homes, and avoiding contact with the pilgrims whenever she could. Ivanka was upset by any form of "prying," including the release of the fact that she had fasted on bread and water during the entire forty days of Lent in 1988.

Jakov also shied away from the pilgrims, though he was easier to find, having accepted a job in the Franciscan bookstore behind the church. For some in the village, it was a scandal even greater than Ivanka's marriage when Jakov left the bookstore and tripled his income by signing on with one of the local tourist agencies, which used him mainly as a drawing card. He stayed in the job only a few months before admitting it had been a mistake and returning to the bookstore.

In 1988, Ivan had become the first of the Medjugorje visionaries to visit the United States. Outfitted in Levi's and Reeboks, the young man amused his hosts with what he chose to partake of American popular culture: Traveling by car, he tuned the radio to country and western stations; in hotel rooms, the TV shows he selected nearly all featured televangelists, who fascinated him. In Chicago, Ivan accepted courtside seats at a Bulls game, and had his picture taken shaking hands with Michael Jordan, but showed no interest when offered a print of the photograph. Ivan's last stop in the U.S. had been Los Angeles, where he astonished his hosts by refusing their invitation to visit Disneyland. "Real people are important to me," he explained, "not mechanical toys or fantasies." He returned home just in time to join the other seers in a nine-day novena before Christmas. Asked about his plans for the future, he said that, as an eldest son, he had an obligation to continue working with his family in the fields. A pilgrim group that inquired about his "philosophy of life" was insulted by Ivan's gruff reply: "People do not need philosophy; they need to live a simple life."

It was shy Marija who emerged as the most unexpected source of sensation and controversy among the seers. Tall and thin, from a family so poor that as a child she had suffered malnutrition, she was perhaps the most reserved of the visionaries during the early days of the apparitions. Yet by the time she reached her early twenties, Marija had become a poised and powerful presence; all the priests, Slavko included, agreed that she had the most intense "prayer life" of all six seers.

Marija increasingly went her own way. For instance, she was the only one of the visionaries who chose not to recite the Rosary when they gathered in the church choir loft to prepare for their evening apparition, explaining that she preferred to read verses from the Bible, then meditate upon them in silence. Some found it disarming, but many were jarred by her habit of describing the most fantastic experiences as if they were not the least bit unusual. All the seers said that the Virgin came to them each Christmas with the baby Jesus in Her arms, swaddled and largely hidden from view. It was Marija alone, though, who reported that one Christmas, she and the others had seen the infant raise His hand from the blanket that wrapped Him and begin to play with the Madonna's veil. Moments later the baby shyly poked His head over the veil, looked straight at the group of them, then ducked back behind His blanket. The child did it twice more, said Marija, before "we realized little baby Jesus was playing peekaboo with us."

In spite of those who rolled their eyes at such tales, Marija was by the late 1980s perhaps the most admired of all the Medjugorje visionaries, and her imprimatur was an enormous boost to the "community of prayer" that had been founded by Father Vlasić just outside Parma, Italy. Vlasić, banned by Bishop Žanić from preaching in Medjugorje, had withdrawn to a monastary near Parma, where he spent a year as a hermit. During this time, the priest prevailed upon the seers to ask the Virgin, on his behalf, "What can I do to serve you, in Medjugorje and in my parish?" The answers the six returned with seemed to discourage him from forming the special and separate prayer community he envisioned, but in February 1988 he did it anyway, bringing together fourteen young people of both sexes for a five-month stay in the Italian countryside, near the castle of Canossa. In less than two months Father Vlasić sent out a letter entitled "An Appeal in the Marian Year" that was designed both to announce his new group and to obtain support for it. "The community wishes to be family, in the example of the first Christian community," he wrote, and would be characterized by "poverty, purity, and obedience." The only activity would be "perpetual prayer, perpetual adoration, eternal love in a wilderness without contact with the external world."

Attached to this letter was a "testimony" from Marija (who had joined the community shortly after its inception), expressing her support for the project. The young woman's friends and family in Medjugorje were distraught over her compliance, wary of the much-loved priest's "ambitions." From the moment of his arrival in Medjugorje, he had been a fount of passion fevers and purpled imagery; when he shouted from the altar of St. James's, "Heaven has been opened to us," people in the pews actually swooned. Father Vlasić's tendency to excess, however, gave pause to the cooler heads of the village. A good many were grateful for the balance provided by Father Slavko, whose reflections had always been more measured.

The two priests had worked well in tandem, and remained dear to each other, but Slavko could not conceal his apprehensions about what was happening in Italy. Like many in the village, he was discomfited by Vlasić's collaboration with an Austrian nurse named Agnes Heupel. Hers was among Medjugorje's most famous healings. In 1974, at the age of twenty-three, she had been stricken with a paralysis of her right side. While a diagnosis had proved difficult, the spinal lesions and pulmonary tumor that accompanied it were verified in examinations by four separate doctors. She spent most of her days confined to a wheelchair, and for her pain took a combination of cortisone and analgesic medicines that gradually eroded her memory; in time, she was unable to recognize even old acquaintances.

In 1983, Heupel claimed that she had experienced a vision of a church with two towers surrounded by light. She did not recognize the church, she said, until she saw it in a book about Medjugorje given to her by a friend. In May 1986, she made the difficult journey to Yugoslavia. Once in the village, she reported that she felt overcome by an urge to discard the crutches and leg braces she had brought with her from Austria: On May 12, she secured an invitation to sit with the seers during an apparition, and entered the rectory using only a single crutch. During the apparition, she experienced a tremendous peace, Heupel said: Time and space seemed not to dissolve but rather to enlarge; the tiny room in the rectory for her became enormous. After the apparition, she stood like everyone else in the room and began to file out the door. Father Slavko came after her, holding her crutch in one hand and shouting, "You forgot something!" But she knew she was healed, Heupel said, and vowed to climb Podbrdo the next day without assistance. A friend (a nurse) who had accompanied Heupel told her that would be impossible: "Your muscles and your legs have been without exercise for twelve years and will not support you for a hundred meters." In the presence of numerous witnesses, however, Heupel climbed the hill of the apparitions on the following afternoon. She used neither her crutches nor her wheelchair again. Her doctors in Austria reopened their files to support her claim that "an organic and gravely irreversible condition" was completely healed. Enthusiasm in Medjugorje palled, however, when she began reporting regular visions and oracles. Concern became consternation after it was learned that she and Father Vlasić were together in Italy, comparing themselves to St. Clare and St. Francis.

While the "testimony" of Marija attached to Vlasić's letter of April 1988 undoubtedly helped with his fund-raising in Western Europe, it only increased the resolve of Marija's friends in Medjugorje to extricate her from involvement with him. Their efforts got results; on July 5, Marija left Vlasić's community, and six days later published a two-page text stating, "I never asked the Madonna for or received any confirmation for the work undertaken by Father Tomislav and Agnes Heupel. " The earlier "testimony" published under her name, Marija claimed, "does not correspond to the truth."

The seer then disappeared for a period of weeks and was said to be traveling in Western Europe. She returned to Medjugorje that autumn, but was gone again by late November, when she made her first trip to the U.S. This journey would not only restore Marija's reputation but considerably enhance it: She was in America to donate a kidney to her older brother, Andrea, who was within weeks of death if he did not receive a new organ. Doctors at the hospital in Birmingham, Alabama, who would perform the operation told her that because of a slight cardiac weakness, there was a 20 percent chance she would die during surgery, and that Andrea had only a 30 percent chance of surviving. She went forward anyway, and reported afterwards that she had experienced an apparition while under general anesthesia. The surgeon who headed the medical team said only that the young woman had seemed to be smiling during the entire time it had taken to cut her open and remove her kidney.

The transplant was a success for Andrea; Marija recovered in time to celebrate Christmas in Medjugorje.

At the very end of 1987, the six Medjugorje visionaries assembled for the last interview they have given as a group. Even the priest who asked the questions, Father Rupčić, later observed that it was difficult to determine whether they had revealed more by the similarities or by the differences in their answers. They spoke as one when asked if the Madonna still came exactly as She had since the beginning of the apparitions. "First we see the light, then Her." When Rupčić inquired whether the six talked regularly among themselves about the apparitions and the messages, they concurred that they spoke to one another infrequently, mainly because they were pressed for time and such conversations served no purpose.

Marija, Ivan, and Jakov admitted it bothered them that Bishop Žanić had been so negative about the apparitions, while Ivanka and Vicka said they couldn't care less. Throughout the interview, Mirjana answered at greatest length, admitting to Rupčić that she had been "embarrassed and upset" when the bishop first spoke against the apparitions: "At the time I was very young and wanted to see justice triumph, but now I have become indifferent. I only experience the need to pray for him, and nothing else."

It was clear from this interview why Mirjana remained the focus of attention for those who wanted an answer to the question more recently posed in print by René Laurentin: "Where is Medjugorje going?" As Laurentin wrote, "The accomplishment of the Secrets had seemed imminent back in 1984, when Mirjana had prepared the mechanism of their public revelation." Inevitably, those who had been waiting in joyful hope began to grow restive as the months and years passed. Laurentin advised the faithful to remember that any prophecy was but "the flashing of fleeting lights about a future which the prophet himself does not understand." Yet Vicka and Ivan each had said at different times that they knew the exact date and time of the Great Sign's appearance, while Mirjana continued to insist that she knew to the minute when each Secret would be revealed. When Rupčić asked the six seers how much longer the Madonna was going to appear to them, Mirjana promptly replied "as long as all the visionaries have not received all the Secrets." Marija told the priest that she and the others had asked the same question years earlier, and that the Madonna's smiling reply had been "Am I boring you?" When Rupčić rephrased the question, asking if they expected the Madonna to one day stop appearing to them, each of the other five answered that they had no idea. However, Mirjana answered, "I am waiting for the other visionaries to receive the tenth Secret."

Mirjana continued to be the visionary who spoke most often of dire events, and of Satan. In January 1987, she had reported a "special apparition" in which the Virgin issued a message intended for both the village and the world. According to Mirjana, the Madonna wanted to warn people that the Devil was gaining on them: "Whenever I come to you, my Son comes with me, but so does Satan . . . You have permitted, without noticing, his influences on you." Mirjana had been reporting such "special apparitions" since late 1985; most were intended, she said, to help her deal with her fears. In March 1986, Milan Mikulich, the little priest who had arranged for my stay in her home, had asked her why the Virgin appeared to her in difficult moments, and not to the rest of us. "I am not speaking of the ordinary problems of life," she had answered. "My difficult moments stem from the Secrets concerning the future of the world, which Our Lady has revealed to me. At times, I can hardly cope when I seriously think of it. In those moments, Our Lady appears and gives me strength and courage to go on."

In September 1989, Father Mikulich was back in Medjugorje to preside at Mirjana's wedding. The groom was Father Slavko's nephew Marco Soldo, with whom Mirjana had kept company at the University of Sarajevo. The ceremony took place at a hunting club in Čitluk. For many people, this event was no less disturbing than Ivanka's marriage, and considerably more confusing: If the end was near, why was Mirjana starting a family? The question took on an even sharper edge when people learned early in 1990 that Mirjana was pregnant. She never had said the world was going to end, she said then, nor had she suggested that people abandon their lives. She and Marco intended to have as many children as God would give them.

A short time later Father Mikulich had convinced Mirjana to come to Oregon. The intervention of Senator Mark Hatfield was necessary to allow a pregnant Bosnian citizen into the country. On January 30, Mirjana arrived in Portland. Her apparition in Our Lady of Sinj Chapel took place on February 2. The message she reported seemed a rebuke. Even practicing Catholics were "helping Me very little," the Madonna said: So many people seemed not to understand that they could neither come to Heaven nor find earthly happiness except with a pure and humble heart, the Virgin explained.

I had read that Mirjana wept all during this apparition, and as well during her birthday apparition six weeks later, but I was unprepared for the photographs of her face taken during these two events that I saw in Medjugorje. It wasn't the red and swollen rims of her eyes that startled me, or even the way the brilliant blue of her irises had disappeared behind hugely dilated pupils. It was the utterly naked quality of her expression; I'd never seen a face more stripped of self-consciousness. Before looking at these pictures, I had been indulging for days in doubts and theories about Mirjana, counting the ways in which the role she played in Medjugorje might soothe the insecurities or serve the vanities she kept hidden from even herself. Her possession and maintenance of the Secrets, it had occurred to me more than once, was a way one could accumulate a sense of power and importance, yet still be credited with a commitment to service and sacrifice. Or perhaps her visions were a benign form of insanity, a madness that meant well. Beneath all the complex processes of the human psyche, maybe it was as simple as this: Believing is Seeing. When I saw those photographs, however, I knew I was not looking at the expression of an actress or a crazy woman. Something really was happening to Mirjana, and I was going to have to live with knowing at least that much, even though I understood nothing else about it.

I would see that same expression—not in a photograph but in person—less than a week later. I had moved out of Mirjana's three days earlier. She needed the space to accommodate a prayer group of thirty and knew I would not be interested in joining the crowd. Marco, whose personality was much warmer than his wife's, had seemed far more concerned than Mirjana about where I would stay next, and was visibly relieved when I told him that Milona Hapsburg had found me a room next to hers at the Pansion Maja on the road between the church and Cross Mountain. I walked out through the fields to Bijakovići on August 2, to arrange a meeting with Mirjana later in the week. When she opened her front door, I took one look at her and forgot completely why I was there. I had never seen such a change in a person's appearance in so short a time. Her face looked as if someone had removed the bones and enlarged the eyes, but such a desciption was inadequate. Mainly what I saw in Mirjana was a sympathetic tenderness that far exceeded the undefended self I had glimpsed during our conversation in the garden two weeks earlier.

Somehow I got inside the house, and the two of us stood in the vestibule, saying nothing. Mirjana didn't even ask why I had come; she just said hello and stared at me. The suspicion and reproach I'd always sensed in her was entirely absent on this occasion. I felt myself swell with some mysterious emotion, and had a nearly overwhelming urge to put my arms around her. This was in no way a sexual impulse; I wanted to offer comfort, and to be comforted. Eventually I remembered that I was there to set up a meeting for later in the week. Mirjana nodded in a way that made me feel she'd agree to anything I asked. There was another awkward pause. "You must excuse me," she said at last. I knew she wasn't asking me to leave, but went anyway. At the gate, I looked back over my shoulder and saw Mirjana still standing in the open doorway. It wasn't until this moment that I realized the date.

After her birthday apparition during the previous March, Mirjana had reported that henceforth the Virgin would be appearing to her on the second day of each month. She had exhausted all her capacity for coping alone with the burden of the Secrets, she explained to me during one of our earliest conversations: "I began to feel that I would really lose my mind. The knowledge of what will happen to the unbelievers was too much for me to live with. I was sad and frightened all the time. When the Blessed Mother came, She said She knew how difficult it was for me, and would help by appearing to me once each month. It has made my life much easier."

Mirjana and I had spoken at that time about my being present during her apparition on August 2, if I was still in Medjugorje. She warned I would have to pray with her for as long as three hours before the Virgin came and seemed to doubt I was capable of doing so, but did not say I would be unwelcome. How curious, I thought, that I had managed both to forget about the apparition and yet to arrive at her front door less than an hour after it was over.

I felt suddenly exhausted and stopped to rest under the giant fig tree where, most days, Gypsy refugees sat amid their displays of cheap plastic and wooden rosaries, waving to pilgrims who passed by on their way to Podbrdo. The Gypsies were absent on this morning, for some reason. Not for the first time, I wondered if I was ever going to get out of this place. I thought again about my conversation with Mirjana in the garden a couple of weeks earlier, and of the sadness in her voice. That led me to recall René Laurentin's description of Ivanka's apparition during the anniversary celebration in Medjugorje in June 1989; I had read it a few days earlier. He had been sitting just a few feet away, on a couch directly opposite Ivanka, Laurentin recalled, and had watched the young woman's "transparent joy" at the beginning of her apparition become an expression he described at first as "somber," then as "grave." She and the Virgin had spoken again of the fifth Secret, Ivanka explained afterward. The French priest admitted being slightly distracted during Ivanka's ecstasy by the presence of the visionary's nineteen-month-old daughter, Krystina, who became extremely agitated when her mother lost contact with her. Staring into the "inexpressible reflection" of Ivanka's eyes, Krystina called, "Mama! Mama!" again and again, Laurentin observed, hitting her mother on the shoulder several times, then finally kicking Ivanka in the stomach to try to get her attention, all to no avail.

I identified with the child, I realized, not with her mother.

Also in the crowd at Ivanka's during her apparition that day was Dr. Philippe Loron, former head of the Neurology Clinic at La Salpietre Hospital in Paris. Dr. Loron, a Catholic, claimed to be present in the spirit of scientific inquiry. Clearly, he was impressed by what he had witnessed.

Ivanka had not blinked even once as the flashbulbs of assorted cameras went off in her face throughout the apparition, Loron recalled, for him convincing evidence that her state of consciousness was neither pathological nor ordinary. He later would classify Ivanka's ecstasy as sui generis, a diagnostic term that can mean either "unknown" or "misunderstood." Urged by Father Laurentin to review the assorted tests previously conducted on the visionaries, Dr. Loron eventually produced an opinion containing language that supporters of Medjugorje found more encouraging: "This is the first time that medical science has been involved to such an extent in evaluating the phenomenon of ecstasy. And, in the process, what was confirmed in several ways was the moral and psychological integrity of the visionaries."

Despite the enormous backlog of medical studies already conducted, Father Laurentin encouraged the seers to cooperate with further scientific testing. Some of what was being passed off as science, however, made even the most earnest researchers snicker. Perhaps the most ridiculous "study" conducted was one intended to test the claims of those who said their rosaries had turned to gold in Medjugorje. Media reports of such supernatural alchemy had long been a source of embarrassment to the Franciscans, who needed nothing more than their naked eyes to see the obvious. A pair of American scientists, one a physician and the other a chemist, had used an electronic microscope to examine four of the allegedly transformed prayer beads before producing a report that read: "The chains of many rosaries are made of brass. Through use, the silver is worn and takes on the orange color of the underlying copper. There is no change in the chains."

René Laurentin's response to this report raised doubts about his own intellectual credibility; rather than mock the niggling absurdity of such scientific inquiry, the priest instead wondered what purpose it served to debunk those "who have drawn spiritual benefit" from their belief that a miracle had occurred. Father Laurentin failed as well to see any humor in the fruitless efforts of a researcher from Toulouse to take infrared photographs of the Madonna during an apparition in Medjugorje, and actually seemed disappointed at the inability of scientists to detect changes in either the magnetic fields or the levels of radiation around the seers during their ecstasies.

Laurentin perhaps was more justifiably distraught over the reception received by yet another team of doctors from the University of Milan who had arrived in Medjugorje during the summer of 1987, this time to perform what they described as "synchotic tests on the muscular state, the diaphragm and the respiration of the seers before, during and after the apparitions." All but Marija had refused to cooperate. And when Laurentin's collaborator Henri Joyeux returned to Medjugorje three months later, hoping to again film the visionaries during their apparitions, he met a similar rebuff. Joyeux flew to Rome and secured the approval of Cardinal Ratzinger for a plan to transport the seers to France, but only Ivan would make himself available. Laurentin bemoaned the "lost opportunity."

In late 1989, however, all six visionaries chose to cooperate with a team of physicians, psychologists, and sociologists assembled by the Vatican, and spent several weeks being interrogated and tested at a monastary near Split. Though no details were released, the French-Canadian priest who headed the Vatican team offered the final paragraph of his report for publication: "The conclusion we draw is that the visionaries' behavior patterns, both socio-cultural and socio-religious, do not give the least indication of any tendancy to fraud, hysteria or self-deception."

CHAPTER THIRTEEN

My room at the Pansion Maja had not only a private bath but also a little balcony with views of both the cross atop Križevac and the twin steeples of St. James's. Beneath these points of inspiration, the pastoral scene looked in places as if a skyscraper had collapsed on top of it. Under towering arbors of grape and kiwi, assorted goats, chickens, and pigs were grazing, pecking, and slopping among concrete slabs strewn with tangles of rebar that covered them like the vines of a petrified plant. In every direction stood the truncated forms of abandoned construction projects that, from a distance, did not look so different than the bombed-out buildings just down the road in Mostar. This detritus of enterprise that lay moldering amid the agricultural verdure of Medjugorje was a testament to the boom years of the parish economy. These had had begun around 1987, when the Communist Party in Sarajevo issued a short press release that read: "The pilgrimage to Medjugorje is a purely religious phenomenon, not political, thus legal."

Up until that year, the government had sent in teams of undercover agents each June to splatter the church and its environs with politically provocative graffiti; the villagers apprehended twelve of these agents during one anniversary celebration alone. Even as late as December 1986, the secret police had organized a raid on the private home where Vicka and Marija were leading the entire populace of Bijakovići in a Christmas prayer novena. Once it decided to abandon all opposition to the devotions in the Medjugorje parish, the government's commitment to its "program of cooperation" was total. By the autumn of 1988, officials from the municipality of Čitluk were meeting with the Franciscans over lunch in the church rectory to jointly plan not just the organization of pilgrimages but also a system of construction codes for the village. Bootleg businesses had operated for years out of orange plastic kiosks salvaged from the Sarajevo Winter Olympics, in spite of almost daily complaints by the Franciscans; now the government sent in teams of men to remove all the kiosks, because they were blocking traffic. The road into town was widened, and construction began on a new bridge across the Lukoc River. In March 1989, when thirty-two representatives of the French media arrived in Medjugorje to conduct an "inquiry," officials of the state feted them with a sumptuous barbecue of roast sheep, answered questions graciously, and insisted they were open-minded about the authenticity of the apparitions.

By 1989, the Emmanuel prayer group was coordinating a network of 130 boardinghouses: Everyone in the parish who owned land and could borrow money was putting up buildings to house the pilgrims. Buses, taxis, and private cars lined the streets; some days, there were traffic jams that stretched halfway to Ljubuški. More than forty confessional booths stood in the courtyard on the south side of St. James's, now jokingly referred to as "Purgatory" because swarms of bees were drawn to the soft drinks and deodorants of the pilgrims. Between the new bridge and the church, and all along the way beneath Križevac and Podbrdo, the street was lined with restaurants, cafés, and souvenir shops. Early in 1990, the secretary of the Communist Party in Čitluk confirmed that more than one-quarter of all the tourists who visited Yugoslavia listed Medjugorje as their destination.

Not everyone was pleased by the impact of prosperity. Father Zovko, who had not preached in Medjugorje since 1985, made a surprise appearance in the pulpit on January 1, 1990, and stunned parishioners by harshly denouncing them for putting profit above religious practice. The village was "disfigured" by the profusion of souvenir shops, said Zovko: "We must understand that all of this commercialism is against Medjugorje . . . I am truly angry about it." Though he spoke in a softer voice, Father Slavko was no less adamantly opposed to the profiteers, and demanded that they withdraw at least from Križevac and Podbrdo. The shopkeepers, many of them non-Catholics, had the government on their side, however, and remained in place.

On June 25, 1990, the homily of the ninth-anniversary Mass was delivered by Father Leonard Kustić, editor of Croatia's largest Catholic weekly, *Glas Koncila*. He never had truly feared the "ideological materialism" of communism, Father Kustić told the crowd, "for one can respond to its arguments." He was genuinely frightened, however, the priest admitted, by "the practical, more ingratiating materialism" that was being imported from the West, and from the U.S. in particular: As Satan surely understood, seduction was a far more effective method of undermining spirituality than was suppression.

The economic juggernaut appeared unstoppable. By 1991, two million pilgrims per year were expected in Medjugorje. Each day, between two hundred and five hundred written "statements" were submitted to St. James's by pilgrims who said their prayers had been answered. A showbiz patina attached even to the apparitions. Each evening's message from the Madonna was now read by a priest over a public address system. When the seers emerged from the church choir loft, they were met by a blast of flashbulbs and touched repeatedly by pilgrims who seemed to believe they could absorb some supernatural power.

Only Mirjana complained publicly about the pilgrims: "There are some who ask for impossible things. They think that I am the Madonna. They think that I can do everything for them, and do not understand that even the Madonna cannot do anything without God. She too must pray to God." All of them had been offered money by pilgrims, said the seers, who added that the Madonna had forbidden them from accepting so much as a penny. "It would be sacrilege," Mirjana explained.

All around them, though, people were growing rich. The cultivation of tobacco was abandoned, and for the first time in village history, grapes were allowed to rot on the vine. But not even those who warned that money would bring damnation were prepared to be saved by the bloodiest European civil war of the century.

It bothered me more each day that it was easy in Medjugorje to gradually forget about the war, or at least to conceive of it as an event that had ended several years earlier, lingering on in aftermath. Whenever I mentioned this discomfort to my hosts, they looked at me with amazement, unable to fathom a mind that could complain about such a blessing.

The nagging sense that I had cloistered myself in fear and denial persisted. Sometimes I would get out my Michelin map of what had been Yugoslavia and with one hand span the distances between where I sat and the besieged cities to the north: Goražde, Tuzla, Zenica, and, of course, Sarajevo. Not one of them was more than two hours away. Among the Loopers, it was considered unfaithful to dine at Medjugorje's secular bastion, the Café Colombo, but occasionally I did anyway, just to sit with the UN crowd and catch up on news of the war. Word-of-mouth reports were just beginning to filter through the front lines of the massacre that had taken place in a town called Srebenica less than a week after my arrival in Bosnia. As many as ten thousand Muslim men had been slaughtered, it was said, and survivors were telling stories of mass graves and of raped women dangling from the trees where they had hanged themselves.

At least I was less oblivious than most American pilgrims, who arrived in guided groups on air-conditioned buses and seemed to feel no closer to the war than they might have in Winnetka or Woodland Hills. Because I made friends among the locals, I heard a story every few days that reminded me how proximate to the horror I was. Ivan Bencun, the splendid fellow who owned Mira's, had a sister in Sarajevo and said that during this past winter she and her family had been reduced to pulling up their parquet floor one piece at a time, boiling the panels in water to make the stock for a soup, then neatly breaking each little bleached square of wood into kindling for the next morning's fire. One of the priests confided that he had nearly suffered a nervous breakdown after hearing the confessions of more than a dozen nuns who had been gang-raped by the Serbs, held in captivity until they were impregnated, then released with three choices: Give birth to a bastard child fathered by a Serbian rapist, get an abortion, or commit suicide; nearly every one of these women had pleaded for permission to kill herself, the priest said.

Early on in the war, Mirjana announced the Blessed Mother's promise that Medjugorje would be protected. And the parish *had* emerged from a series of Serbian air raids and artillery bombardments virtually unscathed, proving even to impious observers that the apparitions were authentic. For me, the evidence was not so clear. It was true that Medjugorje seemed to have been protected from *outside* aggression throughout the war, sometimes in ways so fantastic that only supernatural intervention could account for them. What happened *inside* the parish was at once more troubling and more inspiring. From the very beginning of the apparitions, the Medjugorje seers had reported the Madonna's tearful pleas for peace, as well as repeated warnings from the Virgin that religious divisions were the work of evil. Such messages were unsettling to the people of the region even in 1981: Beneath the rigid structures and sterile processes of communist rule, blood feuds and murderous vendettas had never stopped festering in Yugoslavia. Tales of the travesties inflicted by this or that invader were passed on from generation to generation, as were the family names of those considered collaborators. Each of the three major ethnic groups considered itself a victim of the others. Claims and counterclaims—especially to the ownership of confiscated lands—nourished hatreds that went back centuries. Even under Tito, violence related to such animosities flared regularly in rural areas, and the Medjugorje parish was no exception. In 1978, just three years before the apparitions began, one of Marija's relatives found her son with his throat slit, shot the man who had done it, then took her own life.

Gangs of armed Croats who called themselves Ustaše had again become active in Bosnia and Hercegovina during the early 1970s. Convinced (correctly) that the Serbs intended to keep control of all the country's political and military institutions, these young men vandalized government buildings, robbed weapons factories, and attacked party officials. Medjugorje had its own Ustaše cell, part of a regional network that included several thousand members. Rival gangs of Serbs who cast themselves as Četniks soon battled the reborn Ustaše for turf. More ominously, the Serb-controlled federal army was entrenching itself on the hillsides above nearly every major city in Bosnia-Hercegovina, digging huge bunkers filled with artillery and mortar shells. By the early 1980s, Bosnia was home to both the greatest density of firearms and the largest military arsenal in all of Yugoslavia—perhaps in all of Europe. Munitions plants and armored-vehicle factories dotted the countryside; hardly a village or town was without its own arms depot.

Soon after Tito's death, it became obvious to citizens of every stripe that his iron will had been all that held Yugoslavia together. The favorite slogan of the dictator's successors only emphasized their weakness: "And after Tito, Tito." Huddled around the dead man's legacy, Yugoslavia's second generation of communist leaders recoiled from any sign of change. Every educated person in the country recognized that they had come to a crossroads where the only real choices were reform or repression.

Hope for Yugoslavia's immediate future ended with the rise of Slobodan Milošović. A manicured thug who spoke English and dressed like the international banker he once had been, Milošović assumed control of the Serbian party in 1987, and within weeks purged the Communist Party leaderships in Kosovo and Macedonia. They saw the sign of the beast on Milošović, it was said in Medjugorje, where all anyone really knew about the Serb leader was that he had been raised in a divided household—his father an Orthodox priest, his mother an ardent communist—and that both parents had committed suicide.

In the spirit of perestroika, Milošović agreed that Yugoslavia's "republics" might hold free multiparty elections during 1990. The first votes were cast that spring in Slovenia and Croatia, where nationalist candidates won overwhelmingly. Croatia's new leader was Franjo Tudjman. Once a Partizan follower of Tito, a fervent Marxist, and at thirty-nine the youngest general in the Yugoslav army's history, Tudjman had undergone a meta-morphosis around 1970, emerging from a period of seclusion at the Zagreb Military Institute as a rampant nationalist. Most infamously, Tudjman had produced a revisionist history of the Jasenovac concentra-tion camp, maintaining that very few Serbs had been killed there, and that anyway, the camp had been run by Jews. Tudjman was celebrated, however, for his leadership of what became known as the "Croatian Spring," a democratic-nationalist movement that welled up in Zagreb during early 1971, only to be swiftly crushed by Tito's security forces. When Tudjman was imprisoned for leading the "uprising," he became Croatia's greatest living hero.

It was the elections held in Bosnia-Hercegovina during November 1990 that most accurately foreshadowed Yugoslavia's future. Bosnia had be-come by far the most diverse of the nation's republics: Muslims were the largest group, but with only 44 percent of the population could not claim an absolute majority. Serbs made up 31 percent of Bosnia's population, but there were another six hundred thousand of them living in Croatia, mostly along the old military frontier still known as the Krajina. Croats represented just 17 percent of Bosnia's total population, but owned a majority in western Hercegovina, where towns like Grude, Duvno, and Čitluk were 99 percent Croat. No less important, western Hercegovina was considered the fountainhead of Croatian national spirit (much as Kosovo was for the Serbs); the first Croatian king had been crowned in the city now known as Duvno, less than an hour's drive from Medjugorje. Western Hercegovina's larger cities were decidedly more mixed than its towns and villages: Capljina's population, for example, was 28 percent Muslim and 13 percent Serb, while Mostar, by far the most important city in Hercegovina, was almost evenly divided, 35 percent Muslim, 34 percent Croat, and 19 percent Serb, along with substantial clusters of Jews, Gypsies, and assorted "others."

The slogans and tactics employed during the elections were alarming. Radovan Karadžić had spoken almost incessantly about something called "Greater Serbia," and regularly quoted Milošović's maxim of "All Serbs in One State." Muslims and Croats watched nervously as young Serb men began to publicly and proudly identify themselves as Četniks, growing beards and donning fur hats with skull-and-crossbone emblems, greet-ing each other in the street with the old royalist salute of a two-fingered victory sign, plus a raised thumb. In bars they could be heard singing the old Četnik war song: "Muslims, you yellow ants, your days are numbered!" For the first time in almost fifty years, Europeans were compelled to meet an argument first put forth in the 1930s by Adolf Hitler: The continent's borders must be redrawn to the frontiers of its races.

The Croats responded with provocations of their own, most notably a law that Tudjman pushed through the parliament in Zagreb, requiring an oath of loyalty to the republic "of the Croatian people." Alija Izebegović's rhetoric appealed to ethnic fears and resentments no less than that of Milošović and Tudjman, but the Muslim leader at least came up with a concept he called "co-habitation," suggesting that Bosnia operate with a rotating collective presidency made up of three Muslims, three Croats, and three Serbs. When Izebegović himself was named as the first "president of the presidency," Serbs and Croats alike began to take direction not from Sarajevo but from Belgrade and Zagreb.

One month after voters went to the polls in Bosnia, election returns from Serbia and Montenegro made Slobodan Milošović the new president of Yugoslavia. Upon taking office in January 1991, Milošović immediately ordered the dissolution of all "Territorial Defense" forces controlled by Yugoslavia's republics, and demanded surrender of their weapons to the Serb-controlled federal army. These orders were defied throughout Slovenia and Croatia, and would be as well in western Hercegovina. Armored units of the federal army made straight for every major military base or arms depot that might tempt the "rebels." One of the largest weapons stockpiles in Bosnia and Hercegovina stood about ten miles south of Medjugorje, near Capljina. The village known throughout Yugoslavia as the country's "Peace Center" was about to become a hub of warfare.

Behind an abandoned bakery in Medjugorje was the headquarters of the Croatian army in Hercegovina. Though it was a secret the soldiers kept very well (I wouldn't find out about it until three years after my return home), I shouldn't have been surprised to discover its location in Medjugorje. After all, the war in the former Yugoslavia could be said to have begun on the tenth anniversary of the apparitions, June 25, 1991, a date deliberately chosen by Franjo Tudjman for Croatia's declaration of independence. Tudjman's speech that day invoked the Virgin's appearances in Medjugorje as "a call to the Croatian people."

None of the visionaries endorsed Tudjman's use of the Madonna, but the only one to object was Mirjana, who stirred considerable discomfort by suggesting that the government in Sarajevo—a government headed by a Muslim—should be accepted. "I am not a nationalist," Mirjana had told me on the first day we met; at the time, I could not appreciate the gravity of this statement.

Nearly ever other Croat in western Hercegovina *was* a nationalist, and that included the people of Medjugorje, for whom the towering obelisk at Surmanci long had been the locus of ethnic strife in the parish. The humiliation of the locals by Serbian communists had continued almost unabated since the monument to those slaughtered at Surmanci was unveiled on April 27, 1973, and each spring brought a new cycle of sabotage and punishment that peaked on the anniversary of the monument's dedication. When April 27 finally arrived, so did several dozen carloads of Serbs, driving in from all over the country to celebrate Partizan heroism and Communist Party loyalty. Loud, drunk, and obscene, they freely cursed the villagers, who were assigned to sweep up after "their guests" if they objected.

Even cynics and hard-core communists would acknowledge that the religious revival inspired by the reported apparitions of the Virgin in Medjugorje had seemed to smooth tensions and ease animosities during the early and mid-1980s, not only in the parish, or even just in western Hercegovina, but all across Yugoslavia. The resurgence of Croatian pride that began around 1988 changed everything. "It was very moving at first," recalled Gabriel Meyer, an American journalist then based in Medjugorje. "People were unfurling the Croatian flag and singing national songs for the first time in fifty years." Croatian sentiments would take on some "increasingly ugly aspects" during late 1990 and early 1991, and Meyer's reporting would itself become an element of the conflict spreading across Yugoslavia. As always, Surmanci was the linchpin of local outrage.

During the summer of 1990, rumors began to spread that a Serbian group from Belgrade was on its way to Surmanci, authorized by the government to excavate the great pit where the bodies of the dead had been buried for nearly half a century. At the time, mass graves from World War II were being dug up all across Yugoslavia. Croatians, Serbs, and Muslims all were doing body counts, to demonstrate what had been done to them by the Ustaše or the Četniks or the Partizans. "Especially on Belgrade television, there was just endless, endless footage of these pits being excavated," said Meyer, "restoking the fires that had lain dormant since the forties."

Meyer's position was a peculiar one, even for a reporter. He was well known to the only American priest in Medjugorje, Father Philip Pavich, who first had met Meyer when, as a young man in his twenties, Meyer

had been traveling around the U.S. to speak on behalf of Catholic Charismatic Renewal. Later, Meyer headed Catholic lay communities in San
Francisco and Phoenix, then moved on to Jerusalem, where he purchased
the American Colony Hotel at Damascus Gate, intending to make it into
a Holy Land base for a group called the Covenant Community. Then
Meyer's missionary fervor began to cool, at the same time as his critical
faculties heated up. Somehow he got the idea that his true calling was jour-
nalism, and it was as a correspondent for the *National Catholic Register* that
he found his way to Medjugorje in 1988. His background as a religious
activist, along with a recommendation from Father Pavich, helped get
Meyer into the Loop. An arrangement was made providing him with an
office in the rectory building, where he would set up a semiofficial information center and serve as a contact for the foreign correspondents who
were finding their way to Medjugorje in increasing numbers.

After he began writing about the rise of Croatian nationalism for an
assortment of secular papers, Meyer's reporting took on what several
priests perceived as an irreverent, even disloyal tone. He nevertheless
continued to hold the friars in high regard. "Those guys, the Hercegovinan
Franciscans, are made out of rock," he later would tell me. "They'd take
on anybody. They're mountain-fighters-slash-priests. But there also was
this certain core belief among them that I should be—instead of an objective reporter—just a mouthpiece for Croatian political mythology,
which was that the apparitions were God's way of validating the suffering of the Croatian people."

When calls to battle began to be heard even in the courtyard outside
St. James's, Meyer accused the Franciscans of subverting the Madonna's
main intention: "The great tragedy, in my view, was not seeing that the
messages were addressed first and foremost to the villagers, then to the
country, and only then to the rest of the world. What the Franciscans
did was help turn the message of the Madonna in Medjugorje into a kind
of vague, general piety about peace directed to everyone, which ignored
the tougher questions of what they were going to do about the divisive
nationalism in their own region. Even among the visionaries, Mirjana was
the only one to point out that the messages had a political dimension:
'Love your Serb brothers, love your Muslim brothers.' My view is that
God was trying to create a place in Medjugorje where these divisions could
be broken down, so that it might become a center for a certain kind of
resistance to what was exploding in the rest of the country. That's not to
say the Franciscans didn't do anything. Slavko could argue, rightly, that

he kept the worst from happening in Medjugorje. When people wanted to unfurl the Croatian flag in church, he wouldn't let them do that. But even he went along with this idea that the apparitions were a grace bestowed on the village for all they had endured, and the militant nationalists were able to take advantage of that."

By August 1990, when the Serbs arrived to exhume the human remains at Surmanci, loudspeakers in the cafés began to alternate religious hymns with long-forbidden Croatian folk songs. The red-and-white checkerboard symbol of Croatian national identity (the same one imprinted upon the Ustaše flag) was painted on rocks and signposts all over the parish, even at the bases of Podbrdo and Križevac. Along with rosaries, crucifixes, and statues of the Virgin, several souvenir shops near the church sold swastikas and black busts of President Tudjman.

The situation was already extremely tense when Meyer reached the obelisk at Surmanci on the afternoon he went there with two translators. The three were immediately surrounded by angry villagers who demanded to know their business. "Finally, the Serb leader came by and kind of rescued us. He said, 'You're with me.' And we went down into the pit together, and I talked to some of the men from the village where the women and children who were killed had been from. It was supercharged. These guys had been drinking for days, and there was a lot of anger, a lot of sadness. This one old man in his eighties sat looking at the piles of skulls and bones lined up, then finally said, 'Now I know where my wife and six kids have been.'"

The people of Medjugorje, including nearly every one of the Franciscans, were furious when they learned that Meyer intended to write an article about the excavation at Surmanci. "The attitude was not only 'If you tell everyone what we did, people will forget that worse has been done to us,'" Meyer said. "It was 'We've suffered enough for what we did. We paid three hundred percent, and some of these other things have been almost completely ignored.' The Franciscans absolutely resisted any connection between the apparitions and Surmanci. They said it was sacrilege to suggest such a thing."

His article on the unearthing of the mass grave at Surmanci would appear in the *National Catholic Register* during the spring of 1991, right around the time Serbian paramilitary units began to stage provocations throughout Croatia that were intended to force intervention by the Yugoslav military. Soon after the Croats declared their independence from Yugoslavia, the ethnic Serbs concentrated in the Krajina declared their independence from Croatia, and called for the protection of the Yugoslav federal army. Heavy fighting broke out around the town of Knin, north of Split, and then in Slavonia, near Vukovar. The 180,000-member, two-thousand-tank federal army moved in at once to "protect" Serbian "irregulars." The Croatians answered by occupying the Jasenovac concentration camp, methodically trashing the government's museums and exhibits, leaving only the huge mounds that marked the mass graves of those killed during World War II. Intervention by the European Union produced a short-lived truce, but within two weeks the Serbs were sending army jets to attack Croat villages near Vukovar, and after that the killing would increase week by bloody week.

CHAPTER FOURTEEN

When I finally went into Mostar, it was in the company of the Jesus-hating humanitarian, Karen, and her assistant, a little Londoner named Andy. Probably the most dangerous part of the trip was the descent through the hills into the Neretva River valley. The road was all curves, worn smooth, coated with oil, and notoriously slick, especially after a rainfall like the one we'd had that morning. Heavy vehicles, such as Karen's old Land Rover, frequently found themselves unable to pull out of a turn or stop a downhill slide. The first Americans to die in Bosnia, a group of UN inspectors, would be lost a few months later when their own Land Rover went over a cliff on this same road. Nearly every one of the stone farmhouses along the Neretva had taken fire, and many were pounded to dust. The river valley, deep and dark green, looked deserted from the road above, and felt haunted when we descended into it. The first humans we encountered were soldiers at the Croatian checkpoint, burly, gruff men in olive uniforms who all kept one hand on the machine guns slung from their shoulders.

We entered Mostar from the west, on the Croatian side. The graffiti-spattered, bullet-riddled apartment buildings with their broken windows and fire-blackened walls reminded me vaguely of the South Bronx, circa 1978, and I said as much to Karen. She smiled and told me, "This is the nice part of town." The buildings grew older and more broken as we approached the center of the city. At the Mostar hospital, the one where Mirjana and the other visionaries had been threatened with commitment back in June 1981, several large trucks were backed up to the ambulance bays. Those were the mobile surgeries, Karen told me; when the bombardment was at its height, the Serbs had targeted the hospital, so Croatian and Muslim doctors conceived the idea of treating their most seriously injured patients in semi trailers, enabling them to move a safe distance from the hospital and continue operating whenever the shelling started.

Approaching the river, within sight of the cathedral, we passed onto a long stretch of road that lay in ruins. None of the structures could actually be called buildings; all that remained amid the heaping piles of bricks and rocks were foundation stones and jagged sections of wall, with an occasional shard of roof attached. At one point, in every direction I looked, all I could see was total destruction. "These were the front lines," Karen said. I had never seen devastation on anything remotely like this scale; the place reverberated with death. Before that moment, I wouldn't have believed anything less than a nuclear explosion could accomplish such perdition.

Four years earlier, this city had been among the loveliest in the country: "The jewel in Yugoslavia's crown," one German writer called it. Mostar was divided by the Neretva, and its Muslim east bank had been perhaps the richest legacy left by the Ottomans in Bosnia, renowned for the serpentine cobbled streets of its fabulous Turkish marketplace. The city's beautiful sixteenth-century mosques had been badly ravaged by the Serbs, who used the same phosphorous bombs to incinerate many of Mostar's other monuments, including the Hotel Neretva, the Muslim baths, and the School of Music. Mostar had long been best known for its Stari Most. For more than four hundred years, the Old Bridge had been regarded as the most inspiring structure in all of Bosnia, a stunningly graceful arch of limestone blocks so artfully assembled that the parapet at the center of the span seemed literally to defy gravity. When the sultan Süleyman the Magnificent was shown the design, he warned that his architect, Hajrudin, would be beheaded if the bridge collapsed. Hajrudin saved his neck by creating a mortar mixed with egg whites to cement the stones, and the bridge had withstood not only four centuries of incessant warfare and countless floods but more than thirty earthquakes. It was gone now—a pile of broken stones submerged in the Neretva. Like so many others in the country, I wanted to believe that the Serbs had done this. But they hadn't; it had been destroyed by the Croats.

Until the summer of 1992, the Croat-Muslim alliance had been the one sign of hope to emerge from the former Yugoslavia. The pinnacle of cooperation between these two sides was reached in late June of that year, when the combined forces of the Croatian and Bosnian armies liberated Mostar. Their joint push not only drove the Serbs out of strongholds on the east bank of the Neretva but chased them deep into the hills. Over the next eight weeks, mass graves were found containing more than two hundred corpses, mostly of Muslims who had been slaughtered by the retreating Serbs.

My friend Jozo Ostojić, the former champion sprinter who wept as he chased little Jakov Čolo and the other seers up Podbrdo on the afternoon of June 26, 1981, had fought in the battle to liberate Mostar. The war story he told me was about being stuck in a hillside bunker under fire from Serb snipers. His terror had been so total that for several minutes he sat sobbing and shaking, wondering if he should shoot himself to avoid being taken alive. He had pulled the crucifix he wore on a chain out of his shirt, Jozo said, and held it tight until he became calm, then noticed immediately that he could tell when the Serbs were reloading and began to move downhill in short sprints from foxhole to foxhole. Halfway to the Croatian line, with his testicles in his throat, as Jozo put it, he dove into the foxhole occupied by a Muslim member of his unit. Several months earlier, this young man had been held down with a gun at his head while his parents were murdered, and his sister raped and abducted. He had no family left, the Muslim said when he joined the unit, and lived now only to kill Serbs. "But it looked as if the Serbs had killed him," Jozo recalled. "He had been shot in the face, and was covered with blood." Jozo helped the man out of the foxhole and the two continued their retreat down the hill. They became separated, though, and Jozo reached the Croatian lines first. By the time the Muslim crawled into sight, he had been hit twice more, below a shoulder blade and behind an ear. Jozo and the others watched the Muslim crawl for some distance, before sprinting out to drag him behind a rock. The Muslim asked the Croatians to look for his sister, then died in their arms.

"He didn't want to kill anymore, but he didn't want to live either," Jozo concluded, avoiding my eyes. He had told me the story almost as if a confession, and even in my ignorance I understood what a stretch it had been for him to so fully acknowledge this young Muslim's humanity. As deeply moved as I was at the time, my sense of communion with Jozo became increasingly difficult to sustain as I learned more about what had happened in Mostar during the months that followed its "liberation." For, in both complexity and depravity, the madness of these events perhaps surpassed anything that came before or after.

During the 1980s, at the same time the reborn Ustaše was expanding in towns like Ljubuški and Grude, an even larger organization of young men had been emerging out of Medjugorje. These were the Križari, or "Crusaders," religious brotherhoods that operated both as prayer groups and mutual assistance societies, meeting in houses or barns at least three times a week; occasionally Franciscan priests would attend these meetings and conduct a Mass. By 1991, there were more than seventy Križari groups in Western Hercegovina, and it was from their ranks that most of the leadership of the official Croatian army (known by the acronym HVO) in the region had been drawn.

Those young men who chose to belong instead to the Ustaše had formed the core ranks of the unofficial Croatian army, the Home Defense Force, known as the HOS. The HOS was, among other things, the military wing of the revived Croatian Party of Rights, founded by a former political prisoner who recently had been quoted as saying that the Ustaše government of Ante Pavlević was "too liberal." HOS recruiting posters looked like a Metallica album cover: Black-shirted young men with steely eyes and chiseled chins, who gripped assault rifles with hands covered by fingerless gloves, surrounded by long-legged girls wearing Ray-Bans and motorcycle jackets. "Ready for the Homeland" was their salute, "Death or Glory" their credo. They ran the disco gangs of Ljubuški, which had become HOS headquarters, and gave themselves names like "Dark Falcons" and "Black Legion."

The HOS had supported both the HVO and the Bosnian army during the liberation of Mostar, but almost as soon as the Serbs were pushed back into the hills, the HOS again became a freelance organization, setting up its own "checkpoints" on the roads into and out of Mostar, intent on controlling the lucrative black markets in guns, drugs, cigarettes, whiskey, and stolen cars. The HOS also insisted upon total Croatian control of Mostar, even though the HVO already had agreed to an east-west partition with the Muslims. The city was by now a nest of horrors laid one upon the other. On top of it all were the various "tribunals" going door-to-door to collect and execute collaborators: The Bosnian army were looking mainly for Serbian fifth columnists, while the HVO hunted for Muslim "fundamentalists" and HOS "renegades." The HOS killed dozens of Croats it considered Muslim "sympathizers," but was most interested in capturing Serbian civilians who could be used as hostages in the lucrative prisoner exchange business that was booming throughout Hercegovina.

Almost immediately after their defeat in Mostar, the Serbs had negotiated a truce with the Croats. At the same time, the HVO "requested" that the Bosnian army move its headquarters from the city's protected west side to its exposed east bank, which lay directly under Serbian artillery positions in the hills. Impressed by the success of the HVO in its battles against the Serbs, Alija Izebegović agreed to a partition of Mostar.

The HOS insisted that it wanted the entire city, and that the Muslims must leave. The HVO, which in Mostar was 15 percent Muslim, insisted that the partition agreement be honored. Tensions between the two sides grew so hot that, in mid-August 1992, the HOS commanding general and eight of his bodyguards were shot dead at an HVO roadblock.

The HVO was scarcely an organization dedicated to the rights of its Islamic brethren, of course. In less than two months after they drove the Serbs out of Mostar, the Croatian army had occupied approximately one-third of Bosnia-Hercegovina. The Muslims retaliated by moving to consolidate a "Muslim Triangle" that would stretch its southernmost tip to Mostar. The city of Zenica, where the Bosnian army's Second Corps was headquartered, was the source of stridently pro-Islamic rhetoric, with a number of military and political leaders insisting that Bosnia had been abandoned by the West because Europeans couldn't bear the idea of a Muslim country on their continent.

Determined to hold its ground, the HVO made a fateful decision to incorporate the HOS into its ranks, not only giving these gangs of thugs an offical license to loot and kill, but sending forth "soldiers" who often chose to adorn their Croatian army uniforms with swastikas and other Nazi regalia. In all areas designated as "Croatian," the HVO demanded that the Bosnian army surrender its arms. When, as at Novi Travnik, the Muslims refused to give up their weapons, it was the HOS units that attacked their positions, arbitrarily slaughtering men, women, and children. The Bosnian army would reply by drawing on the support of its own paramilitary units, wild-eyed young men who proudly called themselves Mujahadin (Islamic warriors) drawn not just from Bosnia but from Turkey, Afghanistan, and Iran as well. Soon the Muslims were answering the Croats atrocity for atrocity.

Franjo Tudjman came to Medjugorje in May 1993 for a new round of fruitless "peace talks," and again invoked the Madonna, asserting that Her appearances had heralded "the re-awakening of the Croatian nation." All blame for fighting in the region belonged to the Muslims, who were massacring entire Croatian villages, said Tudjman. By then, everyone who attended the "peace talks" knew that hostilities between the Croats and Muslims were going to come to a head in Mostar. During April, prodded by the government in Zagreb, Croatian paramilitary units had undertaken violent assaults on the city's Muslim population. Just as the Serbs had done one year earlier, the Croats demanded that Muslims hang white flags from their homes. Even Muslim women and children who had sought refuge from the continuing Serbian artillery bombardment on Mostar's west bank were forcibly deported back to the east bank, kicked and beaten by the Croatian troops who herded them across the city's bridges, firing shots over the children's heads if they attempted to turn back. Muslim men caught on the west bank were trucked to concentration camps, where fifteen thousand of them were imprisoned by the beginning of May.

It probably was no coincidence that the final Croatian assault on the city (a nightlong barrage of mortar and rocket fire that set the entire east bank aflame) commenced right around the time Tudjman arrived in Medjugorje. The hell of what took place during the next six months was unprecedented even in a war of remarkable and pitiless savagery; while the Croats kept up a relentless assault of mortar barrage, tank bombardment, and sniper fire, the Serbs continued to rain artillery shells from their positions in the hills. Everyone in the northern section of the east bank by then lived in cellars, cut off even from the rest of the Muslim population, because the open ground made it a shooting gallery for snipers. Some tried to flee down the Neretva; a mother and her two young children who attempted this were killed by an antiaircraft missile fired directly at them.

The tank attack on the Stari Most did not begin until November, by which time the Croatian army had decided that bringing the Old Bridge down might be the only way to completely break the Muslims' spirits. For two solid days, Croat gunners fired 100-mm rounds at the Stari Most, searching for its breaking point. On the morning of November 9, they finally found it, and the bridge Hajrudin had built to last forever collapsed into 158 pieces that sank beneath the gray-green surface of the Neretva.

Karen's Land Rover crossed to Mostar's east side over a road bridge of heavy planks suspended by chains and cables from the steel girders that the Croatian army had chosen to leave in place. Gangs of children loitered about on the Muslim side of the bridge, and I glanced out the window at them without realizing that these faces would prove the most disturbing images I took home from the war in Bosnia. Six, seven, eight years old, they stood smoking cigarettes with expressions of anarchic insolence, either flipping us off or firing with imaginary rifles as we passed. Their eyes were the hardest I had ever seen in a child's face, infinitely more opaque than those of the ghetto gangbangers I'd interviewed as a newspaperman. I stared back at them and wondered aloud, as had so many weak-kneed Westerners before me, "What sort of God could let this happen?"

"Not the sort you'd want living next door, that's for bloody sure," Karen answered.

We dropped Andy off at the entrance to the Turkish market, where his Muslim girlfriend awaited him. During the drive in, Andy had surprised me by saying that he believed the apparitions in Medjugorje were genuine. He had seen too much that was incredible during his year in the village to doubt that something of a miraculous nature was taking place, Andy explained. At the same time, he knew himself well enough to understand that he would never be able to live up to what the seers said the Virgin was asking of us. "So you believe in the apparitions, but not in yourself," I said. Andy thought about this for a moment, then nodded: "Doesn't make much sense to you, I imagine."

I probably made the ride much more comfortable for us all by telling Andy that I understood him perfectly. In fact, his position on Medjugorje was one of several I'd tried to adopt. None had really worked for me, and now I was complicating matters even further by trying to factor in what had taken place in Medjugorje during the war. All the military attacks on the parish had been by the Serbs during the spring and summer of 1992. On April 7 of that year, for the first time in parish history, Mass was said not at the altar in St. James's but in the rectory basement, which had been converted to a bomb shelter, with a sandbag bunker at its entrance. Serbian air force jets had attacked the armaments factories in Čitluk and Široki Brijeg that day, dropping six cluster bombs as well on Medjugorje. Only one had exploded, but the boom was loud enough to send the pilgrims gathered at the church entrance scurrying. Mostly American and British, these pilgrims were evacuated the next day.

Medjugorje was at this point without telephone service, electricity, or water, and the front was just two and a half miles from the parish border. By then, more than four thousand Serbian artillery shells had been fired at Medjugorje, but the only casualties were one cow, two chickens, and a dog. Father Slavko called this a miracle. What most impressed the people of the parish was a failed air raid two weeks later. Serbian jets flew in formation over the village, intending to score a direct hit on St. James's. For some reason, their bombs weren't dropped. "Our Lady prevented them," I would be told by any number of people in Medjugorje, among them Mirjana. The Serb pilots later were quoted in a Belgrade newspaper as saying that they had lost their bearings in a "strange silver fog" that had covered the Medjugorje parish.

All of the seers except Jakov were in the village to celebrate the eleventh-anniversary Mass on June 25, as were nearly three thousand foreign pilgrims. "We have prayed constantly for peace, but if you accept God's will, you accept the war," Vicka told the crowd, then added that the Virgin had told her, "'Only by prayer and fasting can the war be stopped.'" None of the monthly messages reported by Marija during this period made explicit mention of the war, though there were some that seemed to refer to it by implication; the July message urged the faithful to approach prayer as "a joyful meeting with God," even "in these sad days."

By the late summer of 1992, the big Serbian guns had been driven back beyond range of Medjugorje, and despite the astounding scale of the violence that surrounded it on all sides, the parish would never again take artillery fire. However, Medjugorje was under attack of another kind, mainly by Western journalists who demanded to know why the visionaries and the friars had not done more to address, let alone correct, the brutality of ostensibly Catholic soldiers against the Muslims of Mostar. The range of written opinion on the subject was more or less spanned by two pieces published seven months apart in the *National Catholic Reporter*. The first was a stunningly inane "essay" by a writer who demanded to know: "If the Blessed Mother really has been making appearances in Bosnia-Hercegovina over the past twelve years, and if she really is concerned about peace, doesn't anyone wonder why she hasn't radically altered her roster of visonaries by now? Specifically, why has she wasted her time on six young people with absolutely no political clout, connections or credibility?" One might also ask why Jesus was a carpenter, Slavko had observed. The second piece, by Scott Schaeffer-Duffy, was more thoughtful and more troubling. During a visit to Mostar in late 1993, Schaeffer-Duffy reported, he heard one question again and again from the city's Muslim population: "Why do so many thousands of international pilgrims visit Medjugorje, only ten miles away, and then do nothing to stop the war? If only a fraction of them would come to Mostar, the fighting would have to stop." The writer described an encounter with an American nun who was helping to renovate houses for displaced Croatian families, seemingly oblivious to the fact that many of these homes had been forcibly taken from Muslims who now were living in refugee camps. Schaeffer-Duffy was shocked to discover a huge red-and-white checkerboard shield painted on the ground beneath the huge cross behind St. James's. "I could not help feeling ashamed of being a Roman Catholic," he wrote, a declaration that wounded many in Medjugorje when they learned of it.

Perhaps only in Bosnia could criticisms of this sort be both justified and unfair. While the Franciscans of Medjugorje *had* permitted the reported apparitions of the Virgin to become a vehicle for the rampant nationalists of President Tudjman's inner circle, the friars also had done more than any other group of Croatians in Hercegovina to protect the Muslims of Mostar. The friars kept open lines of communications with the city's imams even at the height of the war, and insisted (over the loud objections of the HVO leadership) upon locating the offices of the peace group Medjugorje Mir on Mostar's east bank. When the Croatian army refused to permit convoys of food and medicine to reach the Muslims during the summer of 1993, the leaders of several humanitarian organizations were invited to funnel their aid shipments through Medjugorje Mir.

The young pastor Father Lindeca would insist to me that Medjugorje had proved itself more during the war than at any time since the beginning of the apparitions: "The Croatian people recognized this place as a sanctuary of peace and balance. So in a situation where it was difficult to remain Christian—to remain even human—people were able to come here and find strength. For the families of the fallen as well as the refugees this was so. And it was very moving to me that during the war, Medjugorje became especially interesting to the artists, the writers, the musicians, who had not shown much interest before. They saw the way the aggressions that built up outside were brought here and dissolved."

A couple of days earlier, Postar had explained to me that I could understand what I saw among the people here now only if I knew what they had been like before: "This is the central highlands of the Dalmatian Coast, where people are known to be temperamental, rough, and very hot-blooded. Up until the end of World War II, it was known throughout Europe that the best fighters came out of here." Postar, almost fifty and the father of four, had served with the HVO for two and a half years during the war, dividing that time between the front lines and his home at the base of Križevac. "Every time I went to the front, I prayed that I would not be asked to shoot," he told me. "And I know that most of the others from this area were the same way. Our Lady has destroyed us militarily, and I am very proud that this could happen."

Father Lindeca grinned when I repeated this remark, but grew somber when I asked what he had said to the young men of his parish who came home from the war as killers. "Those discussions are very, very difficult," he said. "What is necessary is to communicate both that these people should be given another chance, and that they should take this chance very seriously. Here, one understands that only if forgiveness is possible will this war truly end."

Karen parked her Land Rover next to the Music School, one of the few buildings in Mostar that had received repairs, thanks in part to money donated by the Italian tenor Luciano Pavarotti. Like living in the city, investing money or labor in Mostar was a calculated risk. The Serbs still were up in the hills, engaged in what had become known in Bosnia as "psycho-terror." Their munitions supplies had dwindled to the point that they now fired only one or two rockets at a time, and they might go as long as three or four days between attacks. "In some ways it is worse," I was told by a Danish relief worker I had met in Medjugorje, "because between each explosion there is a temptation to believe it has ended."

Her closest call, Karen said as we walked up a cobbled lane that led into the marketplace, had come on a morning several weeks earlier, when she found her favorite coffee bar closed. "I went instead to this other place by the bridge, and while I was there, the Serbs fired a rocket. I heard the explosion, of course—you always do—but had no idea where it was. Then on my way back to the west bank, I drove by and saw that the coffee bar where I wanted to go had taken a direct hit. Totally destroyed. That sent a shiver, I must say."

"It could almost make you believe in your guardian angel," I suggested. According to the visionaries, all humans have guardian angels; Vicka and Marija had spoken at length on the subject. Karen steered onto the street where the remains of the blasted coffee bar stood. "The fellow who owned this place had just opened when the rocket hit," Karen said. "He was blown all to pieces. I wonder where his guardian angel was. On holiday, I suppose."

Winding our way through Mostar's souk, past bedraggled men who crouched in doorways amid the pathetic piles of pots, pans, and knick-knacks they were trying to sell to the relief workers as "souvenirs," we arrived eventually at the place where the Stari Most once stood. Aid workers had replaced it with a temporary span of reinforced rubber strung between cables.

"I have to cross it," I told Karen.

"I wouldn't," she said. "Nobody uses this thing; you're totally exposed out there."

I felt utterly compelled, however, and walked out the swaying bridge to its center point, where the graceful parapet of the Stari Most once had peaked amid swarms of swooping swallows. Staring down into the lazy, luxuriously green river that seemed more to nestle than to lap against the pale rocks along its banks, I experienced an odd and no doubt unwarranted sense of protection, as if I had entered, briefly, another time than the one where the snipers and artillery gunners in the hills existed. I didn't know if this time was past or future, but I felt more comfortable out there in the open, suspended above the Neretva River, than I had since entering Mostar. When I raised my head, I could see Karen pacing along the bank, looking out at me with a dubious smile, and experienced an overwhelming surge of compassion for her. I felt for some moments as if I couldn't move. Finally, I walked the rest of the way across the bridge to the west bank, where for the first time I noticed the people who were staring out at me through their broken windows. A tiny dart of fear pierced my serenity, and I felt a bit less steady as I made my way back across the bridge to the east bank.

"You're quite mad, you know," Karen told me.

We walked in silence back through the remains of the market, and were almost to the Land Rover when a boy of about eight approached me with his hand extended. I reached into my pocket and brought out a couple of kuna coins. In an instant, as if materializing out of thin air, a dozen, then two dozen, then I don't know how many ragged children appeared at the entrance of a big white apartment building. The place had looked deserted when we went past earlier, I was thinking, as these kids came sprinting across the gravel toward me. Karen hurried to the Land Rover, waving me to follow. "Quickly," she said. Confused, I climbed into the seat next to her. The children continued to give chase, their hands reaching for me through the open window as Karen sped away.

"Don't ever do that again," Karen said. "They'll tear your arms off."

Mortified by my thoughtlessness, I nodded, grateful to see that the Land Rover was headed back toward the road bridge and the west side. Karen insisted that I must see the Hotel Europa, which had been renovated to house top officials of the EU and UN. I understood why as soon as we stepped through the hotel's front entrance; it was as if the city outside had ceased to exist. The lobby was bright and spotless, with gleaming inlaid marble floors and a huge vase filled with cut flowers on a table near the front desk. On the outdoor dining terrace, we found a table where various flowering vines provided shade and a background of deep, cool green. Karen suggested that I order the fresh trout, and I did, but was more interested in the salad menu; I was desperate for roughage, which was almost unavailable in Medjugorje.

As Karen entertained me with anecdotes about delivering medicines and supplies to assorted towns in Bosnia and Hercegovina, I was struck mainly by the contempt she seemed to feel for those among her fellow humanitarians who imagined themselves as morally superior. "They all have their reasons," she said at one point, "just as I do. That's not saying they don't want to do good, but their motives are always mixed. Mine are, I readily confess. It's the ones who try to pretend that isn't so, they're the people I can't stand."

Both Nicky Eltz and Rita Falsetto had told me that Karen was in Medjugorje because she wanted what only Christ could give her. She wouldn't admit that, at least not to me. "Jesus can bugger off, for all I care," she responded when I raised the subject. "Mary seems kinder somehow, though. Mother of God and all that, I suppose."

She was sober and had been for several days, off the sauce due mainly to the influence of Rita, with whom Karen professed to be in love. She was enjoying the company of a man at the moment, however, and couldn't hide it. Karen probably had been a pretty girl, I thought, but that was just a guess; the ravages of drugs, alcohol, poor diet, and general self-abuse had made her over into an obese and almost aggressively unattractive young woman. Her hunger for my attention, which she never before had revealed, was touching and painful. Perhaps I took advantage of it by steering the conversation toward the subject of her childhood.

We had finished lunch by the time she was ready to tell me about it. Stepping back outside onto the streets of Mostar boggled me. On the lovely terrace of the Europa Hotel, I had begun to imagine I was in some semi-exotic resort setting. For months afterwards, I would recall vividly that moment when the two of us reemerged into the city's streets, unable to comprehend how rapidly my mind had fled the sight of these broken buildings and the broken people who once had lived in them. Karen let me wander in silence for some time, until we came to a block where the buildings all had been razed. The level, empty ground, with its neat stacks of brick and cinder block, was in some way reassuring; perhaps people could start over.

As we walked into that encouraging void, Karen, without any prompting from me, began to talk about growing up as the sexually abused adopted daughter of a wealthy, aristocratic Satanist. Among the most troubling aspects of her story was that part of her always had loved him, and still did. A certain depraved romanticism was part of her father's seductive technique, she explained: "He was quite good at selling me this forbidden love idea. What we had was something special, you see, and that was why we had to keep it secret." As she grew into her teens, her father had resorted to more coercive forms of manipulation, "reminding me of where I really came from, that my mother was 'on the game,' and that I never would have been part of this world of money and proper society that he provided me. The idea was that I could always be sent back. And by then I found that really frightening." Also, knowing that her birth mother had been a prostitute made her feel that she was destined to be a sexual toy, Karen said.

She was both compelling and convincing during this part of her story, but when she began to describe the most terrible ways in which she had been "put to use," I once again found myself on the brink of that vertiginous swoon that seemed to have become an essential part of my Bosnian experience. Her father was a Freemason of advanced standing; there were thirty degrees of rank above the three that the "ordinary lot" knew about, she explained, and those in these upper echelons all were worshippers of the Devil. She had not learned about such details until later in life; all she really knew about the group at the time had been derived from her own participation in Black Masses, which began when she was about five and involved mainly the sexual acts she performed with a variety of grown men at her father's urging, and in his presence.

Karen differed from the young Americans I had read about who claimed similar experiences in that she did not call hers a recovered memory. "I don't believe in that rot," she said. "I certainly never forgot what happened to me. It was something I've thought about, if not every day, at least every week since it began. I escaped by getting drunk and taking drugs, but that's not the same as forgetting." This was where her rage at Jesus came in, she said. "I found out about Jesus and began to believe in Him when I went to school. Right away I began to pray to Him to save me from what was happening. But nothing changed. After a while, I understood that He was letting this be done to me. I still feel that way, and there's no way I can love a God who would let a child be used in the ways that I was used. I believe in God, you see, but I don't love Him."

We had been walking for perhaps half an hour, and I was by then so disconnected from my surroundings that I began to admire the "sunburst designs" in the asphalt under my feet, idly marveling that the people of Mostar had engraved beauty even into the pavement of their streets. Only when I realized that I was looking at the indentations of mortar-shell explosions did the magnitude of my disorientation register. I felt so utterly lost then that I had to stop in my tracks, out of breath and gripped by panic. I had no idea who I was, where I was headed, or what I was doing. I didn't know what to think or who to ask. I had no bearings at all, beyond a vague yearning to survive. And for several moments I was without even that, barely able to fight off the desire to lie down right there in the middle of the street.

Karen was staring at me, concerned in a sort of amused and dispassionate way. "It's all too much," I got out after a few moments.

"I quite agree," said Karen.

I didn't want to give her the idea that I believed her, nor the idea that I didn't. "I think it's time to go back," I said finally.

"Yes, let's go back," she said.

"We'll demand an explanation," I said, seeking to once again find our common ground, someplace on the outskirts of irony.

Karen smiled. "And you know we'll get one."

We left Mostar by a different route than the one by which we had entered the city. This way took us through the foothills on the east side where, three years earlier, most of the Serbian population had lived. It was here amid these terraced homesteads that federal army troops had emplaced their rocket launchers and mortar cannons back in the summer of 1992, hurling more than twenty thousand explosive detonations down on the people of the city during the first three hours of the war. It was here also that, less than one year later, the combined forces of the Croatian and Bosnian armies had slaughtered both the retreating Serbian soldiers and their civilian collaborators. Muslim survivors had moved in since then, creating an intricate system of human shelters and animal pens from the stone and brick remains of the firebombed houses. In Mostar, rubble arrangement had become a kind of art form.

Descending once again into the shattered Ottoman splendor of the east bank, we passed what had replaced the Stari Most as Mostar's most notable feature. This was an immense bonfire built on the foundation of a building that had been leveled during the first week of the war. Into it, for almost two years now, had been thrown nearly all of Mostar's disposable waste and unusable debris, including the assorted body parts of those who had been in the wrong place at the wrong time. The temperature was around ninety-five degrees that day, but the fire still was burning in a circle perhaps forty feet across, with flames that reached fifteen or twenty feet into the air. I would tell myself later that, like Jakov and Vicka, I had been given a glimpse of Hell.

I was in terrible shape by this point, sick not only with the feeling that all hope and faith had been drained from me, but also with knowing how desperately I wanted to forget everything I had seen here. Perhaps even worse was my suspicion that I possessed the capacity for such dishonesty. I hate to think how much worse my condition might have been had I known at the time about Medjugorje's own *mali rat*, or "little war," as the villagers called it.

I would never know how bad it truly had been. The chief outside investigator of intramural violence in the Medjugorje parish, Dutch anthropologist Mart Bax, would report that more than 150 had been killed during the *mali rat*. While Bax had done a splendid job of researching the origins of the blood feuds in the Brotnjo region, his descriptions of events subsequent to the apparitions were riddled with errors, and I knew his numbers should not be trusted. The Franciscans would acknowledge only that there had been "a few" violent deaths in the parish during the war, and that was almost certainly an understatement.

If the dead could not be reliably counted, the reasons they had died were quite predictable. The chain of events went back centuries, of course, as it always did in the Balkans. In this case, it had begun when the Brotnjo's Turkish conquerers had invited the first Serbian family, the Ostojići, to settle in Medjugorje. Bloody conflicts between the Serbs and their neighbors flared and dwindled for hundreds of years, but had remained mostly quiet since the end of World War II, and seemed almost not to exist after the apparitions began. While the Ostojići now considered themselves Catholics and Croats, they were never accorded full membership in the tribe by their neighbors, the Jerkovići and Sivrići, who bitterly resented that the "stone eaters" had prospered from the religious tourism industry that sprung up around the apparitions. By 1990, the Ostojići owned most of the taxi licenses in Medjugorje, had set up a number of restaurants, cafés, and souvenir shops, controlled the supplies of bread and alcohol to the parish, and ran the largest local branches of the government tourist agencies, which according to their neighbors they had obtained by paying bribes.

Tensions began to simmer during the late summer of 1990, when Serb and Montenegrin terrorists closed several resorts on the Dalmatian Coast, resulting in cancellations by several pilgrim tour groups scheduled to arrive in Medjugorje that August and September. By the time Croatia declared its independence in June 1991, most of the boardinghouses in Medjugorje were empty. Only the Ostojići continued to receive a respectable number of paying guests, owing mainly to their good relations with the *biro četnici*, as government officials now were called. Nearly every family in Medjugorje was behind on the loans they had taken out to finance new construction, and almost no money was coming in to pay the bills. The leaders of the other clans began negotiating with the Ostojići to split tourist revenues, but as long-submerged resentments rose to the surface, the family became increasingly reluctant to share.

It was a source of deep shame for the most faithful among the villagers that the *mali rat* had begun in earnest on August 15, 1991, the Feast of the Assumption. Approximately two dozen armed and masked men, all Ustaše members, had prevented three hundred pilgrim guests of the Ostojići from climbing Križevac to pray. A number of the pilgrims refused to retreat until warning shots were fired over their heads. The pilgrim group tried again the next day, accompanied by several Ostojići and a Franciscan priest, but the same armed and masked force blocked their way. The Ostojići, however, had recognized faces behind those masks and promptly reported the names of these men to the police in Čitluk. During an early-morning police raid several days later, a number of Jerkovići men were pulled from their beds and arrested. One week after this, all thirty-two of the Ostojići taxis were trashed by teams of Jerkovići and Sivrići men.

At the same time that these events unfolded, the "big war" was erupting all over Bosnia and Hercegovina. In the hills above the armed camps that once had been cities and towns, the countryside crawled with mobile units whom the Croats called *rezervisti*. Most of these identified themselves as HOS, but nearly all operated as small private armies. The Ostojići naturally felt quite threatened by the breakdown of civil authority in western Hercegovina, especially after learning that a good number of Jerkovići and Sivrići men had joined the HOS in Capljina. By September 1991, their neighbors noticed that the Ostojići men rarely came outdoors except under cover of darkness, and that armed sentries had been posted along the perimeter of their properties.

The first man in Medjugorje to claim he had been fired upon was a Sivrići who said the Ostojići had taken two shots at him when he climbed up on his roof to repair a chimney. The next night, several explosions were heard in Medjugorje, coming from the direction of the cemetery. In the morning, the Ostojići found that nearly every one of their family's gravestones had been shattered by grenades. The situation was made uglier by the incursion of the HOS from Capljina, who at once barricaded the main road from Capljina to Medjugorje, cutting the Ostojići off from family members in the south. Soon after this, the HOS began attacking the Ostojići water supply, blowing up thirty-six of the family's cisterns; almost every day, HOS snipers shot Ostojići cattle.

The Ostojići soon brought in their own reinforcements, a forty-man paramilitary unit from a "cleansed" village to the south reached by mountain paths; by Christmas, these men had managed to destroy twelve Sivrići cisterns. The violence escalated steadily after that: First an elderly patriarch of the Jerkovići clan was shot through the thigh while visiting his dead wife's grave; almost immediately afterwards, two elderly Ostojići were hit by sniper fire, one left paralyzed for life. Then on January 6, 1992, the Feast of the Epiphany, two Sivrići men were shot dead; after that, no adult male from any of the three warring clans could safely show himself on the street during daylight hours.

In March, a drunken Ostojići fired a grenade launcher at a Sivrići stable down the street. The Sivrići answered by setting fire to two Ostojići houses and killing a pair of elderly men. Gun battles escalated, though most of those killed during the spring of 1992 were captured alive, then hanged from trees or ceiling beams. According to Mart Bax, eighty people, sixty of them locals, died this way in Medjugorje during the *mali rat*. That number is no doubt inflated, but several such deaths were documented during the last month of the "little war," May 1992: Among those killed were an elderly Ostojići couple found hanging from a mulberry tree in their front yard, their throats slit and their hands cut off; soon after, a Sivrići man and his two adult sons were found hanging upside down from a pipe, hands tied behind their backs, immersed up to their shoulders in the water of a demolished cistern.

All sides would agree that the *mali rat* was finished when the first HVO troops arrived in Medjugorje. How the little war ended remained in dispute: Mart Bax would repeat the story that nearly a hundred Ostojići men were marched off into a ravine and executed, but everyone I spoke to in Medjugorje insisted that no such thing had happened. By whatever means pacification had been implemented, pilgrim groups once again began arriving in Medjugorje on a regular basis in the late summer of 1992, rejoicing that "the message of peace had triumphed." Peace certainly had not triumphed in Mostar, where nine months later the HVO would lay siege, or in Capljina, where the Croat mayor was about to propose a "breeding program" for Muslims. And just six miles down the road was Ljubuški, a town almost entirely run by gangsters.

Those pilgrims who chose to stay in Bijakovići that August were close enough to hear the huge explosion one afternoon when the towering obelisk at Surmanci was blown apart with dynamite. The pieces of the former monument to Serbian martyrs were used to fill in the pit where the bodies had been buried. Soon afterwards, the Serbian "gatekeepers" at Zitomislići blew up the bridge over the Neretva that for centuries had been the main link between the Brotnjo plateau and Mostar, which was around the same time that members of the Croatian HOS blew up the infamous monastary where a number of Serbian priests were buried alive by the Ustaše in 1941. It was impossible to determine which event had come first, but the Croats clearly had succeeded in "cleansing" Zitomislići, driving the entire population into the mountains. The cycle of violence, and perhaps the process of historical inevitability, came full circle when the dispossessed Serbs settled in a former Muslim village that had been occupied by a Četnik unit several months earlier.

Even in Medjugorje, Gabriel Meyer could find almost no one who would acknowledge that the Croat paramilitary units of western Hercegovina, like the Serbian paramilitary units of eastern Bosnia and the Muslim paramilitary units who operated in the space between, were engaged in ethnic cleansing. "People would tell me, absolutely straight-faced, that everything the Croatians did was part of a defensive action," Meyer recalled. "I saw as I never had before how this self-justifying mythology and denial that is part of the tradition of oral history in Eastern Europe actually operates. The worst part was hearing so many Croats insist that God was on their side, and that the apparitions in Medjugorje proved this. 'The Holy Virgin came to inspire us to fight for our country,' they'd tell you. It was like they never heard that she had come to Medjugorje as the Queen of Peace."

I sought out Father Philip Pavich, Gabriel Meyer's principal sponsor in Medjugorje and the only American among the two dozen or so priests currently living in the parish, largely because of what I had heard about his trips to the U.S. as an advocate for the people of Hercegovina during the early days of the war. What I had not heard, and was startled to learn, was that the war had transformed Father Philip into Medjugorje's most prominent apostate.

Philip was an ethnic Croat. His parents had emigrated to the U.S. during the early years of the twentieth century from two small villages in the Krajina, making their way separately from Ellis Island to Waterloo, Iowa, where Philip was born and raised. He entered an Illinois seminary at fourteen, and at nineteen became a Franciscan novice. Enrolled by the friars at Loyola of Chicago, he had studied philosophy, theology, and psychology, and was still a young man when his superiors appointed him master of clerics (equivalent to dean of students) at a Franciscan college in Quincy, Illinois. His priestly career was moving along quite nicely, Philip recalled, until he became "unraveled" by the 1960s.

I had been warned already that burly, balding, bearded Philip was "sick in his soul." The priest disarmed me with a candid confession that he had betrayed both his priestly vows and his professional ethics by falling in love with a young widow who was seeing him as a counselor: "I didn't even know it was happening. I had no experience with women at all, and seeing this client once a week for a year, and becoming so deeply involved with her, was overwhelming for me."

He reached a crisis in 1969, Philip said, and planned to leave the priesthood to marry the widow. Instead, the two broke up, and he broke down. "It was all very public," he recalled, "and I found myself on the clerical junk pile." He went to Cleveland as an assistant pastor and, while there, "got in on the ground floor of the whole Charismatic Renewal movement," starting prayer groups in several Midwest cities. After three years, he tired of the "showmanship and falseness," and cloistered himself for a novena that ended after fifty-four days when "I obtained in prayer a clear direction to go to Israel."

Things went well in the Holy Land. He spent two years studying the Bible and Italian in Jerusalem, then was assigned to work as an assistant pastor at the huge Franciscan church on the ocean at Jaffa. In 1983, he was appointed pastor of the small Catholic church on the Sea of Galilee. "I took care of UN soldiers, Irish families, Catholic pilgrims, observers from the Golan Heights, plus I guided tour groups. For me, the holy places became a pulpit and I became very well known for these history lesson/ Bible school sermons. It was awesome for me. You went through the whole life of Jesus, walking in His footsteps, Nazareth, the Pentecost, all of it. The first time I walked into the Church of the Holy Sepulchre, I was bawling like a baby. At the Sea of Galilee, the first thing I did was take my little Nikomat camera and go in the water, take it down to eye level, as close to the surface as I could get, and snap, thinking, 'This is what Peter saw as he was going down.'"

He thought he would spend the remainder of his life in Israel, Philip said, until he heard about Medjugorje. "I wanted to come here and see it immediately," he recalled, "but Rome wouldn't let me." When he got a letter from an Irish priest stating that Ivan Dragičević had said he should be in Medjugorje, Philip went into retreat to pray for guidance at Mount Zion. There, he was visited by the only Catholic priest in Israel who had been born a Jew, a man regarded as "quite a local enigma." "Abraham said I must go, that I had been invited," recalled Philip, who spent nearly two years fighting his superiors in Jerusalem before he was able to transfer to Medjugorje in December 1986, arriving just in time to attend Ivanka's wedding.

Philip was in the courtyard in July 1987, when Bishop Žanić gave his "Fires of Hell" speech. "He lambasted the entire parish, but the people barely reacted," Philip remembered. "I didn't realize then that they had this stoical attitude, this sense of a primitive covenant with the earth and the vines and the rocks and the wind: 'The sun will come up, the grapes will ripen, we'll make wine. Bishops come and go, but we will always be here, and so will the Franciscans.' In the sacristy, the other priests were sort of laughing about it, with this condescending attitude of 'We'll pray for the bishop, and he'll catch on.' It shook me, though, to have our bishop calling us rebellious and disobedient. But then Archbishop Franić came to the rescue, with his directive in support of the apparitions."

Any reservations Philip had didn't show in his public statements. For a period of about three years, he would be the principal defender of Medjugorje to the American media. In an interview with the *Miami Herald*, for example, he described Bishop Žanić's opposition as an example of what the Church deplored as "scornful negation." "Anybody who comes here can see that we're not pushing anything," Philip told the *Herald*'s reporter. "We can't convince ten million people all by ourselves."

Philip sighed when I showed him this quote and several others. "Yeah, I was preaching all this big-time," he said. "In fact, I was the one who came up with the Holy Land metaphor of Medjugorje, the trinity landscape, the two mountains and the church between them, the work of the Father, the work of the Son, the work of the Holy Spirit, Nazareth,

Bethlehem, and Jerusalem. I invented that, it was my copyright. The first time I climbed Cross Mountain, I looked out and thought, 'Man, there ain't no place like this in all the world.' There's an ambience to this place, as I'm sure you've noticed. So I preached all this, and I became big here."

Among his duties, Philip explained, was the translation of the Madonna's messages from Croatian to English: "I worked up in the tower, in a little room right under the bell, with the offical journal of the apparitions and my Croatian dictionary, beginning in June of 1981 and working my way forward day by day. And when you do that, you really think about what's being said, because you're going over it word by word. For me, the messages were little Rorschach inkblots and I could read whatever I wanted into them, just take off and fly. I thought I was dutifully interpreting the messages, but I was really just using them for a launching pad."

Philip was thrown into a tailspin when he came to a message that the seers reported receiving from the Virgin in April 1985. "I was already having difficulty with this whole la-la land, Lotto Ball Secrets approach to religion," he explained. "All that stuff with Mirjana and Father Petar, where ten times he fasts for ten days, then three days before it happens he announces each Secret. And the parchment that nobody's ever seen, made of some material that's not of this earth: I guess you need special goggles for virtual reality. I didn't say anything publicly, but I was hearing a lot of stuff that made me think, 'Come on.' Still, though, I believed. I was swept away. I just avoided certain topics because they embarrassed me. But it was the whiny Madonna of 1985 that really got to me, this spoiled Lady who says, 'Well, nobody's listening to Me, so I'm not gonna give you any more messages.' And then a few days later, 'Okay, a few people have listened, so I will go on giving messages.' That doesn't fit my image of Mary of Nazareth, the humble maiden of God who says, 'Do whatever He tells you.' Instead it was, 'Do whatever I tell you.' I'm thinking, 'Hey, just a minute. Whoaaa. This can't be right.'

"So all this stuff that's bothering me starts building up, message by message, as I'm translating. But still I believed, all through '89 and '90, when I flew to Birmingham, Alabama, to appear on EWTN—Eternal Word Television Network—with Mother Angelica, so-called. I did a thirteen-part series for them that ran once a week. *Mary's Offspring* was the title. Sort of a 'Best of Father Philip' talk. That was the culmination of my unquestioning period. It reached a peak, and that peak was put on television. The programs were so well received that they still play them. People come here and tell me they've recorded all thirteen episodes."

Philip laughed bitterly. "It's comical, really. Because right after that everything went downhill."

Philip and I sat in the tiny orange plywood trailer where he had slept for the past three years, sweating through our clothes, pestered by flies. Sixty-five years old, diabetic and disillusioned, Philip was also, I came to realize, alone in a crowd, surrounded by brother priests who could barely stand his company, sought out by pilgrims whose credulity disgusted him. For six long sessions—none shorter than two hours—he led me through the convergence of events that he blamed for his loss of faith. Moaning and sighing, jeering and lamenting, the priest seemed to describe something that was more like the progress of a disease than a process of awakening.

He was convinced that the war had saved Medjugorje: "On June 17, 1991, eight members of the Yugoslav Bishops' Commission came down here for a meeting in the basement of the rectory," he recalled, "four bishops and four theologians. And they gave us this list of pastoral directives they intended to publish. The very first one was 'Let the visionaries refrain from publishing any more messages.' Any future messages, they said, would be submitted to either Bishop Žanić or to the commission itself. This is a bombshell! They told us it would be published in ten days, on June 27, but on June 25, the tenth anniversary of the apparitions, Croatia and Slovenia both declare their independence, and there is no more Yugoslavia, and no more Yugoslav Bishops' Commission either. So the directives were never published. Amazing, isn't it? I've heard a number of people say that Our Lady made the war start then just to protect Medjugorje."

For Philip, the war supplied a new cause; he became an outspoken advocate of the Croatian people, raging against the wrongheaded policies of the first Bush Administration. "I put my reservations on the back burner and said, 'I will die with these people if it comes to that,'" he explained. "The other priests, though, told me I should go back to the U.S. and tell everyone there what was happening. So in May of 1992, I went to Washington, visited senators, congressmen, then went to New York and saw the UN ambassador Jeanne Kirkpatrick. I even delivered a four-page letter to George Bush about what the Serbs were capable of. At the same time, though, my doubts about the apparitions were showing. I just didn't have it in me to hide what I was feeling anymore."

It was what he called "the Medjugorje network" that truly distressed him. Specifically, he was outraged and astonished by the connections between the members of that network and a woman who claimed to channel the voice of Jesus Christ. Vassula Ryden was a Cairo-born, Greek

Orthodox woman who had twice married Swedish Lutherans, worked as a fashion model, and was once the tennis champion of Bangladesh. Vassula had become best known as the author of a multivolume work entitled *True Life in God*. She did not claim merely that her books were dictated by Jesus, but that Christ literally had written them, using her hand. For Vassula's many readers, perhaps the most compelling quality of *True Life in God* was that each volume has been published not as pages of typescript but rather as photocopies of an elegant longhand quite different from Vassula's ordinary penmanship. "So what she's selling is Christ's own handwriting," said Philip. "There are hundreds of thousands of people out there who believe this."

He first had learned of Vassula in the spring of 1991, just before the war began, when two of her representatives (one being the former NBA basketball player Tom Austin) arrived in Medjugorje with copies of *True Life in God*'s first four volumes. "They were offering me a contract to join the first Vassula Dream Team," Philip recalled: "René Laurentin, Michael O'Carroll, Robert Faricy, and me, Father Philip Pavich of Medjugorje. I couldn't believe that Laurentin would support this crap. I thought, 'He's gotta be out of his mind. This is New Age occult spiritualism. This is automatic writing. This cannot be.'" But it was. "Laurentin already had written an endorsement of the fruits produced by Vassula's work," Philip explained, "and O'Carroll had signed on as her spiritual director. These were the Medjugorje gurus, the big guns, and they were backing this floozy."

Four months later, a defector from Vassula's camp provided Philip with copies of the original manuscripts of *True Life in God*. "Kim was this mousy, quiet, little American kid who had been damaged by drugs, but was very good and sincere," Philip recalled. "He wore this kind of self-made hemp monk's robe and this little bent-bun hairdo like a Greek. He was a throwaway Catholic who dropped out and smoked dope and ate magic mushrooms and was on the streets of Athens as a little junk-jewelry dealer, reading St. John of the Cross and living in a tent. He found Vassula and did a meltdown, became completely convinced she was real. But then in September of '91 he shows up here and comes to me with this plastic bagful of papers. He says, 'Father, I really don't want to read Vassula anymore. Will you take these away from me?' He didn't want to just throw them in a Dumpster. Then he said something about how these copies 'have the changes in them.' I didn't know what he meant, but when I looked at them I found out, because the text he had given me was filled

with the red-ink stuff, the stuff she took out before the books were published, because she couldn't dare let people read it. Stuff like how Jesus
instructed her to go to Rome to wash the pope's feet. There were pages
and pages covered with Post-it notes about what to take out and what to
put in, written by Vassula, but in a completely different hand than the
rest of the manuscript. I thought, 'How did this happen?' I said, 'Lord,
what are you tryin' to do to me. It looks like I got a job, a mission to do
somethin' with this stuff.'

"The first thing I did, in January of 1992, was send photocopies of the
pages I had to Michael O'Carroll along with a letter that said, 'Please
consider the gravity of this.' Instead of writing me back, though, O'Carroll
wrote an open letter smearing me, addressed to Father Slavko and to all
the Medjugorje centers in the world. He said he was outraged that I could
be 'actually in Medjugorje,' accused me of teaching rubbish and threatened to write to my superiors in Rome if I did not stop 'defaming' him.

"I don't know entirely what the repercussions were, but in general I
became a pariah. The Irish Medjugorje centers wrote a letter charging
me with acting against the spirit of Vatican II, et cetera, and asked that I
be kicked out of Medjugorje. Vassula herself responded with a fax attacking me," Philip said, and promptly produced the document, along
with O'Carroll's letter, from his file cabinet. "My question for her, from
the start, had been, 'Hey, if Jesus is supposed to control your hand, how
do you dare to just take stuff out? Do you presume to edit God?' So in
her fax she responds by saying Father Pavich has no right to object, because God edits the text. See, she has two notebooks, a 'private notebook' and an 'official notebook.' Listen to this: 'God removes from the
private notebook all that should be diffused and re-writes the messages
in the official notebook.' What crap!

"So, anyway, this whole thing is a big part of why they wanted me to
go back to the U.S. in 1992, to shut me up about Vassula. I kept talkin',
though. I put out alarms, writing to some of the more venerable conservative theologians about how we have to stop this virus from spreading.
And I was also letting people know more of my doubts about Medjugorje.
Still, when I returned here in March of '93, I was glad to be back, feeling
like I'd come home again. I was sort of like the guy who's trying to get a
divorce but just can't do it. You remember all the good times, et cetera,
and you feel very ambivalent.

"Then in May of '94 I went to Rome because the Vatican had asked
me to work for three months as a confessor at St. John Latern. I met

Cardinal Ratzinger on the steps of St. Peter's during a photo op with some Spanish bishops. All of a sudden the group is gone and he's standing there by himself. So I swoop in on him in my American-accented Italian, and I tell him my story briefly and then about my problems with this whole Vassula thing. And he kind of gave me a knowing smile, then took my little notebook from me and wrote the name of the guy at the Vatican, Father Giretti, that I should speak to about all this. I didn't do it right away, because I was planning on a return trip to Rome at Christmastime. Instead I went back to Medjugorje, and worked on all that Vassula stuff, then in December flew back to Rome and delivered it all to Father Giretti. He was very discreet—those guys from the Congregation for the Doctrine of the Faith never tell you anything, they just listen and nod—but I found out later that they already were doing a big investigation of Vassula and already had my materials and knew all about me."

Part of what the Vatican knew about Philip was that his opposition to Vassula Ryden had become inseparable from his flagging belief in the apparitions at Medjugorje. "By this time, Father Rupčić, the first theologian of Medjugorje, has proudly entered into the Vassula cult," Philip explained. "Rupčić huffs and puffs around like he's a giant, but I realized the guy has got feet of clay when I saw that his testimony had been published as the foreword to volume six of *True Life in God.* 'Vassula speaks the very word of God, and oozes with divine love . . .' I thought, 'This is enough for me. I think it's time to terminate my service in Medjugorje.' I flew home to Chicago and went to see my new superior. He said, 'Well, Philip, I've heard about you, that you're negative, that you drive the people away from Medjugorje. And besides that, the province doesn't want you back anymore.' We went on to argue about the apparitions. He was very positive—it changed his life, et cetera. And I don't deny the good, but that is not the issue. The issue is what's really going on. Is it Our Lady? And I have to follow my own opinion on that.

"I didn't know where I was going, but I got back to Medjugorje in January with the intention of packing up. My first weekend here, Father Perevan, who was then pastor, came, and we had a tense meeting. He said some things that were difficult to take. But then in the end he said, 'A lot of people have written to me asking to get you back in Medjugorje to hear confessions.' And I was very touched. It was the last thing I expected, that he would ask me to stay. I took this as permission to have my viewpoint. The problem was what to tell all the people who wanted me out, who had complained bitterly about me. So they had a big meeting here on February fourteenth and decided I could stay, but that I had to be quiet, and couldn't be so controversial.

"And the other side took advantage of that. In the Vassula newsletter, Michael O'Carroll was quoted as saying, 'We have good reason to believe that the opposition to Vassula in Medjugorje is no longer active.' I thought, 'I'm gonna have to let them know that ain't true.'

"But I find myself in this very awkward, limbo-like position. I'm in a kind of semi-retired status, very reduced. I give talks on the glories of Our Lady, but I don't preach the messages. My crisis of conscience is about 'Do I belong here? Is it fair to the people. Is it fair to the priests? Is it fair to myself? Am I living in a kind of unhealthy negation of myself, my own truth?'"

"So what is your truth, Philip?" I asked finally. "What do you believe about Medjugorje?"

The priest blew out a big sigh, then answered, "Well, I exclude hallucination and human invention. Absolutely. After eight years here, I feel certain that the visionaries are in touch with a spirit entity. But is it the Mother of God? There is some testimony I find difficult to deny. Rita Klaus, she's a remarkable miracle story, wonderfully healed, and a very powerful presence. But then, on the other hand, there's the story of Agnes Heupel who also received a miraculous healing and has turned into the leader of a cult. With the fruits, it's sort of a pick-and-choose situation.

"A lot of people hold that it was Mary in the beginning, but somewhere She checked out and the visionaries have carried on without Her. There's also the theory that visionaries are only human and make mistakes. And then the other possibility is that it's a dark spirit disguising itself as the Mother of God. Which is not uncommon; it has happened frequently in the past. In his second letter to the Corinthians, Paul writes that Satan often disguises himself as an angel of light. The Vassula thing sort of points this way.

"I know I haven't spoken clearly about what I believe it is. It's almost like I'm afraid to say it out loud. To say I believe that this entity is not the Mother of God but an evil spirit, one that comes as though benign but leaves a bloody mess on the ground."

CHAPTER FIFTEEN

On the morning I began my seventh and final week in Medjugorje, I noticed a tremendous bustle of activity around the huge tarp tents south and west of the church. Teams of villagers were assembling bleachers, installing lights, connecting public address systems. Nearby, the first teenagers to arrive from the north for the Medjugorje Youth Festival were unloading their bags from blue and green buses.

I stopped briefly to speak with a young man whose white wardrobe identified him as a member of the Oasis of Peace community. Attendance at the festival would be drastically reduced, he told me, by the recent escalation of the war. During the past several days, nearly every government in Western Europe had issued ominously worded travel alerts, warning their citizens not to enter Bosnia or Croatia, and urging those already there to evacuate. The German, Austrian, French, Belgian, Swiss, and Dutch bus pilgrimages already had canceled their plans to arrive in Medjugorje, as had the Irish and English groups that were scheduled to shuttle in from the Split airport. The Polish and Czech buses came anyway, skirting the Serb lines as they drove south out of Hungary, and so did a large contingent of Italians who rounded the Gulf of Trieste and crept down the Adriatic coast. Small groups of Americans, Canadians, and Australians arrived from Split, against their own governments' advice, as did a steady trickle of teens from every part of Europe.

The push against the Serbs had been stalled for months, ever since the seizure of more than 370 UN "peacekeepers" during late May, in retaliation for two NATO air strikes on a Serbian ammo dump. Television footage of UN soldiers chained to Serbian military installations not only humiliated the West but also demonstrated quite effectively the weakness of its resolve.

The UN mission had been "disintegrating" ever since then, as a Reuters dispatch published in mid-July put it. On July 21, NATO had announced "a bold new plan" to deter Serbian aggression; during the next two weeks, Bosnian Serb soldiers fresh from their massacre at Srebenica responded by seizing the supposed "safe area" of Žepa, driving more than five thousand Muslims out of the city, and were on the brink of occupying Bihać as well. The Bosnian army, fed up with the broken promises and empty gestures of the "international community," launched its own offensive against the Serb-held western suburbs of Sarajevo. The UN responded by warning that it might suspend its airlift of food and medicines into the Bosnian capital, leaving nearly four hundred thousand people without any link to the outside world.

It looked as if a dreadful situation was going to get a lot worse, but suddenly, during the last week of July, Croatia once again mobilized against the Serbs. On July 28, ten thousand Croatian troops attacked the Serbs south of Bihać, advancing to within eighty kilometers of the city under a Serbian bombardment that rained shells down on them at the rate of one thousand per hour. Reinforcements were arriving from all over Croatia; I was told that Zagreb's young men had literally disappeared from its streets overnight. The magnitude of what was taking place didn't really register with me until I saw a Jeep loaded with men in dark green uniforms stop outside a market near the church, and realized that one of them was Mirjana's husband, Marco. "I've been mobilized," he told me when I asked what was going on, then gave me a look of raised eyebrows and a slight smile, as it to say, "Yes, it's real."

A Croatian who worked for the Irish tour company Paddy Travel stopped by moments later to tell us, "The war will be over very soon now." I heard that as bravado, but it wasn't. The Serbs who occupied Bihać were already cut off from their supply lines; the Croats had taken Glamoc and now were shelling Strmica. On August 4, the HVO would attack the Bosnian Serb "capital" of Knin, and by August 7, Croatia controlled virtually the entire Krajina.

Cut off from any source of information other than word of mouth, I had no idea what to make of the situation. The UN personnel who still dined at Café Columbo seemed confused and frightened. The American military was lending tactical support to the Croatian offensive, they said, at the same time the U.S. government condemned it, and the Clinton Administration still refused to lift the arms embargo on Bosnia. The Serbs already were reacting wildly, advancing to within three kilometers of the main UN camp near Bihać at Coralici, where thirteen hundred Bangladeshi troops were huddled in terror. If the Bosnian Serbs began to lose too much ground, the UN people warned, Milošović might order the Yugoslav federal army back into the country, and war would envelop the entire Balkans.

Later that morning I heard a group of Canadians arguing about whether they should get out of the country. One woman was upset about being forced to cancel an excursion to Dubrovnik, where the Serbs had renewed their rocket attacks for the first time in three years. "Dubrovnik is half an hour from here," she said. "Our Lady will protect Medjugorje," a second woman said. "But what about Split?" asked the man who sat between them. "I hear they may shut down the airport."

By noon, having verified that the airport in Split was in no danger of closing, I had decided to stay, as planned, through the Youth Festival. In Medjugorje, the war was like a feature of the environment, always in the background, no matter how close it came. "What's happening here is bigger than the war," Nicky said, and for me this had become true.

That afternoon, I decided to climb Križevac one last time. The mountain was crowded with kids who babbled excitedly in at least a dozen languages, occasionally shushed by the locals, but so persistent that I passed through pockets of din throughout my ascent. On a ledge above the ninth station of the cross, I spotted a group of youths staring at the sun, apparently hoping it would perform tricks for them. This was the sort of idiocy I had observed regularly in Medjugorje, and one to which Americans seemed particularly prone. Postar had told me a story about a group from Texas who were staying at his house earlier that summer. One Tuesday afternoon when a *bura* (northeaster) was blowing, two of the Texans had been sitting outside on the veranda when they became very excited, saying they had seen flickering lights at the base of Križevac's cross. Postar told them it was the Italians trying to light candles in the wind, then immediately heard a woman whisper, "This one doesn't believe."

"These people who make up miracles, they hurt all," he said with a sigh. "Worse, though, are the ones who really see lights and wonders, then make something special of themselves for having seen. Watching them is very depressing, especially when they come back here hoping to have their pictures taken with the visionaries."

The most eagerly anticipated visitor to Medjugorje at present was Pope John Paul II. Two months before my arrival in Rome, a mixed delegation of political and religious leaders from Croatia had arrived at the Vatican to invite the pope to visit Split for the city's seventeen hundredth anniversary. He would like to come back to Croatia, the pope had replied in an almost offhanded way, and would perhaps even make a side trip to Medjugorje. Father Philip had described the publication of that remark in Split's newspapers as "like a bomb going off." Various political and evangelical motives were ascribed: Tudjman and his supporters naturally attempted to suggest that the pope was agreeing that Western Hercegovina was part of Croatia. All along the roads between Medjugorje, Čitluk, Ljubuški, and Capljina billboards were emblazoned with John Paul's visage and the caption *"Papa Je s Vama"* ("The Pope Is with You"). Any number of people I met in Medjugorje believed the pope would arrive in the village to formally endorse the apparitions on or before the year 2000. Philip had snorted derisively at the idea—"Can you imagine the pope going somewhere that is basically the Wild West, a place that's more or less run by whoever has the biggest and fastest guns? It'll never happen, and everyone here who has a brain in his head knows it, but you don't hear them saying so, because this enthusiasm is useful."

Even Philip was forced to admit, however, that John Paul's support for Medjugorje appeared unwavering. During 1988, the pope had received a group of Croatian Catholics in his private chapel. Instantly, he recognized two members of the group from photographs he had seen and approached them, observing, "Ah yes, Jelena and Marijana, who have the interior locutions." After greeting each member of the group, the pope returned to the two girls, and then stood staring into their eyes for some time. Two years later John Paul had dispatched his confidant, Bishop Hnilica, to accompany Marija on a visit to Russia; the bishop told her repeatedly how much the pope wished he could visit Medjugorje, Marija reported to friends when she returned to the village.

About a week after my arrival in Medjugorje, John Paul's presence at a meeting between the Congregation for the Doctrine of the Faith and Bishop Gerolmo Grillo of Civitavecchia was front-page news in the Croatian papers. According to these reports, once Bishop Grillo finished his testimony, the congregation's skeptics began to cross-examine him, attempting to trip him up with this or that bit of sophistry. Finally, it was the pope himself who cut them off: "The bishop has described to you what he saw. Can you need anything more?"

I had asked myself that same question several times since. Upon reaching the summit of Križevac, I found myself whispering it once again: "Can you need anything more?" I sank to my knees a moment later but, instead of praying, began to laugh out loud again. It was something the mountaintop brought out in me, apparently. I was thinking of a recent conversation with Father Slavko in which I confided my nagging fear that by some imposition of "secular scrutiny," I would do harm to this holy place. I was aware by then that some of the other priests regarded me as dangerous—a doubting Thomas at least, perhaps even a Judas—and so felt concerned that this most beloved of their brothers might react with alarm to such an admission. Slavko responded with benevolent amusement. "Do not worry about that," he advised me. "The only harm you can do is to yourself."

I woke the next morning to the thought that I had barely seventy-two hours left in Medjugorje. Leaving seemed suddenly an impossibly large task. After weeks of wishing I could get out of this place, I was unable to imagine being anywhere else. Before breakfast, I walked through the fields to Bijakovići and stopped by Vicka's to watch the pilgrims seek her blessing. As usual, Vicka was aglow, smiling at the sun, nodding to the birds in the trees, greeting each wide-eyed soul who stepped toward her with an expression of such resplendent joy that nearly every one of them was moved to tears before she spoke a word.

I stood off to the side, unnoticed, I thought, until Vicka glanced toward me as if she had known I was there the whole time. She looked at me, then at the line of people stretching down the street, then back at me, then back at the pilgrims again, pursing her lips in a smile that seemed wry and knowing and perhaps even a little mischievous. She closed her eyes briefly, then opened them, but never looked my way again.

I walked off feeling pleased and disturbed in equal measure. Five minutes later, I was walking down Visionary Way. I saw no sign of either Mirjana or Ivan, but Jakov was outside watering his flowers. He looked rather anxious at my approach, but seemed to relax when I moved to the opposite side of the street, and waved to me in greeting for the first and only time since my arrival in Medjugorje.

To avoid the pilgrims, I took the long way back through the fields, briefly challenged by a bull whose pasture I invaded, but otherwise left alone. I didn't know what I wanted, except to understand why I felt so reluctant to depart. I'd been in Medjugorje for more than forty days. The grapes, tight clusters of green beads when I arrived, now hung low on the vines, plump and purple. "Nearly ready for harvest," I thought, and suddenly felt like weeping.

When I arrived back at Mira's, Nicky told me that Medjugorje's pastor, Father Ivan Lindeca, was prepared to finish the interview we'd begun nearly two weeks earlier. Grateful for something to do, I went straight to the rectory. In the same room where I had spent most of my time with Slavko, I asked Lindeca about his background. As a young priest he had been assigned to Humac one week after Father Zovko's arrest in August 1981, and "through that window," Lindeca said, had spent seven years studying "the phenomenon" that was Medjugorje. His conclusion that the apparations were genuine came "quite gradually," said Lindeca, who, like so many other visiting priests, had been most deeply affected by what he heard in the confessionals of Medjugorje.

He made no effort to meet the visionaries during those first seven years, Lindeca said, but studied them from a distance: "I was fascinated that they were able again and again to evade or circumvent danger. And the main danger they were able to evade was to become in some false way stars. Even the clergy could not seduce them, which angered some of the priests, I must tell you."

I asked about the criticism that the seers had become "professional visionaries." Lindeca took the question seriously. "In some ways, the people who say this are right," he said. "But it is not that easy to decide what these six are as visionaries, and what they are as ordinary people. One can never really grasp their situation. I have seen some things among them that annoy me, but I have learned, especially as pastor, that one cannot dictate to them. It has always bothered me that this tension must exist, but I have come to accept that it does."

As I sat wondering what else I wanted to ask, Lindeca, without prompting, began to tell me about a day in 1988 that he spent guiding a large group of Germans who were stopping in Medjugorje on their way to Greece: "Suddenly, half the group said it was time to leave, and the other half said, 'No, we're staying here.' So they split in two. Half stayed, half went off to Dubrovnik. It was a very defining moment for every one of them; they had to choose. And in the middle of that I realized this was true of me as well. What I chose was to move to Medjugorje."

The priest paused and studied the expression on my face. "You are traveling through to Greece," he said, laughing, and bid me good-bye a moment later.

*   *   *

I was standing just outside the doors to St. James's early that evening when Father Slavko stepped up beside me and said, "You have been attending the Croatian Mass regularly," then smiled at my embarrassment. It was true. I sometimes even sat through the prayers of the Rosary that were recited each evening at the hour of the apparition.

The church always was filled to overflowing for the Croatian service, and I usually found a seat among the benches on the east side of the building. A cooling breeze invariably stirred at dusk, as the setting sun spread an orange nimbus across the purpled horizon of the Duvno Plains. Above the swallows swooping from their nests in the bell towers soared the beautiful voice of the young nun who sang the call to prayer. Over all, the cross at the summit of Križevac glinted in the sun's fading light. In that place, at that time, I had discovered myself as a person I could not recognize, one who did not need to know the words to understand what was being said, who chose to forgive rather than to forget, who was more moved by the old ladies kneeling in the gravel than by the long-legged girls tottering past on their platform heels.

"There's an ambience to this place," Philip had said, but Medjugorje was more than atmosphere. Even Philip acknowledged that. The visionaries were neither liars nor lunatics, he agreed; something real was taking place. I certainly didn't believe it was diabolical manipulation. In fact, every explanation I had heard still sounded more far-fetched to me than what the visionaries said themselves. "If you can't come up with anything better, consider the possibility that what the seers say is true," Slavko had suggested, more or less. "Then let your heart decide." If only, I thought, I could put my mind to rest.

The next afternoon, Jozo Ostojić sat down at the table where I was eating lunch with Nicky and said, "I wish I could know what it is like to come to Medjugorje as a pilgrim." He longed to see this place with fresh eyes, Jozo explained, in the context of a larger world and a less sacred environment. "Sometimes I can only realize how special Medjugorje is by looking at the faces of those who come here for the first time," he said. He caught himself staring intently into my eyes, shook his head, and laughed.

Part of his problem, I suggested, was that, working as a guide, he heard himself telling the same stories again and again. "It is true," he agreed. "After some time they begin to sound more like something I have made up than something I have experienced." Perhaps what he needed to do, Jozo reflected, was take time off to visit Lourdes or Fátima. Lourdes and Fátima were shrines to events that had taken place long ago, I observed, "but in Medjugorje it's all still happening."

"So you believe something is happening, eh?" Jozo asked, with a sly glance at Nicky.

"Oh yes," I said, "something most definitely is happening."

"What it is, though, that is the question?"

"That is the question," I agreed.

"I think something is happening to you," Jozo said as he left to go meet his tour group.

"Something is happening here, but you don't know what it is, do you, Mr. Jones?" I sang to myself as I watched Jozo disappear into the crowded church courtyard.

"Are you going to confession today?" Nicky asked abruptly.

I stared at him for a moment, took a deep breath, then answered, "Yes."

Father Slavko's confessional was just inside the main entrance to St. James's, against the rear wall of the church. The door was closed. I found myself hoping this meant he wasn't in, but sat down on a bench nearby to wait and see. About ten minutes later the door opened and a Croatian woman my age stepped through it, her cheeks bathed in mascara-tinted tears.

Slavko peered out a few moments after this and looked surprised to see me. "You are waiting for me?" I nodded, stood, stepped inside the narrow wooden booth, and sat down directly across from him, our knees nearly touching. This wasn't how they did it in the movies.

Where to begin was a question I hadn't let myself think about up to this moment. Slavko led me through the ritual repititions of the sacrament, explaining each one. "There is no need for you tell me how long since your last confession," he noted with a smile. We sat without speaking for several moments. "Many sins," he said after a while.

"More than I can remember, Father," I told him.

"Sex?"

"Yes."

"Drugs?"

"Yes." Rock and roll too, I nearly added.

I felt ashamed of a lot I had done, I told him, but not really guilty; it was in the past and I had changed. He nodded. "In your heart, what is it that you most regret?" he asked. As soon as I heard the question, I knew the answer. So obvious, I thought, and so conveniently Catholic. It was also, however, the truth.

"I was party to two abortions when I was younger," I told him. My lower lip had begun to quiver before the words were out. It had all been so abstract until that moment. But now, all of a sudden, I felt as if those two aborted babies were in the booth with me, listening. My feelings weren't a complete surprise; during the past several years I had become very reactive to people who tried to make "terminating a pregnancy" sound like pulling a tooth. I wanted to blame the pro-choice propagandists for all the rationalizations they had given me. But in that booth with Slavko, I couldn't. "I knew it was wrong," I told him, and barely noticed the tears that blurred my vision. "That's what I can't forgive myself for. I knew they were alive, but I went along with it anyway. Twice."

I became too choked up to continue. Slavko's expression appeared neither more nor less kind. He was not one of those who believed abortion was the same as murder, the priest told me. "It is a terrible sin," he said, "but one that God can forgive. And if God can forgive it, so can you. In fact, it would compound your sin to do otherwise."

I should give names to my unborn children, he suggested, and offer Masses for their entrance into Heaven. I nodded. "Anything," I thought. "But that is not your penance," Slavko said. At that moment, I felt ready to eat glass or sleep on nails. "Your penance," he told me, "will be to speak at the most difficult moment and in the most demanding circumstances to an audience that does not want to listen, and to tell them that you are against abortion."

"That sounds too easy," I thought. "It will not be as easy as it sounds," Slavko told me, and smiled. He blessed me, invited me to pray with him, and excused me from the booth.

I left the confessional in such an emotional state that I lost track of the next three hours. I had spent most of that time wandering alone in the fields, sobbing, trying to understand how something I hardly ever thought about could matter so deeply to me. "Am I that good at lying to myself?" I wondered.

The sun was setting by the time I arrived back at Mira's. Karen, who had fallen off the wagon again, was sitting at Nicky's table, drinking plum brandy from a water glass. She stared at me openmouthed when I sat down.

"You look absolutely blown away," she said finally. "What I mean," she added a moment later, "is that you look the way everybody here wishes they looked."

Nicky broke in to tell me that there would be a special outdoor Mass at ten o'clock that evening. It was the big event of the Youth Festival. "You should go," he said.

Crunching across the gravel that led to the benches facing St. James's outdoor altar, I saw Rita Falsetto standing under a spotlight and suggested, for the first and only time, that we sit together.

The attraction between us was sweet and odd and slightly uncomfortable. I was drawn to her in the same way a lot of people were. Slavko called Rita "the pretty soul," a nickname that suited her. She was completely abandoned to God, but in such a clear-eyed, straightforward, unpretentious manner that it disarmed the profane and the pious alike. On the evening after our trip to Tomislavgrad, our young Croatian friend Maja Marić had talked Nicky and me into climbing Križevac with her. It had been nearly midnight when we began our ascent. The three of us were halfway up when we met Rita coming down. She climbed the mountain every night after she finished work, Rita told me (because I asked), and prayed at each station of the cross.

During daylight hours, with her wild blond hair, strong tanned body, and bright blue eyes, Rita stood out in Medjugorje the way an escaped circus animal might have done, and the number of Croatians intoxicated by her seemed to increase week by week. Around me, she made no effort to conceal anything she was struggling with, including her voracious sexuality, but I never detected even the faintest plea to be led astray. Once Karen had tried to convince the lot of us to attend a big Saturday-night bash that the humanitarians were putting together. I said I was game and glanced at Rita, who seemed to waver for an instant, then shook her head and said, "I'm not in Medjugorje to party."

Under that spotlight on the evening of the Youth Festival Mass, I could see that Rita was not entirely comfortable with the idea of sitting next to me. She consented, though, after a moment's hesitation, and we found seats on a bench in the back row.

Father Slavko was to conduct the service, assisted by at least a dozen other priests and backed by a choir of teenagers who had been rehearsing with a small orchestra for several days. The outdoor altar resembled a giant gazebo, with an elevated stage that was partially enclosed by walls of white lattice. The only ornamentation was a large crucifix formed from white tubing that glowed in the dark, as did the faces of those onstage. The choir sang with a fervor that seemed to at once envelop and compact the crowd, which was by far the largest I had ever seen in Medjugorje, perhaps ten thousand strong. Slavko, usually so soft-spoken and understated, read the liturgy in a booming voice, making sweeping gestures with his arms and extending those preternaturally large hands of his toward people in the front row of benches.

As he prepared for communion, Slavko came down offstage carrying the consecrated host in a huge gilded monstrance, followed by two priests who swung large smoking incense burners behind him. He walked through the standing crowd wielding the monstrance like a weapon, I thought, intoning the words "Body of Christ" and sending visible waves of emotion through the people toward whom he pointed it.

In the choir was an Italian girl who had been in the village with her mother since shortly after my arrival. Both were beautiful, but the girl was especially exquisite, though never quite so ravishing before as she was on the stage that evening, swinging her arms back and forth above her head, with an expression on her uplifted face that made my chest ache.

At the same time, I began to hear the strange sounds that were produced by Slavko's swings of the monstrance, cries of pain and gasps of fear, even an occasional curse; several times I heard howling noises and loud, guttural fuck-yous. As Slavko moved in our direction, I began to feel overwhelmed, as if the earth had opened or the sky was falling. The priest's expression was like nothing I had ever seen, fierce and rapturous at the same time. Suddenly he was right in front of me, pointing the monstrance in my direction, and the Presence I felt in that moment was so enormous that not even the smallest part of me could deny it. "Jesus!" Slavko shouted at me, and I knew it was true. I felt as if I had stopped breathing but didn't need breath anymore.

The shouts of rage and cries of agony seemed to be swelling all around me. A young woman to our left began to produce a noise unlike any I had ever heard. It was a cough, dry, but issuing from so deep inside that it sounded as if the girl were trying to bring up an organ. The coughing went on and on, like an echo that did not fade away, but instead amplified in volume with each repetition. The girl bent over, then began to shake convulsively, foaming at the mouth. White lather poured out of her in a stream that was copious beyond belief. She fell to the ground, kicking and writhing, still foaming at the mouth, but now instead of coughing she screamed obscenities. I heard "Fuck you, Jesus" several times, but also curses that were in another language. It was not what she said that terrified me but rather how she said it; her voice had become impossibly deep and guttural. Producing such a sound would have shredded my larynx in seconds, but this girl half my age repeated it again and again.

A crowd of people had gathered around the girl by now and were holding her down as they recited the exorcism prayer of Pope Leo XIII. Slavko continued past without looking back, and the choir continued to sing, only louder and in voices even more ecstatic; it was as if their song and the curses coming out of this girl were at war with each other, and the kids onstage knew they were winning.

I felt petrified with fear and at the same time immune to it. The girl on the ground seemed to go still and silent for a moment, but then screamed louder than ever, in a voice that was horribly desperate. Finally, she arched her back into a position that was unimaginably extended, with her weight resting entirely on her heels and the crown of her head, and issued a loud croaking gasp that must have emptied her lungs utterly. It wasn't the sound, though, but the smell that I would find most unforgettable. Whatever this girl had breathed out in that last hoarse expulsion, the stench of it was so ghastly that I felt too shocked to be sickened.

Yet Rita barely seemed to notice. She was deep in prayer, eyes closed, a faint smile playing on her lips.

The girl on the ground was being helped to her feet. She looked drained but not distressed. People held her by the arms as she turned several times, trying to regain her bearings, then walked off with the crowd of people who had prayed over her and disappeared into the darkness.

I felt as if the bones of my sternum had separated and my heart was about to break through the flesh. Slavko was back onstage with the choir, who continued to sing. The service continued, but I no longer could follow what was happening and barely registered Rita's presence at my side. I had a vague sense of hearing Slavko say at some point that the Mass was ended, and of moving off in the dark with the crowd. Somehow I got back to the Pansion Maja, into my room, and out onto its little balcony, where I awoke at daylight, sprawled on the concrete floor, shivering with cold and happier than I could remember ever being in my life.

*   *   *

I floated through my last full day in Medjugorje, feeling not only lighter than air but as if the reverberations of the previous evening were going to fill me with music forever. The expression on my face brought out a bemused but approving smile from nearly everyone I encountered, including those who barely knew me. "You've really been zapped," Karen observed. I merely smiled back, feeling impervious to either ridicule or interpretation. My senses seemed marvelously acute, and my mind was clear as glass.

Most astonishing was my conviction that this state I had entered was going to last. The Loopers all joined me for dinner that night at Medjugorje's most expensive restaurant, Galija, where I found that all I had planned to say no longer seemed necessary. Karen's giddy relapse into drunkenness, Milona's regret about having revealed too much personal information, Rita's penitential sufferings and pheromonal storms, even Nicky's proud refusal to admit how sad he was to see me go, all these struck me as matters to be worked out between them and God. My own conscience was remarkably clear.

Nicky and I were to leave for the Split airport at about noon the next day. I had planned on a leisurely breakfast, a walk around the village and one last visit to the church before leaving. Shortly after I arrived at Mira's that morning, however, an Irishwoman who was friends with Nicky stopped by our table to announce that Jelena had arrived in the village the night before, then offered to introduce me. At Nicky's insistence, off I went. Five minutes later I was sitting with Medjugorje's "seer of the second generation" at a table in an outdoor garden and feeling quite distracted.

Jelena wasn't exactly the ethereal presence I had expected, but rather a ravishing young woman of Sophia Loren–like pulchritude who could hardly have looked less like my idea of a religious visionary. Yet, Jelena possessed a profound air of gravity, accentuated by piercing eyes and a guarded demeanor. It took me about half a second to realize why so many of the young men in the village were intimidated by her. Jelena was fresh from the completion of her studies at the Franciscan University in Steubenville, Ohio, where she had spent the past three years. She planned to move to Rome in September, to start work on her doctorate in theology at Gregorian University. In the meantime, Jelena told me, she remained torn between her wish to join a religious order and the desire to have a family of her own. "I will not rush my decision," she said. Picturing Jelena in a nun's habit, I felt myself growing a little light in the head.

Despite spending the past three years in the U.S., Jelena had become ever more sternly "orthodox" in her views and was outspoken in condemning American popular culture. The intensity of her frown when she discovered that I had been divorced was such that, for a moment, I thought the conversation might be over. Instead, she took over the interrogation and began asking about my experiences in Medjugorje. She was amazed by how much I knew about the parish and the people in it: "Never have I heard of anyone gaining such access so quickly." It was an odd moment; we were each studying the other so intently that it became a sort of stare-down. Jelena forced me to drop my gaze when she asked, "Do you believe?"

I paused, more anxious about being put on the spot than I would have thought possible an hour earlier. "In my heart I do," I said finally. "My mind isn't so sure."

The answer appeared to satisfy her. "You have a completely different air about you than any other writer, or reporter, or scholar that we have had here before," Jelena said. "I wonder if it's sincere, or a skill that you've acquired."

I almost told Jelena that I wondered this myself, but kept silent.

"If it is a skill, it's a very effective one," she said.

I felt obliged to reply then. "If I'm fooling anyone," I told Jelena, "it's myself."

Nicky and I were on our way to Split by the coastal route half an hour later, winding uphill through the huge rocks and stunted vegetation of the Dinaric Alps, then descending along cliff-hugging curves toward a breathtaking Adriatic vista filled with the Dalmatian Coast's most celebrated islands, Hvar and Korchula.

The countryside surrounding Makarska was gorgeous, much like the Monterey Peninsula must have looked, I imagined, when the only white men around were missionary priests. The town itself, normally crawling with tourists at this time of year, was quiet, almost serene. As we drove past blue and white fishing boats that bobbed in the water between basalt rocks, I marveled at how in tune with this country I had grown. That thought was dispelled by the time of our arrival at the airport in Split, where profiteers and NATO soldiers packed the terminal. Helicopters with machine guns mounted inside their doorways rattled past the windows, while fighter jets taxied off into the distance.

Saying good-bye to Nicky was a wrenching experience: All at once, I realized that from this point on I would be surrounded by unbelievers. "Who's running this show, anyway?" Nicky asked. It was a question I had blurted out in a moment of exasperation several weeks earlier; since then, the Loopers had taken it up a kind of refrain, spreading it to the people of the parish.

Nicky and I each broke into a wide smile. A moment later he was driving back to Medjugorje.

My seatmate on the flight back to Rome was a priest from Imotski who spoke good English and became very excited when I said I was on my way home from Medjugorje. He wanted my psychoanalysis of the apparitions, and when that wasn't forthcoming attempted to engage me in a deconstruction of Karl Barth's crisis theology. I was reduced to a state of near-aphasia by the discovery that I could believe more literally in an appearance of the Virgin Mary than this Croatian priest did. Though the man spoke almost nonstop until we were at the customs gate in Fiumicino, I found it a terribly lonely flight.

Too exhausted to take the train, I hired a taxi. It was worth the expense: As my driver sped up the Via di San Gregorio past Circus Maximus and into the Ancient City, I found myself experiencing Rome in an entirely new way. Somehow I had never before registered the enormity of what took place here during that relatively brief period of history when pagan temples were converted to Christian churches. Out of dozens upon dozens of cults and sects that had arisen in Rome during the first and second centuries A.D., one not only endured but took the entire city in triumph. How could anyone fully engage that thought and dismiss even the possibility of Christ's divinity? I wondered.

After dropping my bag at the Hotel Campo di Fiori, I went back outside and made my way north through the sticky heat of August along streets packed with tourists, stopping at a church near the Pantheon to seek sanctuary in its cool interior. I sat for some time before a rather uninspired statue of the Virgin, fascinated but no longer really surprised by the comfort it gave me.

Long shadows fell across the street by the time I emerged from the church and walked west toward the cooling mists of the Piazza Navona. The only newsstand I could find was out of the *International Herald Tri-*

bune, so I bought a *USA Today* and was greeted by a "cover story" that ran under the headline: "Rise in Cheating Called Response to Fall in Values." According to a recent survey, 70 percent of college students admitted to cheating on tests, claimed the lead paragraph of the article. The survey chief was quoted as saying he had heard the same explanation again and again: "'Everybody's doing it. Why put myself at an unfair disadvantage by being honest?'" The accompanying photographs were of an actor who had been caught in a car with a prostitute, a beauty queen who had falsified her résumé, and a baseball star recently convicted of evading income taxes.

"Welcome back to the world," I thought, feeling sick to my stomach for the first time in weeks.

I left the newspaper on a café table with the dregs of my seven-dollar beer and circled the Fountain of Four Rivers, weaving through throngs of tourists, T-shirt vendors, and street performers, stopping finally to perch on the back of a bench by the lesser fountain at the piazza's south end. I had been sitting for perhaps five minutes when an elegantly dressed man with silver hair came walking in my direction out of the narrow street nearby. He wore a beautifully cut blue blazer with cream linen trousers, a bright yellow cravat, and sharp-toed shoes polished to a high gloss. "Quite the gent," I thought, then saw the man's face and drew a quick breath. His expression was one of the strangest I had ever seen, a sort of malevolent drollery that did not entirely conceal the suffocating rage beneath it. Though all by himself, the man began to speak in a loud voice as he drew near me, in a language that was not Italian. My heart was pounding. I looked around at the tourists nearby, baffled by the fact that not one of them seemed to notice this oddity. It was as if, in some way, the silver-haired man and I were isolated from the scene surrounding us. Suddenly, he let loose with a mad cackle and turned his head to fix me with one eye.

In that moment, I knew he wasn't human. An unearthly calm came over me almost immediately. I clutched the scapular medal that was still around my neck and stared back at him, thinking, "You can't touch me."

He responded with the most obscene leer I had ever seen, and this time I understood exactly what he said: "I'll catch you later."

PART III

TESTING THE SPIRIT

The danger is not that the soul should doubt
whether there is any bread, but lest, by lie,
it should persuade itself that it is not hungry.

—Simone Weil

CHAPTER SIXTEEN

Six months after returning home, I copied out a single sentence from the New Testament's book of Hebrews—"Faith is the substance of things hoped for, the evidence of things not seen"—and placed it beside a handwritten note from Mirjana. The only thing I knew for certain was this: The Miracle Detective was me.

In Medjugorje, I had obtained an annotated list of all the major apparition sites of the nineteenth and twentieth centuries. Though entirely unofficial (the Franciscans, Father Slavko in particular, continued to insist that no public opinion of any other alleged supernatural phenomenon should issue from Medjugorje), the list amounted to a ratings bulletin. Some apparitions were described as false, some as questionable, and some as authentic. Even those listed as authentic were grouped according to their importance, which made this a curious document to behold. The controversial apparitions at Garabandal, for instance, were listed both as authentic and as extremely significant. A number of other alleged apparitions that had generated large devotional followings were listed as false or as doubtful. Some apparition sites that I had never heard of—one at Akita, Japan, for example, and another at San Nicholas, Argentina—were considered to be quite significant. The events regarded as most closely related to those in Medjugorje, however, had taken place in Kibeho, Rwanda.

The apparitions in Bosnia and those in Rwanda had commenced during the same year. In Kibeho, as in Medjugorje, the seers were young, six teenage girls and a boy. In November 1981, the seven began reporting that a shining woman who identified herself as "the Mother of the Word" was appearing to them, warning of horrors to come and and pleading for repentance before it was too late. This had taken place at a time and in a place where the members of their tribe were whispering that something even more terrible than Idi Amin's reign in Uganda would soon be upon them. The atmosphere was "thick with bathos and mystery," as the Belgian priest who would become Kibeho's chronicler, Father Gabriel Maindron, described it. For nearly two solid years a "diabolic fury" had been running through the Central African countryside, Maindron observed, directed especially at Christian churches, where desecrations were occurring almost daily.

The ecstasies of the Kibeho visionaries were quite different than those in Medjugorje (Maindron attributed this to "the African psychology"). The apparitions in Rwanda lasted much longer than those in Bosnia, often going on for three or four hours, once even for eight hours. While the apparitions reported by the Medjugorje children were collective and contemplative, the Kibeho seers experienced their visions singly, but always in public places, and interacted continuously with spectators. The serene expressions and calm behavior of the Medjugorje visionaries contrasted sharply with the bulging eyes, waving arms, and shaking bodies of their Kibeho counterparts. And, most striking, the Kibeho seers invariably ended their visions with a physical collapse, falling heavily to the ground and remaining paralyzed, as if in a coma, for up to fifteen minutes at a time before regaining consciousness.

The Kibeho seven also did not seem to perceive the Virgin as clearly as the Medjugorje six did: "She was not really white like we see her in pictures," explained the first Kibeho visionary to report an apparition, Alphonsine Mumureke. "I could not determine the color of her skin, but she was of an incomparable beauty." Also, in Kibeho, the Mother of the Word had been quite specific and stern about what must be renounced by those who hoped for salvation: idolotry, fornication, and hypocrisy.

Like Vicka, Jakov, and Mirjana in Medjugorje, all seven Kibeho seers would report that they had been taken by the Virgin on a "mystical voyage" to three separate locations that existed outside of time and space. Though they did not call the places they visited Hell, Purgatory, and Heaven, the descriptions matched almost exactly those that had been given in Medjugorje: Mary took them first to a place of fire, the seven said, where souls suffered the greatest punishment possible, "deprivation of God." Next, they went to "a place of reconciliation" where the souls they saw seemed to smile through some sort of terrible suffering. Lastly, they were taken to "a place of splendid lights, perfect joy and absolute happiness."

What made these reports so compelling was that the travelers announced their mystical voyages in advance. Alphonsine had been the first to go, advising the nuns and priests in Kibeho, "I will be like a dead person, but have no fear and do not bury me." At the appointed time, Alphonsine had subsided for exactly twenty-four hours into what observers described as a coma, her body so rigid that two large men were unable to separate the girl's clasped hands. The voyage of a girl named Vestine Salima had lasted forty hours, and was observed by a team of doctors who reported that she was absolutely motionless the entire time, even when pinched or pricked with needles; the girl's pulse and breathing had been that of one in a coma, and her body as stiff as a corpse in a state of advanced rigor mortis. Also, the doctors reported, Vestine's body had taken on an unusual density, as if it existed in some field of gravity quite different than the earth's; it had been difficult for even an entire team of men to lift or turn the girl.

During the Lenten season of 1983, three of the Kibeho seers reported that they had been asked for extraordinary periods of silence and fasting: monitored around the clock by a team of doctors and Red Cross volunteers, the three fasted for eighteen, fourteen, and eight (a total of forty) days, respectively. After Easter of that year, Alphonsine announced that she had been assigned to disseminate the message of the Mother of the Word, which was threefold: one, the Virgin Mary had come to prepare the world for the return of her Son; two, the world is coming to an end; three, the end of the world is not a punishment.

Among Marian Catholics, Kibeho and Medjugorje had been linked from the start, but by 1994 the parallels were astounding even to those who had only a passing knowledge of recent events in the two villages. Bosnia and Rwanda now were the two most violence-racked nations on earth, awash in the blood of so many murdered civilians that a compilation of the dead in either country could only be rounded off to the nearest hundred thousand. In both Kibeho and Medjugorje, the visionaries had warned of terrible events and great sufferings that might be avoided only by repentance and conversion. These warnings were especially intense in Kibeho, where the seers reported early on that the Mother of the Word had asked that a chapel be built in the village and be called "the Gathering of the Displaced." The African priests resisted, unable to make sense of such an odd name, but by the end of 1994 there were an estimated 2.2 million refugees in Rwanda, and, like Medjugorje, Kibeho was a center of relief efforts and a magnet for refugees.

The seers in Medjugorje announced during the first weeks of the war in Bosnia that the Virgin had promised their village would be spared the ravages of war, and it was. The Rwandan village was not so fortunate:

two months before I departed for Rome, several units of Hutu soldiers had swarmed into Kibeho, slaughtering villagers and refugees by the hundreds. *The New York Times* described the nearby Kagera River as filled with headless bodies floating downstream toward Lake Victoria. Among the dead were three of the Kibeho visionaries; the other four had survived only by fleeing into Zaire.

As I read about Kibeho and the other apparition sites on my list, I couldn't help but be struck by the preponderance of young females among the seers, as well as the recurrence of a weeping Madonna who warned that terrible events were imminent. Many of the alleged apparitions had been exploited politically, I discovered. Leftist critics, naturally, had been most passionate about observing the ways in which Marian devotions were embraced by repressive governments (clearly, Generalissimo Franco was able to prop up his Spanish dictatorship by emphasizing the anticommunist element in the Fátima messages), but devotion to Mary also had been essential to numerous liberation struggles, especially in Latin America.

The proliferation of alleged apparitions during the last half of the twentieth century was what most concerned Church officials. The Vatican would provide no numbers, but did pass on a press release observing the "surprising increase" in recent claims of "pseudo-mysticism, presumed apparitions, visions, and messages" associated with the Virgin Mary. René Laurentin had counted more than two hundred reported apparitions of the Madonna since 1950, the vast majority of which were "easily dismissed." Local bishops had gently but firmly rejected claims of divine revelation in places like Ambridge, Pennsylvania, and Marlboro Township, New Jersey, despite enormous devotional followings in those communities. The Church even branded a few reported apparitions—in Bayside, New York, and Necedah, Wisconsin, for example—as outright fakes.

Nothing seemed to embarrass the Church more than publicity about prophecies that didn't come true. During 1988, three parishioners at St. John Neumann's Catholic Church in Lubbock, Texas, claimed they were receiving messages from the Mother of God, and that Mary would appear to all present at the church on the Feast of Her Assumption. Medjugorje, of course, was invoked repeatedly. At just past six P.M. on the appointed day, many in the jostling crowd began to shout and point at the sky, where most impartial observers saw nothing but the sun glowing behind some cumulus clouds. Hundreds, however, claimed to have seen Jesus or Mary in the shimmering light. "It's just like Woodstock, only Hendrix isn't playing," a wry tennis pro from Dallas told *People* magazine. The local bishop simply issued a reminder that the tradition of the Church was never to presume supernatural causes for "things that can have natural explanations."

Some mystical claims, though, had produced inquiries that left many reasonable questions unanswered. An especially intriguing Church investigation involved the members of a family in Damascus, Syria, who on the afternoon of November 27, 1982, began shouting to their neighbors that an icon of the Virgin Mary in their home was exuding a strange oil. A huge crowd assembled, and every person present—Muslims and Orthodox Christians, as well as Catholics—swore they had seen this occur. A short time later, the young woman who owned the icon, Mirna Mansour, began to report that she was seeing apparitions of the Virgin Mary, who had come to deliver a simple message of religious unity: "Christ is the kingdom of Heaven on earth. He who divides it sins. He who is happy with these divisions also sins." Slightly less than four years later, on April 16, 1987, Mansour began to bleed in a band around her forehead, and during the days that followed, wounds opened as well in her hands, feet, and right side. These were witnessed by many, filmed and photographed repeatedly, and attested to by an assortment of medical doctors.

The testimony of skeptics was for me particularly persuasive. During 1985, visitors at Irish grottoes from Armagh to Galway began to report strange fogs that descended on them, then disappeared to reveal that statues of the Virgin in the caves had become animated. "The Irish people had finally done what they threatened to do for generations—lost their marbles," observed a columnist for the *Cork Examiner*, which dispatched a team of twelve observers to Ballinspittle, a village just south of Cork where the epidemic seemed to have begun. Seven of the twelve returned to Cork swearing that they had seen the statue of Mary at Ballinspittle move.

Even more difficult to dismiss are claims of the supernatural made by enormous numbers of witnesses. In 1965, more than a thousand people claimed to have seen an apparition of Jesus and Mary at Turzovka, Czechoslovakia. Communist officials called this a case of mass hysteria, and perhaps they were right, but such a diagnosis is not so easily applied to what took place three years later in the Cairo suburb of Zeitun, immediately after Egypt's Six-Day War with Israel. This apparition event began on April 2, 1968, when a Muslim laborer named Atwa noticed movement on the dome of the city's Coptic Orthodox church. Thinking that he had seen a woman who was about to commit suicide, Atwa began to shout, "Wait! Wait!" Suddenly, he saw bright bits of light that looked like doves materializing out of thin air and hovering above the woman's head, said Atwa, who pointed a heavily bandaged finger, urging the other members of his work crew to look. They, too, saw the woman, as did a group of female pedestrians passing by on the street. The finger Atwa had pointed was so badly infected with gangrene that he was scheduled to have it amputated the next day. When he arrived at the doctor's office, however, Atwa was told that his hand had completely healed. Word got out, naturally, and huge crowds began to assemble, especially after newspapers reported the strange history of the church in question. According to legend, Zeitun was where Joseph and Mary had hid with the infant Jesus after fleeing to Egypt from the persecution of King Herod. The town's Christian church had not been built until 1918; its construction financed by a wealthy man named Khalil, who claimed that the Virgin Mary had appeared to him in a dream and asked that he begin building the sanctuary immediately, promising that, if he completed the project, She would return in fifty years to bless the church.

By the second week of April 1968, crowds outside the Zeitun church grew to more than two hundred thousand on some evenings, and eventually more than a million people—among them Egypt's president, Gamal Nasser—would claim to have seen the "Mother of Light." Members of an investigative team appointed by the local patriarch reported that they also had seen the shining woman on the dome of the church, and needed less than one month to pronounce the apparition authentic. A separate and more rigorous investigation was conducted by the government's General Information and Complaints Department, which employed teams of soldiers and police officers to search the area around the Zeitun church in a fifteen-mile radius to locate any electrical devices that might have been used to project the image of the woman. In the end the department issued a report that read: "The official investigations have been carried out with the result that it has been considered an undeniable fact that the Blessed Virgin Mary has been appearing on Zeitun Church in a clear and luminous body seen by all present in front of the church, whether Christian or Muslim." The alleged apparitions continued for nearly five years, then ended just before the Yom Kippur War.

Even as I learned all this, I was being reminded that such marvels may mean little, or at least little that can be relied upon. What to make, for example, of Maria Esperanza? Scores of witnesses reported that on fourteen separate occasions they had seen a rose—an actual rose, stem and all—break through the skin on Esperanza's bosom and blossom gloriously. Two of those who signed sworn statements that they had observed this phenomenon were medical doctors. Other witnesses claimed to have seen Esperanza transfigure during prayer and levitate during Mass. Holes had appeared in her hands, feet, and right side one Good Friday, as attested to by several physicians. Meanwhile, more than eight hundred people claimed to have seen the Virgin Mary during Esperanza's apparitions at Bettania, Venezuela. When the local bishop (noting "numerous similarities to Medjugorje") issued a report declaring Esperanza's apparitions authentic and Bettania a sacred place, only two of Venezuela's thirty-seven bishops demurred. Esperanza (descended from an aristocratic Caracas family) was hailed by Marian devotionalists worldwide. Yet in Medjugorje I had been warned that Esperanza was not merely a false visionary or a fraud but a witch working in league with Satan.

Interestingly, both the pope and Cardinal Ratzinger had kept their distance from the Bettania devotions, perhaps put off by Esperanza's warnings of the danger posed by a rising of "the yellow races." During a trip to the Vatican, Esperanza's bishop obtained a brief audience with the pope, who made "a general observation about prudence," the prelate reported, then recommended that he read René Laurentin's book on Medjugorje.

I found it fascinating that all four of the alleged apparitions on my list that had taken place on U.S. soil occurred after 1988, and that of these, none had been deemed authentic, though only one (at Conyers, Georgia) was listed as false. Of the three American apparitions listed as questionable, one clearly had generated both the greatest interest and the most divergent opinions. It had taken place in Scottsdale, Arizona, and involved nine young adults. The most noted international investigators of apparition claims, René Laurentin of France and the Irish team of Father Robert Faricy and Sister Lucy Rooney, had endorsed the Scottsdale apparitions as genuine, but their opinions had outraged a number of other observers.

By the summer of 1996, I had decided that I needed to look at an alleged apparition in the context of my own culture. Perhaps, I told myself, I had been overwhelmed by the sheer strangeness of Medjugorje's setting and the palpable environment of devotion that enveloped it, not to mention the stark intensity of Bosnia's wartime atmosphere. Who wouldn't have become at least a little unhinged in such a place at such a time?

* * *

Scottsdale would be another matter entirely, as I understood shortly after checking in to my suite at a resort just off the Phoenix suburb's main drag. On the coffee table, next to a basket of fresh fruit, lay the most recent issue of *Scottsdale Scene*. The magazine's first page was filled by an advertisement that extolled "the new tumescent liposculpturing"; just inside the back cover was a regular column written by a local plastic surgeon who had chosen "laser skin resurfacing" as this month's topic. In between was page after page of ads for condos on golf courses, spa packages, and "shopping opportunities," all wrapped around a main article entitled: "Scottsdale: The Buck Starts Here."

I was still unpacking my bags when the desk clerk phoned to remind me that hotel guests were invited to join the city's regular weekly Art Walk. Just to amuse myself, I told him thanks but no, I was on my way to a prayer meeting.

Actually, I was to rendezvous with a young woman named Mary Cook outside the church, St. Maria Goretti, where her former prayer group was meeting. As if the circumstances weren't odd enough, Mary had learned earlier in the day that her ailing father was near death; she nevertheless agreed to sit down with me briefly before catching a flight back east to say good-bye to him. Mary, a ravishing young woman, was disconcertingly serene, given the situation. She assured me that she was prepared for her father's passing, and completely unafraid. She did concede that she had qualms about discussing her conversations with the Holy Virgin, and about her relationships with the other members of the prayer group.

It was early evening and we were outdoors, but the temperature still was in the mid-nineties. I had chosen what was generally regarded as the worst month of the year, August, to visit the Valley of the Sun. Did something in my mind link searing heat and mystical revelation? I wondered. Or was the connection between sunstroke and religious experience? Mary laughed sweetly when I asked these questions aloud, and within a few minutes was confiding that she no longer knew what to make of her own locutions, which long since had ended. "How much came from inside me, and how much came from outside, I can't say," she admitted. "I believe they were real, but I don't know exactly what real means." Yet for all the conflict and pain she felt about the way things had ended, she still regarded the period when she and the others were reporting regular encounters with the Blessed Mother as the happiest of her life. She had been changed utterly by the experience, Mary said, and remained a devout Catholic, something she had not been before she began hearing the voice of the Virgin. Why had her experiences and those of the others still in Scottsdale ended? She wasn't sure, though the conflict of personalities certainly had played a part. At this point, none of them knew for certain what had taken place during those three years, except, of course, Gianna. Gianna never had doubted, nor had she been doubted by the others, even after they began questioning themselves and each other. Gianna was the key; it all had started with her, and apparently she was where it ended too.

I had read earlier that "the Scottsdale event" began in the summer of 1988, when a young woman named Gianna Talone informed her pastor at St. Maria Goretti that Jesus and Mary were speaking and appearing to her. Actually, the first words Gianna spoke to him during their meeting that day, Father Jack Spaulding recalled, were "I think I may be losing my mind."

Gianna Talone, at age thirty, must have seemed an unlikely candidate for either mental illness or mystical revelation. Successes many and setbacks few, Gianna boasted the résumé of a character from metafiction. The first entry had been made at age five, when her parents found their daughter entertaining the neighborhood children with an accomplished ventriloquist act (using a John Lennon doll). They bought her a real puppet, which the girl named Alfie, and at age six Gianna became the youngest professional ventriloquist in the U.S. The family moved from Phoenix to Beverly Hills when Gianna was seven, and within a few weeks she was working regularly as a child actress and dancer, appearing in numerous episodes of more than a dozen TV shows during the mid-'60s (among them Sally Fields's *The Flying Nun*). At age ten, she became the youngest client of the William Morris talent agency.

When Gianna was thirteen, her father decided he didn't want his daughter to grow up in the entertainment industry and moved the family back to Arizona, settling in the state's wealthiest community, Scottsdale. There Gianna remained an exemplar of straight-arrow success. At sixteen, she was voted first runner-up in the Miss Arizona Teenager contest (and won Miss Congeniality). A straight-A student all through high school, she was awarded a drama scholarship to UCLA, but left after one semester, convinced her father had been right about show business, and returned home to complete her undergraduate education as a science student, first at the University of Arizona, then at Arizona State. She was on the homecoming courts at both schools, and was elected class president at ASU. After graduating with a degree in chemistry, she moved on to the University of Southern California, making the dean's list and earning a doctorate in pharmacology.

She wasn't nearly as wonderful back in those days as a lot of people supposed, Gianna would tell me later. "I ran the race," she observed, seeking honors and awards mainly to impress people, and becoming, by her own description, "a prototype yuppie." The first purchase she made after finishing graduate school, Gianna would recall (sounding more amused than chagrined), was a mink coat. Over the next couple of years, she also bought a condominium in an exclusive neighborhood, filled her walk-in closet with designer clothes, and drove a new 300 ZX. The man she married, commercial artist Michael Bianchi, was famously good-looking.

The only thing about Gianna that seemed in the least peculiar was her claim that Satan had appeared to her one evening during the summer of 1981. She had been napping when she opened her eyes and saw the Devil himself standing at the foot of her bed. He had the lower body of a beast, but from the waist up appeared to be a man, an imposingly handsome one until she looked into his eyes. She still shook with fear whenever she remembered Satan's eyes, Gianna would tell me; the fury in them was total, the hatred absolute. "I was so frightened I couldn't speak. All I could say— not out loud, but just in my head—was 'Jesus.' And then there was this sudden brilliant light in the room, and Satan was gone."

She learned only later, Gianna would tell me, that Satan, knowing the role she was to play in this time when time was running out, had come to scare her off. And he succeeded, at least for a while. "I was so terrified that I wanted nothing to do with anything connected to religion. I wouldn't even go to church, except maybe once in a while on Sundays."

It was during one of her rare attendances at Mass that she first had come across the crazy man, Gianna recalled. After this, whenever she showed up at church, there he was, always doing bizarre things like lighting matches during the service to drive away invisible enemies, or flailing with his arms, or cursing wildly, claiming he heard voices. What disturbed Gianna more was that for a period of a few months, she kept encountering the crazy man at odd places all over Los Angeles (she was at USC then), in shopping malls and at movie theaters, where he did things like kick trash receptacles and demand that whoever was inside come out. "It wasn't like he was stalking me, because he wasn't capable of that," she said. "But he kept showing up where I was. That also was part of Satan's plan, so that when I began to hear voices, I would think I was crazy too."

The purported supernatural experiences that eventually produced the devotions at St. Maria Goretti hadn't started in the summer of 1988, as reported by Laurentin and Faricy, Gianna said, but rather one night in September 1987. She told herself it was a dream that first time: It was after midnight and she was lying in bed when a young woman, beautiful beyond belief, appeared out of thin air and began praying over her. She could see the woman quite clearly, Gianna said, slim and of medium height, wearing a white robe and a semi-sheer veil, with long dark hair, steel-blue eyes, a porcelain complexion, ruby lips, and rosy cheeks. The fingers of the two hands pressed together in front of her were long and perfectly tapered, Gianna noticed; the young woman did not speak, but smiled radiantly, then disappeared.

Gianna kept thinking about this "dream" all during the next day, she said, wondering why it made her so happy. She had an idea who the young woman might be, and felt certain when the same thing happened again the next night. The difference was that this time, she knew she wasn't dreaming, because she turned in bed to see her husband sleeping next to her, then turned again and found the Virgin Mary still standing beside her bed, praying silently and smiling with an expression of love more pure than seemed possible. As she had the day before, Gianna woke up the next morning filled with joy. She wasn't frightened at all, and her elation only increased when the Madonna returned the following night. On the fourth night, though, the Virgin didn't come. Gianna began to wonder if it had really happened. And if it had, what it meant.

All her friends and family noticed was that Gianna, a nominal Catholic at this point, suddenly became quite pious, going to Mass every morning to take communion, praying the Rosary each evening, and making her confession once a week. Being in church, she would explain to me, brought back the tremendous sense of serenity, of delight, and of faith she had experienced during those three nights when the Virgin visited. She didn't get scared until one morning two months later. She was in church, Gianna recalled, and had just knelt to pray when she heard a voice, a male voice, quite clear and perfectly distinct, say, "The Lord seeks favor upon you, for you have cried for the Lord." It was then, Gianna said, that she began to suspect she had gone mad.

She told no one what had happened, except her mother, a devout Catholic born and raised in the Abruzzi region of Italy. Gianna doubted anyone else would believe it. So it was a relief, really, that nothing else of this nature happened to her for the next eight months. By the late spring of 1988, however, she had discovered in herself an overwhelming desire to visit a small village in Yugoslavia.

Most of what she knew about Medjugorje at this point, she had heard from Father Jack Spaulding. Spaulding had visited Hercegovina for the first time in June 1987, and upon his return to Scottsdale had told parishioners the experience was transforming him. He was so moved by what he witnessed in Medjugorje that, during a stopover in Frankfurt on the way back to the U.S., he had cried like a baby. In part because Spaulding was considered a rather cold and cerebral priest, not at all the sentimental type, his testimony made a considerable impact back in Scottsdale, where parishioners formed one of the first U.S. prayer groups devoted to the Medjugorje message.

Pretty and petite Gianna Talone had been attending the prayer group for several months, but the priest knew her only from a distance, and had noted her vivacity, though not any special devotion or reverence. In May 1988, Gianna said she would like to join the group of ninety-seven parishioners whom Spaulding was escorting on a second trip to Medjugorje. She and her mother got the last two seats aboard the charter flight that left Phoenix on June 1. During her second day in Medjugorje, Gianna attended a talk given by a man who was unable to say later what had prompted him to single out one young woman from the Scottsdale group and tell her, "You are going to play a major role in Our Lady's plan." He wished the next day that he had kept his mouth shut, the man admitted, after this same young woman approached him to say that she believed the Virgin had spoken to her.

She could recall verbatim what Mary told her, Gianna said: "Please do not pray for yourself. Pray for others who suffer, so the Lord will bless them, and pray for peace in souls, in families, and in the world. Don't be fearful, for I will protect and guide you."

The Virgin spoke to her each evening for the next week, and on June 6, Jesus appeared to her as an infant. The Virgin told her that Jesus presented Himself as a child only "when He is in joy with someone." The next day, Gianna began to be afraid again: "Remember, I come from a science background," she would explain when we met, "so my rational mind didn't believe something like this was possible; it had to mean I was going crazy." That evening, the Virgin suggested she visit Vicka Ivanković. Gianna walked to Vicka's house the next morning, but at first couldn't get close because of the crowds. Then, magically it seemed, the swarm parted and she found a clear path to the visionary, who listened to Gianna's story, then advised her to remain open and unafraid, and to keep listening.

The young American did not tell her pastor about the voice she was hearing until after their return to Scottsdale. The priest nodded throughout this conversation, but Gianna could see he was shaking his head on the inside. "Father Jack saw me the way I had been and still was, in a lot of ways: aggressive, materialistic, outspoken. Having nice things was really first with me, way ahead of a relationship with God." Spaulding wavered when Gianna showed him some alleged conversations with the Virgin that she had transcribed. "The words were very simple, very clear, and very right on," the priest recalled. "I thought, 'Hmmm.'"

Spaulding's interest—and his apprehension—increased dramatically a few days later, when a young woman named Stephanie Staab came to see him. Like Gianna, Stephanie, then twenty-five, was an attractive and ambitious young woman who had shown little interest in religion. She was a charmer, though, with a winning smile and an unaffected attitude, whose biggest problem seemed to be getting carried away every time she met an "exciting" man. The first words out of Stephanie's mouth were almost the same ones Gianna had opened with, the priest recalled: "Father, I think I may be losing my mind." She had been hearing a voice, Stephanie explained, the voice of a woman who had instructed her to copy out a lengthy disquisition. When the priest read the several pages she handed him, he was visibly shaken. Stephanie was a bright young woman, but not one blessed with either eloquence or imagination; a self-described "number cruncher," she worked as an accountant at a local bank. What she handed him that afternoon, however, was the most moving treatise on conversion of the heart that he had ever read. "I said, 'Stephanie, this is just amazing,'" he remembered, then asked if she knew Gianna Talone. No, she had never met anyone by that name, answered Stephanie, who was not with the group that had gone to Medjugorje. As he had with Gianna, the priest instructed Stephanie to keep silent about all this for the time being, but to come see him "if anything else happens."

Barely a week passed before the young cowboy Steve Nelson showed up at his office, Spaulding recalled. "I think I'm going crazy—" Steve began. "Let me finish," the priest interrupted. "You've been hearing a woman's voice." Stunned, Steve nodded. The priest asked what the woman had said, and Steve told him: "'Come closer to My Son. Pray.'" Steve, who had attended college on a rodeo scholarship and kindled only one ambition, to become world champion in calf roping, seemed concerned mainly that this meant he would have to give up his dream and become a priest. "Did she ask you to become a priest?" Spaulding inquired. No, Steve said. "Then don't worry about it," counseled the priest.

Steve's nineteen-year-old sister Wendy came in next, with essentially the same story the others had told. Spaulding suspected her brother had confided in her, but Steve, who struck the priest as incapable of lying, swore he had said nothing to anyone. At least Wendy had demonstrated some proclivity for the Church, Spaulding knew, having left her sorority at Arizona State to live for most of a year with Mother Teresa's Missionaries of Charity in Calcutta.

Susan Evans, on the other hand, had not until recently shown any tendency whatsoever toward religion. After graduating from the University of Arizona with a degree in business, Susan entered a corporate-executive training program and seemed to Spaulding just "another Scottsdale yuppie" who rarely attended church, and only then to keep her parents off her back. It was Jesus who had spoken to *her*, twenty-nine-year-old Susan told Spaulding. This was shortly after the young woman began to complain of a curious series of undiagnosed ailments that combined acute allergic reactions with hypersensitivity to touch and chronic pain in her joints. She had been sitting with her family at a friend's wedding reception, Susan told Spaulding, when she heard a male voice ask, "Would you give up your family for Me?" She looked around the circle of her relations, then answered, "Yes, Lord."

She was attending the Arizona State Fair a few days later, Susan said, when Jesus began to speak to her again, pointing out particularly unattractive people, one at a time. The first was a man with long, stringy hair and a scraggly beard, wearing greasy jeans and a torn T-shirt, who looked like "the lowest of the low," in Susan's opinion. "Would you suffer for him?" Jesus asked her. She answered that she would. Next Jesus pointed out an immensely obese woman, either Mexican or Indian—"someone I might have looked down on," Susan admitted—and asked, "Would you suffer for her?" She answered yes again and again that day, Susan said.

Her parish priest knew only that Susan began attending Mass every day, then staying after to pray for hours at a time. She would go home, then come back to church an hour later. Spaulding soon learned that the young woman's health was deteriorating rapidly, but that no cause could be determined. Susan had been diagnosed alternately with lupus, fibromyalgia, and scleroderma, but at least two doctors said her condition was psychosomatic. Most of the other physicians who examined her agreed that she showed real symptoms, but that these were so many and so severe that it was impossible to be sure what was producing them. She knew, Susan told Spaulding, that she was suffering for the salvation of souls, as Jesus had asked.

It was all getting to be a bit much for Spaulding, but Gianna said Susan was one of the core six in her vision. This vision, Gianna said, had been given to her by Our Lady, who was requesting a prayer group of young adults between the ages of eighteen and thirty-three. She had been shown six young people, one of them herself, kneeling at an altar, Gianna explained. The others were Steve and Wendy Nelson, Susan Evans, plus two others, Mary Cook and Jimmy Kupanoff. Off to the side were two other young women: one standing, whom she recognized as Stephanie Staab, and another on her knees, whom she did not remember seeing before. In her vision, she had seen one of the group, Jimmy, walk away, but later he returned.

Father Spaulding knew twenty-one-year-old Jimmy Kupanoff as a handsome young man who wanted to be a musician, but instead was majoring in communications at Arizona State, preparing to exploit his good looks as a television news reporter. Jimmy joined the prayer group at St. Maria Goretti that summer, just as Gianna had said he would, but left after only a few weeks, moving to Ohio with his family. Gianna's vision would be tested now, Spaulding told himself. Two weeks later Jimmy returned to Scottsdale, saying the Virgin had spoken to him in his heart, and that he had experienced a conversion. Jimmy was so changed that for a time he lived with the priests in the church rectory.

Mary Cook simply refused the Virgin's "invitation" from the start. To Spaulding, Mary had seemed an unlikely choice. She was perhaps the prettiest young woman in the parish, came from a wealthy family, and at twenty-six already was making money hand over fist, selling cellular phones at a time when they just had begun to penetrate the market. Yet Mary seemed to career from one destructive relationship to the next, barely pausing between. And she was guilty of committing one of the gravest Catholic sins, aborting an unborn baby, not just once but three times.

Gianna told her about the prayer group and her vision and all the rest of it during the month of July, Mary recalled, "but I found the whole idea really frightening, and didn't believe it was real, anyway. I didn't want it to be real, and I knew it wasn't for me." Two weeks later, she announced she was moving back to Wisconsin, where she had grown up. Gianna assured Spaulding that Mary would be back. "I figured, 'Okay, this will be the real test,'" the priest recalled. Two weeks later Spaulding saw Mary Cook's name in his appointment book. Soon after arriving in Wisconsin, Mary explained to the priest when she came in that afternoon, she had heard a woman's voice. She knew it was the Blessed Mother, asking her to return to Arizona and join the prayer group, yet despite this, she had refused. The Virgin asked again, though, requesting that she go back to Scottsdale and meet with Spaulding. The moment she said yes, Mary explained, a sense of peace had welled up within her. She was going to stay and give the prayer group a try.

And she would always be glad that she had, even if things did end so oddly, Mary told me as we sat in the motionless heat outside St. Maria Goretti on my first evening in Scottsdale. Doubt had entered in, no question about that, she said—doubt about herself and about others. "Sometimes I think we lost something, other times I think it was just time for it all to end. I still wonder, 'Did it go wrong, or are we meant to come together again someday, when everyone's ready?' I don't know. But I do have this feeling that I'm waiting for something. I'm not sure it's over. Gianna doesn't think so; she says we're all being 'prepared.'" Mary smiled and shook her head slightly when I opened my mouth to ask a question. "Prepared for what, I can't say," she added. Her tone confused me. "By 'I can't say' do you mean that you don't know or that you can't tell me?" I asked. "Both," Mary answered, and I knew by the expression on her face that this was the best answer I could expect.

From the moment Gianna first confided that she was hearing the Virgin's voice, Father Spaulding told me when we met at his office the next day, "I knew that my, quote, career, unquote, was at a complete end."

Up to that point in time, Spaulding had been known among his brethren in Arizona as "the fast-track priest." A small, clever man with a long, fine-featured face, crippled on one side from the polio he contracted as an infant, Spaulding had become, at age thirty-five, the youngest Catholic chancellor in the country, handpicked by Bishop James Rausch to administer the Phoenix diocese. It was the sort of singling out that virtually guaranteed a priest elevation to a bishopric some day, and possibly even a seat among the college of cardinals. Rausch died nine months later, however, and was replaced by Thomas O'Brien, a modest man who possessed neither great ambition nor exceptional abilities. Spaulding stayed on for a year but felt constrained by Bishop O'Brien, and asked to be reassigned as a parish priest. His hopes of ascendancy to the magisterium were not collapsed, because at St. Maria Goretti, Spaulding had been given the wealthiest parish, per capita, in the state.

Renowned as a manager (his seminary degree was in administration), Spaulding took up his new duties in late 1982 and helped make the parish what one religion writer called "among the best-run in the country." He began to change (and almost everyone thought it was for the better) after his first trip to Medjugorje in 1987, and returned to Hercegovina five times during the next fourteen months. Then, during July 1988, Gianna Talone and Stephanie Staab began to deliver "messages" from the Virgin intended for the entire parish. They were simple, direct, gentle, and repetitive. "Return to God now, while you still can" was the central instruction, though there was also much discussion of mercy, forgiveness, and healing. The Virgin began each message with the salutation "My dear children," according to Gianna and Stephanie, and ended with "Thank you for responding to My call."

By the end of 1988, there would be four separate prayer groups in the St. Maria Goretti parish. The teenagers had their own group, and attendance at the young-adult meeting on Friday nights had grown from thirty to more than three hundred. The core group purportedly selected by the Virgin (which had increased to eight with the inclusion of eighteen-year-old James Pauley) met privately with Father Spaulding on Monday evenings. The Thursday-night prayer group (where Gianna reported each week's message for the parish) was open to all ages and now included more than a thousand members, with as many as seven hundred in attendance on some evenings.

Gianna had sensed from the beginning that Spaulding "didn't want it to be me, because I was too aggressive, too materialistic, too outspoken, not humble at all." He was won over, the priest explained to me on the morning we met, by observing the changes not only in Gianna but in the others as well. He met with each of the eight (they still were waiting for number nine) once a week, "and saw them all suffering but willing to accept it." It was the lack of cohesion among the group, in fact, that convinced him what was happening couldn't be "a copycat thing." "They didn't try to conform to each other at all," he explained. "Exactly the opposite."

And while all eight seemed still able to function normally in the world, they began, one by one, to sacrifice their ambitions. Gianna started it by resigning her high-paying position with a pharmaceutical company to take a job behind the counter at a Walgreens drugstore. Mary Cook abandoned her cellular-phone distributorship to work for a fraction of her former wages at the Good Egg restaurant. Particularly impressive to Spaulding was Steve Nelson, who came in one day and reported that the Virgin had asked him to give up calf-roping; his answer, Steve said, was that She could have whatever She wanted.

And She wanted a lot, apparently. Gianna informed the others that the Virgin was requesting a three-year commitment from each of them, during which time they were not to form any sort of permanent attachment. Some noted that this would be easiest for Gianna, who already was married, but each of the eight consented to give the prayer group the next thirty-six months of their lives.

He had tried to remain skeptical, Spaulding insisted as he recounted the events of this period, "but the depth of commitment I saw in these young people was very persuasive." The priest also was impressed that those who claimed to be hearing the Virgin said She would remind them periodically that they were free to choose. And each of those who were hearing Her said the Virgin assured them that if they chose to say no, they would not be loved any less.

Spaulding was sent reeling again, though, when Gianna came in one day during the fall of 1988 and reported that Jesus now was speaking to her, too. It had happened for the first time on August 10. She was at work when she heard Him say, "My child, know that you are never alone. I am in you, and you are in Me." It was not long after that, Gianna said, that Jesus began to dictate a series of "lessons," and said He wanted them published. Father Spaulding's answer was a firm no. "It just seemed too much, too soon," he explained to me.

Gianna kept coming back, and in November 1989, the priest agreed to help find a publisher for the "lessons," adding that he had no idea how such a thing might be accomplished. Three days later Spaulding received a letter, unsolicited, from the owners of Faith Publishing, inquiring about whether the messages that were being received in Scottsdale might be available for collection. By the time of my trip to Scottsdale, the Ohio company had published more than nine hundred thousand copies of the *I Am Your Jesus of Mercy* books (from which Gianna had not earned a penny).

It was in late 1989 as well that Gianna announced the Virgin had given each of the young adults who was chosen, and Father Spaulding also, a symbol. There were ten in all, which Gianna said signified "the virtues of Jesus' heart." At first, the others thought they were being singled out for their strong points, but Gianna said no, that in each case they were being asked to develop in the areas where they were weakest. This was an especially painful revelation for her, because the symbols she had been given were love and mercy. Father Spaulding got a jolt also, when Gianna informed the priest that his symbol was truth. Susan Evans got charity, and Stephanie Staab joy. Wendy Nelson was given strength, and her brother Steve received faith. Mary Cook got hope, James Pauley courage, and Jimmy Kupanoff compassion.

Taken aback as some were by their own symbols, no one seemed surprised by the virtue that had been assigned to Annie Ross, the ninth and last of the young adults to join the Monday-night prayer group: Annie got humility.

Within moments after Annie Ross opened her front door and said hello, I began to feel as if my feet were losing contact with the earth. Whatever distinctions I made between reality and unreality blurred in much the same way they had during my walk through Mostar with Karen, of whom Annie put me in mind immediately. The two shared that sad combination of obesity and a ravaged complexion, though Annie did not appear to have abused herself with quite the level of commitment that Karen brought to the job. She possessed the same quick, bright, manic quality that marked Karen's periods of sobriety, however. And just as Karen did, Annie seemed to fight against some deep-seated shame with an almost exhibitionistic frankness, sounding at times as if she was boasting about her background even as she described the horror of it.

Like Karen, Annie was from a wealthy family. "My parents were old money on both sides," she began, when I asked about her upbringing. "I had an ostensibly wonderful childhood in St. Louis and Michigan, with gentry farms and camps in the woods that our family owned. Underneath, though, it was a hideous nightmare that I lived in all by myself."

As had Karen's, Annie's nightmare began when she was sexually molested as a child. "It was an adult relative who did it first," she recalled, "but my main abuser was my older brother, who started having sex with me when I was seven years old." These assaults coincided with her earliest apparition experiences. "Our Lady came to me almost every day," she recalled, "mainly to remind me that I wasn't alone, that God loved me, and that She did too. I talked to Her and about Her so often that my parents thought Mary was the name I had given my imaginary friend."

Angels began to visit also, Annie said, and were her only companions after the age of nine, when the other children at school "found out about me." Her brother told only his friends at first, but later showed pictures of her to all of the boys. "After that, nobody wanted anything to do with me. I responded by becoming very gregarious, very outgoing, very aggressive. That may sound odd, but it was the only way I could hide my insecurity. I also was extremely smart; being bored with school was a lot of what drove me to start getting into trouble. By the time I was ten or eleven, I was ending up in the headmistress's office at least once a day. It was a Catholic school and I was the campus troublemaker. My usual punishment was to be sent to sit in front of the Blessed Sacrament for an hour. I didn't know the headmistress was saving my life."

Her apparitions ended shortly after she reached puberty, Annie recalled, "because I wanted them to." She got angry as a teenager and began demanding to know how a supposedly loving God could let such things happen to a child. "And when Our Lady came, I scorned Her encouraging words. I wanted Her to leave me alone, and She did."

At the succession of boarding schools she attended during her teens, she was known as the most promiscuous girl on campus, Annie said, and had sex with almost any boy who showed an interest in her. She also attempted suicide twice during those years, once by slitting her wrists and another time by drug overdose. "But both times people found me and called an ambulance. I not only didn't thank them; I hated them for it." By age sixteen she was either drunk or on drugs—"cocaine and bourbon were my mainstays"—during nearly every waking hour, to kill the pain, Annie explained, because she wasn't one of those who could forget it all. At eighteen, during her first semester of college, she was brutally raped and became pregnant as a result. "I prayed I would miscarry, and I did," Annie told me, her voice shaking for the first time. She began to hemorrhage badly, but refused to see a doctor, and developed pelvic inflammatory disease, which left her infertile.

Annie moved to her parents' new home in Scottsdale that summer, began taking classes at Arizona State, and got a job as a waitress. "My first night at the restaurant, I met a young man and fell in love, I thought. Basically I fell in lust, and he found a sucker." Her new boyfriend was a Turkish national whose only hope for remaining in the U.S. was to marry an American citizen. "I made it so easy for him."

The new pastor at her parents' church, Father Spaulding, refused to perform Annie's marriage ceremony. "I said, 'Fine, I'll get somebody else,'" she recalled. "My attitude was 'How dare you?'" Annie soon found herself in a marriage "where I was beaten terribly almost from the start." Nevertheless, she stayed with her husband for nearly five years, and put him through a master's-degree program in international management. Her family's fortune was nearly exhausted by a series of bad investments and her father's illness, so Annie worked three full-time jobs—as a bookkeeper, a salesclerk, and a waitress—to pay the bills. "I still was drinking heavily, whiskey, mostly, but I had stopped using drugs, so I was feeling more of my pain.

"Finally I decided to go see Father Jack, whom I hadn't spoken to since my marriage. I told him what was happening, and said, 'What do I do?' I remember he told me, 'Annie, there are limits even to perseverance. I suggest you ask the Lord.' I thought he was a little nutty. Somehow, though, just telling someone, anyone, had made me feel what a lie I was living. And I went straight from his office to the church, to attend Mass, which I almost never did in those days. Now, I didn't believe in the Eucharist, but that night, at the elevation of the host, I prayed. I said, 'Okay, Lord, what am I supposed to do? You have to tell me. Am I supposed to leave this marriage? Yes or no, I need to know right now.' And I heard very clearly, 'Yes.'"

Annie filed divorce papers the next day, and had her husband removed from the house. That same weekend, she met Eric Fitch. "The first time I laid eyes on him, I knew he was the man I should marry. And I was heartbroken. He was Catholic, I was Catholic, and now I was going to be divorced. There was no annulment. I crumbled. I just fell apart. I began drinking constantly, which only made my depression worse. After my divorce became final, I was just sitting home alone at night and crying myself sick, because I couldn't cry myself to sleep anymore. I realized I had done things I had promised myself I would never do: an affair to get even with my husband, two abortions at seventeen and nineteen, hard drugs, and dark sex—the boundaries I had overstepped!"

Annie had reached this climax in her crisis during the same period when her mother was imploring her almost daily to attend the special Mass at St. Maria Goretti intended to dedicate a new statue of the Virgin

Mary. "My parents were very involved in the fund-raising for this, and were working with Father Jack," Annie remembered. "And I said, 'I don't want anything to do with him. Father Jack doesn't like me, and I don't like him.' My parents kept after me, though. They were daily communicants, which in a way was part of my anger at the Church, that these people could be so godly and good, and yet so unaware of what was going on with their own daughter. My mom finally got me to agree to attend the dedication, though, by promising to buy me this outfit that I wanted.

"So there I was at Mass that night, March 31, 1989, the date my life changed."

Annie's voice began to alter perceptibly, and it was more than the breathy teariness of her tone. I had noticed it before, though not so dramatically, when she spoke about seeing the Virgin Mary as a child, this rapturous, almost caroling quality. I found it quite compelling, in spite of my best efforts at resistance: I'd be sitting there in a sort of benumbed wonder at the strangeness of the story I was hearing, then somehow begin to feel myself raised to a keener level of attention.

"Now, like I said, I had never believed in the real presence in the Eucharist," Annie went on. "I thought it was a sort of scary joke, really. My attitude was 'Come on, people, get real—it's a cracker.' I always had the impulse to pick the thing up and wave it at them: 'Hello! Does this look like God to you?' Anyway, during the prayer of consecration I was making fun of Father Jack's singsongy voice, like I always did when I heard him speak in church. Suddenly, though, I heard this other voice, this female voice, say, 'My child, you must choose, either for My Son or against My Son.' And I recognized the voice, because it was the same one I used to hear as a child. And I said, literally, 'Okay, You've got me. My life is a shambles, I admit it. Do with me what You want, but I'm out of here in fifteen minutes.'

"I really just wanted to get back to my normal self, but then I heard another voice, a very strong male voice, tell me, 'No. Stop. Listen.' I said to myself, 'Okay, it's finally happened. I've lost my mind for good. No turning back now.' But the thing was, I looked up and I saw the host in Father Jack's hand, and I knew that I knew that I knew that was Jesus. Total conviction, all at once. This . . . is . . . God. Right here, right now. And He's calling me.

"What I wanted to do was go to confession immediately, but then I realized that I didn't know what to confess, or if what I'd done already was so bad that it was too late for me, because I was past confession. My parents stood up to get in the communion line and I couldn't move. My father sort of pulled me along after him. All I could see was Father Jack standing there holding God in his hand. And I was sobbing and shaking as I took the host from him, knowing this is God, pure and complete. Then I go to the goblet. Now, even on those rare occasions when I went to Mass and took communion, I'd never drink the wine—'I'm not gonna drink out of the same cup as all these strangers.' But all of a sudden I didn't care about that. And Father Jack uses white wine, but when I look in the goblet, it's red. It's blood. It even tastes like blood, the blood of Christ, the blood that was shed for my salvation.

"I drink it and I feel like I'm on fire, split right down the middle between the sane, logical half of me that knows this isn't real, and the certain, loving part of me that knows it is.

"I don't know what happened after that. It took me three hours to travel a couple of blocks from the church to my house, and when I got home I had no idea what I'd been doing, or where the time had gone. I walk in the front door and I see my dog, Margaret, crouched down growling at this corner of the room, like someone's there. And then I hear this voice, this woman's voice, say, 'My child, I wish for you to write.' And the dog is growling even louder, so I'm sure there's someone there. Then I realize it's after midnight and this is now April Fool's Day, and I figure someone is making fun. 'Okay, who's there?' But nobody's there. I look under the beds, in the closets, behind the shower curtains, out in the garage.

"Finally I decide that I really have lost my mind, and right in that instant I hear this woman's voice again, saying, 'My child, I wish you to write.' I knew who it was, but I didn't believe I knew. It was too much. My godchild had left her crayons and some construction paper on the floor, and I picked those up and tried to write what the voice was telling me. But it didn't work. So I went to get a pencil and started writing with that, but it broke. So I found another pencil and that broke too. I find a pen, but it won't work, so I look for another pen. And this whole time She's talking, telling me what She wants me to write. Now, I'm dyslexic, someone who can't even copy a phone number unless I ask the person to repeat it a couple of times. But that night I sat down and wrote all night, remembered every word She said, and got it all down."

This went on for a week and a half, Annie said, before she gathered what were by then several dozen sheets of paper covered with "messages," stuffed them into an envelope, wrote, "To Father Jack from Annie Ross (call me if you want to)" on the front, and dropped it off at St. Maria Goretti.

"Father Jack called and asked me to come in a couple days later," Annie continued. "I had just gone to confession for the first time in years, and I went to him, so he knew all about me. He had been really sweet, though, more wonderful than I would have thought possible. So I did go to see him and said, 'What do you think?' He said, 'Has it continued?' I said, 'Yes, Father.' He said, 'Just keep writing, but don't tell anybody. I'm putting you under a vow of Holy Obedience. You understand what that means?' I said yes, but all I really knew was that I had to keep my mouth shut.

"Father Jack said just to come back and see him if this continued, and to write down whatever I heard. So I did. This went on for weeks and months. I had started going to the main young-adult prayer group in April, but I didn't know about the Monday-night group or that others were hearing voices also. I had seen Gianna and Stephanie at Mass, but I didn't even know their names. So I felt really alone. And half of me still thought I was crazy, schizo. I'm thinking, 'Great, now they're gonna lock me up in the loony bin and lose the key. I'll be just another nut, a multiple-personality crazy woman.'"

Later, when I asked Spaulding why Annie had been excluded from the Monday-night group for those many months, all the priest could tell me was "She didn't fit the criteria." Sometime in November 1989, though, Annie learned "from a friend of a friend of a friend" that Spaulding was meeting once a week with Gianna Talone and seven others whose experience paralleled her own. "I was very hurt when I found out," Annie said. "I realized that Father Jack was keeping me out."

It was Gianna who issued the invitation to join the Monday-night group, after seeing Annie in church and recognizing her as the young woman who had been kneeling off to one side in her vision. However, from the moment she walked into that first Monday-night meeting in early December, Annie felt she was not welcome. "When I came in everybody was talking, laughing, chatting. Then it just stopped. The atmosphere became very cold. " She assumed the problem was that "they'd all seen me in action before, seen me drunk, seen me wild."

Annie didn't seem much changed, the others said. "I was verbal," she explained. "I wanted to know what they were going through, what they were feeling. I wanted to be able to talk about all that and get beyond the pettiness. I felt, 'Let's deal with this and help each other out.'"

Nearly everyone else in the Monday-night group, though, regarded Annie as vulgar and unstable. "Most of them approached me at one time or another and told me I was from the Devil," she recalled, "or not part of this, that I was being used by Satan to destroy this group, that I should go away. Some, like Mary Cook, just ignored me.

"Looking back, it does seem as if things started to fall apart because I came in. But it wasn't my entry that made it fall apart, it was their response to me."

That had been a difficult period, Father Spaulding agreed when I asked him about it the next day, but Annie's inclusion in the group was not, for him, the biggest problem. His greatest struggle was with Gianna's announcement several months earlier that the Virgin had told her: "'I will appear to you, and then to the others.'" When this didn't happen, "it started all kinds of doubts in my mind and in my heart," Spaulding admitted.

Then, in December 1989, Gianna reported that the Virgin finally had appeared to her. That first apparition was overwhelming, she said: It began with a feeling of fullness in her heart, followed by a burst of brilliant light. Then, all at once, She was there, a young woman of perhaps twenty, dressed in dazzling white, with unblinking blue eyes and a voice so tender and melodic that Her speech was like singing. "Praise Jesus!" were the only words the apparition spoke. Mary disappeared a moment later, Gianna said, but the emotional intensity of the experience was such that she lay sobbing for hours afterwards.

The next evening, Gianna armed herself with a vial of holy water brought back from Medjugorje; this, she had been told, would drive away any evil spirit attempting to deceive her. At almost the moment the Virgin appeared, Gianna splashed Her with the holy water. The Blessed Mother simply smiled in response, then asked, "Why are you surprised? Didn't I tell you that I would appear to you first?" Gianna continued to be troubled by doubt, but no longer by fear, "because the feeling I had so was sweet and joyful. I didn't even wonder that much why or what for; I just trusted the feeling."

News that the Virgin Mary was appearing to Gianna became public during the seer's first apparition at the Thursday-night prayer group. Those Thursday-night apparitions were especially intense, causing her to lose all sense of her surroundings. She sometimes was aware of people on the periphery of her vision, but they seemed vague and far away. "Our Lady is so beautiful that She takes up all your attention, all your mind, all your feelings," Gianna explained. "You see only Her."

Even as the Virgin's apparitions continued, Jesus continued to dictate daily lessons to her, said Gianna, who reported that the voice of Jesus sounded very different from that of Mary: The Virgin's voice was like the most gentle song she had ever heard, a distillation of maternal love, its very essence. The Lord's voice, though, was more majestic than musical. Yet Jesus had a terrific personality, Gianna reported to the others, and a wonderful sense of humor. He seemed to laugh and cry at the same time in the face of human foibles.

As inspiring, as unsettling, as profound, and as dubious as Gianna's experience was to those who beheld the visionary but not the vision, by early 1990 her apparition claims were no longer even the most controversial development within the Scottsdale parish. Gianna had been upstaged, at least in terms of the furor generated, by Father Spaulding, who announced that Jesus and Mary were speaking not to him but *through* him, using the priest, as he put it, "like a microphone."

All he remembered, Spaulding would explain, was standing to deliver his homily at the Thursday-evening Mass and going completely blank: "I didn't even know who I was. A feeling came over me like I was drained. All of a sudden I heard myself speaking. And it wasn't me speaking. It lasted about forty-five seconds. I didn't hear what was said and couldn't remember later. Afterward, I was so tired I could hardly make it back to my seat."

That had been the Blessed Mother, Gianna informed the priest in the sacristy after Mass; the Virgin was using him so that She might communicate more directly with Her children. About one month later there was a further amplification: While once again preparing to deliver his homily at the Thursday-night Mass, Father Spaulding said, a feeling came over him that he would be "used" that evening. "Only it was much stronger. My whole body tingled. I went out in front, and it started. Only this time it wasn't Our Lady speaking, it was Our Lord."

Up to that time, the events in Scottsdale had been viewed by the rest of the Phoenix diocese with either cautious enthusiasm or disdainful indifference. When word got out that the parish priest there now claimed that Jesus and Mary were speaking through him, outrage and derision erupted. All that quelled the uproar, really, was the announcement that an episocopal commission had been formed to investigate whatever was going on at St. Maria Goretti.

The priest chosen by Bishop O'Brien to head his tribunal was Father Ernest Larkin, a Carmelite theologian admired for both his intelligence and his spirituality. His primary obligation, Father Larkin would say later, had been "to make sure there wasn't some sort of scandal in the making here." Jack Spaulding, however, believed that the main objective of the Bishops' Commission was "to bury this thing as deep as it could."

"The, quote, investigation, unquote, that they conducted was absolutely crazy," Spaulding said. "They met with the kids once. Once! And then only as a group, not individually. And they met with me only once." The meeting with the nine young adults had not been cordial. The commission members did most of the talking, asked a few cursory questions, then told the nine that if there was anything they'd like to add, they could call and set up an appointment. The Scottsdale group sat baffled for several moments, then became indignant. "It is not our job to call you," Stephanie Staab told the tribunal. "You said the commission was formed to investigate us. I mean no disrespect, but if you would like to reach any of us, you have our phone numbers." The nun who sat on the commission, a Franciscan from the cloister at Black Rock Canyon, felt this signified "a lack of openness" on the part of the nine. Besides, she did not like the idea that parishioners might put their faith in visions and messages when they should be "just living a life of faith in the spirit of Jesus."

Most frustrating for Father Spaulding was his meeting with the psychologist appointed to the commission, Dr. James Lange. "I said, 'Am I crazy?'" Spaulding recalled. "He said no, that I was quite sane. I said, 'You think I'm lying?' He said no, he was sure I was telling the truth. I said, 'Just a second. You say I'm not delusional, and you say I'm not lying. But you also say this isn't happening.' He never could give me an explanation." Dr. Lange actually had been the commission member most impressed with the Scottsdale group, noted Father Larkin: "He was probably more reverent than I was, convinced that something truly extraordinary was happening here."

Ultimately, the report submitted by the Bishops' Commission in early 1990 described the events taking place at St. Maria Goretti as "explainable within the range of ordinary human experience," but did not elaborate. The commission's report was not intended to be negative, Father Larkin told the diocesan newspaper: "We don't think these are hoaxes, or that there is any attempt to deceive. We simply maintain that there is not enough evidence to say that these are miracles." Dr. Lange wrote in his section of the report that he found nothing aberrant psychologically in any of the nine young people, and that to him the faith of those involved seemed genuine and great. Larkin added that Father Jack Spaulding "has demonstrated himself to a be a good priest and should be commended for his devotion."

St. Maria Goretti's pastor was hardly appeased. "My assessment is that they wouldn't give us a straight answer," Spaulding said when I asked about the commission's report. "From my point of view, either I'm crazy, or I'm lying, or it's true. This approach of saying it is happening and it isn't happening baffles me."

Ernest Larkin seemed to be pretty baffled himself, and six years later still was struggling to articulate his "admittedly ambiguous" beliefs about what he had encountered among the St. Maria Goretti group. He agreed with Dr. Lange that "all of them seemed to be mentally healthy," Larkin told me when we spoke for the first time a few days into my Scottsdale stay, and believed as well that "they all underwent a very authentic religious conversion." Furthermore, the commission's investigation had found much to support and nothing to contradict the claim that the nine "began having these experiences separately and distinctly, without being aware of the others," which he found particularly intriguing, Larkin allowed. Nevertheless, he could not accept that there had been, literally, a direct communication to them from Jesus or the Virgin Mary. "These young people were, and are, simply reporting their experience," explained the priest, "but experience can be controlled by what you want to happen, what you expect to happen."

I admitted that no matter how often I heard them feathered or fudged, I still tended to accept the three categories of possibility proposed by Jack Spaulding: Either the visionaries were lying, or they were delusional, or they were telling the truth. "Basically, I agree with you," Larkin responded, "but I also think that delusion, which sounds pejorative, needn't be. People may be telling the truth when they say they see this or that, but they may be unaware that the influence of the environment—which can be very subtle—encourages these experiences."

He considered himself "agnostic" in such matters: "I find it difficult to believe that Mary is standing on the edge of human consciousness, and maybe breaking in every now and then, here or there. I don't think these people see the real Mary, I think they see their own image of Mary, an imagined Mary. Mary isn't walking into somebody's life like She was a mortal human being. The Blessed Mother is in this mysterious realm of Heaven."

And there's no interface between that realm and ours? "I don't think so," Larkin answered. So he didn't believe in any apparitions at all? I asked the priest. He became silent for several moments, then sighed. "I can't say that," he finally admitted. "I believe in Lourdes. I believe in Fátima. And I'm very curious about Medjugorje. Something of a profound nature has occurred in each of these places. I don't know how you explain them. I don't know to what extent these are the effect of natural causes and to what extent they are miraculous. It's almost impossible to know what comes from nature and what comes from grace."

We digressed into a discussion of St. John of the Cross; Larkin reminded me that Catholicism's most famous mystic poet had counseled the faithful to resist all supernatural experiences, even their own: "I really believe that these events send as many people away from religion as they draw near, because they seem so bizarre, so much out of the ordinary providence of God." If he went to Medjugorje, Larkin said, "I might be as impressed with the visionaries there as so many others are, but I doubt it. Because I couldn't help asking, 'Why would the Blessed Mother appear here when the world is falling apart everywhere else also?'" That's like asking why Jesus would raise Lazarus when there are so many other dead people, I observed. Larkin laughed. "You're right," he said. "It's the same question. I have to fall back on my a priori principle that we live in a realm of faith from which there is no escape."

Bishop O'Brien was remaining as neutral as possible about the events in Scottsdale, Larkin said. "These sorts of things have to be watched over a long period of time. We have to follow the advice that Jesus gave to his disciples and judge a tree by its fruit." And he had observed nothing but good fruits coming out of St. Maria Goretti, Larkin acknowledged a moment later. More than seven hundred parishioners had agreed to keep a twenty-four-hour vigil, seven days a week, in the Blessed Sacrament Chapel next to the church. Several miraculous healings of a compelling nature were reported, while conversions and confessions, which the church valued most highly, had increased in both number and intensity at St. Maria Goretti. One young woman who joined the Thursday-night prayer group gave a moving public testimony about being present the first time the Virgin spoke through Stephanie Staab: "I knew in the deepest part of me that it was Our Lady. I had no doubt whatsoever. This was the most traumatic experience I have ever had in my life, because it shook me to my roots. I spent the next three days alone, in bed, because I became physically ill from emotional turmoil as I tried to reconcile what

I knew to be true with what I had believed was true . . . I had seriously to evaluate and change my life. God suddenly became One who cannot be taken lightly, and cannot be kept at a distance."

Because his investigative commission found nothing "amiss" in the devotions at St. Maria Goretti, Bishop O'Brien announced, he would permit the prayer meetings and public devotions at the church to continue, although "no unequivocal claim of miraculous intervention may be made."

"The bishop just wishes the whole thing would go away," insisted Jack Spaulding, who probably had been more encouraged than any other member of the St. Maria Goretti group by the arrival from Rome of Father Robert Faricy shortly after the local Bishops' Commission delivered its report. Faricy spent more than a month interviewing each of the principals in Scottsdale before he was ready to issue a public statement, explaining that careful scrutiny was essential in this age of "prevalent false mysticism." He had carefully applied each of the five basic criteria that the Church imposed on reported revelations, Faricy explained, and his conclusion was that the apparitions and locutions in Scottsdale were "authentic."

The odd result of Faricy's positive verdict was to give the devotions at St. Maria Goretti a greater standing internationally than they had in their own community. Spaulding found this a great consolation: "Bob Faricy also helped me tremendously on a personal level. At one point I told him these nine were all good kids, but nobody you'd write home about, as far as spirituality. I admitted that I wouldn't have chosen these kids, because a lot of them drive me crazy. But that was one of the keys to authenticity, according to Faricy—the fact that none of these kids was in lockstep, that they were terribly different personality types."

Spaulding still had a big problem with the inclusion of Annie Ross. "Off the wall," the priest called her, and most of the others in the Monday-night group agreed with him on this point. Several members of the prayer group were unable to deal with Annie's coarse language, shuddering when she described Spaulding's attempts to protect the public image of the nine as "getting a face-lift and a boob job." Annie also had a tendency to flaunt her status as a religious visionary, informing certain younger parishioners at St. Maria Goretti that they weren't looking too good lately in the eyes of the Lord, as if invoking some sort of authority. The others found that highly improper, and said so.

Gianna alone took a longer, more sympathetic view: "At the beginning you see Our Lady, and because She's so beautiful, you can feel you're favored, you're blessed by God, you know it all." Only with the passage of time, Gianna added, did one understand that exactly the opposite was true: "The fact is, the closer you get to Our Lord, the more you know nothing."

Annie's relationship with the group did not improve when she became the second of the nine to report that she was seeing the Virgin. The Blessed Mother had promised a week earlier that it would happen, Annie explained, telling her to fast and pray for three days prior to the event. The moment arrived during a praying of the Rosary at the Thursday-night prayer meeting: As Annie watched, a brilliant light tinted with greens, oranges, and yellows surrounded the statue of the Virgin to the left of the altar, then Mary seemed to step out of the statue and take human form. Gianna, kneeling next to Annie, said she was seeing the Virgin in the same way at the same time.

The others all had the same question: Why Annie? Some had been envious of Gianna, but it was accepted by all that she for some reason was to play the leading part. The choice of Annie made no sense to any of them. And their distress only increased when Annie announced that Jesus was talking to her as well, almost every day. What made this especially difficult to swallow was that the encounters Annie described sounded more like therapy sessions than religious instruction. The Lord was, among other things, helping her deal with her fear of men, she said, coming to her not as an adult male but as a small boy, "so I won't be threatened, so I'll be the older one, the bigger one. He's got enough love to do that." Jesus was teaching her that she had a right to a normal, healthy sexual relationship (within the sacrament of marriage, of course), Annie said, and He allowed her to ask questions about anything, as long as they were put to Him in innocence.

Like Gianna, Annie described not just a person but a personality, a rabbinic teacher (a lot of people felt Annie placed unnecessary stress on the fact that Jesus had come as a Jew) who instructed through questions: "He's not going to tell you, because you already know." Jesus enjoyed a good joke more than almost anything, she said, and made her laugh hardest whenever she asked a question that was not so innocent (these always seemed to begin with the word "why," Annie noticed): "He'll usually come back with 'Are you God?'"

Visitors from all over the planet now were attending the Thursday-night meetings at St. Maria Goretti, and it made a lot of the regulars uncomfortable that Annie had joined Gianna as a featured player: The two sat in the front row of pews and knelt together in ecstasy when the Virgin came. That Our Lady spoke to them separately struck some as odd, at least. But Gianna, whom few doubted, said Annie's apparitions were real.

The other members of the Monday-night group could not accept Annie's claims. "Choosing Annie was Jesus testing us," Gianna explained. "He has said, 'I give mercy to those whom I choose.' And our mistakes are what teach us. Yes, it's incredible that the Lord chose Annie, but that's why, because she's able to touch what's broken in people, and that's our greatest common bond, our brokenness."

Be that as it may, many of the faithful at St. Maria Goretti publicly expressed their relief when, in the fall of 1990, Annie announced, unexpectedly, that the Virgin had said She no longer would appear to her on a regular basis (promising, though, to come on her birthday for as long as she lived). After this, she saw the Virgin not as a person during the Thursday-night prayer meetings, but only as "a form of light" during Gianna's apparitions. Gianna continued to report seeing the Virgin daily, but now even she bore the stigmata of flaw and failure. In early 1991, Gianna's husband, Michael Bianchi, left her and filed for divorce. She was nuts, he told people.

Religious visionaries in the midst of divorce proceedings are not exactly a commonplace of Catholic culture, and news that Gianna Talone had become one rocked the Scottsdale parish. "A number of people nearly had breakdowns," recalled Carol Ameche, who had become a sort of scribe to the St. Maria Goretti seers. "They are won over, enthralled, and then—boom—they are confronted by this human reality and lose faith completely."

For some, it wasn't so much the divorce as that "they wondered why Gianna ever had been married to this guy," Carol said. Bianchi's looks seemed to be all he had going for him: He owned a reputation—deserved or not—for exploiting women financially, and had worked sporadically as a commerical artist during his marriage to Gianna, who was the family breadwinner most of the time. As for his wife's mystical experiences, "I think he just rejected it all from the outset," Father Spaulding said. Observed Carol Ameche: "He had no degree of faith, and wanted out because it got to be too much, more than he could handle. Saying she was crazy was his excuse for bailing."

I spoke to Bianchi by phone in the midst of my Scottsdale stay, and the man brought out the worst in me. We fenced at length over the question of why he should speak "on the record," and for several minutes I was completely convinced that Gianna's ex-husband knew something that might ease my mind. In the end, though, I realized he had nothing of any real value to tell me. Perhaps Bianchi was more of a gentleman than people understood, I decided: He had, after all, spared Gianna the disapprobation of the Catholic Church by declaring publicly that he did not want children, providing his ex-wife with grounds for a speedy annulment. By that time, though, the dissolution of her marriage was just one scene in the public spectacle that surrounded Gianna.

A documentary about the "Scottsdale visionaries" had been broadcast on a local television station, and made the nine public figures in the Phoenix area. Gianna, featured in the TV special, was working then as pharmacy coordinator at one of the city's largest hospitals. "All at once, everyone at work knew," she remembered. "People shunned me, mocked me. I heard about the jokes and remarks secondhand, but sometimes I would walk into a meeting and everyone would stop talking; I knew it was about me. Some couldn't keep from laughing. The only thing that kept them in check was that I continued to do my job."

During that time, the Virgin gave her a message for the other eight: "My dear children, do not be upset or worried by the humiliation which comes from this present world . . . You can benefit from your weaknesses and failures, fears and doubts, by drawing good from infirmities."

Gianna kept just one friend from her former life, a non-Catholic whose job as an investigator for the state hardly encouraged her to credulity. "I really didn't know what to make of the religious experiences Gianna said she was having," this woman told me. "But watching the way she dealt with things was very impressive. I knew she was suffering, over her divorce especially, but there was this calm about her that I had never seen before. When we were younger, I'd always thought of Gianna as high-strung, emotionally intense, so to see how serene she was with everything that was going on in her life really made me pause, and not pass judgment."

Among those at St. Maria Goretti who did not turn away in disillusionment, it became an axiom that the divorce and what followed had happened so that Gianna "could experience rejection, just as Jesus experienced rejection," one prayer-group member told me. Gianna herself believed she had entered a "spiritual night" that would last for almost three years. What she experienced was a form of grief, she explained, a period of mourning that all who undergo real religious conversion must pass through. "You're gaining something, of course, but you're also losing something, and that's the ability to be in the world like other people. Your attachment to things and appearances is fading, but not gone completely, so you have a conflict inside. Also, because you see how beautiful and how loving Our Lady is, you become aware of all your own faults and sins, your pride, your lack of generosity and compassion. You feel the pain of all that, of being so far from that beauty, that peace, that perfection. You feel ashamed of yourself, and despondent."

Sensing her weakness, Gianna reported, Satan began to attack her physically during the night, and she woke up many mornings covered with bruises: "I was exhausted so much of the time," she recalled, "just spent." Within a few months, she took a leave of absence from her job, which turned into a resignation when the hospital filled her position with another pharmacist. Her spiritual director said Gianna's situation had gone beyond his scope of understanding, and suggested she find someone "more experienced with this sort of thing."

Gianna amazed everyone with her selection of a new spiritual director: The priest she chose was the same one who had headed the episcopal commission that had concluded there was no proof her conversations with the Virgin were authentic, Father Ernest Larkin. "Very impressive," said Larkin of Gianna's decision to place herself in the hands of an admitted skeptic. He came to admire the young woman enormously during the next three years, the priest told me: "I would constantly bring everything back to faith, that we live by faith, not by sight . . . And Gianna was a very beautiful person in this regard; she never became defensive or argumentative. Not even once."

He still could not accept that the experiences she described were "objectively real," Larkin admitted, but was compelled by her character and conduct to allow that something extraordinary was taking place. He certainly believed Gianna was not mentally ill, and also that neither she nor any of the others at St. Maria Goretti was after wealth or power. That left, of course, the desire for attention—"which is a big one," the priest noted: "To have ten thousand people looking up at you and waiting for your word, that's a tremendously seductive temptation." He had been forced to concede that most of the St. Maria Goretti nine not only didn't seek attention but actively avoided it. In fact, as Gianna became absorbed by her personal struggle, the public devotions in Scottsdale grew increasingly private.

By 1991, both Mary Cook and Wendy Nelson said that they, too, were seeing the Virgin, but what they described had a more nebulous quality than the apparitions reported by Gianna and Annie. "Interior" was the word Mary and Wendy each used to describe their visions, and neither of the two appeared comfortable with a public role. Wendy in particular balked at the pressure from Father Spaulding to "be out front," often refusing even to attend the prayer meetings. The sense of mission that had imbued the parish during the first couple of years grew diffuse, and the group of young adults at the center of events was drifting apart.

The "Unraveling," as some called it, happened slowly but inexorably. Stephanie Staab went to Dallas for three months in the fall of 1990 to work as a financial consultant on a mortgage portfolio, then in 1992 married a banker from Chicago and moved with him to the Midwest. Wendy Nelson's brother Steve married that year also, and took up residence on a small ranch outside the city, supporting himself as a carpenter; like his sister, Steve stopped coming to the prayer meetings. Susan Evans, whose physical condition had steadily worsened, was traveling back and forth from Scottsdale to an apartment in Vancouver, British Columbia, where she spent her days in virtual isolation. Jimmy Kupanoff began leading youth groups to the Mexican mission at Guaymas; James Pauley went off on a speaking tour in England, then matriculated to the Franciscan University in Ohio. Mary Cook worked for a time running a preschool, then married the Christian singer Michael John Poirier and moved with him to Payson, Arizona; they came back to Scottsdale, but Mary, who was raising a new baby, said she felt it was her role now to be private and prayerful, removed from the public eye.

Annie Ross had ceased attending services at St. Maria Goretti early in 1991, choosing instead to join a smaller parish nearby. A few months later Annie left Scottsdale to go on the road with the charismatic New Orleans–based Father Robert Degrandis, traveling to seventeen foreign countries and thirty-two American cities. "I know people have said I'm horrible, going around promoting myself as a 'visionary,'" she said, "that it's so vulgar and vain. But I never told any of the people I spoke to that I was one of the Scottsdale visionaries." Annie ostensibly was teaching "on prophecy and charisms," but often her presentations amounted to personal testimony, and she found herself doing things like describing the events of her childhood to an audience of twenty-five hundred in Guatemala City.

Even those who criticized Annie, I noticed, kept adding that she'd "come a long way." Her new spiritual director was a priest who worked as a psychologist, and he had to be doing her a world of good, because during the succeeding years Annie became a much calmer and more mature presence. Hardly a more conventional one, however. Annie said she spoke daily with Jesus, Mary, and various saints, among them Bernadette of Lourdes, Teresa of Avila, and Padre Pio. Her hands, she said, had begun to exude a watery oil; Jesus told her it was to be used for anointing the people with whom she prayed. Annie's first marriage was annulled by the Church in February 1991, and exactly one year later, after vacillating for months about entering a convent, she married Eric Fitch. The Virgin appeared to her during the ceremony, she said, to bless the marriage. Annie published a book, *Inner Healing Through the Rosary*, a few months after the wedding. Those members of her former Monday-night prayer group who read it said they were surprised and impressed by its simple clarity.

It was to Gianna, though, that most of the believers at St. Maria Goretti still looked for inspiration. And she appeared to be floundering. She had attempted to put together a health-care collective serving the poor and the homeless in Phoenix, but was unable to pull it off. During a visit to Rome, she was inspired to create a "lay Catholic community" that would include single men and women, married couples, and even members of various religious orders, but that never came to fruition either. In the summer of 1992, Gianna went to live at a cloistered Carmelite monastery in Wisconsin, where she planned to spend six months deciding whether to become a nun. She had been there only six weeks when the convent dog, a collie who never had shown the slightest sign of viciousness before, bit her face so savagely that she nearly lost an eye, required surgery, and was blind on one side for more than a month.

She came back to Scottsdale in August, and by September was once again attending the Thursday-night prayer meetings at St. Maria Goretti. Early in 1993, the parish learned that Gianna was leaving Scottsdale once again, this time to move across the country and marry a man she barely knew. It was "God's will," she explained.

My last full day in Scottsdale exhausted me utterly. I began the morning by speaking at length over the phone with Jack Spaulding. I was troubled by any number of discoveries I had made during the past week. For one thing, it had become clear to me that several former members of the Monday-night prayer group at St. Maria Goretti felt he had wounded them, and that at least three harbored no small antipathy to the priest. Spaulding professed to be unaware of this. "I was very involved with all of them for quite a while, and then they started going their own way," he said, as if this should serve as sufficient explanation. When I pressed for more, Spaulding sighed. "I didn't totally agree with any of them," he admitted, "and I told them so, and sometimes that did hurt their feelings. So they would go to other priests to talk, which was their prerogative." Acid leached into the priest's voice on that last word.

Nearly every one of the nine had complained at one point or another that he was trying to "control" them, I told him. "It was my duty to control them," the priest said. "I couldn't let this whole thing turn into a circus." The remark struck me as odd, given that the main complaint I had heard about Spaulding was that he insisted upon creating a "spectacle" at St. Maria Goretti. I had learned just a couple of days earlier that he had been very involved in theater as a boy and had wavered between choosing the priesthood and a career as an actor all during his late teens and early twenties. This bit of information kept adhering in my mind to what I knew of Gianna Talone's background as a child star, and to Ernest Larkin's expressed concern that a desire for attention might explain much of what had taken place at St. Maria Goretti. Looking in from outside, I told Father Spaulding, it appeared as if everyone involved had just let the whole thing drop. "Not everyone," he said. "I was still at prayer group every Thursday—they weren't. And that, too, was their prerogative." That word again, sounding just as corrosive as it had when he spoke it the first time.

I brought up Annie's belief that her entrance into the group had been the catalyst of dissolution. "A lot of them didn't like her," Spaulding conceded, "because of her personality. The group already had coalesced, the trust level was fairly deep, then Annie came in and nothing was ever quite the same." What did that mean? I asked. "There was division," he replied, then sighed again. "Like I said, I had a lot of trouble with a lot of their personalities. And I still do, maybe. They drive me crazy, to be perfectly honest. I wished many times that it wasn't these people. But you know, I already had hit that with the visionary Ivan in Medjugorje. When I met him, I thought, 'Give me a break.' Father Slavko talked to me at some length about the need to be humble and to accept God's choice, and I tried to do that, in Medjugorje and here in Scottsdale. I think I succeeded, but maybe others don't see it that way."

Bishop O'Brien had personally ordered the priest's reassignment from St. Maria Goretti one year earlier. Father Spaulding clearly believed he was being marginalized: "Bishop O'Brien and I have had many conversations about this. The last time I met with him, I said, 'Bishop, I wish I could say to you that I didn't believe this, because it would make your life easier, and it would make my life one heck of a lot easier. But I can't do that, because I believe this with all my heart. And Bishop, it's gonna continue as long as Our Lady wants it to continue.'"

Spaulding sounded almost fiery for a few seconds there, but in the next breath he grew morose. "I know the bishop doesn't think I'm lying, and I don't think he thinks I'm crazy. I don't know what he thinks, really. No one ever has been able to give me an answer."

I empathized with Father Spaulding in that moment, and perhaps should have ended our conversation there. I felt obliged to raise the subject of Carol Ameche, however. According to Gianna, the Virgin Mary had specifically chosen—or rather, invited—Carol to become secretary to the prayer group at St. Maria Goretti, and the woman grew closer to the nine than any other member of the parish. Though we had spoken only briefly, and mostly over the phone, I found Carol a reliable source of information; both her recollections of and opinions about Father Spaulding and the other members of the prayer group were borne out by what I learned later. However, I also had discovered that the woman posed a rather large problem, not only for me but for the entire St. Maria Goretti parish: Since May 1992 she had been reporting that Jesus was using her as a prophet of revelation, a claim that not even one of the other prayer-group members accepted. Father Spaulding had gone so far as to urge me to avoid all contact with Carol. Why? I demanded to know.

"Because I believe she's misled," he said. What did that mean? By "misled," was he implying the involvement of some evil spirit? "No," answered the priest. I reminded him that we had agreed earlier that there were three core possibilities: The person is lying, the person is mentally ill, or the person is telling the truth. "I don't think Carol is lying and I don't think she's telling the truth," Spaulding said. So you think she's mentally ill? I asked. "That's the remaining possibility, isn't it," he replied in a tone that was chilly indeed. Spaulding did not hide his displeasure when I told him that I would be meeting with Carol late that afternoon to hear her version of events at St. Maria Goretti. "That's your prerogative," he said, and hung up on me a few moments later.

Thoroughly unsettled, I hurried off to my appointment with Susan Evans's mother, Dawn. Mrs. Evans kept her house cool and dark, two points in her favor on a day when it was 116 degrees outside. Still, I began to grow lightheaded during the interview and when I stepped back outside after it was done, the stunning blast of light and heat nearly bowled me over. "By tomorrow night, I'll be home," I thought as I stumbled toward the rental car I had been forced to park in full sun. The temperature inside the vehicle had to have been 140; I was sopping wet and so dizzy I could hardly see the road in front of me. By the time the air-conditioning kicked in, I realized I was coming down with something. Back at the resort, I cooled my fever in the shower and was sprawled naked on the floor when the phone rang. It was Annie Ross, calling up to finish the conversation we had started face-to-face three days earlier.

She wanted mainly to discuss the whole problem of victimhood, but first felt obliged to say that she had agreed to speak to me in the first place because "I asked and was told you needed this." Asked who? I inquired, and wiped the beads of sweat off my brow, wishing I had a thermometer. "The Lord," Annie said. "He explained to me that you weren't here mainly as a writer; you're here because you want to find God. You're here because you doubt God's love, and you doubt God's love because you doubt you can be loved. You're also here to discover that you don't have to drop everything in your life to discover God. You want to know how you're going to fit God into your life, or, more to the point, how you're going to fit you into God's life. You're terrified that if you do that, you're going to lose everything that's important to you, and you won't. You won't lose it. It's not going to happen to you. Just because you've seen it happen to others, that doesn't mean it's going to happen to you. God wants you to know that. He has a different plan for every one of us."

Annie listened to my silence for a few moments, then giggled and said, "But enough about you. Let's talk about me. Let's talk about how you recover from an experience like I had as a child. Real recovery for me began with my Advent offering four years ago. I asked Our Lord what my offering should be, and He replied by asking what I'd like from Him. I said I'd like to get over hating my brother, that I'd like to have a normal marriage and sex life. I said, 'I want You to help,' and He agreed. I asked how, and He said, 'Stop complaining and start praising Me.' I said, 'Praise You for what?' He said, 'For being there during that time.' I said, 'You weren't there. I prayed and I prayed and You didn't answer. You didn't

do anything to stop it.' He said, 'It's the anger at Me you have to overcome first.' With His help, I began to look back, and I saw the times when
people offered help and the love of the Lord, and I couldn't accept it.

"Forgiving the Lord was the first step, but then I had to start working
on forgiving my brother. By now he was married to his second wife and
had three beautiful daughters. I called him up and we began to talk. He
acknowledged everything. I found out that he had gotten counseling and
had really dealt with a lot of this already, but hadn't been able to deal with
me. Up to that time, he and I couldn't even be around each other physically. He would be consumed with guilt if he had to be in the same room
with me, and I hated him bitterly. But in the space of a few months, with
Our Lord's help, I was able to go from absolute bitter hatred of my brother,
which had gone on for years, to realizing that the same things he did to me
had happened to him. His anger about what was done to him turned in on
himself, then came out on me, because I was the vulnerable one.

"Eventually, together, we told the rest of the family what had happened. I was even able to discuss it all with his present wife, who already
had heard everything from him. I'm sure it sounds incredible, but we've
actually become close, like a normal brother and sister. Just yesterday he
called me, excited, to say he had been offered a position with a French
bank. On the phone, I told his wife I was so happy for him. I have prayed
for his healing and happiness. For me, the ugliness is in the past."

Annie's voice had taken on that rich, full, vibrant tone that so entranced
me during our face-to-face meeting. It was the sound of someone speaking through tears that already had been cried but were not yet dry. The
strange and broken purity of it made me want to weep myself.

"The Lord is saddened by the claim to victimhood made by so many
people of our generation, and the generations behind us," Annie continued. "It's all a crock. Because how we respond to what happens to us is
what decides who we are. I'm not the victim. You're not the victim. Jesus
was the victim. Understanding that is the road to recovery.

"So there's my story," Annie added after a brief pause, and giggled
again. "If you decide I'm a loon, I'll try not to take it personally."

An hour later I was wondering if Carol Ameche would take the same
attitude. Carol's home was the nicest I had visited during my stay in
Scottsdale. Though it had the look of an adobe bunker from the street,
inside, the place felt like a large enclosed terrace, brightly tiled, cool but
full of light, with walls of windows and lots of well-made white wicker
furniture. Carol, a slender woman with expertly dyed blond hair, looked

a lot younger than seventy, and no doubt had been quite stunning in her day. Her husband, Don Ameche, Jr. (son of the two-time Oscar-winning actor), had made a fortune as a stockbroker in Chicago, and the two of them lived on his investments now. As a young woman, she had worked as a nightclub singer and was pretty well known for being "a party girl" during the 1960s. Her life had been saved, Carol said, by a nun she met shortly after reaching the end of her rope: "I went through a very long and painful conversion process. I had to confess a lot, because I had a lot to confess." After marrying Don, she gave birth to six kids in nine years. The couple moved to Scottsdale after his retirement, and she began attending services at St. Maria Goretti shortly before the Thursday-night prayer group formed.

I was struck by how sane and sober Carol sounded as she described her background. The only curious note was how unaware she seemed to be of the low regard in which she now was held by the former members of the Monday-night prayer group. Oh, she knew there was some "resistance," Carol acknowledged, but she felt certain that more of them believed than didn't. "The reason some people don't accept me or my messages is that they're pretty apocalyptic in character," she observed, "and frightening. They're downers. People don't want to hear it."

Carol said she received her first message on May 5, 1992, when she woke up at midnight and heard a man's voice say very clearly, "I wish to speak with you." She asked for some time to prepare, ate a bowl of cereal, drank a glass of orange juice, prayed the Rosary, "then said, 'Okay, let's go.'" I was less taken aback by what Carol was saying than by the way she said it. Her transformation when she spoke of her dialogues with Jesus was no less remarkable than Annie's, but completely opposite. Rather than the exalted, emotionally intense tone Annie took on, Carol's voice spiraled into a giddy, coquettish squeal. Alternately giggling and panting, she sounded as if she couldn't believe her own story, and yet as if she still found the whole experience thrilling beyond description. For a few minutes, it became unnerving to sit in the same room with her, but then suddenly Carol seemed to get control of herself and once more began speaking normally.

Tell me about this voice you hear, I suggested. "It's like a voice giving dictation," she said, "but one you hear only inside your head." My disturbance must have shown on my face, because Carol began to assure me that she had done much "testing of spirits," praying to God for protection against any tricks of the Evil One or of her own imagination, before taking her messages public. Her main message was that the Warning prophesied at both Garabandal and Medjugorje was very near, and that when it came, there would be worldwide chaos and confusion. "Every person on earth will see Christ crucified in the sky," Carol said. "Yet still, some will not believe. This event will not only galvanize the faithful, but also the enemies of the Church, who will do their best to explain it away. The current pope will be gone by the time this happens, and in his absence the Church will split, and its importance in political terms will increase. Both before and after the Warning, there will be widespread devastation. Our own country will be especially hard hit, and there will be a general breakdown of society. We will have no choice but to call in an outside agency—the UN, or something that replaces the UN—to solve our problems. And that's how the bad guys are going to take control. The face of evil, well hidden now, will come out into the open very rapidly, and the situation will be obvious to everyone almost immediately."

Carol paused to take a breath and studied my reaction. To avoid showing any, I asked a question: Where exactly is the face of evil hidden presently? "In the media, mainly," she answered. "Taking over the media has been their main objective for most of the twentieth century. They're also very involved in international banking and the weapons industry." I nodded but said nothing, having decided there was no choice but to ride this out. "Jesus says that the complacency of people is the most dangerous thing in the world," Carol told me suddenly. "And pragmatism is part of complacency, this whole idea of progress for its own sake, with no idea where we're going." Her voice now had become very firm and clear, commanding, actually. I was impressed in spite of myself. "Our Lady has told me that man was never meant to live at the rate of speed we do today," she said, "and that Satan does everything he can to make us go even faster. Abortion, though, is what has made the cup run over. The rejection of His gift of life, God's justice cannot accept this, and His hand must come crashing to earth, though He waits and waits and waits until the last possible moment."

That moment *was* coming, and soon, Carol said. Scottsdale had been chosen to serve in that terrible time as Christ's Center of Divine Mercy. "Many, many will die, especially on the West Coast," Carol went on, "and the remnant people will be coming here by the tens of thousands, desperate, frightened, feeling as if God is attacking them. They will have lost everything, and it will be our job to explain to them that this is justice, to help them make sense of God's mercy, to understand that this is the only way God has left to reach them."

This all would happen in her lifetime, Carol assured me—"and I'm not a young person, as I'm sure you've noticed." That was why Jesus was giving such clear lessons, because time was short. "Jesus is my spiritual director," she said. "He has told me I must separate myself from the world, that I must stop going out at night, that I must learn to pray early in the day, when I'm most awake. He has told me I can't spend time with my friends like I used to, that I have to pull away. He is calling me to one-ness with Him, to that quiet place where heart and spirit heal."

Carol brought out a copy of her book, *As We Wait in Joyful Hope*, and pressed it into my hands. "We have to avoid this idea of a vengeful God that Jesus and Mary are holding back with their prayers," she said. "God the Father has spoken to me also, and it's the most loving, the most delightful, the most nurturing voice you could ever imagine. When I first heard God the Father, my feeling was 'The Buck Stops Here.' Because you feel that finality, that majesty, and yet He's very dear, very easy to listen to. It was through that experience that I finally came to understand that true fear of God is not terror but awe. God is quite simply giving us the gift of Himself."

She took my hand in hers for a moment, then said, "I think you've had enough. I won't tell you about the part you are to play in all this, because Jesus wants you to find that out for yourself."

I was so woozy my knees nearly buckled several times as I walked through the crushed white rock and cactus plants that filled Carol's front yard and climbed back into the oven of my rental car. My fever was growing worse. Back at the resort, I filled the bathtub with cold water and buckets of ice, then sat in it for the next hour drinking rum and Cokes. It was just getting dark when I wrapped myself in a sheet, lay on the floor next to the air conditioner, and dozed off.

I awoke three hours later to the sound of thunder. Rising to my knees, I looked out the window to see the sky streaked by lightning bolts and the air filled with whirling debris. I threw on a pair of shorts and a T-shirt, then stepped out barefoot onto my room's patio. I stopped there for only a moment, then continued on a pathway that wound through the resort's grounds. Huge palm fronds were torn loose by the wind and cartwheeled past me. Tremendous skeins of lightning flashed in the sky, reflecting off the ridges of Camelback Mountain, and the thunder was deafening. I would learn the next day that this was the most violent thunderstorm the Phoenix area had seen in several years; stories of the deaths and damage it had caused filled the front page of my morning newspaper.

Soaked to the skin, I wandered in the storm for more than an hour and never saw another soul. I had entered a sort of delirium that had little to do with my fever. At one point I began to shout into the wind, the same phrase, over and over: "God exists! God exists! God exists!" I intended this less as a declaration of faith than as demand to be either struck dead or released from further involvement. "Who gives a shit?" I murmured finally, and walked back to my room. By the time I climbed into bed, all I felt was grateful to be going home.

I wasn't quite there yet, though, and another phone call from Annie Ross caught me just as I was about to check out the next morning. She was calling, she said, because she had forgotten something important, which was that I needed to be convinced—or at least reminded—that Satan was real. The Devil existed because free will did; if I could just get my mind to fully engage that idea, I would understand. "Satan is determined and Satan is clever," Annie said. "Satan has tried to trick me at various times by pretending to be Jesus or Mary, and it's hard to tell the difference, except by the feeling you have inside. It's the feeling you have to trust. Doubt is our biggest obstacle and Satan's greatest weapon. Doubt is what blocks the Lord's voice, and the first doubt is that we're making up the voice in our head. I still struggle with doubt. I know when the Lord and Our Lady are speaking to me, and yet I doubt. That's because I'm human. I can only say that I believe that I'm experiencing what I'm experiencing. But I always question, even though I always know.

"So, just remember that we're not so different."

I said thank you, though I didn't really mean it, and promised to pass along a greeting to Gianna when I saw her, which at this point I doubted I ever would. I arrived back in Portland late that afternoon, went straight to bed, and stayed there for the next two days. By the time my fever had broken, I was pretty thoroughly convinced that this whole enterprise, all the way back to Boardman, had been an exercise in self-delusion that need not continue with a trip back east to meet Gianna Talone. Drained and despondent, I spent my first day out of bed moping about the house, feeling vaguely angry at a God I really didn't believe in. My own susceptibility astonished me now that I was in a position to consider it; this renegade self inside me that insisted upon feeling over thinking very nearly had driven me to madness. I was drinking a beer on the deck when I remembered the CD Annie Ross had given me. *O Holy Angels*, it was called, a collection of gospel tunes that Annie had recorded for M.A.R.Y. Ministries a couple of years earlier. More out of boredom than curiosity, I put it on the stereo, hit the "random" button, and headed for the kitchen to get another beer. I had just opened the refrigerator door when Annie's rendition of "Taste and See" came on and stunned me into immobility. The voice in which Annie sang was one of the purest and most soaring contraltos I had ever heard, enormous in volume and resplendent with emotion. I closed my eyes and stood in a sort of exalted shock, unable to comprehend that this magnificent sound could issue from the misshapen body of Annie Ross. I never did get that beer, and by the time Annie began to sing "Breathe on Me," I was gasping for breath and blinking back tears.

My head was still between my knees half an hour later, when the music stopped and I realized that I had no choice but to head east.

It was January 31, 1993, Father Al Pehrsson remembered, when a tall man with a beard approached him in the parking lot outside St. Joseph's Church in Emmitsburg, Maryland, and introduced himself as Dr. Michael Sullivan. He was the assistant medical director at the Geisinger Clinic in Pennsylvania, Dr. Sullivan explained, so as to establish the professional credentials that might persuade the priest he wasn't a lunatic. "Do you know anything about what has been happening at St. Maria Goretti in Scottsdale, Arizona?" the doctor asked. He did indeed, the priest replied; the question was a marvelous coincidence, actually. Just a few weeks earlier someone had given him a tape of Father Jack Spaulding's testimony before his congregation in Arizona. He found it fascinating, Father Pehrsson said, and listened to the tape again and again on his headset as he walked through the cemetery at the nearby shrine to America's only native-born Catholic saint, Elizabeth Anne Seton.

Pehrsson began to tell the doctor all about it, how these nine young people from Scottsdale had reported receiving locutions from the Blessed Mother; four said they actually *saw* the Virgin, and one young woman claimed to have taken dictation directly from the Lord. "Yes, Father, I know," Dr. Sullivan interrupted, and gestured to the large-eyed young woman who had stepped up beside him. "I'd like you to meet my fiancée, Gianna Talone."

Stunned, the priest stopped smiling. "Why are you here?" he asked. Dr. Sullivan explained: They had come to the Lourdes Shrine in Emmitsburg (the oldest in the U.S.) to dedicate their marriage to the Sacred Heart

of Jesus in front of the grotto's crucifixion scene; at the shrine, the Virgin
Mary appeared to Gianna and invited the couple to move to Emmitsburg.
The Holy Mother told them to think about it for three days, and ended
the apparition by suggesting that they drive into town and introduce themselves to the pastor at St. Joseph's. "So here we are," Gianna finished.

And now I was, too. Well, I actually was eight miles away, in Gettysburg, Pennsylvania, as I listened to Father Pehrsson's story. Through the
window of my motel room I could see a line of Civil War cannons and
assorted monuments to the three bloodiest days in U.S. history. "Experts
in the field of paranormal activity" reported that Gettysburg was haunted
by more ghosts than any other place in America, I read in a brochure
that I had picked up in the motel office. Why was this easier to believe,
I wondered absently, than Gianna's claim that the Virgin Mary was appearing to her each evening just across the state line in Emmitsburg?
Perhaps because ghosts asked us to worry about their souls, not our own.

I drove with my wife to Emmitsburg, arriving at St. Joseph's Church
in the midst of a swarming crowd. Gianna still made her only public
appearance of the week each Thursday, when a special Mass was celebrated around her evening apparition. On top of this, Father Pehrsson
was retiring and would be saying good-bye to his parish that evening.
People were lined up all the way back to the rectory, where seating as-
signments were being given to the lucky few who would be admitted to
the church for this Thursday service. So it was not surprising, really, that
my wife and I should be the object of many aghast expressions as we were
ushered past the crowd and into the sanctuary by a pale bald man who
led us to a pew near the front, then insisted that two older women give
us their seats. Embarrassed and confused, we slid into the pew amid a
chorus of indignant murmurs and no small number of nasty glances.

The people around us began praying the Rosary only a few minutes
later. I had no idea where Gianna was until a strange hush fell over the
church. Then I spotted the small woman who had risen from her seat in
the front row and was kneeling before the altar. Even then, I found it
difficult to focus on what was happening up there, distracted as I was by
a group of women who sat in the next pew, alternately fingering their
beads and shooting me dirty looks.

When the Mass was ended, we joined the crowd shuffling shoulder to
shoulder toward the exit. Suddenly I heard my name called over a microphone and saw a woman at the altar waving me toward the front of
the church. My wife and I pushed against the surge of the crowd in that

direction, but it took us nearly ten minutes to travel fifty feet. The woman at the microphone ushered me to a door behind the altar that led into the sacristy. A moment later, I found myself face-to-face with the person I had come three thousand miles to see. Gianna was attractive in a rather exotic manner, with a beautiful olive complexion, large features, and enormous, slightly protuberant eyes that seemed to search me out as I shook her hand and said hello. She also was a good deal plumper than the young woman with the size-two figure I had seen in photographs, owing mainly, I would learn, to the baby girl to whom she had given birth only a few months earlier. Gianna's appraising glance reminded me a lot of the one Mirjana had met me with in Medjugorje. She greeted me warmly, though, then asked if I was in church for the full service, and nodded approvingly when I answered that I had been.

"Our Lady wanted you here tonight," Gianna explained. I could feel my face growing red as I searched for something to say in reply. All I could think about, though, was how I might escape this claustrophobic room. I asked Gianna if we could meet privately the next day, but she already was waving over a tall man with carelessly combed hair and a scraggly gray beard. "This is my husband, Michael Sullivan," Gianna said. The intelligence in the man's pouchy hound-dog eyes made me like him immediately, but I still wanted out of there. However, before I could stop her, Gianna had sent someone back into the church to retrieve my wife. I barely contained my agitation as introductions were made, then immediately explained that we had a dinner reservation in Gettysburg and said good-bye. Gianna and her husband both appeared taken aback, but offered no protest. My wife shot me a questioning look (this was the first she'd heard of any reservation), but went ahead of me through a side door that led into the parking lot.

Outside it was twilight. As we walked back to our rental car, I asked my wife to remind me what exactly we were doing here. "I thought we were here to find out what you believe," she told me. I said I really didn't like hearing it put that way.

Before my meeting with Gianna the next day, I took an hour to explore "historic Emmitsburg," a place so rooted in its past that the local walking tour was laid out building by building, with elaborate descriptions of each eighteenth-century house that lined Town Square. I hadn't been nosing about long before I met the local Realtor who had found Gianna and

Michael a house when the couple moved here almost three years earlier. "A lot of local people were very concerned about those two at first," the woman told me.

Emmitsburg was the best-known parish in the nation's oldest archdiocese (Baltimore's), and provided a home not only to the Seton Shrine (where the Daughters of Charity still maintained their provincial house) and the Lourdes Grotto but also to Mount St. Mary's monastery. The parish was proud to be described as "the cradle of American Catholicism," but no one here had seen anything like what ensued after Gianna's arrival in the autumn of 1993. Within a few months, attendance at the Thursday-night prayer meeting in St. Joseph's was well into the hundreds, and while most of the worshippers were well behaved, seeing cars with out-of-state plates stream into town each week and prowl the side streets for parking places agitated some residents. This concern had been insignificant, the Realtor told me, compared to the distress that spread when she and a couple of other local Realtors began getting calls from people all over the country who wanted to move to Emmitsburg because they believed it would be among the world's few safe places when the Chastisements came.

"People wondered if we might have another Jonestown here," the Realtor recalled, "but those of us who met Michael and Gianna told everyone how nice and normal they seemed, and that soothed some of the concerns." Also, the mobile medical clinic that Michael and Gianna operated, Mission of Mercy, had brought high-quality health care to a lot of lower-income people who couldn't get it otherwise, so at this point there were probably as many people who wanted them here as there were people who wished they would leave.

Her voice dropping to a whisper, the Realtor added, "I asked Gianna once if this place really did have some sort of special protection, and she said it did."

I drove back to St. Joseph's and parked across the street. The church was an ornate Georgian box, white with black doors, the sort of solidly built manor of God preferred by citizens of previous centuries. Emmitsburg no doubt had its charm, but the village on the whole possessed a static quality that most of us raised in the American West find unbearable; no one even slightly interesting would move *to* such a place, we feel instinctively, and so assume the citizenry must consist entirely of those who lack the will to get out. I was wondering how a young woman who had spent her whole life in California and Arizona could bear it here, when I spotted Gianna, sitting alone in the shade of a tree not far from the side door by which I had escaped the previous evening.

Gianna laughed through a grimace when I asked the question. "Those first few months might have been the most difficult of my life," she said. "Remember, it was January when we first came to visit, and there was snow on the ground. I had no idea it got that cold below ten thousand feet. And it was the worst possible time for me. My mom just had been diagnosed with lung cancer and had three months to live. We were very close. Knowing I would not be with her during her last weeks of life, not to mention saying good-bye to all my friends and my home to move across the country to a place where I knew absolutely no one—it seemed impossible."

Then why do it? I demanded. Gianna looked straight into my eyes. "Because Our Lady asked me to," she answered. I stared back at her for as long as I could, then dropped my gaze. "You're shaking your head," she observed. I looked up at her again. "I knew Our Lady would never invite me to do anything," Gianna said, "unless it was for the good. So I made it all—leaving my mom, especially—a great offering of penance to the Lord."

I asked her if she could describe to me the circumstances in which this "invitation" from the Virgin had been made. Mary's request had been preceded by an announcement Gianna found no less astounding, she told me. This had taken place in November 1992, on the evening she first met Michael Sullivan. Michael was at the time a physician with a flourishing career as the chief of medicine for the Geisinger Clinic hospital near the Penn State University campus. He had come to Phoenix ostensibly to attend a cardiology clinic, but readily accepted an offer to attend a prayer-group meeting in Scottsdale. Michael was in the midst of a personal religious revival that had climaxed eleven months earlier in December 1991, when he flew to Dubrovnik to volunteer his services to the Croatian army. He spent the next three months on Dubrovnik's front lines, tending to the wounded. During this period, he took two short leaves, both to visit Medjugorje, and returned home in the spring of 1992, convinced that he was being called by the Lord to some extraordinary service.

She hadn't even wanted to attend the prayer service in Scottsdale on that November evening, Gianna recalled, "because it was at the time when Our Lady usually comes. But my friends convinced me." She barely spoke to Michael that evening, but invited him and the other pilgrims at the prayer meeting to attend the "private apparition" held each Saturday evening at her home: "There were about twenty people present that night, including my mother. When Our Lady came, the first words she said to me were 'Allow me to introduce you to your husband.' And these rays went onto Michael Sullivan. I thought, 'You're kidding.' I mean, not in a million years did I think I'd strike up a relationship with him." The problem, Gianna readily admitted, was Michael's appearance. "I mean, Michael Bianchi was a strikingly handsome man, very GQ. That was my type. I was still very vain about things like that. So I decided not to say anything about this to Michael Sullivan. I really had no interest in him, and no interest in marriage either. I thought, 'Okay, if this is what God wants, fine, but it will have to develop on its own.'"

That seemed unlikely when Michael failed to show up on the following evening for a dinner party at which Gianna was one of the guests, but the two met again only a month later at a Marian conference in Denver. By New Year's Day, they were engaged. Later that January, the two made their first trip to Emmitsburg. But when she informed Michael that the Virgin had appeared to "invite" them to relocate to Emmitsburg, he resisted, feeling that the sacrifice of the career he had built in Pennsylvania was too much to ask. "He could say no to me," Gianna said, "but not to Our Lady. So here we are."

What she was mainly hoping to discuss with me today was what it meant to be a visionary. She knew I had questions about what had taken place in Scottsdale, so we got those out of the way first. For the next twenty minutes, though—each time I asked a specific question—Gianna insisted that I turn off the tape recorder before she answered. What happened in Scottsdale was a case of "humanity's interference with God's plan," she said in summation, when I was finally permitted to record her. "It was ego, mostly, people wanting it to go their way, or to take control, or being jealous of one person, or suspicious of another. Pride and hurt feelings, that's what got in the way." Even when the tape wasn't running, Gianna had refused to criticize anyone in Scottsdale personally, though she did make it clear that anything Carol Ameche said should be met with skepticism. "You should pray for the gift of discernment, Randall," she said, "because you need it tremendously." For instance, the fact that Carol was a warmer and more likable person than Father Spaulding meant nothing, Gianna observed: "Feelings aren't facts," she said, an observation that would provide me with much wry amusement when I listened to it later.

Gianna made no attempt to conceal her curiosity about Michael Bianchi, and showed me the ordinary and girlish sides of her personality without a great deal of self-consciousness. The short, flat replies she made to questions about her former life didn't seem to reflect avoidance so much as a lack of interest in the subject. Her personal and psychological issues seemed more and more trivial as time passed, she explained. And as a visionary, she had to struggle constantly to avoid interference with God's message. "I try to be very careful to say only what Our Lady has said," Gianna told me with an earnest expression. "Yet even in that, there's human interpretation. I'm a sinner. I have defects in myself. Sometimes I have to try to help people understand what Our Lady is saying, but I know that I make errors. So I try not to pretend that I'm anything special. I let people know that I didn't lead such a great life, and that I still see all the sweet enticements of this world.

"The enlightenment of your soul also casts light on your nature, and that can be very difficult and very painful. There have been times when I felt more cursed than blessed. I spent almost three solid years in darkness. I was exhausted most of that time. Something most people don't realize is that when you see Our Lady, when you see how loving and beautiful She is, you become that much more aware of your own faults and sins, your pride, your unkindness, your lack of generosity and compassion. You feel ashamed of yourself, and despondent in some ways. You're no longer of this world, but you're not in the next one either."

How had her period of darkness ended? I asked. "I just woke up one morning and found that the sadness was gone," she answered. "The doubts, the fears, the feeling of loss—all of it. I realized that what I had gained was so much greater. The one thing I did right during that period, I think, was stay with it. I didn't try to avoid my own suffering. I went through it and kept trusting, even when fear and doubt and pain were overwhelming me."

I grew somber during the last part of this discourse, and Gianna noticed it. "I had Our Lord and Our Lady helping me in a very special way," she said gently. "I couldn't have made it through otherwise."

Which raises the question of, Why you? I observed. "I know a lot about what my role is, but I don't know anything at all about why I'm in that role," she said. "I used to think about that all the time, because of my own egotistical pride. But I don't much anymore, and I'm a lot happier."

We got off onto the nature of Gianna's locutions and apparitions. She made her encounters with the Virgin sound almost conversational, I commented. "In a lot of ways, it's just like talking to you or anyone else," Gianna said, "only a lot more absorbing." She described the voices of Mary and Jesus in much the same language I had heard from others earlier:

"When Our Lady speaks, it's almost like singing, so melodic. Jesus is different. His voice is deeper, for one thing, but also the tone is different. He's gentle also, but more commanding. The Lord has a terrific personality and a wonderful sense of humor. I can't remember Our Lady ever making a joke, but the Lord does it all the time."

I was writing a note to myself about being disappointed by Gianna's lack of eloquence when I asked her, rather absently, what sort of jokes Jesus made. "Well, this isn't the best example," she answered, "but sometimes He'll use a word that I don't understand, and He'll tease me about needing to work on my vocabulary. He tells me I'm not exactly a poet. Jesus jokes with me about choosing someone who isn't good with words. He understands that my intelligence is more of a scientific, quantitative, numbers kind. I got straight A's all through school, but I always had to work really hard to get A's in English classes. The Lord always tells me just to do my best, and to accept the way God made me."

I was so rattled by the coincidence of Gianna's answer and my unspoken thought that for the next several minutes I barely tracked what she was saying. She kept talking, though, and when I tuned in again, she was telling me about the various penances that had been asked of her. Back in Scottsdale, she had been the only one of the nine who was asked to physically experience the agony of Christ's crucifixion. This was in August 1991, she remembered: After a single day of overwhelming physical pain and interior darkness, she had decided to ask for an end to her apparitions and a return to normal life. "But when Our Lady came that evening, She recommitted me to the Lord. We said a prayer together, a beautiful prayer, and since that day I've never asked again if this could stop."

I had reached my saturation point, but Gianna couldn't see it. She was not naturally sensitive to others, I had realized, yet for some reason I didn't hold this against her. Only when I stood to say good-bye did she understand that the interview was over. "You know," she said as she shook my hand, "what Our Lady said last night is that the power we hold in our hearts is directly proportional to the amount of confidence we have in the Lord's mercy. The message was given to us all, but I think it was meant especially for you. I hope you'll meditate on it while you're here."

I promised that I would, but only because I wanted her to let me go.

CHAPTER SEVENTEEN

Father Larkin's line about how he didn't mean anything "pejorative" when he used the word "delusional" kept coming back to me. It was as if I had been shown an escape hatch by someone who didn't know how to operate it. I spent weeks looking for directions in the collected works of Carl Jung and came away bitterly disappointed. Marian apparitions were perhaps the purest example that existed of an archetype emerging from the collective unconscious, wrote Jung, who regarded Bernadette's visions in the grotto at Lourdes as among the most significant events in human history. When I probed for what he meant by this, I found that Jung repeatedly described visions resulting from mystical raptures as both actual and as imaginary, as natural and as synthetic, as projections and as precognitions. God existed, he asserted, but perhaps only in our minds, and that should be good enough. For me, it wasn't. "Jung was always very careful to 'dodge'—your word—the ultimate question," conceded the director of Chicago's Jung Institute, Dr. Peter Mudd, when I sought his opinion. "All he would say is, 'There is something in the human psyche that acts *as if it* were divine.' And he would leave it at that." Contemplating the great man's equivocation, I felt dull and frightened and increasingly bereft. "At least Sigmund fucking Freud knew what he believed," I told Dr. Mudd, who chuckled into the telephone.

The birth of my twin son and daughter in May 1997 brought relief. Finally, I had two answers bigger than any of my questions. I called myself a born-again parent. As months passed, though, I became increasingly aware of the melancholy growing inside me. It began with an acute awareness of vulnerability. All that was dark and dangerous disturbed me in ways I had never experienced, at least not since my own early childhood. Knowing my children were at risk, knowing that the world was full of people who didn't give a damn about them, and most of all, knowing that I could never protect them completely made me sad and frightened and, finally, angry. I began to take evil personally, and in some way to blame God for that. The Greek philospher Epicurus had framed the problem for me quite succinctly when he observed that there were two logical possibilities: One, God can prevent evil and chooses not to (and therefore is Himself not entirely good), or, two, God chooses to prevent evil and cannot (and therefore is Himself not entirely powerful).

During the spring of 1998, I grew distracted by the question of a diabolical presence in the world. Jung's answer was exactly the sort of obfuscatory twaddle that had made him such a disappointment to me: "Evil is terribly real for each individual. If you regard the principal of evil as a reality, you can just as well call it the devil." I grew more knotted by anger with each passing day, unable to see any semblance of divine plan or invisible hand in the course of events, but only the random pulse of a chaos that could turn ugly in an instant. I found myself compulsively clipping crime stories out of the newspaper. Most of these involved juvenile offenders: A sixteen-year-old girl who had slit a man's throat to steal his money for drugs; two high school boys who were arrested for torturing a cat to death at the same school where seven students, four of them football players, had videotaped themselves setting an opossum on fire, then shown the tape in a classroom; a "gang" of seven- and eight-year-olds who had tried to suffocate a second-grade girl for "breaking up" with one of them. All I knew was that I for some reason felt driven to document the presence of evil in the world. I finally began to see some purpose on the morning before my children celebrated their first birthday, when a magazine editor phoned from New York to say that there had been a shooting involving more than two dozen victims at Thurston High School in Springfield, and that he wanted me to write a profile of the fifteen-year-old killer. The wise thing would have been to say no, but wisdom was by now among the virtues I scorned.

I didn't know if I was losing my mind, but I felt pretty sure that no other journalist assigned to the story was asking himself so openly whether the voices inside Kip Kinkel's head were symptoms of psychotic delusion or of demonic possession. Jung would have said these were equally valid descriptions of the same phenomenon. During that week I spent in the Eugene-Springfield area, living out of a hotel room on the Willamette River, I felt more hollow and hopeless with each passing day. The context of the shootings at Thurston High was what really got to me; in a lot of ways I was more horrified by the kids who surrounded Kip Kinkel than

I was by the killer himself. The levels of desensitization I was encountering in these teenagers created a mood of surreal desperation. As I listened to a story about a friend of Kip's who liked to boast that he had tortured his pet hamster to death by running it over with his skateboard (told to me by a girl whose main claim to fame was having had sex with six boys at the same party), I felt as if my brain were being eaten by ravenous imps.

My condition only worsened during the next several weeks, and by August the cackle of that creature I had confronted on the Piazza Navona three years earlier seemed to ring in my ears unceasingly. I understood only that whatever part of me I had opened back then was rapidly becoming a void, and that if I didn't find something to fill it with, life soon was going to be unbearable. On the morning of August 8, the day the Catholic Church officially celebrates the birth of Mary, I told my wife I was thinking about returning to Medjugorje. Three weeks later I was on a flight to Rome. Like just about every decision I was making at this point, it was one I would regret.

Split had changed tremendously in the past three years and in ways I knew I should applaud. Why then did I find so disheartening the abundance I discovered along the city's seafront promenade? The little grocery store at the southeast corner of Diocletian's Castle, where I had perused pathetically bare shelves on my first visit to the city, was now a supermarket with track lighting that cast a lustrous shine on mounds of oranges and baskets of asparagus. Huge tubs of filleted fish and pork chops reposed inside glass cases, while the aisles teemed with women who pushed shopping carts and wore silk dresses. Tourist boats rocked against one another in the crowded harbor, and the traffic on the street was bumper to bumper. The people still were not particularly friendly, but now an American alone was more likely met with indifference than hostility. Life here was good again, but for some reason I couldn't see it that way.

I found a symbol for my disdain of Split's new prosperity when I followed a broad brick path to what was now the city's busiest and most expensive restaurant, a McDonald's where dozens of Croatians stood in line to pay more for a Big Mac than it cost for a huge platter of fresh calamari at the restaurants on the harbor. Was this what they had fought the war for? My begrudging attitude shamed me, but I couldn't shake it. Wandering among the shops and cafés inside the castle walls, I felt rank and feral and utterly nasty. "Out of shape but spoiling for a fight," I had described myself to an old friend shortly before leaving home, and his knowing laugh was one of the few sounds I'd heard lately that pleased me.

I'd barely left my hotel room in Rome. The whole city seemed draped in scaffolding as it preened for the Catholic Jubilee that would begin on Christmas Eve, 1999. I went no nearer to the Vatican than a twilight view from above the Spanish Steps; sheathed in steel bars, wood planks, and crisscrossing cables, St. Peter's looked as if the barbarians were not only at the gate but over the walls. Walking back to my hotel in the gathering darkness, I cut from the Via del Corso onto a side street and was confronted immediately by three young men bristling with badass swagger. When they tried to walk over me—common behavior among the young men of Rome—I reacted by banging shoulders with the most aggressive of the three. He threw up a forearm and I caught it with my own, shoving him off the curb. His two companions turned in belligerent amazement, but the wildness in my eyes backed them off. "I'll rip your lungs out," I told the one I had collided with, and realized the depth of my fury only when I saw his defiance turn to terror in an instant.

My knees trembled all the way back to the hotel, and I became physically ill the moment I was alone in my room, but even my retching was unaccompanied by remorse. "What is wrong with me?" I wondered. No one was answering. I slept badly that night, wracked alternately by chills and sweats, then dozed off around dawn and awoke just in time to catch my afternoon flight to Split. And now here I was, jet-lagged and sleep-deprived, waiting for a bus to the Bosnian border.

Shortly before I left home, my application for a half-million-dollar life insurance policy had been rejected when I'd admitted to the underwriter I was about to take a trip overseas. I hadn't mentioned Bosnia, but I did say I'd be "stopping over" in Croatia, and that alone was enough to delay coverage until I returned safely home. I'd had a feeling of foreboding ever since. This trip was ten times safer than it had been during the war, yet I felt at far greater risk. My greatest asset in dangerous situations, I long had believed, was an intuitive recognition of the right moment to move forward or back away. Somehow, though, I'd lost my reverse gear. Deep inside me was a hysteric who shrieked ceaselessly at God to prove He was there for me. My wife had used the word "possessed" several times during the last week before my departure to describe what she saw in me, and there were moments when I believed it might be true.

I knew in some pre-rational part of myself that this was not the right time for a return trip to Medjugorje. The sense of being summoned that had impelled my journey in 1995 was entirely absent in 1998. Yet I continued to forge ahead, heedless of every warning or apprehension. By the time the bus finally arrived, I had begun to picture my qualms as tiny, malevolent entities that swam in my bowels. "I'll drown you little fuckers in whiskey and Pepto-Bismol," I thought as I climbed aboard, then wondered a moment later if everyone was staring at me because I was American or because I was crazy.

The trip began with a long drive south along the Adriatic shore. A pair of German couples who chattered away in the back of the bus were heralds of Dalmatia's transformation. Though not nearly at prewar levels, tourists were returning to the Croatian coastline. The Germans got off the bus in Makarska, and we turned inland at Ploče, following the Neretva past young men who sold watermelons cooled by fountains they had drawn from the river. Only when we arrived at the border just outside Metković did it occur to me that I hadn't seen anyone carrying a gun since deplaning at the airport. The Bosnian soldiers who lounged in unbuttoned uniforms at the border crossing sat with their machine guns at their feet, and barely glanced at me as I walked past and climbed aboard the bus to Medjugorje.

Bad roads, narrow and broken, were the only significant change I noticed as we passed into Bosnia, or "B-H," as I was obliged to call it from now on, out of regard for the Croatians who continued to emphasize the Hercegovina half of their country's formal name. The rubble of bombardment had long since been cleared, and neither soldiers nor any other armed authorities were to be seen in Gabela. I yearned for familiar sights and found a certain comfort in the bullet holes and mortar damage that still pitted the walls of many buildings in Capljina, the last stop before Medjugorje. I knew this place only as a country at war, I reminded myself.

If I required an atmosphere of death and destruction, Kosovo was less than 150 miles southeast. The Serbs had burned scores of villages and displaced more than a quarter million ethnic Albanians since February; how many had been killed was anybody's guess. The fighting was finished here in Bosnia, replaced by an undercurrent of personal grudges and ethnic hatreds that made travel dangerous for locals but merely difficult for visitors. Most of the foreign currency available in Sarajevo these days was being brought into the country by American and Japanese tour groups, which followed what by now had become an almost standardized itinerary: Their guides always took them first to Sniper Alley, then to the Markale market, where sixty-nine people had been killed by a single mortar shell in 1994; from there, the groups usually stopped by the Catholic cathedral where twenty-one people lining up for bread had been blown apart by a Serbian artillery shell; then ended their day in the charred skeleton of the Olympic Stadium. What was the difference between me and them? I wondered, and couldn't come up with anything of substance as the bus lumbered down out of the hills and onto the Brotnjo Plateau.

I'd imagined that the sight of the cross atop Križevac would stir my soul and enliven my thoughts, but it did neither. I had fallen as flat as I could remember ever feeling by the time the bus stopped to let me off in front of the rebuilt Medjugorje post office. I passed at least a half-dozen new construction projects during my half-mile hike toward the twin spires of the church; for much of my walk, a cacophony of power tools drowned out all human sounds. Pulling my backpack on wheels behind me, I paused for only a moment in the courtyard of St. James's, then headed across the street to Mira's, imagining that I might find Nicky at his old table. But Mira's was no more; the café's space had been incorporated into the Dubrovnik restaurant. I didn't even recognize the waiters. I sat down to reconnoiter over a beer, hoping to spot someone I knew, but every person who passed was a stranger to me. My dolor was spiced with a generous measure of chagrin; before leaving home, I had not bothered either to announce my arrival or to make arrangements for housing, trusting that I would be taken care of upon my arrival in Medjugorje. Now I sat at a table in what was no longer Mira's, with no clear idea of where to go next.

By the time I finished the beer, I was so blue that I thought seriously about catching the first available ride out of here and heading home. But there wouldn't be another bus until the next day, so I walked up the road to the first house offering rooms for rent, paid twelve dollars to stash my backpack, then stepped back outside, still feeling lost. I walked toward Križevac as far as my old digs at the Pansion Maja, then veered off into the fields, looking for something I couldn't name and didn't expect to find. I was walking through a cow pasture, aiming myself vaguely in the direction of Bijakovići, when I looked down at the ground in midstep and saw that my foot was about to come down on a viper that lay coiled in the middle of the path. I was barely able to extend my stride so that my foot came down right next to the snake's head, then stood frozen. Several seconds passed and the viper didn't move. Finally, I lifted my foot and in that moment felt, if not protected, at least very lucky. Ten feet away I turned to watch the snake slither off into the grass, then just stood for some time, listening as a cooling breeze rustled the leaves of the fig and maple trees at the edge of the field. After a few minutes, I noticed that my mood had lightened considerably.

I turned and went back the way I had come, remembering all of a sudden that Nicky had recently opened an art gallery, the White Lily, not far from the church. I found the place in no time, built into a corner on the ground floor of a four-story building still under construction. The gallery was closed, but there were a table and chairs under an umbrella just outside the front door, so I sat down in the shade. Nicky drove up two minutes later, immediately followed by Ivan Bencun.

My jubilation was short-lived. Within the next half hour I learned from Nicky that I had arrived in Medjugorje at the worst possible time. Mirjana and Vicka both were out of the country and would not be returning before my departure; Jakov was in the U.S.; Marija had been in Medjugorje for almost a month but planned to leave for Italy the day after tomorrow. Rita had taken off two days earlier for her annual prayer retreat and was not coming back until right around the time I had to catch my return flight from Split to Rome. Worst of all, Father Slavko was in England and, after that, was scheduled to spend several days in the Netherlands; he might or might not make it back before I had to leave.

Nicky understood my disappointment, especially at Slavko's absence, but even that was beside the point, Nicky said, "because Our Lady is here. It's Her you've come for, even if you don't know it." I nodded in a sort of patronizing despair. He laughed, not unkindly. "Doubt it all you want, old boy," he said, "but the fact is, you've come back." Bencun, who couldn't understand a word we were saying, nodded vigorously and gave me a wide smile. Our friend had given up Mira's, Nicky explained, in order to finance construction of the Hotel Marben, which was what he called the building that provided the shade in which we sat. The place was still months from completion, but Bencun had begun receiving guests several weeks earlier and insisted through Nicky that I must stay there, at a substantial discount, of course.

Nicky and Bencun both looked about the same as they had three years earlier; I could see in their eyes, though, the toll that the past several months had taken on my appearance. Nicky actually seemed to feel a little sorry for me, and said he could imagine how exhausting having two babies at the same time must be. I asked about the other Loopers. Most were gone, he said; Karen had called once from a treatment facility in Victoria, British Columbia, but was never heard from again. Milona had married Charles, as I knew, and was now a mother. Her husband and daughter had accompanied Milona when she arrived from Paris for a two-week stay in June that had been a complete fiasco, Nicky reported; Charles broke his own arm during one of his fits and had to be driven to Split to have it set. Rita had remained, of course, and was now essentially a fixture of the place, said Nicky, who was himself spending only about half the month in Medjugorje, and the rest traveling in pursuit of his latest obsession, tracing the true lineage of the French royal family. I possessed no interest whatsoever in the subject, and could barely pretend even slight enthusiasm.

When the call to evening Mass sounded, I headed in the direction of the church, taking my old seat on one of the benches just outside the northeast entrance to St. James's. The nun with the beautiful voice still sang "From All Quarters," the swallows still spiraled and swooped from the bell towers, the old ladies in black dresses still clutched their rosaries as they knelt on the paving stones. Why, then, did everything look so much dimmer, as if the holy glow that bathed this scene three years earlier had been brushed away with the back of some indifferent diety's hand? As the congregation rose to recite the Our Father and prepare for the Eucharist, I felt as if I were standing outside looking in. When my benchmates shook my hand and said, "Peace be with you," I repeated their words but felt like a fraud. For the rest of the service I kept struggling to come out of myself, to simply be present, but no matter how I tried to rise above it, misery continued to overwhelm me. By the time the Mass was ended, all I wanted was a pillow for my head. Jet lag, I told myself; in the morning, I would feel better.

And I did, sort of. After breakfast with Nicky, I moved my bag to the Hotel Bencun, then spent most of the rest of the day walking. I went through the fields to Bijakovići first, then up Podbrdo to the site of the first apparition, where perhaps a dozen other people sat or knelt in silence. I took my own seat on a rock that was right in front of the steel cross that marked the spot where the six seers had assembled on a June evening seventeen years earlier. Cards marked with prayer requests were piled at the base of the cross, but I couldn't bring myself to read even those. My gaze kept drifting to the village below, where the sound of hammers hitting nails suggested a telegraph operator in the grip of an epileptic fit.

I made a brief stop at the Blue Cross on the way back down the hill, then entered Visionary Way out of the fields. The curtains were drawn at Mirjana's house, and at Jakov's too. A sprinkler watered the flowers on one side of Ivan's house, but I saw no other sign of life. I kept walking until I arrived at Križevac, then trudged to the top, stopping at each station of the cross to kneel on the rocks just as the true believers did. I even recited the Our Father and the Hail Mary at the first couple of stations, but my prayers felt so forced that I simply knelt in silence at the third station, as if waiting, for what I did not know. Beneath the cross on the summit, I sat with my chin in my hands and allowed myself to wonder how much of what I remembered was true. For a moment, I wanted so badly to be certain of something, anything, that I felt like beating my head against the rocks and wailing. Instead, I hiked back down the mountain, and along the way ordered myself to stop whining.

When I arrived back at the Hotel Bencun, Nicky was out front, and suggested that he take me to meet Marija Pavlović before she drove to Split to catch a flight to Milan early the next morning. I hadn't met Marija during my previous stay in Medjugorje, and rode back to Bijakovići in Nicky's new VW Golf, hoping the seer would break this evil spell that had been cast over me. When we arrived, Marija and her husband, Paulo, were standing out front, watching a backhoe dig up their front yard. The sewer pipe had burst, and the two of them were intent upon seeing that it was repaired before they left for Italy. Tall, with long limbs and sloped shoulders, Marija was warm but distracted. We made innocuous conversation for a few moments, but even then most of what Marija said was drowned out by the machine's roar.

Marija's sister Milka soon drove up in an enormous black Mercedes sedan, then climbed out wearing a linen pantsuit and a Rolex watch. Milka was now in her thirties, and had married a wealthy businessman from Ljubuški, Nicky explained. I felt staggered by the idea that this was the same little goatherd girl who, along with Mirjana and Ivanka, had been the first to report seeing the Virgin Mary back in June 1981. Nicky interrupted Marija's conversation with her sister to ask if we— I—might sit with her during her apparition that evening. It would not be possible, Marija answered, and suddenly seemed not to want to look at me. "There will be another chance," she said, but I doubted that.

On the way back to the Hotel Bencun, Nicky observed that it was Marija's last night in Medjugorje, and that she obviously had plans. Something about his expression, though, made me feel that even he had noticed that the light around me was much weaker than it had been three years earlier. Ivan and Mira Bencun insisted we eat dinner with them that evening. Between bites, I asked who had been the most memorable recent pilgrims. Nicky said he had become quite involved (as a sort of spiritual adviser, apparently) with a pair of homicide detectives from Dublin. "Rock-hard guys," he explained, "until the day one says to the other, 'My life is going nowhere.' 'Neither is mine.' 'Let's go to Medjugorje.' So they come in with a tour group, looking totally out of place. The first thing they do is climb Križevac. They're almost to the top when all of a sudden they both see flames all around them, knee-deep, flaring up out of the rocks. 'Harry, do you see what I see?' The other one nods, then asks, 'Why doesn't anybody else see it?' 'And why isn't there any heat or smoke? There's a fire, but nothing's burning.' They come down off the mountain and vow that they will never breathe another word to anyone else. But one talks, and for the rest of their stay those two were surrounded by people assuring them they should trust their experience, not their minds. By the time they left, their faces had softened so much that the other people on the tour group said they wouldn't have recognized them if they hadn't watched it happen."

The visitor who had most affected Medjugorje's parishioners that summer was a middle-aged Canadian woman who almost half a century earlier had been famous as one of the first thalidomide babies, born with no hint of an arm or leg on one side. "On the other, she has just a little baby arm with an even tinier hand at the end of it, and the stump of a leg that ends about midthigh," Nicky said. "Beautiful face, though, and this magnificent red hair. She arrives and immediately announces she has come here to climb Križevac." And this the Canadian woman had done, refusing all offers of assistance to literally drag herself over the rocks with her stump of a leg and little baby arm. "That face when she came down," Nicky recalled. "No one could stop looking at it. I've never seen determination and joy in such perfect harmony." I could almost see the woman myself, reflected off the faces of Ivan and Mira, who sat smiling broadly even as their eyes filled with tears.

Hearing this story seemed to unhook me from my misery for at least a few hours, and that night I slept soundly for the first time in weeks. In one of my dreams, a woman who may have been the Virgin Mary seemed to call to me through a fog, repeating again and again a short phrase that I couldn't make out until she had disppeared into the fog and I heard the words "Carry your cross."

I was jarred awake by the sound of a concrete drill that had gone to work on the roof of the Hotel Bencun right above my room. I lay still for a moment, feeling pounded by the big tool's vibration, then burst out laughing. For some reason, I had remembered a story told to me during my previous visit to Medjugorje, about a group of British pilgrims who happened to arrive in the village on the day of the annual pig slaughter. Following a tradition that went back nearly two centuries, the parishioners of Medjugorje had agreed that they would all kill their pigs on the same day; among other things, it permitted them to sell the skins in bulk to a tannery and the offal to a dog-food manufacturer. Anyway, the British pilgrims had stepped off the bus at midmorning that day just as the slaughter was about to commence, and within moments were greeted by the sounds of pig after pig after pig squealing in its death throes. So horrified were these pilgrims that they insisted their driver take them straight back to Split and away from this hellish place. The story hadn't amused me much when I first heard it in 1995, but for some reason I now found it gut-bustingly funny. People who couldn't understand that pigs had to be killed before they ate bacon, or that even a religious visionary might become distracted when the sewer pipe broke, weren't ready for this place.

After breakfast, Nicky suggested I come along on a drive to Ljubuški, where he intended to buy his first cell phone, or "handy," as they were called here. I jumped at the chance to escape, even if only for a couple of hours. Ljubuški was transformed: The city center I remembered as grimy and ravaged now was lined with shiny new sidewalk cafés and stores that sold knockoff Nikes or bootleg Ray-Bans. The older buildings all bore patches of mortar where bullet holes had been filled in, but a good deal of the town had been rebuilt. The most impressive change was that Ljubuški no longer seemed dangerous. Immediately after the signing of the Dayton Accords, Nicky explained, the Croatian army had surrounded the town with troops, tanks, and artillery, demanding that the HOS thugs who had ruled Ljubuški for the past four years surrender their weapons. The disco gangs were dismantled almost overnight, and if there were any guns left in town, their owners kept them well hidden. However, when Nicky and I sat down for lunch on the terrace of what was supposed to be the best restaurant in town, we heard a good deal of vehement conversation at the tables around us; a couple of shouting matches actually broke out.

I had arrived in Bosnia three weeks before the country's national elections, and at a time when ethnic tensions were perhaps higher than they had been since the signing of the Dayton Accords. All sides were most concerned with how the Serbs would vote. Moderate candidates were receiving strong support from NATO, and the United States was being particularly aggressive; Secretary of State Madeleine Albright recently had warned that only those committed to the Dayton Accords would receive U.S. support. This implied threat had backfired immediately; the UN-backed candidate for the Bosnian Serb presidency was promptly labeled a Western stooge by her chief opponent, a rabid nationalist who was destined to win the election by a wide margin. The leading Croat contender already had promised to divide Hercegovina from Bosnia and join the Croatian government in Zagreb. Within a few weeks, the Serbs blew up the homes of ninety-six Muslim families who applied to return to native villages near Prijedor, and the Croats had done the same to the homes of sixty Serbian refugee families in Drvar. The "process of peace," as Albright and her boss, Bill Clinton, liked to call it, was going nowhere fast. Meanwhile, the situation throughout the rest of the Balkan states was growing more volatile by the day: Romania was a de facto military dictatorship run by not-so-ex-communists and ethnic nationalists; Bulgaria's most powerful economic and political force was the Russian mafia; Greece, like Macedonia, was waiting to see if NATO would follow through on its threats to intervene against the Serbs in Kosovo, where ten thousand ethnic Albanians were being driven from their homes each week. Violence and chaos were so much a part of the atmosphere in Bosnia-Hercegovina that even Western diplomats were admitting that a new outbreak of war could be avoided only if the thirty-five thousand NATO troops in the country remained well into the next century. The Queen of Peace, I observed, was reigning over a principality that seemed to shrink second by second. Nicky insisted this meant only that the Warning and the Great Sign were imminent. They had been "imminent" for almost twenty years now, I observed; "Waiting for Godot" was holding up a lot better than divine prophecy.

"So now you scoff," he said as we sat among retired killers on a sunny terrace, eating trout almondine.

"'Blessed are those who do not see, yet believe,'" I replied. "P. T. Barnum would have taken that line to the bank."

"I see. You want to be clever and 'with it' again."

"It's getting a little late for 'with it,' whatever that is," I told him. "I'd just like to know what's real. Sometimes I think I'd welcome even bad news if I could believe it."

"Our Lady is what's real!" Nicky shouted so loudly that heads turned at every table on the terrace.

I nodded, but only as a way of suggesting we change the subject.

The silence between us lasted until we were in the car and on our way back to Medjugorje. On the long curve beneath Ljubuški's ancient hill-side fortress, Nicky announced that he was leaving in forty-eight hours to attend a series of meetings in Vienna, and would not return to Medjugorje before my departure. "You can't do that!" I said. "I can't?" Nicky asked. Yeah, well, of course he *could*, I allowed, but he shouldn't. If Father Slavko and Rita were around, or if Mirjana and Vicka weren't out of the country, it would be different, I said, but in my present condition I didn't think I could handle this place without companionship. "You need to seek Our Lady's companionship," Nicky replied. "She's there for you in a very unusual way. We've all recognized that since you first showed up three years ago, but for some reason you never have."

I was thrown into a vaguely guilty silence. Why, I didn't know, but I'd never had "a big thing for the Virgin Mary," as I found myself putting it, even in the immediate aftermath of my first visit to Medjugorje. My experience—even while I was here—had been of Jesus. Christ's majesty and mercy were what I made the objects of my religious practice, to the degree that I had one. Even when I sailed into the spiritual doldrums and discovered myself becalmed in a sea of blood-streaked bile, the one part of the Catholic liturgy that never failed to move me was that "Lamb of God" litany just before the consecration of the host. Mary, though, had always remained an elusive and doubtful presence. I ruminated on my lack of a "personal relationship" with the Madonna during much of the next two days, sitting for long spells among the crowd of mostly old women who gathered around the statue of the Virgin in St. James's courtyard. Nothing seemed to change, though, and then it was time for Nicky to leave.

We ate a late dinner together on the evening of his departure. At one point, he demanded an accounting of my stay so far, and I admitted being bitterly disappointed that my experience of Medjugorje this time was so much less profound than it had been three years earlier. "Who do you think you are?" Nicky demanded. He sounded as if, against his will, he was more astonished than angered by my attitude. "Do you expect fire-works every time you show up?" I thought about this for several seconds, then said I was more guilty of anticipation than expectation. "Whatever word you want to use, it doesn't work that way, old boy," Nicky said. "Not for you, not for anybody. Very few people who come here have an experience that even approaches what you were given, yet some of them are fed for a lifetime by what they find here. You've come back in less than three years, insisting your plate is empty and that you need a second helping. Your ingratitude is enormous." I was still sitting with that thought when Nicky said good-bye.

My distress only increased after loneliness was added to the mix, and the next three days were dark indeed. I strove to shake my black clouds in a closed circuit of aimless wandering between the base of Križevac, the Blue Cross on Podbrdo, and the altar of St. James's. I spent hours alone in the fields. The other pilgrims seemed increasingly pathetic and absurd to me, pitiful souls who had traveled thousands of miles to look for something they could not find in themselves. I knew I was no different, yet could not stop searching for the invisible thread that connected me to what I had experienced three years earlier.

I attempted escape by making a day trip to Dubrovnik with Postar's son Mate, who was just finishing his military duty and had become intent on a trip to the U.S. All during the drive to the Adriatic, Mate peppered me with questions, opinions, and items of gossip involving assorted Medjugorje characters. His descriptions of extramarital affairs between people I knew and still faintly admired made me feel increasingly ridiculous as we cruised south along the magnificent coastline in Mate's Mercedes.

Dubrovnik's restoration was remarkable, and even a glimpse of the old city from the hilltop where Mate parked his car cut through my crust of cynicism. A volunteer army of artisans from all over Europe had replaced the red-orange roof tiles and patched the limestone facades of buildings that absorbed the blasts of more than two thousand artillery shells during the Serbian siege of 1991–92. More than five hundred of the old city's buildings were hit by shells during that thirty-six-week bombardment, but Dubrovnik's magnificent high walls, nearly twenty feet thick in places, had held up under the shelling. Six years later, the sandbags were gone and the shrapnel scars on the buildings had nearly all been filled in. The enormous limestone paving stones of the old city's main street, the Placa, had been either repaired or replaced. The church bells rang and the Onofrio Fountain splashed. Tour groups assembled under Dubrovnik's magnificent clock tower. Nearly every Croatian who visited Dubrovnik for the first time since the war burst into tears when he entered the old city and saw how beautiful it still was, Mate told me.

The two of us spent a couple of hours ascending to and descending from the old city's walls. For Mate, climbing the stone staircases that rose steeply from the Placa provided numerous opportunities to look up the short skirts of young women who were coming down. He could hardly contain himself, and I, as an American, could scarcely imagine what hormonal storms raged inside a twenty-two-year-old male virgin. A series of long climbs combined with Mate's increasingly hilarious struggle with his lust made us both a little light-headed. He attempted again and again to make me his accomplice in lechery, rolling his eyes in derisive disbelief when I insisted that I had long since investigated what was up the skirts of as many young girls as I needed to know.

When I asked Mate if he thought he would remain a virgin until marriage, he became quite serious and said he hoped that he would. Like me, though in a very different way, Mate was living in two worlds, at one moment insisting breathlessly that the tall blonde in the orange dress was wearing nothing underneath, then in the next asking if I would like to meet his best friend in Dubrovnik, an elderly nun who guarded the relics of the the city's most famous saint.

He had been five years old when the apparitions began, Mate reminded me when we sat down for lunch at a restaurant perched on a seawall above the harbor, and could hardly remember a Medjugorje that had not been a center of religious devotions. He was and would remain a believer, Mate assured me, but during his adolescence had developed an increasingly scornful attitude toward many of Medjugorje's foreign pilgrims, especially those who were reluctant to leave. "As far as I am concerned, anyone who stays in Medjugorje for more than three months has something wrong with him," he said. "They think they can only believe when they are here. They are afraid to face their lives." What about someone like Rita Falsetto? I asked. "Rita should either become a nun or go home and get married," he answered curtly. "She stays here so that she will not have to decide what to do." What about Nicky? I asked. "Nicky thinks there are one set of rules for him and another for everbody else," Mate said. "He tells everyone they have to go to Mass every day, but Nicky's idea of attending Mass is to walk around the church smoking cigarettes. He is a hero for what he did during the war, for sure. But there are a lot of people who think he should go home and be remembered, instead of staying until everyone forgets he is here," he stated with startling vehemence. "And I do not believe his story about his wife," the young man railed. "I met Nicky's youngest daughter when she came here to visit, and she was a great girl. There is no way she was raised by a mother who is possessed by demons. Nicky is full of crap." I smiled in spite of myself; Mate's stridency was spectacular.

He became distracted again a moment later, when three attractive young women in sundresses sat down at a nearby table. "What do you think of the dark one?" he asked. Nice, I assured him. Yet when our meal arrived, Mate prayed aloud over it, ignoring the curious stares and uncomfortable expressions of the girls at the next table. Will you do that even when you are in the U.S.? I asked. "I will do it wherever I am," he answered. "I know that God exists. I will never forget *that*." Mate spoke respectfully of the visionaries, and was particularly admiring of his cousin Jelena, the inner locutionary, who still was studying theology in Rome. "Jelena goes so deep that when I am with her, I can only listen; I know I have nothing important to say." Nevertheless, he was skeptical about the Secrets, Mate admitted: "The people who are waiting for the world to end bother me even more than the permanent pilgrims. I want the world to go on. I want to be part of it. Like you."

For a moment I didn't know whether to laugh or cry. Instead I kept my mouth shut and let my young friend have his illusions.

I descended again into an oppressive loneliness after returning to Medjugorje. The Bencuns treated me like a member of the family, but neither Ivan nor Mira spoke more than a few words of English. After an evening Mass, I ran into the Irish tour guide Philip Ryan in the church courtyard and felt like clinging to his sleeve. I had misread the young man as a bit of a prig back in 1995, spreading infantilism and inhibition with a spiritual scorecard and a self-satisfied smile, and had decided then that he would be one of the Medjugorje characters I didn't have time or space for in my book. I apparently had failed to realize the excruciating pain he was in from a mountain-climbing accident that had nearly crippled him. Now fully recovered, Philip was proving to be considerably more thoughtful and tough-minded than I had imagined, and not nearly so stiff or self-involved. He even had confessed to a core of romantic vulnerability. Back in 1995, I had been astounded and even a little annoyed by Philip's indifference to the assortment of young women who tried to capture his attention. Now I understood this was merely a matter of high standards: He was carrying a torch for the beauteous, brilliant Jelena Vasilj, and ached for her with touching grace and fidelity. I had learned only the day before from Jelena's cousin Mate that Philip had no chance, but as we stood in the twilight on the edge of a crowd that had gathered around the Virgin's statue, I didn't have the heart to tell him, and knew it wasn't my place, anyway.

So instead we talked about my faltering faith, and how difficult I was finding it these days to distinguish between experience and interpretation, thought and understanding, perception and imagination. Philip remarked that prayer was the only defense we had against our confusion, then told me what would become one of my favorite Father Slavko stories: About a year earlier, a couple of unusually earnest German reporters had spent a week in Medjugorje preparing a report for one of the country's largest newspapers, and on the day they were to leave admitted how moved they had been by their experiences here. They still believed that the apparitions were a psychological phenomenon, the reporters said, some exalted work of wishful thinking, but thought the place was wonderful anyway, because of the deep worship they had witnessed, the moving faith and the astonishing conversions. "The fruits, you mean?" Slavko had asked. Yes, the reporters replied. "Well, you are much more mystical in your thinking than I am," the priest said. The reporters laughed. What? they said. "I am merely a man who has walked out into a field and found apples on the ground that I know have fallen from a great tree," Slavko explained. "You walk out into the same field, see no tree, yet find the apples, and insist that they must have fallen from the sky. That is truly miraculous."

I was still laughing at my mental image of Slavko's deadpan expression when Philip asked me bluntly, "Do you believe in God?" I stopped laughing, stood blinking and stammering for a few seconds, then found myself answering in a surprisingly strong voice, "I believe in God, but I'm not sure God believes in me." It was the most succinct expression of my inner state that I had managed in months. I was marveling at how good it felt to speak the truth, even if it was a truth that damned me, and barely listened as Philip began talking about the "dark night of the soul," a phrase coined by St. John of the Cross to describe the period when a convert feels that God has abandoned him, and told me the stories of several saints who had lived through it. Philip did not capture my attention again, though, until he went silent and closed his eyes, as if listening to some inner voice. "You know," he said a moment later, "I've been struggling myself lately. And I've had this recurring thought that what I need to do is climb Križevac barefoot, to really feel the rocks against my flesh, not so much as a penance but as a way of experiencing myself as human, in all my weakness and vulnerabilty. But it just struck me that maybe you're the one who needs to do that." He smiled. "I don't know where the thought came from," he said, "but I'm pretty sure it wasn't Satan."

I laughed but dismissed the idea in the same breath. I felt I had gotten to know my weakness and vulnerability well enough during the past year. All through the next day, the idea of climbing Križevac with bare feet kept entering my thoughts, and I kept saying no to it. Finally, at just before six P.M., I headed toward St. James's with the intention of sitting through the Rosary service that preceded the Croatian Mass. I walked past the church, though, and continued toward the Mountain of the Cross. I didn't feel I was making a decision so much as clearing my mind of interfering thoughts. At the base of Križevac, even as one part of me stood apart and mocked the enterprise, I sat on a rock , removed my boots, and slung them over one shoulder. I could hear the prayers of the Rosary by the time I had ascended to the third station of the cross, and already was wondering how I would make it to the top. I placed my feet more and more gingerly, trying to find a spot on their soles that hadn't been bruised, moving so slowly that it took me several minutes to negotiate a single switchback. At around the fifth station, though, something in me released and I began to walk through the pain rather than trying to go around it. I moved much more rapidly, listening as those seated outside the church finished the prayers of the Rosary and joined the Mass. I stopped to pray at each station, my mind gloriously empty. By the time I reached the summit, my feet felt incredibly hot, as if I had been walking on coals, but there wasn't a mark on them. Below, I could see the faithful assembled in a long line around the church, waiting to take communion. There was no epiphany, but my head stayed clear; thoughts seemed to flit past, deflected by some invisible shield.

I didn't stay on the mountaintop long; the sky already was turning dark above the horizon, and I knew that I would be lucky to make it to the bottom before the light was entirely gone. I had descended only as far as the thirteenth station, though, when I nearly had a bad fall. My feet were so sore that they seemed to slip off the rocks the moment I placed my weight on them; I attempted to compensate by hurrying, which nearly pitched me headfirst over a boulder when I lost my balance between strides and saved myself from serious injury only by catching my hip on the big rock. I persisted but slipped twice more before reaching the twelfth station, where I decided enough was enough. As I sat down to put on my boots, I spotted two figures struggling on all fours across the rocks below me. I couldn't tell if they were coming up or going down. When I tied my laces and climbed down to their level, I discovered two women, one middle-aged, the other in her sixties. Both were overweight, bathed in perspiration, and looked terribly frightened, the older woman especially. As soon as they saw me, the two began to cry out in German as if they had found their deliverer.

Waving her arms and gasping for breath, the older woman seized my arm and hung on tight, speaking to me nonstop even after I told her I didn't *sprechen Sie Deutsche*. With the aid of hand signals and my tiny German vocabulary, the two made me understand that they had intended to climb the mountain, but that the old woman's legs had given out and then they both were too afraid to try climbing down in the gathering dark. Convinced they would be forced to spend the night, the two women had been looking for a place to lie down and were wondering if they would survive until morning.

Barely able to see more than twenty feet myself at this point, I used my hands to tell the pair they needed to follow me down the mountain. The older woman insisted she could not continue on her own, so I was forced to take each of the women by one hand and lead them, walking backward on the rocks, toward Križevac's base. Imagining how ridiculous we must look made me slightly giddy, but the old woman's fright was so palpable that I had no choice but to take her seriously. Also, finding my footing as I tried to look behind me over one shoulder in the dark very quickly became an absorbing task. And the old woman never stopped talking. She must have said "*Gott segnen Sie*" ("God bless you") a hundred times by the time we reached the relatively easier ground at the fourth station. I had realized about two stations earlier that this would be the defining moment of my return trip to Medjugorje. From somewhere inside me, whether out of my imagination or my intuition, came a voice that said I had taken my portion of grace three years earlier, and that all I could receive this time was an opportunity to give. I actually felt grateful for it, and listened with an odd, almost embarrassed detachment as the older woman continued to thank me profusely. When we reached the bottom of the mountain, I led the women to a café, sat them down at a table, bought them each a soft drink, and said good-bye. The older woman grabbed my arm again, said "*Gott segnen Sie*" another six or seven times, then pulled a rosary from her pocket and pressed it into my hands. I hung it on the statue of the Virgin outside St. James's as I headed back to the Hotel Bencun, then slept peacefully until the concrete drill woke me at seven the next morning.

I was drinking espresso at a café across the street from the Hotel Bencun and thinking about going home when Philip Ryan popped his head in to say that Father Slavko had arrived back in Medjugorje during the night, but would be leaving again tomorrow, this time for three weeks. A line of people had formed already outside his office door, Philip said, and if I held out even the slightest hope of seeing Slavko, I had better get over to the rectory at once.

Most of the people waiting on the steps outside and in the hallway that led to Slavko's office were Croats who wore expressions of either distress or determination. A handful of pilgrims loitered on the periphery, perhaps hoping just to catch a glimpse of Medjugorje's globe-trotting holy man. My chances didn't look good, but I pushed through to the open doorway of Slavko's office, where a nun sat in the chair playing receptionist. I knew Slavko must be on the other side of the closed door that led to the room where we had sat together so many times before. The nun shook her head as soon as she saw me, but spoke very little English, so I pretended not to understand that she was trying to send me away. I inched into the room feigning a baffled expression while the nun responded by speaking to me more loudly in Croatian. Her tone grew increasingly menacing, and I was preparing myself for a scene, when the door behind the nun opened and Slavko stepped out to see what was going on. He barely seemed surprised to see me, raising his eyebrows slightly, then knitting them into a frown. "I have heard you are here," he said, sounding none too thrilled about it. I knew he had to leave again the next day and that there were many people who wanted to see him, I told the priest. Nevertheless, I had come by to ask for a little of his time. Slavko looked exasperated for a moment, then seemed to force himself to smile. "Speaking of time," he said, "I wish you had chosen a better one." The door behind him opened wider; inside I saw a grim-faced man and a woman whose face was bathed in tears. Slavko watched my reaction for a moment, then told me in a clipped tone, "Come back at one o'clock and I will make an hour for you. But know it is difficult."

I avoided the eyes of the people in the hallway as I stepped back outside into the sunlight, feeling more guilt than relief, and more relief than satisfaction.

When I returned at one, the nun quickly opened the door to the meeting room and waved at me to get inside quickly, before anyone noticed. I sat alone for a few minutes before Slavko stepped through a second door, clasped my shoulder briefly in greeting, then sat down opposite me looking harried and exhausted. He said he was glad to hear I had not abandoned my book, asked the names of my children, then told me that he had just come from The Hague, where he had stopped to take the confessions of the Bosnian Croats who were about to stand trial as war criminals. It had been one of the worst experiences of his life, Slavko said. The moral suffering of these men, and especially of their families, was terrible to witness. But perhaps even worse was the hypocrisy of the United

Nations and of the "Euros" in particular. "These trials are not about justice, they are about politics and they are about power. Who has it and who does not." I had never seen Slavko angry or anguished, but now he was both, and the force of his emotions startled me. For three years, I had been thinking about seeing this priest again, almost daily expanding my agenda of confessions and questions, imagining how he would supply the words that eased my mind and restored my trust. Slavko didn't want to talk about me, though, and I sat in a sort of benumbed disassociation as he went on about how Radovan Karadžić—"a man responsible for the deaths of thousands"—continued to live like a feudal lord in Pale. The former Bosnian Serb leader could be seen every day in the backseat of his Mercedes sedan as it drove from his hilltop chalet to the Famos factory where he maintained his office, escorted by three Jeep Cherokees filled with armed guards. "There are perhaps twelve of them," Slavko said. "NATO has thirty thousand soldiers in Bosnia, and they are afraid to arrest Karadžić. Yet they arrest a Croatian police officer who let the militia use his home as a command center and tell this father of four children that he must go to prison for twenty-five years because some of those men killed Muslim civilians. It is the injustice that hurts these men, that hurts us all. Those who order the killing, those who orchestrate the horror, those who spread the evil, they cannot be brought to justice, but those who are swept up in it, who have seen their own families butchered, they must be punished. Hypocrisy is too good a name for this."

I sat stunned, nodding, wondering what to say as he ranted on. Arming and training the Muslim and Croat federations soldiers to create a balance of military power in the region had been an absolute condition of the Dayton Accord, Slavko observed, but the Europeans had blocked this at every turn. Nearly a million Croat and Muslim refugees who had been told they could return to their homes in Serb-controlled territory still were being denied entry, while their houses were either occupied by Serbs or burned to the ground. "Instead of confronting the conditions that led to war and trying to change them, NATO and the UN insist that if they stay in this country long enough, its troubles will go away. In fact, they are only creating more hatred, more pain, more bitterness. Real peace must be based on justice, and justice must be based on truth, but you cannot tell this to men who care nothing for justice and even less for truth, and who do not know the difference between a country at peace and a country occupied by foreign armies. The opportunity to create a climate of forgiveness and reconciliation is slipping away in front of their faces, and they either do not or will not see it." Slavko was practically shouting, his face drawn, his expression tortured. "You should go to The Hague and talk to the men there," he told me, "then go to Pale and see what is happening there. This is a situation the world must acknowledge, or the next war will be even worse—much worse—than the one before."

Almost before I could grasp what was happening, Slavko told me that he had given me all the time he could and that he had to meet with the families who had been waiting to see him since early that morning. "I hope that if you come again, we will have more time and less distraction," said the priest as he stood, then smiled at me almost as kindly as he had three years earlier. "I know you are struggling," he said. "So are we all. I will pray for you. Go with God." He touched my shoulder lightly, turned, and walked out of the room. I stood alone, feeling stupefied and vaguely ill for several minutes, then finally went back out through the office into the hallway, studying the faces of those who waited for Slavko. By the time I stepped outside, I was aching for home.

Rita would be returning to Medjugorje in a couple of days, and I wanted to see her, but not nearly as badly as I wanted to be with my children again. That evening I told the Bencuns I was leaving, presented the copy of Graham Greene's *The Power and the Glory* that I had brought for their daughter Ivana, and said good-bye. When the Globaltours bus pulled up in front of the post office at seven the next morning, I was waiting for it.

I arrived at the airport in Split that afternoon just in time to catch the flight to Rome, then rode back to New York seated next to a jeweler from Philadelphia who offered me a lesson in how to buy pearls. "The most important thing to remember," he said, "is that you get what you pay for."

CHAPTER EIGHTEEN

A week to the day after I left Medjugorje, Jakov delivered a short but startling written report to the parish office. "On Friday September 11 during the regular apparition Our Lady told me to prepare myself specially by prayer for tomorrow's apparition because she will confide the tenth Secret to me. On Saturday September 12 Our Lady came at 11:15. When she came she greeted me as always with 'Praised be Jesus!' While she was confiding the tenth Secret to me she was sad. Then with a gentle smile she said to me: 'Dear child! I am your mother and I love you unconditionally. From today I will not be appearing to you every day, but only on Christmas, the birthday of my Son. Do not be sad, because as a mother I will always be with you, and like every true mother I will never leave you. As you continue further to follow the way of my Son, the way of peace and love, try to persevere in the mission that I have confided to you. Be an example of that man who has known God and God's love. Let people always see in you an example of how God acts on people and how God acts through them. I bless you with my motherly blessing, and I thank you for having responded to my call.' The apparition ended at 11:45."

This left only Vicka, Marija, and Ivan (each of whom claimed to have received Secrets one through nine) continuing to report daily apparitions, and set off a wave of speculation among many of Medjugorje's faithful that the time of the Warning was very near. Y2K was now only fifteen months away, as countless Internet postings reminded believers, and the world needed to prepare itself for far more serious events than a glitch in computer programs.

During the months that followed, the e-mailed auguries of Hopi medicine men and Mayan astronomers flitted across my computer screen, chased by the forecasts of Edgar Cayce and Nostradamus, all of them subsumed by verses from the Apocalypse of St. John the Divine. From the red calf in Jerusalem to the white buffalo in Wisconsin, portents of Our Savior's return were surfacing all across the earth, one missive noted, while another advised me that evangelical Christians by the hundreds were taking up residence around the Mount of Olives, where Jesus was said to have ascended to Heaven. The Garabandal seer Mari Loli was talking again, I discovered early in 1999, and had been telling people that the Warning was "very close": She couldn't give the exact date, because the Miracle would take place during the same year, but did feel compelled to tell us that during the Warning everything on earth would stand still, even the planes in the sky. "It will be a terrible thing," said Loli, who was now praying fifteen decades of the Rosary each day. "It will make us feel all the wrong we have done."

While the voices of those who insisted things could not keep going on this way forever grew increasingly shrill, the Medjugorje visionaries, I noticed, would not respond to the millennial anticipation that swirled about them. Mirjana was alone when she appeared at a question-and-answer session for the media on the day after Jakov announced that his apparitions had ended, and what she offered was little more than an admonition to live day by day. No one should imagine they could prepare for what was coming by retreating to some supposedly holy sanctuary, she told her interrogators: "You won't have to leave home." She did not know if Jakov's Secrets were the same as hers, Mirjana reiterated a few moments later, because the six of them understood they were not to discuss these matters even among themselves. "I can just tell you that we don't have private Secrets," she added. "The Secrets are for the whole world." When one interrogator asked, "Does Mary think the Secrets will be revealed by the year 2000?," Mirjana seemed almost to mock the question. "Secrets are secret," she said. "When they begin, we will see what will happen and when."

Perhaps the most interesting remarks Mirjana made were about the Madonna's reported statement, "This is the last time I will be on earth in this way." Though no clarification had since been offered by the Blessed Mother, "I came to think that what She meant was that this is the last time that She will appear for so long a time, and with so many visionaries," Mirjana explained, "not that She will never come to earth again." The media in both Italy and Croatia would make much of this "clarification," suggesting that it sounded as if Mirjana was underplaying the importance of Medjugorje.

For me, the most jarring words Mirjana spoke were in reply to a question about impending disasters: "I don't know where it is that people are getting the idea that the ten Secrets are so horrible, because we never said that." But during her tape-recorded interviews with priests during the early 1980s, Mirjana had spoken at length about how frightening some of the Secrets were, and in 1995 had told me that she was overwhelmed by sadness and dread each time she thought about the terrible things that would happen after the Sign appeared on Podbrdo.

This was one of those inconsistencies that lodged in my mind like tiny, toxic beads of doubt. Sometimes I found it difficult to remember why I had found Mirjana so convincing during the time I spent with her in person. Medjugorje's gadflies, in particular *Fidelity* magazine editor E. Michael Jones, had increasingly focused on Mirjana as the instigator of an unintentional conspiracy that had evolved over time into a massive moneymaking scheme. At once the most sensitive and the most intelligent of the seers, Mirjana had, through some "mediumistic ability," divined the "psychic forces" of the region and transmitted them to the other five visionaries, according to Jones (who early on had insisted that the apparitions were simply a fraud copied from Lourdes), then over time had realized that she could serve not only the political ambitions of her Franciscan mentors but also the material needs of her friends and neighbors. I knew from earlier readings that Jones was outrageously irresponsible in marshaling facts to support his arguments, but I had to concede that a compilation of the seers' remarks on the subject of the Secrets would be a troubling document. And yet I could dismiss none of it.

I found myself lapsing into a sort of psychic limbo during the last months and weeks of the millennium, observing it all with an increasingly detached fascination. I began to tell people I found the entire subject of Y2K tedious. I did not realize that my dispassion was a disguise until the afternoon of December 31, 1999, when blaring sirens announced a leak of poison gas at Oregon's Umatilla Chemical Depot, where the site of the proposed Our Lady of Grace Shrine still stood empty. It turned out to be a false alarm, set off by someone at the local Emergency Operations Center who was trying to warn drivers on the nearby interstate of fog and ice. That adrenaline-flooded moment in which I had found myself thinking, "It's all true!" came back to me again and again, however, as a mortifying reminder of how altered I was by my time in Medjugorje. The Church doctrine that seemed to apply was *semel credidisse*. What it meant, roughly speaking, was that anyone who had believed, even for an instant, would forever carry that belief within him. Jung had been fascinated by *semel credidisse*, and cogitated upon it throughout his lifelong battle with Catholicism. Unlike him, I wasn't trying to reinvent Christianity, but even learning to live with religion as an open question was proving no easy feat. While those around me celebrated the new century, I found myself wishing I could change the past, undial my first phone call to Irma Munoz, cancel my plane ticket to Rome, obliterate all memory of Bosnia, and visit Scottsdale only to play golf during winter months. What I really wanted was to let someone else do my thinking for me. It was in that spirit that I turned to science for answers.

Early in the year 2000, I discovered a passage in a book by a contemporary Catholic theologian that concerned the frustration of early-nineteenth-century prison chaplains ministering to inmates so simpleminded they were unable to "imagine" the existence of God. Within a period of less than a hundred years, the author noted, this dynamic had reversed itself entirely, and by the middle of the twentieth century, it was educated people who found it most difficult to hold the idea of God in their minds. Scientific breakthroughs had produced this paradigm shift, in the opinion of the author, and I couldn't disagree, yet found myself wondering if the change had more to do with perspective than proof.

According to a poll published by the National Science Institute shortly before the dawning of the new millennium, 78 percent of America's physicists and astronomers reported that they did not believe in God. This was an impressive statistic, given that, according to the scientist-priests who worked at the Vatican Observatory, these fields had produced more evidence of a divine majesty than all others combined. The Holy See has been especially ardent in its embrace of the big bang theory, and likes to remind secularists that the first astronomer to suggest it was a Catholic priest, the Belgian abbé Georges Lamaître. Back in 1927, applying Albert Einstein's theory of relativity to the notion of an expanding universe suggested by the work of American astronomer Edwin Hubble, Lemaître proposed the idea of a "primeval atom" that contained all matter and energy in existence before exploding into space. Hubble, in turn, drew heavily on Lamaître's ideas to develop his hypothesis that stars and galaxies not only are receding from Earth in every direction, but that the speed of this recession increases as does its distance from us. Seventy-five years later, every major theory that has resulted from the big bang theory relies upon Lemaître's suggestion that the universe was once a "singularity"of matter and energy condensed in an extraordinarily tiny and infinitely hot mass. And the Belgian priest's idea that an immense explosion sent matter and energy expanding in all directions has led to any number of testable deductions, the most significant of which is that the temperature in deep space must be several degrees above absolute zero. This has been confirmed repeatedly, most persuasively by readings sent back to earth by the Cosmic Microwave Background Explorer satellite, which confirm that the background radiation field in space has precisely the spectrum predicted by the big bang theory.

Since Lemaître, many major scientists have observed that the big bang theory is consistent with a theistic concept of creation. The work of Max Planck suports the idea that prior to the "Initiating Event" there was only one force and one particle in existence, and that from this microdot of mystery both time and space originated. Stephen Hawking has suggested that the early universe blended space and time in some way that makes a definite beginning point impossible. No great mind has been able to construct a viable theory of how aggregates of mass, such as galaxies, could have formed, given the speed of the universe's expansion; all they know is that whatever holds things together had to exist before atoms did. At the same time, scientists have been forced to concede that the universe could not have emerged out of pure nothingness, since there is not and can be no complete vacuum. Contemplating what there was before there was anything has inclined many great minds to a mystical point of view. Even as Einstein rejected the concept of a personal God, he regarded "cosmic religious feeling" as the supreme state of human consciousness. "Everyone who is seriously involved in the pursuit of science becomes convinced that a spirit is manifest in the laws of the Universe—a spirit vastly superior to that of man, and one in the face of which we with our modest powers must feel humble," Einstein wrote in 1936.

While Steven Weinberg's famously dour observation that "The more the universe seems comprehensible, the more it also seems pointless" is a favorite of contemporary intellectuals, any number of equally important contemporary physicists have drawn an exactly opposite conclusion from the same data. This is perhaps because they go beyond extolling the laws of physics and ask, Where did the laws of physics come from? As quantum physicist and philosopher Paul Davies has put it, "Why a set of laws that drives the searing, featureless gases coughed out of the

Big Bang toward life and consciousness and intelligence and cultural activities such as religion, art, mathematics, and science?" The question has taken on more and more resonance in the face of scientific tests which show that randomly selected laws of physics almost inevitably result in either utter chaos or numbing stasis. Many physicists have perceived a clear indication of purposefulness in the growing body of evidence that the universe exists in a balance of freedom and discipline, one that seems to guide evolution along a clear path toward some unknown goal. As the avowed atheist Heinz Pagel put it, the laws of nature seem to be written in some cosmic code, and the job of the scientist is to crack that code and deliver the message in which it is written.

At the same time, more and more scientists speak of a "cloture" built in to the universe that makes it impossible to arrive at a full and final Theory of Everything. The more they know, these scientists observe, the more they realize how little they know. This is driven home every time a new breakthrough reveals that the hypotheses it was based upon are no longer viable. As scientists at the Brookhaven National Laboratory began preparing to test their new Relativistic Heavy Ion Collider—or "time machine," as it was being called—they spoke of re-creating the big bang and of producing the quark-gluon plasma that must have existed in the first nanosecond of creation, so that they might understand how protons and neutrons formed, then combined to produce atoms. All tests would, of course, be conducted in accordance with the standard model that for some time has been the basis of subatomic theory. Yet when the Brookhaven Laboratory reported its first important results, they were accompanied by an announcement from the lab's associate director, Dr. Thomas Kirk, that henceforth the standard model would be "insufficient to describe our universe": Subatomic particles called muons had reacted to magnetic fields with a "large numerical departure" from the standard model. The finest scientists from more than a dozen countries were at a loss to explain this and in fact could only conclude that the universe must contain other particles they didn't know about that behave in ways they can't understand, and that these had somehow influenced the muons' movements. In other words, what their $600 million machine had taught the most brilliant scientific minds on the planet was how little they actually knew about a universe that is scarcely less mysterious than it was to our tribal ancestors.

For those at the Vatican Observatory, this was but one more demonstration of Holy Mystery. The Vatican's scientist-priests like to tell the story of an historic meeting between Georges Lemaître and the amateur astronomer they know as Pope Pius XII. Excited by early test results that seemed to support the big bang theory, Pius suggested that the Church endorse it (making special note that a priest had been instrumental in its development). Lemaître advised him not to. A religion that tied itself to twentieth-century science, the abbé observed, was bound to look foolish in the twenty-second century.

The question of whether research supports or undermines belief in the Almighty can be argued by either side, but all one can truly know is that God has been neither proved nor disproved by modern science. The über-Darwinists of evolutionary psychology are determined to convince us that our brain is a computer that has been programmed by natural selection, while Edward O. Wilson argues that morality has developed entirely as a response to our material conditions and that we need a new religion, independent of God, based upon scientific empiricism. Yet the majority of us persist in some form of the "transcendentalism" that Wilson and company reject, and a good many who do so are themselves scientists, "the roving scouts of the empiricist movement," as Wilson calls them. In fact, polling services continue to report that members of the largest profession made up of college biology majors still believe by a fairly significant majority in the existence of a personal God.

These are physicians. Based almost entirely on their professional experiences, medical doctors are perhaps the most religious professionals on earth. According to a survey conducted in 1999 by Yankelvich Partners, 99 percent of doctors believe that religious faith can heal a sick patient. Perhaps even more remarkable, 75 percent of physicians believe that the *prayers of others* can contribute to a patient's recovery. And scientific research bears them out. During the past twenty-five years, study after study has shown that seriously ill patients who are prayed for—including those who don't know about these prayers—fare better than those who are not prayed for. The man who has done the most to integrate the results of these studies, Dr. Larry Dossey, former chief of staff at Humana Medical Center in Dallas, sums them up in two words: "Prayer works." Or, as Dossey's admirer Dr. Herbert Benson of the Harvard Medical School puts it, "If spirituality was a drug, we wouldn't be able to make it fast enough."

Very few investigators of "medical miracles" come away unaltered by the experience, no matter how passionately they strive to protect their scientific reputations from the taint of marvelism. Among the most impressive, and certainly the most famous, conversion produced by bearing witness to a miraculous healing is that of Alexis Carrel, the French-born Nobel laureate who was present at Lourdes in May 1902, when a young woman named Marie Bailly was brought from the brink of death to perfect health by the application of waters from the spring that Bernadette Soubirous had discovered nearly half a century earlier.

Carrel was only twenty-nine, and had just delivered the paper delineating the breakthroughs in vascular ligature and related surgical techniques that would not only save thousands of lives and win him the Nobel Prize, but also lay the foundation for modern organ transplants. He visited Lourdes in May 1902 as a favor to a former medical school classmate who asked Carrel to replace him as the physician assigned to a train transporting sick people from Lyon to the shrine in the Pyrenees. On that same train was Marie Bailly, who had been more or less smuggled aboard by family members in defiance of a ban on those near death. She was at the time semiconscious, suffering from a case of tubercular peritonitis so advanced that her abdomen was hideously distended by the rock-hard masses that encased her viscera. During the train ride, Carrel eased her pain with morphine, and told her traveling companions that she would not make it to Lourdes alive. Marie Bailly survived the trip, but when she reached the shrine, doctors at the hospital there refused to allow her submergence into the sacred pool, explaining that she was too far gone. The young woman pleaded her case, asking if someone might pour water on her swollen belly. Alexis Carrel was present as three large cups of water were poured onto her body, and was among those who watched as the blanket covering her lower torso lowered perceptibly. When Carrel pulled back the blanket, he discovered that Bailly's abdomen was flat, that the hard masses that distended it had disappeared, and that no discharge of any sort could be observed. That evening, Bailly sat up in bed for the first time in months, and ate dinner without vomiting. She got up early the next morning and had dressed herself by the time Dr. Carrel appeared to ask what she intended to do with her life now. "I will join the Sisters of Charity to spend my life caring for the sick," the young woman answered. During the following six months, Dr. Carrel investigated her case thoroughly, confirming that Marie Bailly had left Lyon in critical condition, released from the hospital there by doctors who did not think she would live another week. Unable to accept that her healing had been simply "miraculous," Carrel could not conceive of an empirical explanation either, and so proposed a theory of "natural psychic force." He arranged for Bailly to be examined not only by physicians but also by psychiatrists during the next six months, until, as promised, she joined the novitiate in Paris during December 1902. She lived without relapse for the next thirty-five years as a Sister of Charity.

Carrel declined to publicize his involvement in the case of Marie Bailly, and did his best to conceal the fact that he had so much as made a trip to Lourdes, fearing that it would discredit him among his colleagues on the medical faculty at the University of Lyon. A local newspaper outed him, however, and published an article suggesting that the doctor did not accept Bailly's cure as a miracle. Carrel answered with an article of his own that alienated parties on both sides of the "controversy" and resulted in his departure from Lyon less than a year later. Carrel moved first to Paris, then to Montreal, then to the University of Chicago, before making his permanent home at the Rockefeller Institute, where he became a major New York celebrity after winning the Nobel Prize in 1912. International luminaries from every field of endeavor made pilgrimages to his lab, hoping to see the heart from a chicken embryo that he kept alive in a special solution. So many newspaper articles reported that Dr. Carrel was on the verge of discovering the secret of immortality that the claim soon began to appear in print almost every time his name did.

Carrel remained reluctant to discuss the case of Marie Bailly, and his written account of the five days he spent with the young woman in 1902, *The Voyage to Lourdes*, was not published until 1948, four years after the doctor's death. Though raised as a Catholic, Carrel never resumed practice of the religion he had abandoned as a university student. On his deathbed, however, the doctor called for a Trappist monk he had met ten years earlier, confessed that he believed Bailly's healing had been a miracle, and received the sacraments with his last breaths.

The story doesn't quite end there, unfortunately, but includes the sort of confounding postscript that so troubles the relationship between the Roman Catholic Church and the medical scientists it employs: In 1964, the International Medical Committee, in conjunction with the Medical Bureau at Lourdes, announced that it could not approve Marie Bailly's healing as miraculous, because doctors at the time had not considered the possibility of pseudocyesis, the psychologically induced mimicry of pregnancy. Evidence that Marie Bailly was of sound mind and that the doctors who treated her in Lyon had repeatedly noted discharges of the heavy mucous consistent with peritonitis mitigated strongly against such a diagnosis, the International Committee conceded, but since at least a seed of doubt remained, no miracle could be confirmed.

Remote possibilities, scientific skepticism, and theological biases not only muddy the healing waters at Lourdes but continually plague those who endeavor to employ medical science to authenticate supernatural cures. During the past century, more than sixty-five hundred individuals have reported miraculous healings to the Bureau Médicale at Lourdes, which has categorized twenty-five hundred of these as "remarkable." Yet of that number, only sixty-six have been approved by the International Committee, and the last of these took place in 1987. None of the cures at Medjugorje have as yet obtained formal recognition by the Church. The healing of Rita Klaus is probably first in line for approval, but the process seems interminable to those who have been part of it. Among the physicians who have investigated the case is Dr. Richard Casdorph, a non-Catholic from California who first reviewed the medical records of Klaus back in 1989. Dr. Casdorph had begun investigating purportedly miraculous healings almost thirty years earlier, when he undertook an inspection of the medical records of people who claimed to have been cured during prayer meetings conducted by the evangelist Kathryn Kuhlman. The first case he considered involved a teenage girl who had been treated by an assortment of doctors at the Children's Hospital in Los Angeles for a malignant tumor in her hip bone. While seated in a wheelchair at Kuhlman's service in the Shrine Auditorium, the girl suddenly stood and walked. She rode a bicycle that same evening. Doctors at the Children's Hospital, who had warned only a week earlier that if the girl so much as tried to stand her hip bone might shatter, reported that her tumor had vanished. "The evidence was absolutely overwhelming," Casdorph told me.

Even though Kuhlman called him "the most skeptical man I've ever met," Casdorph recalled (not without a certain pride), she agreed to open all her records. After he had thoroughly documented twelve utterly inexplicable healings, he collaborated on a book, *The Miracles*, that was published in 1975, the year before Kuhlman died. Success as an author did not help his medical career, however, as Casdorph was shunned by most of his professional colleagues, saw his practice drop off dramatically, and lost his position on the faculty at the UCLA Medical School. "Science and religion seem to be incompatible as a matter of philosophy rather than of fact," he observed during one of our conversations.

I found myself recalling Rita Klaus's clear, kind eyes, and the faint odor of talc she exuded, as Casdorph described the process by which he had become involved in her case. For years after Kathryn Kuhlman's death, he had been unable to sit through a conventional religious service, the doctor explained: "Nothing else seemed to register with me at the same depth." But then in the mid-1980s, he read an article about Medjugorje and experienced the same sort of "call" that had led him to Kuhlman. After returning home, tremendously moved by the two weeks he spent in Medjugorje, Casdorph began to correspond with Father Slavko, who asked if he would review Rita's medical records. "It was an incredibly well-documented healing," Casdorph recalled, "because she had such an excellent work-up from several doctors who had treated her in the previous months and years." While multiple sclerosis could be misdiagnosed in its milder forms, he allowed, a case this advanced was beyond dispute. And the fact that Rita's deformed and atrophied legs had been restored to perfect health within a few hours made her healing especially remarkable.

He was quite impressed by the rigorous standards imposed on his investigation by the Vatican officials with whom he corresponded during 1988 and 1989, and assured them that if her healing did not qualify as a medical miracle, he could not imagine what would. Nevertheless, Dr. Casdorph's work proved to be for naught. Someone connected to the investigation learned that he was not technically a Catholic, and he was immediately removed from the Klaus case. "I almost had the feeling they were looking for some way to disqualify or discount me," Casdorph said, "not out of any sort of malicious intent, but simply because they wanted this thing to drag out for as long as possible." For them, the worst-case scenario was not one in which a genuinely miraculous healing never received official Church sanction, the Vatican officials told him, but rather one in which a miracle was confirmed by the Church only to be called into question by later discoveries. Twelve years after Dr. Casdorph was removed from the investigation, the Church still had made no determination as to the miraculous nature of Rita Klaus's healing.

"The most fundamental laws and facts of physical science have all been discovered and these are now so firmly established that the possibility of their ever being supplemented in consequence of new discoveries is exceedingly remote," the German-born physicist Albert Michelson pronounced back in 1903. "Only two things are infinite," the Swiss-born Albert Einstein remarked not so very much later, "the universe and human stupidity, and I'm not sure about the former."

As if to confirm Einstein, I waited until pretty late in the game to ask myself what I really wanted from science. Information, of course, but then I already had more of that than I knew what to do with. "Reassurance" was another thought, yet I felt driven by an impulse to shed the religiosity that had covered me like a second skin for six long years now. To some degree, I was looking for a kind of vocabulary that would allow me to communicate with unbelievers, a principal reason that the Church embraces science, according to Catholic catechism. But that wasn't quite the heart of the matter for me. Pope John Paul II had said, "Science can purify religion from error and superstition. Religion can purify science from idolatry and false absolutes." This was a position I could support, but my motives, I knew, were a bit more selfish than the pope's. I was looking, I realized, for a bridge that would allow me to live and work on opposite shores of the same river.

What tormented me was the way my dilemma seemed to drag on. I had published two other books since my first trip to Medjugorje, but I still couldn't let go of the one I had begun in Bosnia, and it wouldn't let go of me. After all this time, I was still utterly unable to reconcile my belief that what I had seen and heard and experienced in Medjugorje was true, with my equally embedded conviction that it wasn't *definitively* true, that it was, in fact, as much a phenomenon of human nature as of divine will. At least I had gotten past demanding a clarification.

The problem was that, just when I began to feel I had achieved a kind of equanimity about the futility of my inquiry, some new revelation would shake me. In early 2001, I discovered that the Medjugorje visionaries had been subjected to their most extensive scientific testing in more than a decade—perhaps ever—and that this had been conducted, in part, during my second stay in the parish. The doctors who conducted these tests (which went on for eight months) were mostly Italian, though Austrians from the Institute for the Field Limits of Science in Innsbruck had collaborated. Their specialities ranged from internal medicine, neurology, and gynecology to psychiatry, psychophysiology, and hypnotherapy. The psychological tests alone were smothering in their scope: MMPI, EPI, MHQ, Tree test, Person test, Raven Matrixes, Rorschach, Hand test, and Valsecchi truth detection. Physiological tests that included an electrocardiogram and a computerized polygraph were conducted concurrently. Four separate states of consciousness had been tested: waking state, visualization of mental images, hypnotically induced ecstasy, and the raptures of the three seers who still reported daily apparitions. All of the visionaries had cooperated (although only after considerable pressure from Father Slavko), excepting Jakov, who consented to just a psychological examination conducted at his home in Bijakovići.

While the Parish Office in Medjugorje had "requested" the examinations, the Holy See insisted upon control of the results and was sparing in what it would reveal. The report provided by the Vatican press office was nevertheless perplexing. While the doctors involved in the study agreed that the seers tested had been and continued to be free from "pathological symptoms," the visionaries did demonstrate a greater level of "stress" than previously noted, reported the Vatican. The tests again had demonstrated that, during their claimed apparitions, they entered an altered state of consciousness quite different from the other three mental states in which they were tested. Most interesting to both the medical team and Vatican officials was that the pyschiatrists who had examined the seers during a pair of two-day sessions conducted in Como, Italy, and in Medjugorje were able to induce a hypnotic trance in each instance, but were unsuccessful in producing any visions of the Virgin Mary, despite repeated attempts.

For me, the most arresting sentence in the Vatican report was one that came very near the end of that concise and cautiously worded document: "Results of the investigation demonstrate that the ecstatic phenomenology can be compared to those from 1985 *with somewhat less intensity*" (italics mine). How, I wondered, could a conversation with the Mother of God be somewhat less intense in 1998 than it had been in 1985? Were the visionaries fatigued? Were they distracted? Was familiarity breeding a kind of unconscious complacency? Could one learn to take daily dialogues with the Queen of Heaven for granted? All I knew was that this single phrase in the doctors' report became an impediment that my mind could not get around. Suddenly, asking the right questions was no longer much of a consolation. I again wanted answers.

The one person I imagined might be able to put this in perspective for me was Father Slavko, who after all had orchestrated this most recent study, and was the only wise man I had ever met. But it was barely a week later that I learned Slavko was gone from this world.

It was as perfect as any death could be. On the afternoon of November 24, 2000, Slakvo had led the faithful on his weekly "Way of the Cross" hike to the summit of Križevac. Five years earlier, I had scribbled this passage about the little priest: "Each Friday afternoon he led a prayer procession up Križevac, climbing the mountain through the sticky heat in his wool habit and leather sandals, megaphone in one hand, breviary in the other, sweating prodigiously, his skinny chest heaving under the brown cloth that covered it. Walking alongside, I observed his exhaustion and his frailty and his determination and his strength with an admiration that grew into the deepest affection I could recall ever feeling for one of my fellow men. In the presence of this particular priest, it was impossible to tell oneself that some people were born to be saints, while the rest of us were destined to struggle fecklessly. Slavko had become the man he was largely by dint of effort in a life given over wholly to devotion and service. During the past ten years he had taught himself four languages while managing to write a book every few months, praying for six hours each day, and giving at least another twelve to his ministry. Catnaps, I had been told, were the only sleep he permitted himself. What Slavko did that was truly remarkable, though, was to make every word, every deed, every gesture somehow an expression of love. And his wasn't some smarmy, smug, self-congratulatory sort of sentiment, either, but a love that was tough and durable, composed in large part of suffering and sacrifice, offered to all, and given with absolute humility." The man was using himself up before our very eyes, I had remarked on at least a few occasions during my first stay in Medjugorje, and local people always knew what I meant. He continued his processions up the mountain week after week, even in the bitter months of the *bura*. On that particular Friday he made it all the way to the frigid summit of the mountain but did not finish his prayers at the base of the big cross, as was his custom, instead reciting his final Hail Mary in front of the bronze relief at the fifteenth and final station, "The Resurrection." Finishing, he turned to lead the descent, but made it only to the next station, "Jesus Is Buried in the Tomb," where he stopped, seemed to lose his balance for a moment, then sat down on the ground. Rita Falsetto, with him as always, ran to his side, and as Slavko lay down, he rested his head in her lap. He tried for a few moments to draw another breath, then went unconscious and died in Rita's arms.

The next day, Marija reported the Madonna's monthly message. During the past fifteen years, these messages had mentioned only one living person—Pope John Paul II—according to Marija, but Mary's message for the month of November ended with these words: "I rejoice with you and desire to tell you that your brother Slavko has been born into Heaven and intercedes for you." All six seers issued a public statement through

Jakov on Saturday; the most lengthy and moving section of it recalled Slavko's visits to their homes and how he delighted in playing with their children, all of whom had adored him as "a true friend." On Sunday, the parish laid waste in honor of his funeral; every bar, every café, every restaurant in Medjugorje was closed, despite the presence of thousands of people who came from all over the world to be there. More than one hundred priests concelebrated the funeral Mass. The seventy witnesses who had been on Križevac when Slavko died all swore that at the moment of his death, the cloud cover had broken and the sun had shone directly on the mountaintop. A rainbow had appeared in the sky, they said, that seemed to rise up from the spires of St. James's.

If it isn't true, it should be, was my response to these reports. Tears filled my eyes within moments after I opened the letter informing me of Slavko's death. My children, who had never seen me cry before, were frightened by my stifled sobs and asked what was wrong. "My friend Father Slavko has gone to Heaven," I choked out. Slavko's soul belonged in paradise, so there had to be such a place, I had decided in that instant, and it was remarkable how uplifted I was by the simple ontology of this equation. My absolute conviction that I had known a saint sustained me even when I learned how miserable the last year of Slavko's life had been.

Twelve months exactly before his heart failed him at the summit of Cross Mountain, Slavko had been banished from Medjugorje to the most remote corner of the Bosnian woods by Mostar's new bishop, Ratko Perić, who gave him until December 8, 1999, to depart. His fellow Franciscans could save him from this fate only by ascending to the pulpit of St. James's and, one by one, reading aloud a written statement in which they admitted the apparitions were false and that "it was all Slavko's invention," their bishop informed them. An Irish theolgian named Chisholm received permission from Cardinal Ratzinger (and by implication the pope) to mediate, but returned to Medjugorje after a single meeting with Bishop Perić to announce that it was pointless. Perić was "completely possessed" by his animosity to Slavko and the other friars, Chisholm said. Perić set a new deadline of January 9, 2000, for Slavko's evacuation, and warned that he would see the man defrocked if he refused to obey. Slavko stayed, of course, but endured more than ten months of threats and attacks. Those who worked with the man said they had never seen him suffer more.

Many in the parish blamed Perić for their beloved friar's death, but the crowd had remained mostly silent when their bishop appeared at Slavko's funeral. Could Perić possibly have been unmoved as Marija stood at the graveside laughing through tears as she repeated again and again, "*Slavko u nebo! Slavko u nebo!*" (Slavko in Heaven), I wondered. And what did Mostar's bishop make of the fact that a cause of Slavko's beatification had been undertaken within weeks of his death, replete with reports of miraculous healings and conversions through his intervention?

I sent Perić a copy of the letter I had written testifying to Slavko's heroic virtue, but didn't mention that with Slavko gone, my connection to Medjugorje seemed increasingly tenuous. I doubted I would ever return, and mostly ignored news reports that issued from the village—at least until the morning of September 12, 2001, when I received a copy of the letter that Father Zovko had sent to "All People of America." He was "deeply shaken by the events and images" of the previous day, and at the same time overwhelmed by memories of what had happened during the war in Bosnia: "Know that our prayers and compassion are with you in the pain and suffering of this difficult trial. We are with you upon our knees in prayer and vigils for your peace and strength; for light in this darkness. Our large prayer community is praying and is celebrating the Eucharist for all of those who have died, for the wounded and for all those who grieve." Most of the village would have been there, I knew, kneeling on the marble floors of St. James's, sincerely believing that through the graces of Our Lady, they could comfort strangers from the other side of the world.

Some Medjugorje enthusiasts, especially in America, insisted that the terrorist attacks of 2001 signified the beginning of the end, but the visionaries themselves made no attempt to link the horrors of September 11 to their Secrets; what had happened that day, they said, was as great a shock to them as to anyone else. Any suggestion of an imminent apocalypse was further diffused when Vicka became the sixth and final seer to begin a family, marrying Mario Mijatović of Sarajevo on the afternoon of January 26, 2002. She would be pregnant within three months, giving birth to her daughter, Marija-Sofija, shortly before the first anniversary of her wedding. Two months later she gave a lengthy interview to an American film crew whose director asked her immediately about "maintaining peace" in the face of an impending war with Iraq.

In her answer, Vicka said more about how she and the other visionaries were prepared for the carnage in their own country than she ever had before. The Virgin never spoke of the war, even as it drew close, Vicka said, "but you could tell, you could see—on Her face, from Her behavior, the way She presented Herself—She had a great pain. Nevertheless,

She did not frighten us by saying that war was going to start, that we should do this or that. Yet so many times before the war began, She told us—as She does now—that by our prayers and fasting, wars could be stopped."

I experienced a familiar sense of ambivalent bemusement as I read the other questions and answers. Vicka was and always would be a simple peasant woman, yet however uninformed her opinions might be, they were always disarming in their sincerity. She and the other seers would remain true to the Virgin's message of ecumenicism, Vicka said, and at present were praying for both Saddam Hussein and George W. Bush, for the people of Iraq and for the citizens of the United States. For what did they ask? "We recommend them to Our Lady," Vicka replied, as if explaining the obvious, "so that She may help."

Reading these lines, I wished for the thousandth time that I were capable of so simple a faith. By then, though, I was on a plane to Rome, where complications were currency.

CHAPTER NINETEEN

Rainbow-colored "*pace*" signs hung from half the city's balconies, and peace marchers by the thousands paraded through the streets, streaming toward a rally in St. Peter's Square. There was "still time to negotiate," the pope would tell them when they arrived, "still room for peace." John Paul might be down to measuring hope in seconds and centimeters, but if the past ten days had demonstrated anything, it was this pope's unique position of moral authority. One non-Catholic world leader after another—from Kofi Annan to Tariq Aziz to Tony Blair—had arrived at the Vatican to plead his case before the pontiff, each one conceding that no other public figure could command such a broad spectrum of influence. I would be meeting John Paul myself in less than seventy-two hours, but by then even the pope recognized that whatever room for peace remained would have to be made in the aftermath of one more bloody war.

I had arrived in Rome in March 2003 with an agenda that almost nobody at the Vatican seemed to share. My exploration of the hazy border separating science from religion had become a blundering search for whatever vague connections might exist between the rational and the rapturous. A theologian I had interviewed on the previous morning joked that I was attempting to forge "a unique brand of non-Catholic Catholicism," yet he and most of the other priests I met on this trip to Rome seemed to be struggling with their own definitions of the true faith. It was not, of course, an easy time to be a member of the Catholic clergy. Accusations of sexual abuse that surfaced in one diocese after another in the United States during the past year had enveloped the Church in its most threatening scandal in at least a century, and were forcing many in the Vatican to publicly address subjects (such as the prevalence of homosexuality among American and European priests) that traditionally had been kept to the confessional. A related problem was the continued shortage of clerics; the only continent on which younger priests were being ordained faster than older ones died off was Africa, but the vast majority of African priests did not obey their vows of chastity, and many were either secretly married or living openly with their mistresses.

Political controversies, meanwhile, were overwhelming theological considerations in even the most occult corners of the Vatican. My erstwhile mentor Peter Gumpel, the Jesuit priest I had interviewed at the Vatican back in 1995, was embroiled in the most painful contest of his long career in Rome, the result of the veteran postulator's efforts to secure the beatification of Pope Pius XII. John Cornwall's 1999 book, *Hitler's Pope*, not only had revived accusations that Pius was an anti-Semite who ignored Nazi atrocities, but alleged that, as the Vatican's secretary of state during the 1930s, the future pope had helped Hitler's rise to power. The Holy See employed unusually blunt language to condemn the book (calling it "trash," among other things), but assorted activist groups, most notably the Anti-Defamation League, had taken up the case against Pius, warning that his beatification would be the worst blow to Catholic-Jewish relations in fifty years. Peter Gumpel, now nearly eighty, had devoted more than two decades to a four-volume report on Pius's heroic virtue, and urged the Magisterium not to yield, accusing Jewish historians who took part in a panel studying Pius's wartime record of "clearly incorrect behavior." A month before my arrival in Rome, Gumpel had persuaded the Holy See to open archives showing that Pius had attempted to protect not just the four thousand Roman Jews who were given sanctuary inside the Vatican, but many others across Europe, and that he had not issued more scathing indictments of Jewish deportations for fear that the enraged Nazis would respond by increasing the scale of their slaughter. The result of Gumpel's actions was not a vindication of Pius, but a vitriolic attack on his elderly Jesuit defender, who found himself also accused of anti-Semitism. Clearly angered, Gumpel was now declaring that the internal processes of the Roman Catholic Church should not be influenced by the "worthless" arguments of Jewish propagandists.

Troubling as it was to my hosts, the martial atmosphere I found in Rome invigorated me. The impending war with Iraq seemed to produce the same clarity of perspective I had experienced during my first trip to Bosnia, almost eight years earlier. Even the ambitious felt little inclination to posture or obfuscate in a world where everything seemed up for grabs, and scarcely anyone I met professed unfamiliarity with the inner conflicts I described. The main obstacle my inquiries met was bad timing; not only were people distracted by the war, but the passing of the millennium had moved the investigation of prophetic revelations to the Vatican's back burner. Throughout the Holy See there was an attitude that these matters would sort themselves out in due course, and that as long as they were resolved before the end of the twenty-first century, no one need rush to judgment. The Congregation for the Doctrine of the Faith, in fact, had just announced its intention to publish a list of "up-to-date criteria" for distinguishing between true and false visions, asserting that the plethora of reported apparitions and locutions during the past two decades had forced the Church to protect itself from the "negative consequences of unwarranted devotions" that "multiply by imitation."

Any doubt that what some in the magisterium called "the Medjugorje virus" had prompted this decision was removed by this sentence in the Congregation's announcement: "Sometimes there is a long and worrying tension between the faithful who believe in these phenomena and the local bishop who is unwilling to give recognition to them." Bishop Perić promptly sent forth his vicar general to remind the Catholic press that "threats to the local Church are particularly pronounced in Medjugorje where [events] have been characterized by disobedience to the pope and to the bishop." Perić's man also repeated the accusation that the Medjugorje seers had attempted to blackmail Bishop Žanić into an acceptance of their apparitions by threatening him with "heavenly judgment." It was this tactic that had convinced Žanić that the apparitions were a fraud, the Mostar vicar general added.

"We are not taking sides, we are merely preserving our options," Father Augustine DiNoia, an American theologian recently assigned to the Congregation for the Doctrine of the Faith, told me. "Medjugorje has produced many strong reactions, pro and con. I think it would be fair to say that watching and waiting is the preferred approach of the Holy See at this point." As the congregation's recent announcement on its updated standards of authenticity had noted, only eleven of the 295 alleged apparitions that were investigated by the Church between 1905 and 1995 had been approved, meaning that "fewer than one in twenty-five are believed to be authentic," DiNoia noted. The embarrassments to the Church caused by instances of credulity that bordered on mass hysteria within various dioceses around the world, but especially in the U.S., were increasingly worrisome. "I think most bishops would rather find out they had a pedophile in their parish than a bleeding statue," he said. "The complications are greater, and the damage may be also."

Time was perhaps the greatest investigative tool the Church could employ in these cases, DiNoia observed. False claims of revelation had a way of revealing themselves over the years, often because the devotional cult they inspired simply dried up and blew away, or in some cases because the supposed seers felt the need to confess their "doubts and errors" as they approached death. Even some truly mystical events were simply personal phenomena, and not intended to result in any sort of broader impact, DiNoia added. Apparitions that involved matters of real importance to the Church as a whole, on the other hand, tended not only to sustain the devotions they inspired, but also to prove themselves by the fruits they yielded. Hadn't Medjugorje's fruits been impressive enough already? I wondered. "I personally know any number of people who have visited Medjugorje and been deeply moved by the experience," DiNoia allowed. "There's no question that the prayerful atmosphere of that parish is very inspiring. That, of course, doesn't by itself make the apparitions authentic. We need to let the local and regional authorities come to their conclusions, then let those remain in force until or unless new information comes to light." It had not helped the Medjugorje cause that the most powerful Church official in all of Bosnia-Hercegovina, Cardinal Vinko Puljić of Sarajevo, in an October 2001 address to the Synod of Bishops in Rome, had denounced the reported apparitions as "divisive," lambasting the Franciscans for their "disobedience" and asserting that their "pseudo-charisms" were a serious threat to the Church in his country. DiNoia had no comment on any of that, but did point out that negative judgments by bishops had been overcome, most notably at Lourdes, but in several other instances as well. The two younger seers at Fátima had been beatified eighty years after their deaths, he observed, and the Medjugorje visionaries might wait just as long to be recognized, or never be accepted at all. It was simply too soon to tell.

What the Church could not escape, the theologian conceded, was that many of its most influential figures, even in the modern era, had been inspired by what they considered mystical revelations. It had come out recently that Pope Pius XII claimed to have been visited by both Jesus and Mary during World War II: Mother Teresa's private letters had revealed that she began her ministry in Calcutta after receiving an interior locution from Jesus in 1947. And of course the assorted charisms of Padre Pio continued to make him at once the most controversial and compelling Catholic mystic of the twentieth century. No formal judgments had yet been made about Pius, Mother Teresa, or Padre Pio, Father DiNoia reminded me: "We have to acknowledge how little we understand about these things, and that the position of the Church can change as its understanding grows." As if to illustrate his point, the priest informed me that Vassula Ryden, the banned visionary who claimed that Jesus was the true author of her books, had recently taken up residence in Rome, and that her case was being "reconsidered" by the Holy Office.

One problem with waiting was that anticipation grew and rumors spread as time passed. The fabled third Secret of Fátima at last had been revealed on May 13, 2000, a date that had been chosen carefully. It was not only the nineteenth anniversary of the failed assassination attempt on John Paul II but also the eighty-third anniversary of the apparition at which Lucia dos Santos claimed to have received her three Secrets from the Virgin Mary. The third Secret had been a prophecy of the attack on the pope, Cardinal Angelo Soldano, the Vatican's secretary of state, informed a crowd of six hundred thousand who had gathered in the Portuguese village to celebrate what the Holy See designated as "Fátima Day." Soldano explained that because the secret involved John Paul personally, the pope (who sat nearby) had asked that he make this announcement. The cardinal then quoted from a passage in the third Secret that described how a "bishop clothed in white," while making his way through the corpses of martyrs, "falls to the ground, apparently dead, under a burst of gunfire." The Holy Father remained convinced that the Virgin of Fátima had saved his life, Soldano told the crowd, insisting that her "motherly hand" had guided the bullet's path, enabling him to halt "at the threshold of death." Those in the crowd who waited for more were disappointed. They said afterwards that they had hoped "the rest of the Secret" would be revealed when the pope himself spoke, but John Paul said little to amplify what Soldano had announced earlier. The pope had come to Fátima to conduct the Mass at the beatification ceremony for Jacinta and Francisco Marto. Ninety-three-year-old Lucia dos Santos, better known now as Sister Lucy, arrived at the tomb of her cousins wearing a black nun's habit, assisted by a pair of Church officials as she walked with a cane. She and John Paul met, held hands, and spoke briefly, but what they said was not shared with the crowd. When the pope delivered his homily, he began by stating, "I desire once again to celebrate the goodness of the Lord toward me when, severely struck on that May 13, 1981, I was saved from death." John Paul made no mention of the Secrets, other than a fleeting reference to the horrors of World War II that Lucia said had been predicted in the first two Secrets. "So many victims during the final century of the second millennium!" he lamented, but left it at that.

Catholics worldwide expected that further revelations—especially about the future of the Church—would be provided when the full text of the third Secret was released, but they discovered on June 26, 2000, that there was nothing new to disclose. Word that the Fátima Secrets all concerned events in the past came as a shock to many, and more than a few Catholics said they felt cheated. A story swiftly spread that some part of the third Secret had been withheld. This rumor was not dispelled until December 2001, when Sister Lucy herself announced (through Cardinal Ratzinger's secretary, Archbishop Bertone) that "everything has been published—no secret remains." Sister Lucy also dismissed reports that she had received new messages from the Virgin. "If I had received new revelations I would have communicated them directly to the Holy Father," she said.

The sense that they had somehow orchestrated an anticlimax still rankled any number of priests at the Vatican, who became quite testy whenever the subject of Fátima was raised. "It is what it is," Father DiNoia told me. "The pope believes that the third Secret predicted the attempt on his life, and that it was somehow instrumental in saving his life. If that's not enough for people, then perhaps they expect too much."

The Holy See intended to continue playing its cards close to the vest when it came to matters such as these, I was told by DiNoia and several other priests I spoke to. Disappointing people fifty years from now remained a better option than feeding their fears and speculations in the present, it was explained. The controversy that still raged around the Church's handling of "the Civitavecchia matter," I was advised, was a prime example of why "the three Ps" (prudence, patience, and perspective) were necessary to the administration of such phenomena.

The drama of La Madonnina had played out in the courts, in the newspapers, and in the Vatican's Palace of Congregations for eight long years, and what little had been resolved was still being argued among the various parties. Bishop Gerolmo Grillo continued to suggest, but never to state unequivocally, that he believed the statue's tears had been of supernatural origin. Grillo's refusal to turn the statue over to the police, however, had convinced the public prosecutor that the bishop was in cahoots with Fabio Gregori and his family, and that the lot of them had perpetrated an outrageous hoax. The courts attempted to craft a compromise (ordering that La Madonnina remain sealed in Bishop Grillo's cupboard while the state's inquiry continued) but were undercut when the Holy See made a very public gesture of support for Fabio Gregori. This came when the pope dispatched his close friend and countryman Cardinal Andrej Maria Deskur to Civitavecchia to address Gregori's congregation at an Easter Mass, where the cardinal presented Fabio a blessed copy of *La Madonnina*, and compared what was taking place to events in Poland during 1967, when communist authorities had sequestered the revered Madonna of Czestochówa in Kraców.

For the next six years, *La Madonnina* stood behind a screen of bullet-proof glass at St. Agostino's, attracting thousands upon thousands of pilgrims. Long after every other one of the other claimed miracles—and there had been scores of them—that surfaced in Italy during the years leading up to the millennium had been debunked, the bleeding statue from Medjugorje remained an object of veneration that boasted its own Web site, despite the best efforts of multiple agencies to discredit it. The public prosecutor continued to press a criminal complaint of pious fraud, still flanked by his unlikely allies from Codacons and the Anti-Brainwashing Hotline. While Codacons officials chose to wait silently for a ruling by the courts, the head of the hotline, Giovanni Panunzio, remained vocal in his opposition. However, the various tricks and ruses Panunzio suggested might be the source of *La Madonnina*'s tears had been disproved by separate investigations.

The Church itself seemed to be inching toward an endorsement of *La Madonnina*'s tears as a genuine miracle. Bishop Grillo had become increasingly outspoken in his remarks, insisting during the Christmas season of 1996 that he could categorically "exclude the possibility that this is a product of artifice, or tricks motivated by bad faith," and that "the statue truly weeps." He had appointed an investigative commission headed by René Laurentin to examine the evidence, Grillo announced that same month, but was back in the headlines during February 1997, when he disputed a report in *Il Messaggero*, which said that all eleven members of the panel had concluded *La Madonnina*'s tears were the result of "supernatural forces," and that a positive ruling on the little statue from Medjugorje would be issued soon. While refusing to discuss the panel's opinions, Grillo reminded reporters that the members had only a "consultive role" in studying the case, that he alone would make the final decision on the question of supernatural agency, and that "many problems remain to be solved" before he could do so. What these were, the bishop declined to say, but most observers assumed he was waiting to see what happened with the court case.

La Madonnina's would-be debunkers were heartened when they were joined by the Italian Committee for Investigation of the Paranormal (CICAP), whose cofounder Luigi Garlaschelli, the head of the organic chemistry department at the University of Pavia, was considered the leading scientific investigator of claimed miracles involving tears and blood.

Garlaschelli enjoyed displaying for the media the various frauds he had exposed, many involving mechanisms built in to the heads of statues, but it had already been established by X-ray evidence that no such devices were behind *La Madonnina*'s eyes. There were other ways to perpetrate such a fraud, Garlaschelli replied, such as the use of a colorless compound that turns red when it comes into contact with the vapor of ammonia; a smear of this under each eye might have gone undetected. That was unlikely, said the scientists who had examined *La Madonnina*, but Garlaschelli was undaunted. Photographs taken at various times during the five-day *lacrimazioni* in Civitavecchia proved that the bloodstains on the statue's cheeks did not change shape, the professor asserted. When it was reported that more than sixty persons had sworn before Bishop Grillo's investigative commission that they had seen *La Madonnina* weep tears of blood, all at various times on different dates, Garlaschelli insisted that "emotionalism" had fevered their imaginations.

The refusal of Fabio Gregori to submit to a DNA test was regarded as suspicious by Garlaschelli and many others, but Gregori's defenders were even greater in number. While the attorney representing Gregori in the criminal case pending against him took pains to point out that the original forensic analysis of the blood lifted from the statue's cheeks had been profoundly flawed (a point on which a majority of scientists involved in the case agreed), those who were close to Gregori portrayed him as a simple, earnest man who had been emotionally devastated by the efforts of all sides to exploit the miracle of *La Madonnina*. "Mistrustful" and "withdrawn" were the words they most often used to describe a man who was increasingly appalled by the efforts of Civitavecchia mayor Pietro Tidei to create a tourist industry around the weeping statue. The mayor already had allocated billions of lire for the construction of roads, streetlights, toilets, and parking structures (along with a large "consecrated" marquee directing pilgrims to St. Agostino's) and was bitterly complaining of Bishop Grillo's refusal to authorize construction of a large new sanctuary to house *La Madonnina*, or to approve of plans to tie in with tour operators who would direct pilgrims through Civitavecchia on their way from Rome to Lourdes. By the spring of 2000, Gregori and his attorney were aggressively pursuing those who attempted to commericalize *La Madonnina*, obtaining an injunction against the Austrian bank Hypo when it used a photograph of the weeping statue in an advertisement and preparing another against Benetton that was abandoned only when the clothing manufacturer ceased using its own ad featuring *La Madonnina*. Gregori and his family were most

upset by the recent stunt of a popular magician, Alfredo Barrago (a frequent collaborator of the Anti-Brainwashing Hotline's Panunzio), who had
attempted to demonstrate for TV cameras how tears of blood might be
manufactured by shining a red laser beam onto the cheeks of La Madonnina from a position in St. Agostino's gallery. The effect had been so startling that a woman praying in front of the shrine fainted on the spot.

While Gregori (whose home had been searched by police nearly a
dozen times) became more and more reclusive, communicating only
through his attorney, the debate that raged all around him was increasingly messy and absurd. Bishop Grillo had thrown fuel on the fire by
asserting that laboratory tests indicating that the tears on La Madonnina's
cheeks contained the DNA of an adult human male had proved to his
satisfaction that the blood was that of Jesus Christ. An organization that
billed itself as the Institute for Secular Humanism answered that the presence of male DNA in the blood on La Madonnina's cheeks established
only that the Madonna was a transvestite, and took to calling her "The
Virgin Larry." A reporter for Il Messaggero admitted that she had been
among those who saw the statue weep tears of blood, but insisted she
believed it had been a clever trick of some unknown origin. Giovanni
Panunzio said he believed that both Fabio Gregori and Bishop Grillo had
been duped by the members of an anti-Catholic conspiracy who were
using them to mock the Church.

The person in possession of the greatest number of facts from the broadest spectrum of sources involved in the investigation of La Madonnina,
Judge Carmine Castalado, who was hearing the pious fraud case brought
by the Procura against Fabio Gregori, seemed more and more unhappy
with the position in which he found himself, and had let the trial drag
on for months, then years. A clamor of criticism from the media eventually forced Castalado to announce early in 2001 that he would soon issue a ruling. And on March 20 of that year, he did, announcing that there
had been "no trickery" by Gregori or anyone else connected to the weeping
statue of Civitavecchia.

Gregori made his first public statement in many months that day. "I
am happy that the case has been closed," he told reporters, "but in conscience I must say that I was absolutely always at peace. I was prepared
to face an eventual sentence, so long as I could defend the truth to the
end." Bishop Grillo hailed the judge's decision as a personal vindication.
"Today I say: Let's hope that the world will at least believe the court."
The Vatican, however, would not react to the court decision. The Con-

gregation for the Doctrine of the Faith issued a statement that it continued to analyze the case, and reminded the public that the Church nearly always took "many years" to declare a miracle.

I was advised that the Holy See would take no formal position on *La Madonnina* until it made a decision about Medjugorje, and that was not likely to happen until most if not all of the principal figures—both in Bosnia and in Civitavecchia—were deceased. Of course, if the Great Sign were to appear on a hillside in Bosnia, one priest told me with a faint smile, "that might accelerate the process."

Few discoveries I had made during the past eight years revealed more about the Holy See's attitude toward visions, locutions, apparitions—all of the phenomena that Roman Catholicism lumps together as "private revelations"—than that those the Church assigns to investigate them are, most often, theologians. Authenticity and theological correctness are inseparable in the eyes of the Church, explained Father Gabriel O'Donnell, who had been called in as "consultant" by numerous U.S. bishops compelled to investigate reports of mystical events in their dioceses. This might sound overbearingly dogmatic, Father O'Donnell agreed, until one understood that "usefulness to the Church as a whole" was the time-honored standard of a mystic's significance.

I met with Father O'Donnell at the Angelicum, home to the Pontifical University of St. Thomas Aquinas, where he had been in residence for the past year. To get there from my hotel just off St. Peter's Square required a long walk along the Corso Vittorio Emmanuel, across the Piazza Venezia to the intersections of Via Panisperna and Salita del Grillo. The sensations of this plunge into secular Rome were amplified by the mad roar of rush-hour traffic, yet it was strangely quiet on the little knoll where the Angelicum reposed. About the place was a sense of redoubt, separated by city blocks from the prying eyes of the Holy See, yet elevated above the commercial hubbub of the crowds on the streets below, a place where the centuries-old search for truth had survived human appetites for power and money. The University Biblioteca housed one of the greatest collections of religious manuscripts on the face of the earth, the Casantanense; and students who divided themselves between the schools of philosophy and theology still took many of their classes in Latin.

Father O'Donnell was a plump, pink-cheeked man with a slightly breathy voice, whose hair and beard were nearly the same shade of white as his

Dominican habit. His demeanor was kind but careful. I couldn't help but wonder what the years since 1995 would have been like if I had stuck with my original intention and written a book in which O'Donnell or someone like him provided the protagonist's point of view. "A lot less interesting" was the priest's opinion. The redundancies he cataloged in his work as a miracle detective made it a generally tedious process, O'Donnell explained, and this wasn't simply because the purported seers he investigated had lacked wit or imagination. Bernadette Soubirous, Lucia dos Santos, the six seers of Medjugorje, and assorted other peasant children were the best-known Catholic visionaries of the modern era, he said, but "not all the people who have these experiences are intellectually undeveloped. Some are actually quite gifted. I've dealt with cases involving physicians, college professors, even scientists." Nevertheless, the messages delivered by even these mediums tended to be "very similar," O'Donnell told me in a weary voice, "especially in their literary style, which relies heavily on the prophetic language of the Old Testament. Very often one instruction will be linked with another, and there's at least the hint of a warning."

The messages of the Madonna at Medjugorje were "prototypical" of what he had observed in parishes all over the U.S., said O'Donnell, who conceded that he found it difficult to separate the upwelling of "extraordinary events" reported by Catholics during the past two decades from the apparitions in Bosnia: "Medjugorje and the millennium seem to have sparked many if not most of these things." Yet while he believed that just about every reported revelation he had probed contained social, political, psychological, and "imitative elements," he added, he did not think these should by themselves invalidate claims of divine intervention. During the past two decades, O'Donnell probably had investigated as many alleged miracles as any cleric in America, and during that entire time, the priest said, he encountered not a single case that he believed to be diabolically inspired, and only a handful that were the results of fakery or mental illness.

His assignment in most cases was to interview the seer or locutionary and to write a report. He almost always began with a half-dozen or so face-to-face meetings in which the subject told his or her story. "I generally become their spiritual director, and they visit me or I visit them over a period of months," he explained. "Now, the point of spiritual direction is not to authenticate or validate supernatural experiences, but to help you grow in virtue. I find that many of these people have difficulty in keeping these two things straight and separate, and that this is usually because they feel they have some special mission or duty. I also find that the more they feel this, the more I tend to doubt the importance of their visions." Of course, the prosaic nature of most messages reported by mystics was a factor as well: "In the vast majority of cases, what you get is a pious expression of moral forms that are more or less within the confines of the Ten Commandments, with nothing that really bears in a unique way on the Church today and the times we live in. General complaints about the moral decay of our times are not terribly interesting or helpful."

There was one common characteristic of such messages that "puzzled" him, O'Donnell admitted: "The threat of punishment if a warning is not heeded." He had come to believe that nearly all such messages were the result of human distortion, and that they usually were related in some way to the vainglory of the person who delivered them. "I watch very closely how people respond when I tell them, 'You know, you're not really important here. You're just the instrument, the vehicle.' As soon as you see them react to that with anything other than humble agreement, you know you have a problem. That doesn't mean the vision or locution is inauthentic, however, only that it is problematic and therefore not of use to the Church."

The most troubling cases to him were the ones in which "these things begin as authentic and become something else, because the visionary somehow confuses or even co-opts the message. It is entirely possible to corrupt what is good and holy. Spiritual pride is especially insidious, because you're feeling good about doing good or about being good." The temptations faced by mystics were very real, in his opinion: "The experience of an apparition or locution is incredibly seductive. That's what St. John of the Cross kept telling people. Not 'Don't listen because it isn't real.' But 'Don't listen because it's so seductive to discover that you are the Chosen Vessel.' I think a lot of genuine mystics enter religious orders because it's the only place they can hide, where they aren't constantly tempted to think of themselves as stars."

Those who allowed their motives to mix were amusing and alarming in just about equal parts, the priest said: "I'm thinking of the sort of person who will tell me something like 'Our Lady really doesn't like your suspicious, questioning attitude, and you really should be more docile to Her.' I always reply, 'Well, the next time you talk to Her, perhaps you could ask Our Lady to let me know this Herself, because I find it very difficult to accept this sort of correction through a third party.'"

Only in a few cases had he encountered visionaries who seemed to recognize inherently that extreme humility was their best protection against error. These almost always were the most compelling mystical claims he encountered, yet even in these instances of what he deemed to be authentic revelation, O'Donnell's position was usually that the messages received be treated as personal and private: "I most frequently end my quote, investigations, unquote, by advising these people simply to keep these things to themselves, because no good will be served by publishing them. I think it's very rare to encounter a seer or locutionary who is truly called to speak to the Church at large." Only twice in all the years he devoted to this work had he met mystics whose revelations were worthy of wider dissemination. One had been a recent case that involved messages "concerning sexual abuse by priests in the United States," O'Donnell told me. "I really can't say a lot about it to you, but there was this notable absence of the ominous Old Testament prophetic language so common in these cases. It was a very clear, simple message that concerned the interior lives of priests and clergy in general. It was profound, but not at all portentous, and much more instructive than threatening." Both the message and the person who reported receiving it had passed all three of his primary tests, O'Donnell added: "Theological correctness, usefulness to the Church, and a clear relationship between the messages the person reports and changes in the quality of their own lives."

And yet, after six months of investigation and the submission of a lengthy report that urged the publication of these messages, the bishop had elected not to issue a judgment. "The same thing happened in the one other instance where I submitted a positive report," said O'Donnell. "All I can say is that bishops are very afraid to make a mistake, so they find a way to shelve this stuff. In both instances the bishop ordered the seer not to go public, in order to avoid generating a cult."

While admitting to a measure of "frustration" in these two cases, he understood that the Church was a hierarchy, and wondered if keeping a lid on things might not be the approach that best served the seers themselves. "The public nature of a vision complicates it immediately," he explained. "Which is why, to whatever degree this is true, the integrity of the visionaries in Medjugorje is so remarkable."

He had decided some time ago not to visit Medjugorje, mostly because of what he understood about himself. "I know so many people who have gone to Medjugorje and come back reporting this profound experience of faith. I might have it too, but I don't think it would change me, because even if Our Lady were to convert me, my intellect would keep working away, wondering , questioning, 'What is this for me?' And 'Is it authentic?' Because while I think God uses a place such as Medjugorje,

I don't believe that makes what's reported there authentic. And all this doom and gloom that's associated with the Secrets is very troubling to me. I don't understand its necessity." And yet the length and frequency of the reported apparitions, so perplexing to some in the Vatican, bothered him very little, O'Donnell said: "There has never been anything like it, but that by itself is no real criticism."

He was curious about but largely unimpressed by the results of the scientific tests conducted on the Medjugorje seers. As a young priest, he had participated in what he believed was the first "brain study" of mystical experiences. "It was at Yeshiva University in New York," he recalled. "They hooked us up to these machines, then asked us to meditate or pray. Some of us were Catholic, some Jewish, some Buddhist, some Muslim—every religion you can imagine. And of course it registered that we went into an altered state as we prayed, and that the deeper we went, the more it registered. There clearly is physiologically something that happens to you, but that isn't evidence of the supernatural. In fact, it conforms entirely to the laws of nature."

When I mentioned that perplexing line in the Vatican's summary of the 1998 tests run on the Medjugorje visionaries, the one about how their experience seemed to be the same as before but slightly less intense, O'Donnell smiled wanly. "Perhaps it is that She has refused to speak about things that are so personal, and this makes it less intense for them," he suggested. "These are, after all, human beings that we're talking about."

I repeated the same question I had asked Augustine DiNoia one day earlier, the one in which I described an apparition as a door opening, and wondered if it was possible to open that door from either side. Like DiNoia, O'Donnell promptly answered in the negative: "The door can't open from this side and be authentic." Although he had worked with many psychiatrists over the years, and found followers of Carl Jung to be the most engaging, he ultimately rejected a Jungian description of these events. "I think they deceive themselves because, like most modern people, they have convinced themselves that man is at the center of things. But the heart of religious life is that God is the center." On the other hand, he did believe that "a person who has had the experience of the door opening from the other side can, through some process of the subconscious much like Jung described, re-create the experience," O'Donnell said. "This isn't a religious vision, however, but an illusion, and a very dangerous one.

"No person can control that door opening," the priest continued. "It's a grace. Why it's bestowed we really can't know. I draw on the Gospel of St. John to explain these things to myself. 'God so loved the world that

He sent His only begotten Son so that we might be saved.' Well, God so loves the world that He keeps sending us these messages through angels, His Mother, the saints, so that we never perish."

O'Donnell was intrigued when I asked him what he imagined a Buddhist who happened to be walking past Podbrdo on June 24, 1981, would have seen. "I think it's entirely possible that a Buddhist would have seen something other than the Virgin Mary," he replied after a considerable pause. "So I suppose that means I think the vision depends on the seer. But that's only because the seer is a vessel, and each vessel is different. But I don't think the seer creates the vision. Not if it's authentic."

O'Donnell then made a remark that startled me: "You know, this is probably the first real conversation I've ever had about these matters." He smiled at my expression. " To be quite honest, we don't talk about this stuff amongst ourselves," the priest explained, "probably because we understand how dangerous these subjects are."

I hadn't recognized those dangers at first, and then later had chosen to ignore them, I told him. "That's probably why you've chosen to write the book you've described," the priest said, and smiled again. "I don't know if you made a brave choice or a foolish one, but at least it's interesting."

While I was trying to decide whether to tell O'Donnell that I had felt early on as if this book were choosing me, rather than the other way around, the priest again caught me by surprise, this time by repeating, almost verbatim, the statement Augustine DiNoia had made at the end of our interview the day before. "There's one person you absolutely must speak to before you finish this book," he said. "That's Benedict Groeschel." I knew Groeschel, a Capuchin monk, as the author of what was considered Catholicism's most important modern work of "mystical theology," a brilliantly concise volume titled *A Still, Silent Voice*. With the publication of the book, Groeschel had assumed the roles played in earlier centuries by St. Ignatius Loyola, whose *Rules for the Discernment of Spirits* was the fundamental work in the field, and Father Augustin Poulain, a nineteenth-century Parisian whose *Graces of Interior Prayer* was regarded—especially among theologians—as an even more authoritative source. Father DiNoia had seemed almost reverential when he spoke of Groeschel, saying that the Capuchin was "a very important figure in the Church, regarded as very deep, even profound, someone whom a lot of people already consider a saint." Gabriel O'Donnell widened his eyes in wonderment when I repeated DiNoia's remark. "Well, I'm not sure Ben is a saint," O'Donnell said, "but he is Groucho Marx in a monk's habit."

Even better, I thought, but unfortunately, Groeschel was not in Rome, and in fact was known to avoid the eternal city and its political machinations. The man was difficult to contact and perhaps impossible to interview, said O'Donnell, but the Dominican promised to "ask around" for a phone number where I might leave Father Groeschel a message. "In the meantime," O'Donnell added, "you have your meeting with the pope to look forward to." I was approaching that encounter with high hopes, I confessed. O'Donnell laughed. "Now, those," he said, "are really dangerous."

This would not, of course, be a private audience. I was to meet John Paul II in the presence of more than ten thousand people on the morning of March 19, 2003, separated from them only by the stone steps that led to the entrance of St. Peter's Cathedral. These were "hours of trepidation," as the pope would put it in his address to the crowd; everyone present knew that the bombs would begin falling on Baghdad very soon (though few expected the air assault to commence that evening), and the hope that John Paul might make this occasion a historic one hung over the cathedral square like the bated breath of anxious angels.

I'd been kept awake by my own sense of anticipation for most of the previous night, and now found myself stifling yawns as I looked through swollen eyes at the ranks of cardinals and bishops who awaited His Holiness's arrival. Overprepared as I was for this event, a rush of exhilaration still coursed through me when the white Isuzu jeep known as the "popemobile" zipped out of the colonnade to my right. I was practically giddy within seconds, watching the jeep make passes through the cheering crowd in the courtyard, and caught my first live glimpse of John Paul, right arm swinging like a metronome as he waved to people who had come from all over the planet to be this near him.

Try as I might, during the past several days I hadn't been able to keep myself from imagining that I was on the cusp of a climactic moment—perhaps *the* climactic moment—in what was now a years-long struggle with Catholic arcana. This trip to Rome had felt from the first like a resumption of the journey I began in the summer of 1995, mainly because, like my first visit to Medjugorje, it seemed to happen on its own, with things falling into place as if planned—though not by me—and a familiar sense that I was being guided had grown in me from the moment I set a date for my departure. Even this opportunity to meet the pope had seemed to come out of nowhere, the gift of unseen forces that had rewarded me for nothing more than falling in love with the right woman. By the time I had taken my seat on the mezzanine outside the front entrance to St. Peter's, I was convinced that something John Paul said or did today was going to provide the resolution I longed for. As I watched the popemobile climb the ramp to the platform where I waited, I felt certain that soon everything would be clear to me.

John Paul's papacy was already the third longest in the history of the Church, and he would surpass that of Leo XIII if he lived another year. During his quarter century as pontiff, John Paul had logged more than seven hundred thousand miles in visits to 120 countries, had issued a record thirteen papal encyclicals, had canonized nearly three hundred saints, and had beatified more than eight hundred other individuals. He had done more to bring down the Iron Curtain, topple the Soviet Union, and end the Cold War than any other person on earth. However, my expectations of him had been conditioned less by John Paul's accomplishments than by the fateful role into which this pope had been cast by a string of prophecies that stretched from Medjugorje all the way back to Fátima. Ever since the attempt on his life in 1981, he had put his Marian devotion and his belief in the Virgin's apparitions at the center of his papacy. This was a pope whose personal motto was "I am completely yours, Mary," and who, I had been told, insisted that the letter *M* be embroidered on every robe he wore. In *Crossing Threshold of Hope*, he had written, "If victory comes, it will be brought by Mary. Christ will conquer through Her because he wants his victories now and in the future to be linked with Her!"

John Paul had credited the Virgin of Fátima with saving his life even as he lay in a hospital bed recovering from bullet wounds, and now was said to have recognized himself as "the bishop clothed in white" described in the third Secret even before the assassination attempt took place. Malachi Martin had written that this pope actually believed it was his duty to live at least a few years into the new millennium, until the day an awe-inspiring sign from Heaven appeared in the sky, placed there by Mary as a signal to all mankind that the world as we know it was at an end. The apparitions at Garabandal were still viable within the Church because of the pope's interest in them, and because more than fifteen years before Karol Wojtyla became John Paul II, Conchita Gonzales had claimed the Virgin told her that this pope would be the last. Conchita had delivered this revelation in October 1962, on the day the bells of the village church began to toll the death of John XXIII: "The pope is dead. Now there will be only three more," Conchita had told her mother. "How do you know that?" the older woman had asked. "Because the Virgin told me," Conchita had replied. When asked later what this meant for humanity, Conchita said that the Virgin had told her the third pope's death would signal the end of time but not the end of the world. She didn't know what this meant, she said. John XXIII had been followed to the papal throne by Paul VI and John Paul I. John Paul II was the third.

Almost no priest I had met at the Vatican doubted this pope was privy to secrets that would shake the foundations of world order. When Mehmet Ali Agca, the gunman who had attempted to kill Pope John Paul II twenty years earlier, was pardoned by the Italian government in June 2000 (the same month the Vatican released the full text of the third Secret of Fátima), then flown home to Turkey, it was widely reported that the pope had not only approved but encouraged the decision. Prosecutors made it clear they did not believe Agca's claim that he had been working for members of the Bulgarian secret service employed by the Soviet KGB, and conceded that they probably would never know the true story of the assassination attempt, but asked what other choice they had when John Paul himself insisted that it would be wrong to hold the man in prison simply to make him talk. I had heard many reasons for the Vatican's decision to encourage Agca's release and to withhold what it knew about his attempt on the pope's life, but everyone I spoke to agreed on one point: John Paul regarded the man as no more than a minor actor in the drama of God's plan, and had long ago forgiven him.

The pope had made it clear that he regarded the events at Medjugorje as pivotal to the unfolding of this drama's third act, and in return the Bosnian seers extolled him repeatedly over the years. Until Father Slavko's death, John Paul was the only living person to have been mentioned in the monthly messages at Medjugorje, most portentously in August 1994, when, according to Marija Pavlović, the Virgin had asked that she and the other visionaries pray for the pope's health, referring to John Paul as "My most beloved son, whom I have chosen for these times." Marija said she had been amazed how often the pope's speeches echoed phrases she had heard first from the Madonna during her apparitions. Jelena said she had been told this was the pope who would "defeat Satan." After meeting with John Paul in private for twenty minutes in 1987, Mirjana said that meeting the pope's gaze was "just like looking into the eyes of the Blessed Mother."

What most struck me when John Paul drew near was how visible were the ravages of his debilitation. An advanced case of Parkinson's and assorted other ailments had left him looking as if he literally carried the weight of the world. His osteoporosis had produced a startlingly large dowager's hump on the pope's upper back, and as he shuffled out of his vehicle onto the small, wheeled hydraulic platform that carried him to his throne, he seemed almost impossibly bent and shriveled. I had learned only in the past few days that the strapping Karol Wojtyla had been quite the ladies' man in his day, even authoring a treatise on the female orgasm that was regarded as the most important work on the link between sexuality and spirituality to have been produced by a Catholic theologian in several centuries. Now, though, it hurt to watch the old man lift the large feet that were the only remaining physical evidence of his robust youth.

I assumed he must be heavily drugged, and wondered if the pope actually understood what was taking place. Yet when he began to speak—in seven different languages—his voice rang out, clear and commanding, even as the paper he read from fluttered in his trembling hands. As John Paul blessed those present, I found myself recalling the promise I had made to Slavko in the confessional shortly before my departure from Medjugorje in 1995. The opportunity to speak out against abortion in a public setting had never presented itself, so the most I had done was mildly irritate the feminist sensibilities of a few friends' wives. I had, however, offered Masses to my lost babies, and given them names. I silently prayed for them now as the pope turned the focus of his address to St. Joseph, whose "solemnity" was being celebrated by the Church this day. Leaning forward in my chair, I listened intently as John Paul observed that St. Joseph was, among other things, the patron saint of workers, then asked those present to reflect on "the importance of work in the life of man." I did not begin to take the pope's remarks personally until he described St. Joseph as a "just man," then explained that by "just" he did not mean that Mary's husband was merely a man of moral rectitude but also one who had responded to a heavenly call with "docile responsibility" and "never presumed he had the right to question God's project."

The same, I knew, could have been said of me only during the weeks I spent in Medjugorje. My expectations of the pope and of this day were just the latest example of how contrary I remained to the "total openness to the will of the heavenly Father" that John Paul was recommending to the crowd in St. Peter's Square. I made a visceral effort to abandon all my preparations for this encounter, drawing deep breaths and digging my fingernails into the palms of my hands as I told myself that if one could simply approach the pope with a humble acceptance of the moment, then perhaps one might receive what one needed.

It was an attitude few journalists could adopt, as evidenced by the looks of disappointment on the faces of the media when it became clear that John Paul did not intend to use this occasion to make a major antiwar speech. The pope closed, in fact, with a simple prayer that St. Joseph, "man of peace that he was," obtain for all mankind, and "especially for the peoples threatened in these hours by war, the precious gifts of harmony and reconciliation."

A series of introductions, greetings, and benedictions followed, then suddenly a factotum wearing a waistcoat with a white sash was summoning our group toward the pope's throne. I recognized only a split second later that the occasion was about to be hijacked by a single member of our group. Florence was a major donor to the Vatican's art collections, a woman born into the Italian nobility who had married the American owner of a huge supermarket chain. Her husband had been lost at sea more than twenty years earlier; the boat was found, but never the man's body. Many rumors about his rich widow had circulated since then, and following his death, Florence had become possessed by a sort of religious mania that she channeled mainly into her support for various restoration projects undertaken by the Vatican museums. Her garish makeup, gaudy jewelry, and haughty manner had made her a distracting, somewhat unnerving presence at the functions our group had attended earlier in the week, from the cocktail reception at the ultraexclusive Circolo degli Scacchi, where she upbraided one young woman for failing to wear an appropriate blouse, to the private tour of the restored Sistine Chapel where she carried a jewel-encrusted purse worth more than most people's houses.

From the moment we arrived at St. Peter's that morning, she had insisted that the rest of us defer to her, demanding the chair closest to John Paul and informing us in no uncertain terms that she would lead the way when we approached the throne. Apparently doubting our obedience, she charged to the lead when the chief of protocol waved us forward, and was already at the pope's side by the time the rest of arrived to have our pictures taken with His Holiness. As it happened, I was positioned immediately behind John Paul's throne, on his right shoulder, and had a pope's-eye view of Florence as she leaned forward, nose to nose with the vicar of Christ, then pulled from the folds of her cloak a large envelope wrapped in showy flowers and began to repeat in a hoarse, almost raspy voice the same word over and over: "*Dollare, dollare, dollare.*" I wasn't sure the pope understood he was being handed a wad of cash. He quickly passed the envelope to a cardinal, but as he did, Florence grasped his hand, the one on which John Paul wore the papal ring. I waited for her to kiss what many regard as the most venerable object in all of Catholicism, the "Ring of the Fisherman," as it was known, hoping that we might proceed from there in a more orderly fashion, but Florence was squeezing the pope's hand with such ardor that she somehow managed to remove the ring, which fell onto the paving stones at our feet and disappeared into a maelstrom of gasping, grasping Vatican officials who bumped heads in their frenzied rush to retrieve it. Never before in the history of papal audiences had such a thing occurred, I would be told later, but then I had pretty much guessed that already. The ring was recovered, of course, and swiftly returned to the pope, who wore an expression that was either absolute aplomb or utter exhaustion as he permitted a cardinal to return it to its rightful finger. Everyone else in the vicinity looked shocked or horrified—even the two Swiss guards who stood at stiff attention in their striped pantaloons and metal helmets, armed with ax and spear, seemed to twitch as they exchanged questioning glances. The chief of protocol, needless to say, was at this point in some hurry to dispatch our group. White gloves waved at us to move on without further delay. Stunned, I slowly complied, letting my left hand brush the pope's shoulder as I moved to his side, where Florence had been a moment earlier. At this close range, I was taken aback by how pink and smooth John Paul's complexion was, given the severity of his physical impairment. "Cherubic," I thought at the time. His eyes were the same shade of blue as Mirjana's, and equally translucent. I hadn't yet abandoned hope for some last-second revelation—a profound word, a dramatic gesture. What I got was a sidelong glance and a faint, flickering twinkle of amusement. I had turned and taken several steps toward the white gloves that still gestured frantically, when a chuckle percolated out of my innards and burst forth before I could stop it. I felt overcome by a glorious kind of reckless abandon; this was the same sacred guffaw of liberation I had discovered at the summit of Križevac almost eight years earlier, my kind of communion with a God who was wild and free and totally unpredictable, a God who laughed at me if I made Him, but with me if I would only allow myself to join in. I threw my head back, gaping upward at the statues of Jesus and His Apostles where they stood atop the entrance to St. Peter's, and grinned at them like a chimpanzee. "I get it," I heard myself say, and in that moment actually believed this to be true.

CHAPTER TWENTY

I did not learn until the day I left Rome that Cardinal Ratzinger was about to sign a letter endorsing the negative judgment of the apparitions reported by Gianna Talone-Sullivan that had been submitted to the Vatican by Baltimore cardinal William H. Keeler. The cardinal was permitted to announce officially that Gianna's visions were not supernatural, Ratzinger wrote, and Keeler promptly went public with the news, advising the new pastor at St. Joseph's Church in Emmitsburg that this ruling from the pope's right-hand man should "relieve doubts of the faithful regarding the alleged apparitions and any public dissemination of their message." That wasn't likely, though, and Cardinal Keeler probably knew it.

The cardinal had first moved to end the public devotions surrounding Gianna's claimed apparitions during the late summer of 2000. On September 8, the Feast of the Birth of Our Lady, the archdiocese of Baltimore issued a three-sentence statement announcing that, after careful consideration, it found "no basis" for the alleged apparitions and messages attributed to the Virgin Mary by Gianna. The archdiocese published a "bulletin" six days later in which it expanded on its judgment that Gianna's visions contained "negative elements," and ordered that the Thursday-night prayer-group meetings at St. Joseph's Church be "discontinued" immediately. The archdiocese also asked that sales of a video featuring Gianna, *Unbridled Mercy*, cease at once.

Certain representations made by Gianna about what the Virgin Mary had told her were cited repeatedly by the archdiocese in subsequent news reports about the commission's verdict and the cardinal's position. Specifically, it was explained that Cardinal Keeler and the theolgians who advised him took umbrage at Gianna's claim that Jesus would return as a child, and that the catastrophes which would precede this Second Coming would include the death of every fish in the ocean. That prediction especially delighted Internet satirists, who mocked Gianna as a failed actress who had attempted to revive her career in show business by targeting a religious audience.

While I bristled at such cheap shots, I understood how the Baltimore archdiocese might conclude that Gianna and Michael were forcing their hand. The *Unbridled Mercy* video wasn't intended as a provocation, I felt sure, but Cardinal Keeler and his crew had not been entirely unreasonable to see it that way. Michael must have known, even if Gianna didn't, that predictions of trials and tribulations—including not only a global fish kill but also a "fire of purification" that would cover the earth—were the sort of stuff that offended the Church as an institution. And it could not have come as a surprise that the Baltimore archdiocese was disturbed by a "message" reported by Gianna in July 2000 (just as an Israeli-Palestinian summit was convening in nearby Camp David) that a miraculous sign would appear in Emmitsburg during the following October. "Wait and see," the message had ended. Cardinal Keeler had decided not to, and in explaining why echoed much of what I had heard at the Vatican. "Given the present circumstances throughout the world of what may be called a growing addiction to the spectacular, we think that the Church should not promote or encourage persons claiming to have extraordinary channels to God," Keeler would write to the pastor at St. Joseph's. The cardinal did acknowledge in this letter that the Thursday prayer service at the church had produced some "impressive results," including conversions, confessions, and several seemingly authentic physical healings, but agreed with his commission that there was "no necessary connection" between Gianna's claimed apparitions and the apparent benefits.

Michael, who was handling all public matters for Gianna these days, responded to the archdiocese's orders at first by telling the cardinal's judicial vicar, "We will be obedient." He and Gianna then issued a statement on their Internet site reading, "This is a gift. Be at peace. Continue to pray. God's hand is in all of this. Watch and see!"

Many of those who watched to see did not hide their disappointment when October came and went without the appearance of the promised sign. Except for Mission of Mercy, which they continued to operate, Gianna and Michael virtually disappeared from public view for almost two years. Several eminent advocates, however, continued to speak out on their behalf. At the forefront was René Laurentin, who in August 2001 sent Cardinal Keeler a five-page document describing his "ten years of study on Gianna Sullivan," complete with a cover letter in which he lauded "her fully dedicated faith, her human worth, and the fruits of her initiatives."

Laurentin devoted considerable space to the assorted medical investigations of Gianna, including one by his colleague Dr. Philippe Loron (the neurologist who had previously tested the Medjugorje seers) indicating that during her apparitions, Gianna was "disconnected from the exterior world by the ecstasy, does not sleep or dream, and is not in an epileptic state." But of course, in considering a reported apparition, "the fruits are the most important," Laurentin wrote, "and in Gianna's case the fruits have always been positive, without anything negative. Around herself she has awakened and supported the faith in a world where the faith is asphyxiated by secularization, laicization, and ambient materialism."

Gianna emerged from her self-imposed silence in August 2002, when she released her first "public message" from Mary in twenty-three months. This had been done "at Our Lady's initiation," Michael would tell me when I phoned the house overlooking the cow pasture. I had to admit I was disappointed when I read the message in question, given that it was nothing new. "Little children, darkness can be overcome only through the Light of Love," it began. "There is no other way to silence evil and defeat it except through the Light of Love."

"We have to be told the same things again and again, because we don't listen," Michael told me.

At almost the same moment Gianna explained to the local newspaper in Emmitsburg that she would continue to publish Our Lady's messages, if asked to do so, Cardinal Keeler announced that the theological commission he had formed to investigate Gianna was finally ready to render a decision.

Gianna's supporters had been encouraged in June 2001, when the three members of Keeler's commission were identified as a respected canon lawyer, a priest-psychiatrist, and a theologian who had been a member of the committee that voted, finally, to beatify Padre Pio. On September 28, 2002, however, Gianna was informed in a letter from the archdiocese that the commission members had agreed unanimously on a verdict of *constat de non supernaturalitate*, or "consistently not supernatural." Three noted Marian theologians, among them Robert Faricy, the Marquette University professor who had investigated Gianna in Scottsdale, and Father Edward O'Connor of Notre Dame University, had flown to Baltimore to testify on Gianna's behalf, but were told that no theological issues existed in this case, only pastoral ones, so there was no need to hear from them. Yet when the commission's report was published, the three were astounded to discover that the principal bases for condemning Gianna's visions were, in fact, theological. Specifically, the commission's report explained, the three members were disturbed by Gianna's "apocalyptic prophecies." "It is our impression that the Commission has made some very serious errors," O'Conner wrote in a letter dated October 7, 2002, to Cardinal Keeler.

Michael was even more outspoken. "It was a joke," he told me when I called him after returning home from Rome. "The commission spent a total of three hours with Gianna, and I was present for most of that time. I was shocked by how superficial the questions were. It was obvious they had already made up their minds." Especially frustrating to him, Michael said, was that since September 2000 the cardinal had smothered any expression of support for Gianna within the archdiocese: "Keeler has controlled all the information. Hundreds of letters supporting us have been sent to the diocesan newspaper, and not one has been published. Letters attacking us, though, do get published."

A few days later he sent me a copy of the letter he had written to Cardinal Keeler on Mother's Day (other copies, I noted, had gone to Cardinal Ratzinger, President George W. Bush, and U.S. foreign relations adviser Condoleezza Rice). Reading the letter, I had the distinct impression that Michael was daring the cardinal to take action against him. "Releasing what has been released to the media without providing Gianna any decree or declaration signed by you personally, Cardinal Keeler, is morally wrong," Michael had written. "Using Latin words like *constat de non supernaturalitate* in the media without any formal declaration signed by you and delivered to Gianna at her residence is morally wrong. Paraphrasing comments by Cardinal Ratzinger in the newspaper without allowing Gianna or her spiritual directors or advisors to know on what information Cardinal Ratzinger based any comments is morally wrong. To totally disregard the detailed scientific studies done on Gianna during her ecstasy by Fr. René Laurentin and his team of American and French scientists is morally wrong. Where has honesty and Christian charity gone?"

Michael had ended his letter by declaring, "We are now living in a time in salvation history when God Himself will soon reveal the Truth and ratify His prophets."

Gianna's husband had left himself no room for doubt. Once I had admired this approach. Now, though, I wanted only to find the wise man who would show me how to avoid it.

*   *   *

Obtaining a phone number for Benedict Groeschel proved considerably easier than making actual contact with this legendary priest. Father Groeschel took calls during only two hours out of every week, I was informed when I dialed the number, but after waiting three days for this window of opportunity to open, I discovered that I was playing a sort of lottery, hoping to be one of the lucky few who rang in at the right moment. On my fourth failed attempt to reach Groeschel, I was able to win the sympathy of a woman who had answered an earlier call. Unfortunately, I found it almost impossible to communicate with her. The woman didn't just ramble, she repeated herself so many times I lost count. I found myself doing the same after a while, as we stopped and started a conversation that the woman interrupted with one non sequitur after another. She was extremely sweet and obviously wanted to help, but I doubted she understood a word I was saying. Her capacity for digression was breathtaking. At some moments she seemed to imagine that I sought to serve the poor, and at others that I wanted Father Groeschel's help in investigating a haunted house. Several times, her voice trailed off in mid-sentence and the line went quiet until I started again from the beginning, hoping that I might register my request if I repeated it often enough. Finally, I gave up trying, and at least a minute passed without either of us speaking a word. Then, out of nowhere it seemed, the woman repeated nearly every word I had said to her, and suggested that I send Father Groeschel a fax explaining my project and let him know exactly when I intended to follow up with another call. If I interested him, Father would come to the phone, she assured me.

I already knew that Groeschel was esteemed for his work in any number of fields, and that the priest's time and attention were coveted by legions of petitioners. What no one had told me was that one of Groeschel's callings involved ministering to the mentally ill, several of whom served as his assistants. The priest's patron saint was Benedict Joseph Labre, the only presumed schizophrenic to have been canonized by the Roman Catholic Church, an unwashed beggar who was driven from town to town during his life, yet whose death resulted in a funeral attended by thousands of people who made hundreds of miraculous claims on his behalf. Father Groeschel, considered to possess one of the keenest and most versatile intellects in all of Catholicism, was not himself mentally ill. He did question *my* sanity when I made yet another call to his number two days later. "I don't know how you got into this, kiddo," said the priest by way of introduction when he came on the line, "but you couldn't have chosen a subject more certain to make a person crazy. You must love to suffer." I had no idea what I was getting into back at the beginning of this, I explained. "That, you didn't have to tell me," he said. "You wrote a good letter, though. So come and see me." If I was at his door at five o'clock in the afternoon a week from today, the priest said, he would find a couple of hours for me.

Groeschel also insisted "ipso facto" that I had to find Poulain's book and read at least some of it before we met. This required searching out the all but invisible Sisters of St. Paul bookstore on East Fifty-second Street in Manhattan to buy an excerpt from *Graces of Interior Prayer* that had been published under the title *Revelations and Visions*. I caught the New Haven Line at Grand Central and studied the book all the way to the Larchmont station. Poulain had written his masterwork during the first year of the twentieth century while working as a spiritual director in Paris, a position in which he reported thirty-three instances of authentic "supernatural graces" and only nine cases of "false visions." While this ratio of true to false seemed high by the Vatican's contemporary standards, Poulain was considered to have understood better than any other commentator the writings of St. John of the Cross and Teresa of Avila, and his book remained a standard work throughout the Church.

I was startled to discover that among Poulain's categories of authentic visions were not only Exterior Visions ("perceived by the bodily eyes") but also Imaginative Visions ("seen without the assistance of the eyes") and Intellectual Visions ("perceived by the mind alone without any interior image"). And while Exterior Visions were considered to be the most remarkable of these graces, the most profound Catholic mystics had reported visions primarily of the latter two categories. St. Teresa's visions, for example, had begun as intellectual, then become imaginative, but were never of the exterior variety, Poulain reported, even if she had imagined otherwise. And while Exterior Visions were purely divine gifts granted without any preconditions, Imaginative and Intellectual Visions seemed to be both given and taken, a product to some degree of the receiver's holiness. Exterior Visions (which might be of either divine or diabolical origin) themselves came in four distinct varieties, according to Poulain. Those of the first manner involved perception of the true heavenly bodies of Jesus or Mary, while those of the second manner involved seeing the "borrowed body" of a heavenly being "formed by the ministry of angels." In cases of the third manner (called "semi-objective" by Poulain), the visionary did not perceive a true body, but rather saw the "luminous rays" of a body in Heaven with the assistance of angels who "produce these undulations as they would produce sound waves." In the fourth manner, which was "purely subjective, angels imprint the image of the object directly upon the retina."

Poulain was a bit easier for the modern mind to digest when he explained the multiple ways in which visionaries err in understanding and reporting their visions, all of which involved the imperfect natures of human beings whose ignorance, vanity, or simple inability to distinguish their own thoughts from the message of a divine authority could garble, obfuscate, or even falsify its content. St. Teresa, Joan of Arc, Simon Stock—even St. Peter himself—had been subject to such failings, Poulain pointed out, and were evidence that nothing even the greatest mystic said should be accepted without critical analysis. The separation of the divine from the merely human was what made the adminstration of mystics and their revelations such a thorny problem for the Church.

To shun claims of the miraculous, however, was to deny God, Benedict Groeschel and I would agree as we sat nearly knee to knee in his crowded study a short time later. Miracles were the essence of every major religion, not just Christianity. Jesus raising Lazarus to demonstrate His power over death was in this sense of a piece with Buddha rising from the ground, dividing His body into pieces, then rejoining them in midair to demonstrate His liberation from the laws of karma. Without the "supernatural graces" that Poulain dared to catalog, there would be no religions, only philosophies.

Father Groeschel had posed what he called "our mutual dilemma" minutes after we were introduced: "If you do no more than dismiss these things, you're simply an obscurantist. If you mindlessly embrace them, you're just a dope. We have to resist the obsessive-compulsive demand for a clear, definitive answer to these questions. This is a field for people who don't have to have it all figured out, who don't need it cast in black and white. There's a lotta gray mist around this stuff, and you have to be prepared to deal with that. Once in a while a bright, shining light comes through, and we should be grateful for it. Because the rest of the time we have to feel our way through the twilight."

I didn't try to hide the fact that I found this unnerving, and Groeschel seemed to appreciate my discomfort. "Tread lightly," he suggested with a smile.

Groeschel certainly looked the part of a Catholic sage. What little hair he had on top curled around his ears like the overflow of a full beard that was trimmed close on the sides but fell to the middle of his chest in the center. The priest was past seventy, and his whiskers were a considerably whiter shade of pale than the rough gray robe that hung loosely on his small, slender frame. His eyes were gray also, and so intense that they might have been called piercing, except that there was more kindness in them than this word suggests. The man sounded more worldly than he looked. Groeschel's speaking style was staccato, pointed, almost acerbic, with a thick accent that had been formed by his upbringing in Jersey City. He came across at first as a cutting-edge curmudgeon who had long since lost his patience with small talk and other superficial niceties. At the same time, there was a palpably tender quality to the man. When I told Father Groeschel how differently he had been described by the priests I met in Rome—by Augustine DiNoia as a saint in the making, and by Gabriel O'Donnell as Groucho Marx in a monk's habit—the elderly priest laughed ruefully and said, "Well, Gabe probably knows me better than Gus does."

We were meeting at Groeschel's principal residence, an estate on Long Island Sound that had been donated to the Church and was now called Trinity Retreat. The priest also spent a good deal of time in the South Bronx, where he ran a number of programs for the poor, among them a residence hall for homeless mothers and their children. The scope of his ministerial activities overwhelmed me, given that he also served as director of spiritual development for the archdiocese of New York, had managed to produce a shelf of slim books on weighty subjects, preached at churches all over the metropolitan area, worked as a clinical psychologist (he had earned his doctorate at Columbia), and was continually called upon to investigate supernatural—or at least strange—phenomena in locations all over the country. He had been ready to die for more than two decades, Groeschel told me at one point, but was burdened with so many obligations that, "unfortunately," he would have to live another ten years.

I had begun the conversation with my "door-opening" analogy, asking Groeschel if he believed the portal could open from either side. "It all depends on what you're talking about," he replied. "If you're talking about a supernatural event whose origin is an intrusion of the divine will into the world in which we live—the action of God—then you're talking about something that has to begin on the other side. On the other hand, if you're talking about what Poulain calls an 'intellectual vision,' then the question is open. An intellectual vision is when the ideas and thoughts of the grace-filled person become so powerful that they seem to be a visible or auditory reality." He placed one of the most famous private revelations in Catholic history, St. Teresa of Avila's "Transverberation," into this category. "She says this angel pierced her heart with a flaming sword, and it's by no means clear whether in her own mind she thought that was an apparition. But John of the Cross, who was there, said, 'These people are so drawn to divine love that it *seems to them* an angel has pierced their heart.' We're talking about a conceptualization of grace so powerful it seems it is there. But what you're receiving is a contact through the ordinary processes of grace, which also has a supernatural origin, but of a different order. So did the door open from this side or that one, or did both sides work together?"

His studies and investigations had led him to any number of persons involved in the Charismatic Renewal "who feel they are speaking words, or sounds, that God has put in their mouths," Groeschel said. "Some even feel that the Lord is telling them to get out and give a teaching. I don't believe anybody who's got any perspective thinks that what they're experiencing is a direct intrusion of divine power into the world, and yet what they're saying is ninety-nine percent truthful. Because to them it *seems* like an ego-alien experience—an experience coming from someone else. But in fact it's assumed to be, and assumed to be by me, as part of the ordinary processes of grace, which are so powerful that they take on an ego-alien aspect or feeling. But they are not. What's essential in dealing with these people is not to dismiss the profound experience of God they've had, but at the same time not to validate their delusions about where it came from."

For Groeschel, and for the Catholic Church, "the benchmark of private revelations" were the apparitions of Bernadette Soubirous at Lourdes. This wasn't a value judgment about *what* Bernadette had experienced, Groeschel emphasized, but about *how* she had experienced it. "Bernadette is the best because she makes the least possible subjective interpretation," he explained. "Even when told that the words 'Immaculate Conception' referred to the Virgin Mary, Bernadette continued to say simply, 'I saw a lady, a young woman.' And they said, 'Yes, but she told you she was the Immaculate Conception, which means she was the Virgin.' And Bernadette said, 'No, I saw a young lady who told me she was the Immaculate Conception.' Neither the priests who believed nor the priests who disbelieved could influence her. And Bernadette never added a syllable to what she was told during her apparitions. She was a witness par excellence. Bernadette was a smart kid, shrewd and fresh as a daisy. The monsignor says to her, 'Do you expect me to believe you saw the Virgin?' And Bernadette says, 'No, I don't expect that at all. It's not my job to get you to believe. It's my job to tell you what She said.'"

The visions of the Sacred Heart reported by St. Margaret Mary Alacoque may have been no less extraordinary than Bernadette's apparitions, Groeschel observed, yet had to be regarded with a level of caution that was not required in dealing with the phenomena at Lourdes: "Margaret Mary was a deeply spiritual person who fell into a profound ecstasy of a supernatural dimension, no doubt about it in my mind. At the end of the great feasts she would kneel down as the other sisters were retiring and she wouldn't move a muscle. She wouldn't cough, she wouldn't shift her weight, nothing, until six o'clock the next morning. On three occasions she had to be roused and assisted back to her room at the time of morning prayers. And these were the three occasions of the visions of the Sacred Heart. Now, I believe entirely that these were supernatural phenomena. But in her descriptions of them, you are, I believe, getting the subjective ideas of a devout Frenchwoman who had read some theological treatises about the Sacred Heart and then injected some of her own thoughts. Understand, I feel certain that she received genuine revelations, but the account of the revelations has the subjective in it, and so has to be handled with kid gloves. See, here's the basic problem: On the one hand, you have an infinite reality that is impenetrable and incomprehensible to us, touching a finite reality here on earth. The person is going to feel like they are talking to *someone*. And they were being contacted by another world, but in order to grasp it, they have an image—probably put into their mind by divine providence—so they can relate to the source of this experience. We can never know exactly what took place, because even the person it happened to doesn't know. All they know is how it *felt* and what they believe about that. We have to decide what we believe all on our own."

I had been told in Rome that Groeschel's intellectual daring, his willingness to poke fun at (and holes in the mythology of) Catholicism's most venerated figures, combined with his ability to communicate a heartfelt regard for their experiences and accomplishments, was what had made him such a respected figure in the Church, not to mention the most influential thinker in all of Christendom on how to deal with reports of supernatural experiences. What delighted me, though, was his disdain for the flocculence in which most Catholic commentators felt compelled to cushion their appraisals of the saints.

"We are never going to have anything more than the vaguest clue as to why this or that person is chosen to receive such graces," he told me. "About all we can hold on to is what St. Paul told us about it: 'The poor things of this world hath God chosen, things that are nothing.' Look at St. Catherine Laboure. Poor Cate, she was absolutely a klutz. She was a super-klutz. But St. Catherine Laboure predicted any number of things that happened exactly as she said they would. She also predicted a couple of things that didn't happen. When they asked her about that, she said, 'I got it wrong.'" Groeschel cracked up as he repeated the saint's words. "Good for you, Cate," he chortled. "Let them deal with the truth.

"And Joan of Arc, there's a girl," he went on. "She said she spoke to the saints, when what she really saw were statues. But they spoke to her. Was she crazy? I don't know. I do know that she stopped the longest war in European history. Winston Churchill, no less, said of Joan, 'There is no purer figure in all of European history for a thousand years.' Freud, on the other hand, called her a schizophrenic. Who's right? You decide. Was she both mad and blessed? It's entirely possible, my friend. Entirely possible."

"Devotionalists" liked to imagine that receiving an extraordinary grace resulted in an exemplary life, Groeschel continued, but this was often not the case. "Look at La Salette," he said. "Those two kids never amounted to anything. The girl ended up being a flake and the boy was a kind of crook. Yet it's widely accepted within the Church that they received authentic visions of the Virgin. I accept it."

He did not see it as his job to encourage the sort of pious embroidery that framed even the major apparitions, but to strive for a perspective in which reverence and critical thinking could coexist. Even Lourdes was not exempt from his scrutiny. "What happened there was miraculous and extraordinary, but it may very well have been what Poulain calls an 'imaginative vision,'" he said. "That isn't in any sense a pejorative description, by the way. It doesn't diminish what took place, but it does put it in a category called 'nonperception.' The eyes can't see it, but the brain does. The reason you can say this about Lourdes is that when Bernadette saw the Blessed Mother, there were ten thousand other people present, and none of them saw anything. St. Thomas Aquinas says that the best explanation of this is that she had an 'inner experience,' because otherwise you gotta have ten thousand miracles. What Bernadette experienced was an apparition, but it was not a theophany."

Theophany? I asked. I'd never heard the term. A theophany was a supernatural event of the highest order, Groeschel explained, "literally a divine manifestation." The greatest theophany in modern times, he told me, had occurred at Fátima in 1917, with the appearance of a whirling sun. "Which was not the sun," he pointed out. "The Greenwich Observatory is not very far away, and they didn't pick up anything, but over an area of about forty square miles, everybody who was there—everybody—believers and nonbelievers, attentive people and inattentive people, saw this thing that looked like a whirling, multicolored sun descending toward them. Many people present actually fell to the ground. There were cases like that of a Freemason, a socialist who had gone there to laugh, and afterward he had to be hospitalized for three days. He was taken away from the scene in shock. That's what a theophany does, because it registers in the external world."

There had been another theophany during the nineteenth century at Knock, Ireland, Groeschel said. "Nineteen people, not related, directly saw these visions, and—perhaps more tellingly—people in the distance saw the lights, and thought it was some kind of fireworks." There no doubt had been others, at Zeitun in Egypt, perhaps, and possibly at that peasant village in the Ukraine. But even with a theophany, he noted, the result was determined largely by how those who had received the revelation dealt with it. Externally, the phenomena at Fátima were more impressive than the phenomena at Lourdes, but Bernadette had been a better, a more reliable, a more exemplary vessel than the Fátima seers, in his opinion, and therefore had yielded more impressive fruits. I was mulling this over when Groeschel startled me by announcing that he was skeptical—"to say the least"—about the Fátima Secrets. "I believe what happened at Fátima was the most astounding theophany in modern times, but I don't believe they were given any Secrets," he said. "If you look at the documents closely, it's obvious the Secrets came later. I think the nun came up with them. But who knows. I certainly wouldn't want to make an official, binding pronouncement on Fátima, or on the Secrets. I've stated my opinion, and the pope has decided I'm wrong. He can do that, you know. It's a perk of the job."

Groeschel surprised me again by stating that the Church had long ago recognized novelty as a feature that marked an apparition or locution as authentic. Never once in any of my interviews at the Vatican had this been mentioned. "For their own, essentially political reasons, the priests in Rome don't want to spread the word on this, but one of the signs of a divine revelation is that it departs from the accepted notions of the moment," he explained. "It goes a bit against the time. Otherwise it's assumed to be derived." He wasn't talking about exotic descriptions or fanciful forms, Groeschel cautioned, but about the actual content of a reported communication from a heavenly being. Originality was among the qualities that had most distinguished *The Chaplet of Divine Mercy*, produced by the Polish nun Faustina Kowalska during the years between the First and Second World Wars. "Polish Catholicism of the early twentieth century was not known for its emphasis on divine mercy. It was pretty heavy-handed, almost fascistic. And yet it was in this atmosphere that this simple peasant child, with three years of formal education, delivered this incredibly deep book, which she obviously does not understand on an intellectual level." Groeschel read aloud the long passage titled "Conversation of the Merciful God with the Despairing Soul" in which Jesus calls again and again to a soul that "remains deaf and blind, hardened and despairing." In a grant of "final grace," the mercy of God "exerts itself without any cooperation from the soul," and only if even this is refused does the soul pass into an eternal separation from God, the passage explains. "Today, just about anyone who reads this knows they are hearing something both totally original and profoundly true, but it was startling to the Polish Catholics of that period," Groeschel said. "Faustina was accused of heresy at the time, and the book was banned. Only later, when it was read more carefully, did the Church recognize that the book contains not a single theological error. Faustina walks right up to heresy, but she doesn't fall in, and the subtlety with which she navigates these distinctions is astonishing, especially when it comes from a woman with three years of education. And today Faustina's description of Prevenient Grace, by which the divine mercy gets to exert itself without any cooperation from the soul, has become dogma.

"Faustina is about the best example you could find of how powerful what Poulain calls an 'intellectual vision' can be. This is a vision that comes up from within oneself in response to grace. It's ecstasy. And what is ecstasy? I like Aldous Huxley's description: 'Ecstasy is the tribute the mind pays to that which is beyond it.' That may be an incomplete definition, but it's cute."

Unfortunately, new and original ideas were rarely a feature of the purported supernatural phenomena that were brought to his attention, Groeschel sighed. "I get dozens and dozens of letters about supposed divine revelations, and it's the same old stuff, over and over," said the priest in a voice that was hilariously soporific. "But these are people who read this kind of literature, and they conjure up these kind[s] of intellectual experiences. You can't dismiss them, even when they put you to sleep, but you don't have to read their letters twice either."

We had been talking for more than an hour by then, and Groeschel seemed to be avoiding the subject he knew I most wanted to discuss. "I'm deeply perplexed by Medjugorje," he said with a heavy sigh. "It might be the most puzzling of all these phenomena. Clearly a profound event occurred there, but I couldn't tell you what it was."

He had visited Medjugorje just once, in 1986, and while there spoke to only one of the visionaries. "Even that was an accident. A bunch of us were on the Hill of Apparitions, and we got caught in a sudden rainstorm, so we retreated back downhill and sought refuge in the first building we came to, which just happened to be Marija Pavlović's house. I didn't ask her a lot of questions, didn't do the sort of formal interview I might have, because she didn't know why I was there, and so I thought it was unfair. Actually, I had decided before I went not to seek out any of the seers. But I did ask Marija, through an interpreter, 'How long has the Blessed Mother been appearing to you?' And she said, 'About five years.' I said, 'How do you feel when She comes?' And she said, 'Happy, very, very happy.' I said, 'Does that mean you've been happy for the whole past five years?' And she said, 'Don't be silly.' That, I thought, was a great answer."

My conversation with Vicka back in the summer of 1995 immediately came to mind, but I didn't share it with Groeschel, especially after he began to describe his experience of the group apparitions he had witnessed during his stay in Medjugorje. "Without introducing myself, I sat in on several," he explained. "And yes, I was impressed by the synchronicity. You had the feeling you were looking through a closed window and that you couldn't see who they were talking to, but that there was someone there. It was almost a physical sensation. But at the same time I was troubled that they were reacting in totally different ways. It was as if each was having his or her own individual experience. Their gestures and facial expressions were very different from one another. Vicka sort of upstaged the others, I thought."

How did he explain that, again and again, the seers reported hearing the same words from their vision of the Madonna, even when they were separated from one another immediately after an apparition? I asked. "As I said, I find Medjugorje extremely puzzling," he answered. "There are a lot of inexplicable elements, but that can mean either that the phenomena is supernatural, or that people haven't been able to explain it. I know I can't. I only know that there are a lot of things that bother me." For the first moment since I'd met him, Groeschel seemed uncomfortable with a subject, and more than a little hesitant about explaining why. After several ambiguous replies to my questions, he finally blew out a deep breath and said, "It would seem to me that there very well may have been an original supernatural phenomenon, perhaps a very powerful one. It may have been an apparition, but I don't think it was a theophany. Then again, it may have been. There are people I respect who believe so. Whatever it was at the beginning, though, I'm inclined to believe it changed into something else."

I was reluctant to ask why he believed that. I found Groeschel in some way a threatening presence. Not forbidding or even intimidating, but daunting, nevertheless. I already liked, admired, and trusted him more than any priest I'd met since Slavko, yet from the moment we'd first looked into each other's eyes, I'd been filled with apprehension. My fear was of that "gray mist" Groeschel had described. I felt that if I became disoriented one more time, I might actually be lost. Still, there was no choice but to let him explain his "perplexity."

He frankly blamed the Franciscans for a lot of what troubled him about Medjugorje, Groeschel said, and then distressed me to no end by focusing most of his criticism on Slavko. "I don't think the priests there could have made more mistakes if they tried," he said. "They fell into every hole there is. The Franciscans could have read a book on this, but they're Croatians, and God forbid that they could learn anything. But they should have read Poulain." Like him, Poulain would have been scandalized by "the monthly and weekly bulletins after the apparitions, the interpretations, which were done by Father Slavko," Groeschel said. "This is completely useless material. Worse than useless. I mean," he explained through a thick Jersey City catarrh, "you gotta get the real stuff." And he found it incredible that "these simple Croatian peasants were capable of articulating such complicated ideas about ecumenism, which is a pet cause among the Franciscans." The disobedience of the bishop troubled Groeschel also, although he was no defender of Žanić: "All he ever proved is that he was not the man to pass judgment on Medjugorje. Calm objectivity clearly was not his approach. But I find it very, very difficult to believe the Blessed Mother would criticize him. This simply isn't the sort of thing that happens." The duration of the purported apparitions was unprecedented also, as was the change in the nature of the apparitions over time. Furthermore, he considered "this whole story about the secrets" to be "pure hooey." And yet, and yet . . . Based on his own observations, he felt certain the six seers weren't frauds, Groeschel allowed. And the results of the scientific and medical testing "made a very convincing case that these kids were not mentally ill."

I told the priest that I had never been able to convince myself that there were more than the three choices I had given myself at the beginning about what was taking place in Medjugorje: Either they were faking it, or they were crazy, or they were telling the truth. "Well, I would say those are the three *categories* of choice, along with the possibility of a diabolical plot," Groeschel responded, "but what you seem not to recognize is that these elements can be mixed. Religious visionaries can be a little dishonest or a little crazy, or both, at the same time they are experiencing and reporting genuine apparitions. It can happen. It *has* happened."

He hesitated, then opened a subject he seemed to find even more difficult than Medjugorje. When he had described the events in Bosnia as the most puzzling phenomena of this kind that he knew about, he probably should have said "Catholic phenomena," Groeschel confessed. Because he was certainly no less perplexed by what he had witnessed more than thirty years earlier, when he had been present at the inception of a book now considered to be the "New Age Bible." He had been a graduate student in psychology at Columbia University during the late 1960s when one of his professors, a woman named Helen Schucman, had written—"which is not to say authored"—*A Course in Miracles.*

Helen Schucman was nearly sixty when they met, and Groeschel, who was then almost forty, knew her not only as a teacher but also as a friend. "Helen was a very scientific lady," he recalled, "a Jewish intellectual who considered herself to be an extreme agnostic, though not quite an atheist, and very skeptical about everything having to do with religion or spirituality." Schucman was also witty and engaging, and Groeschel, who was writing his dissertation on the relationship between science and theology, found her to be one of the most stimulating conversationalists he had ever encountered. The older woman became a good deal more fascinating to him when she announced in 1969 that she was taking dictation from a disembodied voice she knew only as the "Son of God."

It had all started one day when she was riding the subway uptown and experienced a vision, Schucman explained: A beautiful light suddenly filled the car and shone on the faces of the people all around her. A short time later she felt compelled to begin writing page after page of blank verse that eventually grew into *A Course in Miracles.* Groeschel still could vividly recall his "dizzy astonishment" as the professor explained that she knew the meaning of each sentence she was writing, but had no idea what was coming next. "The interesting thing is that it scanned," the priest remembered. "It was written in iambic pentameter, and some of the passages were quite beautiful." The result was a series of discourses by the "Son of God" in which the narrator/teacher/protagonist came across as the figure Jesus Christ might have been if born a Hindu rather than a Jew. Sin, sacrifice, and suffering all were dismissed as illusory, the maya (though this word was never used) of those chained to earthly existence. Only forgiveness is real, and all things, even the most heinous acts, are forgiven, the "Son of God" says again and again, without any need for penance or punishment.

He eventually came to understand the book as the product of "an intellectual experience called 'sequential words,'" Groeschel said. "It's actually very common and probably the least impressive of all these things. St. John of the Cross nailed it. He said, 'They're calling the words of God the thoughts that they address to themselves.' Now, there's an ice-cold glass of hot water."

What Groeschel found to be at once most thrilling and confusing about Helen Schucman's process was that, during the time she wrote *A Course in Miracles* (a book that any number of fundamentalist Christian ministers have called the most dangerous ever published), she became intensely attracted to the Catholic Church, attended Mass regularly, and was devoted to the Virgin Mary. Only under close questioning did Schucman admit that, many years earlier, she had briefly been a Christian. This had resulted from an "accidental" childhood visit to Lourdes, where she had been so moved that she received baptism upon her return to the U.S. She also had prayed the Rosary for years afterwards, Schucman claimed, until she adopted scientific skepticism as her creed, and lived by it for most of her adult life.

When he suggested she apply for membership in the Catholic Church, Schucman replied that this was unnecessary because, as a Jew, she had been Catholic before "you Gentiles came along and made all these rules." No less fascinating to the priest was the sharp distinction between Schucman's own stated convictions and the content of *A Course in Miracles*. "I hate that damn book," she often told him, and regularly disavowed its teachings.

Groeschel continued to try to "open the doors of the Church" to Schucman, but his influence was subverted by her husband. William

Thetford, also a Columbia professor, was a mysterious character, and "probably the most sinister person I ever met," the priest recalled. Only after he retired from teaching did Thetford's Columbia colleagues (who knew him best as a rare-books expert) discover that all during the years they worked with him, the man had been employed as an agent of the CIA—one who was, among other things, present at the first fission experiment conducted by physicists assigned to the Manhattan Project. Thetford also was "the most religious atheist I have ever known," Groeschel recalled, and conceived a great enthusiasm for *A Course in Miracles*, personally arranging for its publication. Schucman was embarrassed, Groeschel remembered, and confided to the priest her fear that the book would create a cult, which of course it did.

Groeschel initially read the *Course* as "religious poetry," but grew steadily more negative in his assessment of it as the years passed and sales of the three volumes passed into the millions of copies. From his point of view, *A Course in Miracles* served to undermine authentic Christianity more effectively than just about any other work he could recall, and while he was inclined to reject the position of St. John of the Cross that "these things are diabolical unless proven otherwise," doubts had crept in over the years. Most troubling to him by far was the "black hole of rage and depression that Schucman fell into during the last two years of her life," the priest explained. She had become frightening to be with, Groeschel recalled, spewing psychotic hatred not only for *A Course in Miracles* but "for all things spiritual." When he sat at Schucman's bedside as she lay dying, "she cursed, in the coarsest barroom language you could imagine, 'that book, that goddamn book.' She said it was the worst thing that ever happened to her. I mean, she raised the hair on the back of my neck. It was truly terrible to witness."

Only during Schucman's last weeks of life did Groeschel learn that the woman's mother had been a Christian Scientist, one who read to the girl from the writings of Mary Baker Eddy all during her childhood. This information had contributed to the appraisal of the woman he found easiest to live with, the priest said: "I decided that *A Course in Miracles* was a fascinating blend of poorly understood Christianity inspired by her visit to Lourdes and poorly understood Christian Science inspired by her memory of Mary Baker Eddy's writings, all of it filtered through some profound psychological problems and processes." Yet doubts persisted. The morning Schucman died, Groeschel said a funeral Mass for her. "Only when I opened the missal did I discover that it was the Feast of Our Lady of Lourdes," the priest recalled, "and I tell you, I shivered. The odds are one out of three hundred and sixty-five."

He had been sifting his experiences with Helen Schucman through his mind for more than three decades now, Groeschel said, and over the years had realized that any attempt to define them was futile. "What I learned, I think, is that these things can be both real and imaginary, paranormal and spiritual, divine and diabolical. And that when you enter the world of the supernatural, the worst mistake you can make is to impose a ultrarealist point of view. You can't make those kinds of distinctions about experiences that are beyond our comprehension. You have to do as Moses Maimonides instructed and teach your students to say, 'I don't know.'"

He was inclined to apply the same wisdom to his consideration of Medjugorje, and felt it was his duty to warn me that the truth might be more complicated than I would prefer. "Some of these things that the seers manifested, like the ability to run up that hillside at an impossible speed, for example, are as likely to have a paranormal explanation as a supernatural one," said the priest. And while he agreed that stories like the one Dr. Margnelli told about the silence of the birds during the apparitions were "very affecting, and clear evidence of the profundity of what has taken place there," they were not, Groeschel told me, "proof that it is miraculous."

Father Groeschel had investigated inexplicable phenomena about as thoroughly as any priest in the Catholic Church, and continued to believe that the paranormal and the supernatural were separate realities, but that it would be difficult to distinguish between them now and for a very long time into the future. When I asked what exactly he meant by paranormal, he went silent for a moment, then answered, "The paranormal are physical and psychological phenomena that are not comprehensible by our present understanding. Now, I firmly believe that some things we can't understand are of supernatural origin, but a good deal is not. One of the things I've learned is that because a phenomena is inexplicable does not make it miraculous. You can't make that jump. I've dealt with poltergeists, and I know they're real. I agree they're inexplicable. But I don't believe they're supernatural." As it happened, Westchester County was the poltergeist capital of the country, Groeschel said, and he had been called in to consult in quite a few local cases. One involved a house nearby, where the walls were full of dents, "but they don't go in, they go out," the priest explained. "I had a tube of Prell thrown at me in one house. It went right over my shoulder. That could be diabolical, I suppose, but I don't think so." He then told me a long story about a thirteen-year-old boy who recently had been traumatized when his father abandoned the family to run off with a younger woman. Since that event, the boy's home had been filled with strange phenomena—lights turning on and off, faucets doing the same, cassette players exploding and spewing out tapes that unraveled in long streams. "One night, he and his brother and their mother are in bed, and this étagère moves across the floor, then falls forward in a loud crash," Groeschel recalled. "They called and I went over to meet with them. I spoke to the boys, and the one kid says, 'I know it's me.' His mother had already told me it happened only around him, and that it happened even in his sleep. And I think it *was* him, even though he didn't know how and had no intent to do these things. It was just something that was generated by the psychic energy of his distress. Yet no one can say it doesn't have a spiritual component."

For his money, the fullest and most admirable consideration of the paranormal had been that of the noted psychologist Benjamin Wohlmann, Groeschel said, then insisted that I listen while he read, very slowly, a long passage from Wohlmann's *Handbook of Parapsychology:* "There are at the present time two guiding philosophies within parapsychology. According to one, the concept of the paranormal has no permanent validity, but is simply an expression of our ignorance. In the fullness of time, parapsychology will be integrated into a unified consensual framework embracing all the sciences. Such a framework may have to be extended in various unexpected ways, but there is no danger of it being stretched to the breaking point. According to the other school of thought, the significance of the paranormal is precisely that it signals the boundary of the scientific world. Beyond that boundary lies the domain of the mind liberated from its dependency on the brain. In this view, parapsychology, using the methods of science, becomes a vindication of the essentially spiritual nature of man, which must forever defy any strict scientific analysis. Which of these two antithetical philosophies will prevail remains a question for the future. In the meantime, there is no reason whatever why both parties should not cooperate in furthering our knowledge of this, the most perplexing field of inquiry ever to engage the curiosity of our species."

Groeschel let that sink in for a few moments, then remarked that he had been reading a great deal of Einstein lately and found the man's ideas to be of great use in contemplating "the subjects, plural" that we were discussing. "Einstein understood that it's important to have a well-developed sense of the mysterious before considering any truly important matter," the priest explained. "And that you must respect the mystery enough to understand that you are never going to solve it. As he grew older, he understood better and better that science is limited to the measurable. Einstein recognized that science can never affirm or deny the existance of God, and that only stupid people put their ultimate faith in science." When I observed that Einstein had rejected the idea of a personal God, Groeschel waved me off. "He may have said so when he was younger, but as a mature man, he became, I believe, quite a religious person. He was fascinated by the Blessed Sacrament. He surrendered to his sense of mystery more and more as he approached the end of his life." Groeschel couldn't help but contrast Einstein to Alexis Carrel, whose *Voyage to Lourdes* he had been recently rereading: "I believe Carrel actually witnessed two miraculous healings in his life, and yet he remained trapped in this limited mentality that tries to reduce things to the orderly study of the interactions of physical qualities or entities on each other. Unlike Einstein, he didn't grasp the fact that truly great scientists are the ones who understand the limitations of their fields."

Hardly anything about the contemporary Catholic Church depressed him more than the fact that the Vatican was now "full of people who worship science," Groeschel said. "The ones who have the brains to say that the emperor has no clothes don't have the guts to do it. The pope does, but the rest of them toady to the secularists. We've got the greatest case of wimpitude I've ever seen."

He wondered—and worried—about the future of the Church when it was without John Paul. Medjugorje, for example, had been spared a negative judgment only because the head of the Church was determined to protect the devotions in Bosnia. "I can tell you for a fact that the pope loves Medjugorje from afar and would go there in a minute if the theologians would let him," Groeschel said, then observed that it was clear to him I loved Medjugorje also.

Though I hadn't intended to, I found myself telling the priest about what had happened to me on the summit of Križevac back in July 1995. Since that time, I had lost virtually every vestige of the faith I imagined I had found in Medjugorje: I not only hadn't honored my pledge to formally join the Church, but within a few months found myself doubting almost every miracle that was at the core of Catholic dogma. I didn't know if there truly had been a virgin birth or if Jesus had really walked on water or if he had actually cast out demons. And yet my experience of God's mercy on that mountaintop had never left me; nor had my knowledge of Christ's divinity. Those were with me in every moment, and even now I was more sustained by them than by anything else that I had ever felt, thought, imagined, or believed.

There were tears in my eyes by the time I finished, and Groeschel was a little choked up also. His intellectual rigor, however, was intact. "*That* is a religious experience," he told me. "But it doesn't necessarily validate Medjugorje. People have been converted in brothels. Still, I think it's fair to ask, 'Why did it happen there?' And I have to tell you that when I went to Medjugorje, what impressed me was the faith of the people who live there. To me it was more extraordinary than any of the phenomena reported by the visionaries. The prayerfulness of that place is mysterious beyond all analysis."

He sighed. "Look, I'm not anti-Medjugorje. Far from it. I believe God has used Medjugorje. I believe Medjugorje is part of the providential plan. But I also believe it would be a great mistake for you to hang your faith only on Medjugorje, or even on what happened to you in Medjugorje. I also think that you don't have to be afraid to be completely honest with yourself about what you believe has happened there and what you believe *is* happening there."

When I replied with a questioning expression, Groeschel said he wasn't trying to read my mind, but merely to interpret what he had seen and heard during the two hours we'd spent together. "It's obvious to me that you are convinced a major supernatural phenomenon, a breaking of God into this world, took place in this situation," the priest said. "You are not so sure it continued, however, and in fact strongly suspect that it got altered or corrupted or lost or replaced by something else." This was not so far from what he himself believed, Groeschel added, "except that, unlike you, I am willing to say I think that what goes on now, and has gone on for some time, may be a form of hysteria. A deeply devout hysteria, to be sure, almost a positive kind of hysteria, because it's an echo of the original event. Or it could still be real but somehow not pure and so not real in the same way. Not wholly real."

He believed that the apparitions might have begun—probably had begun—as a means of preparing the people there to survive, in a spiritual sense, the war that had commenced ten years later, Groeschel said. "You look back through history, and the number of times these events have taken place, especially the ones accompanied by apocalyptic prophecies, and it's astounding how often they seem to have anticipated terrible and bloody events. Each time people believe they are preparing for the Apocalypse, because we tend to forget that apocalypses, lowercase, occur regularly. I think all this stuff about the ten Secrets is a crock, but I also think it may have been produced by the warning given to those six kids that something terrible was coming and that only faith in God would see people through it.

"Of course,"Groeschel added with a smile, "I'm only talking about my belief here. I don't actually *know* anything. Nobody does."

He wanted to leave me with two pieces of counsel, Groeschel said in conclusion. "One, I believe that you will serve both God and yourself best if you end your book by leaving the question open. Don't try to answer it, because you never will. Two, I hope you come to understand that even if you were capable of making an airtight case about Medjugorje, that wouldn't result in true belief. True belief is a decision. It's also a gift. Accept the gift and you will make the decision."

CHAPTER TWENTY-ONE

The end, it seems, is always back at the beginning. I had embarked on this voyage of discovery with a mind-set that was a bit like a second-rate scientist's, naively assuming that I might arrive eventually at an objective reality. At least I had learned that, for a human being, the truth is and must remain entirely subjective. After my meeting with Father Groeschel, I realized that I had absorbed one other lesson, which was this: Faith is no more the elimination of doubt than courage is the absence of fear.

In my own way, I was reconciled. I could live even with questions about my sanity, because I understood that those came with the territory. Immediately after my session with Groeschel, I dined with the two nuns who were to take the priest's psychological examinaton, Sister Cate and Sister Clare. They asked me what had been my most memorable experience in Medjugorje, and I repeated the story about my first climb up Križevac. The older of the two nuns, Sister Cate, at once asked me if I had ever imagined that I knew who that young girl had been, the one who gave me her hat and covered my shoulders with a towel. I feigned confusion at first—"How could I know that?"—but I knew what she meant. The nun persisted, and finally I said I didn't want to answer that question. I certainly didn't want to tell Sister Cate that about two years after my return from Medjugorje, I'd seen a photograph of Bernadette Soubirous that had literally stopped my heart, because for a moment I'd felt absolutely certain it had been her. I also didn't want to explain that by lying on the floor and taking deep breaths for nearly an hour, I had been able to dispel this notion, and had never looked at that photograph again. As I sat with the nuns, it occurred to me that I hadn't told Father Groeschel about my encounter with that diabolical creature at the Piazza Navona. For that matter, there was one other experience I'd had in Bosnia that I never intended to describe to anyone. In part, this was because I knew I could be incorrect, or even crazy, but Sister Cate understood the deeper reason. "Some things we just don't want to talk about," she said, "because they seem a little less true if we do."

"There's the subjective truth for you," I thought, as I was boarding the plane home from New York, and in that moment realized there was one more place I had to go.

Irma was gone and the peach tree was dead. The little trailer, dilapidated as ever but now painted bright blue, was occupied by a new family of migrant workers, none of whom had heard of Irma Munoz or the apparition of the Virgin Mary that had been front-page news in these parts nine years earlier. Someone had chopped all but two branches off the dead tree, and those pitiful stumps were being used to support a pair of clotheslines where laundry hung drying in the sun.

It was understandable, Marge Rolen said. Few families stayed more than a year, and Irma's had left the Boardman trailer park almost six years earlier. "Irma struggled with what it was all about," explained Marge, who hadn't heard from the younger woman in more than three years. "She kept her faith, though. She prayed with us for a whole year, and helped us with our work for the shrine, believing the whole time that we would make it happen."

They had come close. At one point the plot of land outside the Umatilla Army Depot had been dedicated in a ceremony attended by two bishops and a cardinal. The group of them had ringed a clearing with volcanic rocks, and in the middle planted a statue of Mary atop a juniper tree log where the thirty-foot sculpture of the Blessed Mother one day would stand. Hundreds of people came to worship and pray. But then a man who owned a neighboring farm had purchased the mineral rights to the land and demanded that all traces of the incipient shrine be removed. He was anti-Catholic, Marge believed, but who knew? The man said he was going to dig a gravel pit at the site, but for the time being the thirty acres were being used to grow crops of corn and alfalfa.

They hadn't given up, even when Joe Locke died during cancer surgery in August 1999. That had been a blow, of course. Joe didn't have the money to pay for the shrine himself, and the six wealthy friends he had convinced to serve as the shrine's board of directors all abandoned the project after his death. Charles Parks, the sculptor they had chosen to execute the statue, said he would proceed anyway with the first stage of the project, a sculpture of Mary's heart surrounded by a crown of thorns, if he got a down payment of sixteen thousand dollars. "Only at that time our bank account was empty," Marge recalled. "I said, 'There's no way we can come up with sixteen thousand dollars"; but Kim Hickey said, 'Let's believe.'" So in the autumn of 2000, twenty of them got together to pray to Our Lady of Good Remedies, on October 8, Her feast day. "And in two weeks we had seventeen thousand one hundred dollars," Marge said. Kim and her mother drove all the way back to Delaware to collect the heart sculpture, and brought it back to eastern Oregon in the trunk of their car. For the time being it hung in the vestibule of Our Lady of Angels Church in Hermiston, where the shrine group was permitted to hold a small adoration service on the first Saturday of each month, and take collections. A bank account, fed by Mexican farm workers who were being generous if they laid a dollar bill on the plate, was still several zeros short of the $2 million the shrine would cost, however.

"Irma got very discouraged," Marge said. The visionary was by then living across the Columbia and on the other side of the Horse Heaven Hills in Yakima, Washington, where she had gone to take a job in a farmworker's medical clinic. Tongues wagged, naturally, when Irma became seriously involved with an Anglo named Leon Wagner who had spent most of his adult years in the state prison at Walla Walla. It certainly had seemed as if Irma's determination to redeem Leon had corresponded to her abandonment of the shrine foundation back in Boardman, but then perhaps that been mere coincidence.

"The truth was that Irma just sort of shied away," said Irene Virgen, who had accompanied Marge and me to the trailer court. "She felt unworthy of what had happened to her. Some people tormented Irma, telling her she wasn't good enough. She wasn't holy, they said, so why would something like this happen to her?" Irma had fought so hard for the shrine—even carrying a petition door-to-door to convince the city to donate land—because "she needed to see something real and solid come of all this," in Irene's opinion, "something for everyone, not just her."

"You gotta get over the 'good enough' idea," Marge said as we stood in the dust outside the little blue trailer. "'Cause it ain't gonna happen."

I nodded emphatically. I wasn't sure if I'd changed or she had, but Marge seemed a considerably more compassionate and far less overwrought kind of Catholic than the one I remembered. She sounded sad but not the least bit judgmental as she described how Irma "got tired of nothing coming of it," then explained that Kim had given up finally also, after she decided to leave her husband and move back east to Maryland, where her mother lived. "You need a solid base to stand on when you're dealing with setbacks," she said, "and they didn't quite have that."

Marge and Irene had carried on, organizing one of the most vital Schoenstatt communities in the western United States. Schoenstatt was a movement of Marian devotion that had begun in 1914 when the citizens of a small German village dedicated their chapel to the Virgin. Replica chapels now served as centers of worship centered on the Blessed Mother in cities all over the world. Working together through Schoenstatt, Marge and Irene had generated the first real union of the Anglo and Hispanic communities ever to form out here in the High Desert. "Before, there was virtually no contact between us," said Marge. "But now we've realized we have to work together if we want to get things done." Irene nodded solemnly. "That's a fruit," Marge told me. "A major fruit."

There had been others, small things that added up. The train trip to Milwaukee, for example. During the previous May, they had decided to organize a pilgrimage to the main Schoenstatt shrine in the U.S., the one in Milwaukee, Wisconsin. They weren't sure what it would cost, but got a computer printout from Amtrak guaranteeing them tickets at $170 per person: "A lot for people who live out here, but less than we had imagined," Marge recalled. "Twenty-five people had signed up, but when we went to pay for their tickets, the man at the station looked at our printout and said, 'Where did you get that?' It turned out that the cost of a round-trip ticket to Milwaukee was almost four hundred and fifty dollars. But it was their mistake, so they had to honor our tickets. And then because we agreed to a certain departure date, the price went down to a hundred and twenty-nine dollars. That meant everyone had paid forty-one dollars too much, which came to a total of one thousand and twenty-five dollars. I said I'd figure out refunds later. Well, we got to Milwaukee, and it turned out we were a day early, so everyone needed a night's lodging and three meals. That came out to forty-one dollars apiece, a total of exactly one thousand and twenty-five dollars. This is how the Blessed Mother gets things done. We keep having these sorts of things happen out of the blue, and that's what keeps us going."

I told Marge I knew exactly what she meant. Then I looked at the peach tree and sighed.

Marge and Irene knew that Irma had moved from Yakima back to Texas sometime in 2000, but didn't have either an address or a phone number for her, and had been unsuccessful in finding one. Irene was a lady of no small pluck, however, and refused to give up. As Marge and I watched, the Mexican woman began to go from trailer door to trailer door, inquiring in Spanish after Irma Munoz, the girl who had seen the Virgin. The first few people she questioned wrinkled their brows in confusion and said they had no idea who or what Irene was talking about, but finally our friend found a woman who not only recognized Irma's name but said there was another Munoz girl living in the park, in a trailer painted purple. We found the purple trailer a couple of rows over, and Irene rattled the flimsy screen door. A young girl, who said she was Irma's niece, answered and, after some discussion, gave us a phone number with a Texas area code.

I phoned the number the next morning, the Fourth of July, and Irma answered. She was back in Mission, the little border town on the Rio Grande just west of McAllen, where she had been born and raised, working now as an MRI technician at a diagnostic imaging facility. She knew who I was and why I had called without needing to have it explained.

Marge and Irene were right, Irma said, she had struggled for a long time with feelings of unworthiness. "It could have happened to so many other people," she said. "It should have happened to so many other people. I couldn't stop thinking, 'Why me?' I was the furthest thing from a holy person. But now I understand that God does things for a reason, and whether or not we understand the reason isn't the point. I just feel thankful that it did happen, and that this was part of God's plan."

When I asked if she had ever doubted that her experience had been real, Irma answered in a very firm voice. "Not for one second. It changed my life, and it's impacted me right up to this moment." She went to church every Sunday and read the Bible every day, but more important was that "I've never stopped trying to be a better person," she said. "I owe the Blessed Mother for that, because She brought Christ into my life."

Only recently had she realized what a deep depression she was in back in 1994, Irma said: "My son dying just really took the heart out of me. I was so messed up. But what happened helped me accept it. I came to truly believe he's with God, and that I will be, too, someday. I never feel sorry for myself anymore."

She knew that a lot of people back in Boardman found it difficult to accept her relationship with Leon, "but I know in my heart that God put us in each other's lives for a reason." They were married now, but Leon was back in prison, this time at Fort Worth. He would be released in November, and she intended to try again to make the marriage work. "I know it sounds incredible, but I still have hope for him. He's had a very hard life, but I believe that with God's help—and mine—he can overcome it."

She wanted to tell me a story, Irma said. Back before they were married, and while he was still in prison, she and Leon had lost contact with each other. Weeks passed, during which she tried to accept that he was gone from her life. "Then I get a letter from him saying he's in Fort Worth, and that when he arrived and was shown to his new cell, the first thing he saw was a rosary that someone had left hanging on the wall. And suddenly he felt this incredible urge to write me." Irma paused as if she expected me to speak, but I had no idea what to say. "I believe God placed him in my life for a reason," Irma told me finally.

When I asked her if she had confided in many people down there in Texas about her apparition experience in Oregon, Irma laughed. "I told a few people at first, but they didn't believe me, so I stopped talking about it." It was all right, she added a moment later: "I don't need anyone to know. When I moved down here to Texas, I didn't bring any newspaper clippings, any videos of the TV coverage, any pictures or anything like that. I didn't need it. My mom has a lot of that stuff, but I never look at it." Lourdes Munoz also kept the *Desert Aglow* painting stored in her garage, but her daughter hadn't looked at it in more than five years. "I know what happened," Irma explained. "I carry it with me. I consider it a very personal thing."

She still hoped and prayed for the shrine, "but I don't *need* it anymore either," Irma said. "I would like it to happen for everyone else in the area, and I would move back to Boardman in a minute if it did. But I got my benefits already. I don't need more."

In the meantime, she was returning to Boardman more often than some people suspected. In fact, her last visit had been less than a month earlier. Someone had tried to give her Irene Virgen's new phone number, but she said no, Irma recalled. "I made a decision right then and there that I don't want to deal any more with all the people who were part of that time. Because whenever we got together, it seemed like all we talked about was why the shrine didn't happen, and that we were so disappointed. I don't want what happened to leave me with a feeling of disappointment. I want it to leave me with a feeling of gratitude. And that's what I feel now."

We let a few seconds of silence pass between us, then Irma told me that while she had let go of her relationships with Marge and Irene and

Kim and the others, she always returned to the trailer whenever she came back through Boardman. "Every time I go there," she said, "the memory comes back so strong. I know it was the most important thing that ever happened to me, and the most important thing that ever will happen to me. God gave me this great gift, and I would be wrong to expect anything more."

I mentioned how sad I had been to see that the peach tree was dead, and Irma said she felt the same way. "But you know what?" she asked. "Those rosebushes that my mom planted, the ones we were given that bloomed so huge that next summer? She dug them up and brought them with her when she and my dad moved back here. And they're blooming again. They're blooming outside my window right now."

"Some things you don't want to speak about," I thought, "because they seem a little less true if you do." I thanked Irma for her time, wished her well and said good-bye, knowing this was the last time I would hear her voice.

After hanging up, I stepped outside my office and listened to the wind blow through trees where the birds did not go silent. After a few moments, I whispered a Hail Mary, and for a moment let myself experience the joy that is belief. It was gone as quickly as the gust that had rustled the branches overhead, but I knew it would come back, and that even if it did not, I would never forget that I had felt it. *Semel credidisse.*

"All this time," I thought, "all this effort," and all I had demonstrated to myself was that I could not live without God's love, and that the only way I knew to get it was to love Him back. I looked up at the light sparkling on Oregon pine needles and saw rosebushes blooming in Texas. It was a miracle, I knew, even if I could never prove it. All I had to do was ask.

SOURCES

By far the greatest aids to me in writing this book were the Medjugorje Parish Archives and a stupendous compilation of documents, transcripts, recollections, articles, and book excerpts titled *What They Say About Medjugorje: A Contemporary Mystery* that was self-published by Andrew B. Thul in 1991. Especially helpful were the translations of the meticulous records kept by the Croatian priests who monitored the apparitions during June and July 1981.

The "authoritative-looking volume" mentioned in the second chapter of this book is *Encountering Mary* (Princeton University Press, 1991), by Sandra L. Zimdars-Swartz, a thoroughgoing description of every major apparition of the Virgin Mary that was investigated by the Roman Catholic Church during the nineteenth and twentieth centuries. An altogether admirable work.

Evelyn Hill's *Mysticism* is, as the jacket of the current edition describes it, "the preeminent study in the nature and development of spiritual consciousness." This superlative book was first published by Methuen in 1911. The 1990 edition is published by Doubleday.

Marina Warner's *Alone of All Her Sex: The Myth and Cult of the Virgin Mary* (Alfred A. Knopf, 1976) has been praised by secular critics as the most erudite work on the subject ever written. I am not an admirer of the book, which seems to me more driven by Ms. Warner's sexual frustrations than any intellectual or spiritual force, but did learn from it.

Kenneth Woodward's *Making Saints: How the Catholic Church Determines Who Becomes a Saint, Who Doesn't, and Why* (Simon & Schuster, 1990) is far and away the most comprehensive and readable book on its subject. I am at once indebted to Mr. Woodward for his research and frustrated by the difficulties I encountered at the Vatican due to his book's reception there (owing mostly to a controversial section on the Opus Dei movement). Nevertheless, he remains the finest religion writer—at least on the subject of Catholicism—working for a mainstream publication in the United States.

Benedict Groeschel's *A Still, Small Voice* (Ignatius Press, 1993) is, as I've described it, "a brilliantly concise volume" and the most compelling work of mystical theology produced by a Roman Catholic in years.

Augustin Poulain's *The Graces of Interior Prayer* was first published in 1901 and translated to English by Leonora L. Yorke Smith in 1910. The book is difficult both to find and to read. Brother Frank Sadowski has produced a very skillfully edited excerpt of the book that was published by Alba House in 1998 under the title *Revelations and Visions*.

Linwood Urban's *A Short History of Christian Thought* (Oxford University Press, 1995) was for me an enormous education.

The theolgian/novelist Malachi Martin is the one writer on the subject of Catholicism who cannot be ignored. His most notable nonfiction works on the subject of the Church are: *Keys of This Blood: Pope John Paul II Versus Russia and the West for Control of the New World Order* (Touchstone, 1991); *The Jesuits: The Society of Jesus and the Betrayal of the Roman Catholic Church* (Linden Press, 1987); and *The Decline and Fall of the Roman Catholic Church* (Putnam, 1981).

Father René Laurentin is the author of *A Short Treatise on the Virgin Mary* (Ami International Press, 1991), widely regarded within the Roman Catholic Church as the finest work on Marian devotion, and of the similarly esteemed *Bernadette of Lourdes* (HarperCollins, 1979). Fr. Laurentin's first book on Medjugorje, *Is the Virgin Mary Appearing at Medjugorje?* was published in 1984, and then followed by annual reports that continued into the mid-nineties, all published either by the Riehle Foundation or its subsidary, Faith Publishing.

Medjugorje: Religion, Politics, and Violence in Rural Bosnia (Vu University Press, Amsterdam, 1995), by Mart Bax, is a perplexing work. Bax has done a remarkable job of researching the historical context of the apparitions, yet undermines his own work with careless errors and dubious assumptions about events after 1981. This is a profoundly instructive book, but also a deeply flawed one.

Other books about Medjugorje:

Father Ljudevit Rupčić's *The Apparitions of the Virgin at Medjugorje* (Ljubuski-Humac, 1983) is an invaluable record of early events in the parish. Father Rupčić is also the author of *The Truth About Medjugorje* (Ljubuski-Humac, 1990), written as a retort to Bishop Pavao Žanić's pamphlet "Medjugorje."

Equally helpful is Father Svetozar Kraljevic's *The Apparitions of Our Lady at Medjugorje* (Franciscan Herald Press, 1984), a surprisingly clear-eyed and unassuming account of the same period.

Father Milan Mikulich's *The Apparitions of Our Lady in Medjugorje* was self-published in 1985.

Mark I. Miravelle's *The Message of Medjugorje* (Franciscan Herald Press, 1986) is the most thorough theological examination of the messages reported by the seers.

Father Michael O'Carroll's *Medjugorje: Facts, Documents, Theology* (Veritas Publications, 1986) is a compendium of the earliest investigations of the apparitions by outside agencies.

Father Janko Bubalo's *A Thousand Encounters with the Virgin Mary* (Ceres, 1987) is essentially Vicka Ivanković's edited journal of her apparitions.

Wayne Weible's *Medjugorje: The Message* (Paraclete Press, 1989) is the most popular of all the devotional books on the subject. Though neither well written nor very informative, it at least seems an earnest work.

Janice T. Connell's *The Visions of the Children* (St. Martin's Press, 1992) is the "devotionalist drivel" referred to in the second chapter of this book. The visionaries have attacked it as inaccurate, and claim that quotes attributed to them were invented.

Mary Craig's *Spark from Heaven* (Ave Maria Press, 1988) is superior to both the Weible and Connell books.

E. Michael Jones' *Medjugorje: The Untold Story* (Fidelity Press, 1989) is the broadest attack on the authenticity of the apparitions produced to date. Jones is not a good writer, makes no attempt to be fair or balanced, and is often simply inaccurate, but he does raise at least a few legitimate questions.

I found Father Ivo Sivrić's *The Hidden Side of Medjugorje* (Psilog, 1989) to be without merit. The book was "edited" by Louis Belanger.

Dr. Nicholas Bartulica's *Medjugorje: Are the Seers Telling the Truth?* (Croatian Franciscan Press, 1991) is a spirited defense of the apparitions written by a psychiatrist who has tested and interviewed each of the visionaries.

Heather Parsons' *Marija and the Mother of God* (Robert Andrew Press, 1993) is a touching (if entirely uncritical) chronicle of the apparitions from Marija Pavlović's point of view during the early days of the war.

Father Slavko Barbarić's *Mother! Lead Us to Peace!!* is a collection of the beloved priest's "Reflections on Mary's Messages" that was published by Nicky Eltz in 1995.

Books on the Scottsdale Apparitions:

Our Lady Comes to Scottsdale (Queenship Publishing Company, 1993) by Father Robert Faricy and Sister Lucy Rooney is an approving examination of the apparitions there. Father Faricy and Sister Rooney are also the authors of *Return to God: The Scottsdale Message* (Queenship Publishing Company, 1994).

René Laurentin's *Our Lord and Our Lady in Scottsdale* (Faith Publishing, 1992) is similarly positive about the apparitions of Gianna Talone and the others.

Gianna Talone's *I Am Your Jesus of Mercy* books all have been published by Queenship Publishing Company.

Father J. Michael Sparough's *Not Seeing is Believing: A Skeptic Goes to Scottsdale* (Medjugorje Book Center, 1992) is quite sincere, though not very skeptical.

Healing Through the Rosary by Annie Ross Fitch was published by M.A.R.Y. Ministries in 1992.

Carol Ameche's *As We Wait in Joyful Hope* was published by the Colorado Mir Center in 1994.

Books about other apparitions:

Father Gabriel Maindron's *The Apparitions of Our Lady at Kibeho* was published by the Marian Spring Centre in 1996. It's a compelling document.

René Laurentin's *An Appeal From Mary in Argentina* (Faith Publishing, 1990) was interesting to me mainly for what it revealed about the response to such events in Latin America.

Jody Brant Smith's *The Image of Guadalupe: Myth or Miracle* (Image Books, 1984) is a fascinating consideration of the various scientific investigations of the Image that have been conducted during the past three hundred-plus years.

Books about Marian Catholic eschatology:

Michael H. Brown's *The Final Hour* (Faith Publishing, 1992) is an overripe but quite informative argument on behalf of those who believe the end is at hand.

Apocalypse: The Book for Our Times (Faith Publishing, 1991) by the Rev. Albert Joseph Mary Shamon is interesting mainly for how it places the Book of Revelation in a Jewish context, and interprets the work of St. John the Divine in terms of Old Testament symbolism.

Books about Bosnia, Croatia, Serbia, and the war:

Why Bosnia? (The Pamphleteers Press, 1993) is a collection of essays and articles by writers from all over the world, edited by Rabia Ali and Lawrence Lifschultz. If I were to recommend only a single book about how that horrible war in the former Yugoslavia happened, this would be the one.

Roy Gutman's *A Witness to Genocide* (Macmillan, 1993) is a collection of the reporter's Pulitzer Prize-winning dispatches on ethnic cleansing in Bosnia. As literature, the book enjoys both the advantages and disadvantages of coming so early in the conflict, but it stands still as one of the relatively few works that have probably saved human lives. Father Slavko was so insistent I read it that he forced Rita Falsetto to give me her copy.

Love Thy Neighbor (Alfred A. Knopf, 1996) by Peter Maass is the finest work of literature to emerge from the war in Bosnia.

Ed Vulliamy's *Seasons in Hell* (St. Martin's, 1994) is an angry, harrowing book that places the war in a rich historical and cultural context.

Alex Dragnich's *Serbs and Croats* (Harcourt Brace, 1992) offers a clear and concise history of the troubled relationship between these two peoples.

No book I read about what was once Yugoslavia gave me more pleasure than Rebecca West's *Black Lamb and Grey Falcon* (first published by Viking Press in 1941, and in a current edition by Penguin).

ACKNOWLEDGMENTS

Acknowledgment can mean confession in some contexts, and I must admit that it feels awkward to be thanking people whose contributions are described within this narrative. However, a last word of thanks to Father Peter Gumpel, Monsignor Robert Sarno, Father Augustine DiNoia, Father Gabriel O'Donnell and assorted other priests who assisted me during my visits to the Vatican seems appropriate. Their patience with me was and is much appreciated. I also want to thank Father Allen Duston for his hospitality during my stay in Rome during the spring of 2003, and for making my encounter with Pope John Paul II possible. Father Duston's assistant Elizabeth Heil was a whirlwind of efficiency, and the staff of the Hotel Bramante was wonderfully helpful. Carl Battaglia was a boon companion.

Janet Knez arranged my meeting with Father Milan Mikulich, who facilitated my stay with Mirjana Soldo during my first visit to Medjugorje, and thus made much of what I was able to accomplish possible. Ratko Mikulić and Aquarelle Travel Agency in Split, Croatia not only provided me with transportation and translation but also orientation to surroundings that seemed strange indeed. Ivan and Mira Bencun of the Hotel Marben, and Zarko and Ljilja Juricic of the Pansion Maja were gracious hosts, and Ivan Bencun became a valued friend who demonstrated that courage and humility stand together.

Mirjana Soldo and her family accommodated me to a degree I appreciate better now than then; Marco Soldo's consideration told me much of what I know about their family values.

Rita Falsetto and Nicky Eltz were friends who shared heart and soul. My memories of speeding with Nicky through the war-torn countrysides of Bosnia and Herzegovina still come back to me in dreams, and to this day I can close my eyes and see Rita trekking to the top of Križevac at midnight, after putting in a sixteen-hour day at the parish office in

Medjugorje, praying every step of the way. Milona Hapsburg divulged much that appears between the lines of this book. My thanks go out also to Philip, Michelle, Rafaella, and all the Loopers who were my companions in Medjugorje, and to Jozo Vasilj and his son Mate, who made me feel like members of their family, and to Rita Klaus, for telling me what to fear, and to Karen, for the ride to Mostar. Gabriel Meyer offered both knowledge and perspective in the months after my first trip to Bosnia.

Father Ivan Lindeca, pastor of the Medjugorje parish during the summer of 1995, was a man of depth, humor, and generosity who gave me better answers to my questions than they deserved. Father Philip Pavich spent many hours with me describing his experiences. And it was a delight to get so much personal attention from Father Jozo Zovko when I visited him at the monastary in Humac. Father Slavko Barbarić was and is my model of heroic virtue.

Thanks to all at St. Maria Goretti in Scottsdale, Arizona for welcoming warmth, and to Father Ernest Larkin for being so forthcoming. During my visit to Emmitsburg, Maryland, Michael Sullivan and Gianna Talone-Sullivan were exceptionally kind, and I remember them fondly.

Irma Munoz, Kim Hickey, Irene Virgen, and Marge Rolen shared their experiences with me in the most sincere manner possible during visits to the high desert, in the beginning as at the end.

I thank Father Benedict Groeschel for being a guy who actually knows something.

Finally, thanks to my publisher, Morgan Entrekin, for sticking with me over a haul that was a lot longer than we anticipated, and to my editor, Brando Skyhorse, for steering this book to a conclusion that satisfied us all.